The Double Eagle Guide to

CAMPING *in*

WESTERN

PARKS *and* FORESTS

VOLUME I
PACIFIC NORTHWEST

WASHINGTON
OREGON
IDAHO

A DOUBLE EAGLE GUIDE™

DISCOVERY PUBLISHING
BILLINGS, YELLOWSTONE COUNTY, MONTANA USA

The Double Eagle Guide to Camping in Western Parks and Forests
Volume I Pacific Northwest

PUBLISHED BY
Discovery Publishing
Editorial Offices
Post Office Box 50545
Billings, Montana 59105 USA

Discovery Publishing is an independent, private enterprise. The information contained herein should not be construed as reflecting the publisher's approval of the policies or practices of the public agencies listed.

Information in this book is subject to change without notice.

Cover Photos (clockwise from the top)
      Humboldt National Forest, Nevada
      Lake Owyhee State Park, Oregon
      Memphis Lake State Recreation Area, Nebraska
      Big Bend National Park, Texas

Frontispiece: Belfair State Park, Washington

10 9 8 7 6 5 4 3 2 1

November 30, 1994   5:18 PM Mountain Time

Produced, printed, and bound in the United States of America.

ISBN 0-929760-27-1

TABLE OF CONTENTS

(Continued on the following page)

INTRODUCTION TO THE *Double Eagle*™ SERIES

Whether you're a veteran of many Western camps or are planning your first visit, this series is for you.

In the six volumes of *The Double Eagle Guide to Camping in Western Parks and Forests*, we've described most public campgrounds along or conveniently near the highways and byways of the 17 contiguous Western United States. Also included is basic information about jackcamping and backpacking on the millions of acres of undeveloped public lands in the West. Our goal is to provide you with accurate, detailed, and yet concise, *first-hand* information about literally thousands of camping areas you're most likely to want to know about.

The volumes which comprise the *Double Eagle*™ series constitute a significant departure from the sketchy, plain vanilla approach to campground information provided by other guidebooks. Here, for the first time, is the most *useful* information about the West's most *useable* public camping areas. We've included a broad assortment of campgrounds from which you can choose: From simple, free camps, to sites in deluxe, landscaped surroundings.

The name for this critically acclaimed series was suggested by the celebrated United States twenty-dollar gold piece--most often called the *"Double Eagle"*--the largest and finest denomination of coinage ever issued by the U.S. Mint. The *Double Eagle* has long been associated with the history of the West, as a symbol of traditional Western values, prosperity, and excellence.

So, too, the *Double Eagle*™ series seeks to provide you with information about what are perhaps the finest of all the West's treasures--its public recreational lands owned, operated, and overseen by the citizens of the Western United States.

We hope you'll enjoy reading these pages, and come to use the information in the volumes to enhance your own appreciation for the outstanding camping opportunities available in the West.

Live long and prosper.

Thomas and *Elizabeth Preston*
Publishers

CONVENTIONS USED IN THIS SERIES

The following conventions or standards are used throughout the *Double Eagle*™ series as a means of providing a sense of continuity between one park or forest and other public lands, and between one campground and the next.

State Identifier: The state name and number combination in the upper left corner of each campground description provides an easy means of cross-referencing the written information to the numbered locations on the maps in the Appendix.

Whenever possible, the campgrounds have been arranged in what we have determined to be a reasonable progression, and based on *typical travel patterns* within a region. Generally speaking, a north to south, west to east pattern has been followed. In certain cases, particularly those involving one-way-in, same-way-out roads, we have arranged the camps in the order in which they would be encountered on the way into the area, so the standard plan occasionally may be reversed.

Campground Name: The officially designated name for the campground is listed, followed by the park, forest, or other public recreation area in which it is located.

Location: This section allows you to obtain a quick approximation of a campground's location in relation to nearby major communities.

Access: Our *Accurate Access* system makes extensive use of highway mileposts in order to pinpoint the location of access roads, intersections, and other major terminal points. (Mileposts are about 98 percent reliable--but occasionally they are mowed by a snowplow or an errant motorist, and may be missing; or, worse yet, the mileposts were replaced in the wrong spot!) In some instances, locations are noted primarily utilizing mileages between two or more nearby locations--usually communities, but occasionally key junctions or prominent structures or landmarks.

Since everyone won't be approaching a campground from the same direction, we've provided access information from two, sometimes three, points. In all cases, we've chosen the access points for their likelihood of use. Distances from communities are listed from the approximate **midtown** point, unless otherwise specified. Mileages from Interstate highways and other freeway exits are usually given from the approximate center of the interchange. Mileages from access points have been rounded to the nearest mile, unless the exact mileage is critical. All instructions are given using the current official highway map available free from each state.

Directions are given using a combination of compass and hand headings, i.e., "turn north (left)" or "swing west (right)". This isn't a bonehead navigation system, by any means. When the sun is shining or you're in a region where moss grows on tree trunks, it's easy enough to figure out which way is north. But anyone can become temporarily disoriented on an overcast day or a moonless night while looking for an inconspicuous campground turnoff, or while being buzzed by heavy traffic at a key intersection, so we built this redundancy into the system.

Facilities: The items in this section have been listed in the approximate order in which a visitor might observe them during a typical swing through a campground. Following the total number of individual camp units, items pertinent to the campsites themselves are listed, then information related to 'community' facilities. It has been assumed that each campsite has a picnic table.

Site types: (1) Standard--no hookup; (2) Partial hookup--water, electricity; (3) Full hookup--water, electricity, sewer.

We have extensively employed the use of *general* and *relative* terms in describing the size, separation, and levelness of the campsites ("medium to large", "fairly well separated", "basically level", etc.). Please note that "separation" is a measure of relative privacy and is a composite of both natural visual screens and spacing between campsites. The information is presented as an *estimate* by highly experienced observers. Please allow for variations in perception between yourself and the reporters.

Parking Pads: (1) Straight-ins, (sometimes called "back-ins")-- the most common type, are just that--straight strips angled off the driveway; (2) Pull-throughs--usually the most convenient type for large rv's, they provide an in-one-end-and-out-the-other parking space; pull-throughs may be either arc-shaped and separated from the main driveway by some sort of barrier or 'island' (usually vegetation), or arranged in parallel rows; (3) Pull-offs--essentially just wide spots adjacent to the driveway. Pad lengths have been categorized as: (1) Short-- a single, large vehicle up to about the size of a standard pickup truck; (2) Medium--a single vehicle or combination up to the length of a pickup towing a single-axle trailer; Long--a single vehicle or combo as long as a crew cab pickup towing a double-axle trailer. Normally, any overhang out the back of the pad has been ignored in the estimate, so it might be possible to slip a crew cab pickup hauling a fifth-wheel trailer in tandem with a ski boat into some pads, but we'll leave that to your discretion.

Fire appliances have been categorized in three basic forms: (1) Fireplaces--angular, steel or concrete, ground-level; (2) Fire rings--circular, steel or concrete, ground-level or below ground-level; (3) Barbecue grills--angular steel box, supported by a steel post about 36 inches high. (The trend is toward installing steel fire rings, since they're durable, relatively inexpensive--50 to 80 dollars apiece--and easy to install and maintain. Barbecue grills are often used in areas where ground fires are a problem, as when charcoal-only fires are permitted.)

Toilet facilities have been listed thusly: (1) Restrooms--"modern", i.e., flush toilets and usually a wash basin; (2) Vault facilities--"simple", i.e., outhouses, pit toilets, call them what you like, (a rose by any other name.....).

Campers' supply points have been described at five levels: (1) Camper Supplies--buns, beans and beverages; (2) Gas and Groceries--a 'convenience' stop; (3) Limited--at least one store which approximates a small supermarket, more than one fuel station, a general merchandise store, hardware store, and other basic services; (4) Adequate--more than one supermarket, (including something that resembles an IGA or a Safeway), a choice of fuel brands, and several general and specialty stores and services; (5) Complete--they have a major discount store.

Campground managers, attendants and hosts are not specifically listed since their presence can be expected during the regular camping season in more than 85 percent of the campgrounds listed in this volume.

Activities & Attractions: As is mentioned a number of times throughout this series, the local scenery may be the principal attraction of the campground (and, indeed, may be the *only* one you'll need). Other nearby attractions/activities have been listed if they are low-cost or free, and are available to the general public. An important item: *Swimming and boating areas usually do not have lifeguards.*

Natural Features: Here we've drawn a word picture of the natural environment in and around each campground. Please remember that seasonal, even daily, conditions will affect the appearance of the area. A normally "sparkling stream" can be a muddy torrent for a couple of weeks in late spring; a "deep blue lake" might be a nearly empty hole in a drought year; "lush vegetation" may have lost all its greenery by the time you arrive in late October. Elevations above 500' are rounded to the nearest 100'; lower elevations are rounded to the nearest 50'. (Some elevations are estimated, but no one should develop a nosebleed or a headache because of a 100' difference in altitude.)

Season, Fees & Phone: Seasons listed are approximate, since weather conditions, particularly in mountainous/hilly regions, may require adjustments in opening/closing dates. Campground gates are usually unlocked from 6:00 a.m. to 10:00 p.m. Fee information listed here was obtained directly from the responsible agencies just a few hours before press time. Fees should be considered **minimum** fees *per camping vehicle*, since they are always subject to adjustment by agencies or legislatures. Discounts and special passes are usually available for seniors and disabled persons. The listed telephone number can be called to obtain information about current conditions in or near that campground.

Camp Notes: Consider this section to be somewhat more subjective in nature than the others. In order to provide our readers with a well-rounded report, we have listed personal comments related to our field observations. (Our enthusiasm for the West is, at times, unabashedly proclaimed. So if the prose sometimes sounds like a tourist promotion booklet, please bear with us--there's a lot to be enthusiastic about!)

Editorial remarks (Ed.) occasionally have been included.

A Word About Style...

Throughout the *Double Eagle*™ series, we've utilized a free-form writing concept which we call "Notation Format". Complete sentences, phrases, and single words have been incorporated into the camp descriptions as appropriate under the circumstances. We've adopted this style in order to provide our readers with detailed information about each item, while maintaining conciseness, clarity, and conversationality.

A Word About Print...

Another departure from the norm is our use of print sizes which are 10 to 20 percent larger (or more) than ordinary guides. (We also use narrower margins for less paper waste.) It's one thing to read a guidebook in the convenience and comfort of your well-lit living room. It's another matter to peruse the pages while you're bounding and bouncing along in your car or camper as the sun is setting; or by a flickering flashlight inside a breeze-buffeted dome tent. We hope *this* works for you, too.

A Word About Maps...

After extensive tests of the state maps by seasoned campers, both at home and in the field, we decided to localize all of the maps in one place in the book. Campers felt that, since pages must be flipped regardless of where the maps are located, it would be more desirable to have them all in one place. We're confident that you'll also find this to be a convenient feature.

A Word About 'Regs'...

Although this series is about public campgrounds, you'll find comparatively few mentions of rules, regulations, policies, ordinances, statutes, decrees or dictates. Our editorial policy is this: (1) It's the duty of a citizen or a visitor to know his legal responsibilities (and, of course, his corresponding *rights*); (2) Virtually every campground has the appropriate regulations publicly posted for all to study; and (3) If you're reading this *Double Eagle*™ Guide, chances are you're in the upper ten percent of the conscientious citizens of the United States or some other civilized country and you probably don't need to be constantly reminded of these matters.

And a Final Word...

We've tried very, very hard to provide you with accurate information about the West's great camping opportunities But occasionally, things aren't as they're supposed to be .....

If a campground's access, facilities or fees have been recently changed, please let us know. We'll try to pass along the news to other campers.

If the persons in the next campsite keep their generator poppety-popping past midnight so they can cook a turkey in the microwave, blame the bozos, not the book.

If the beasties are a bit bothersome in that beautiful spot down by the bog, note the day's delights and not the difficulties.

Thank you for buying our book. We hope that you'll have many terrific camping trips!

Washington

Public Campgrounds

The Washington map is located in the Appendix.

Washington 1

WILLABY
Olympic National Forest

Location: Western Washington on the west side of the Olympic Peninsula north of Hoquiam.

Access: From U.S. Highway 101 at milepost 125 +.6 (38 miles north of Hoquiam, 66 miles south of Forks), turn east onto South Shore Lake Quinault Road (paved); proceed east for 1.6 miles, then turn north (left) into the campground. (Note: If you're southbound on '101, you can save a mile by taking a short cut from mp 126 +.6 at the south end of the Quinault River bridge, then southeastward on a short, paved local road to the South Shore Road; the amount of time you'll save taking the short cut is about equal to the few seconds it took you to read this note.)

Facilities: 19 campsites; most sites are medium-sized, with fairly good separation; parking pads are paved, mostly short straight-ins which may require some additional leveling; some units have large, framed-and-gravelled tent pads; paved pathways; fireplaces; firewood is available for gathering in the vicinity, but may be wet much of the year, so b-y-o is suggested; water at faucets throughout; restrooms; paved driveway; nearest supplies (limited) at the small general store in Quinault, 0.6 mile east; complete supplies and services are available in the Aberdeen-Hoquiam area.

Activities & Attractions: Self-guiding nature trail, 0.2 mile west; boating; boat launch; trout fishing on the lake (Quinault Indian Reservation permit required).

Natural Features: Located on a relatively steep hillside a few yards from deep blue (when the sun shines) Lake Quinault; Willaby Creek enters the lake near this point; very tall conifer forest with an abundance of ferns and other low-level vegetation; mild temperatures year-round; annual rainfall averages 145 inches; elevation 200'.

Season, Fees & Phone: May to September; $7.00; 14 day limit; Quinault Ranger Dist. (206) 288-2525.

Camp Notes: About half of the campsites provide you with somewhat of a view of Lake Quinault through the trees. Only smaller trailers are recommended due to the narrow driveway and small parking spaces. The trail system in this area consists of interconnecting segments which allow you to begin at the nature trailhead, hike through the forest over to Falls Creek Campground and back along the lake shore to Willaby (or vice versa).

Washington 2

FALLS CREEK
Olympic National Forest

Location: Western Washington on the west side of the Olympic Peninsula north of Hoquiam.

Access: From U.S. Highway 101 at milepost 125 +.6 (38 miles north of Hoquiam, 66 miles south of Forks), turn east onto South Shore Lake Quinault Road (paved); proceed east for 2.3 miles, then turn north (left, by the ranger station) into the campground.

Facilities: 31 campsites, including 10 park 'n walk tent sites; sites are small to medium-sized, with fair separation; parking pads are paved or packed gravel, medium-length straight-ins; ample space for tents; parking area for tent sites; fireplaces; firewood is available for gathering in the general vicinity, but may be wet, so b-y-o (or b-y-o kindling) is suggested; water at several faucets; restrooms; paved driveways; nearest supplies (limited) at the small general store in Quinault near the campground; complete supplies and services are available in the Aberdeen-Hoquiam area.

Activities & Attractions: Boating; boat launch; lake fishing for rainbow, dolly varden and cutthroat trout (Quinault Indian Reservation permit required); hiking trails.

Natural Features: Located on rolling terrain along the shore of Lake Quinault near the southwest corner of the Olympic Mountains; vegetation consists of medium-dense, very large conifers and lots of ferns; Falls Creek flows down through the campground; elevation 200'.

Season, Fees & Phone: May to September; $7.00; 14 day limit; Quinault Ranger Dist. (206) 288-2525.

Camp Notes: The campsites here are somewhat closer to the water's edge than those at neighboring Willaby. Indeed, a secondary reason for the annual winter closure of the campground (other than most campers' lack of enthusiasm for 'sleeping out' in the rain) *is* its closeness to the shore. During lengthy winter downpours, portions of the campground may be slightly submerged by the lake's swollen waters. But the Olympic Peninsula is made to handle such events, and the place dries out handily by the time camping season rolls around.

Washington 3

KALALOCH
Olympic National Park

Location: Western Washington on the west coast of the Olympic Peninsula south of Forks.

Access: From U.S. Highway 101 at milepost 157 +.7 in the small settlement of Kalaloch (34 miles south of Forks, 70 miles north of Hoquiam), turn west into the campground.

Facilities: 179 campsites in 6 loops; (a group camp is also available, by reservation only); majority of the sites are small+ and fairly well separated; parking pads are paved, short to short+, reasonably level straight-ins, a few are pull-offs; most sites have medium to large, level tent spaces; fireplaces; b-y-o firewood; water at faucets in each loop; restrooms; paved driveways; ranger station nearby; camper supplies at a nearby resort; adequate supplies and services are available in Forks.

Activities & Attractions: Beachcombing; amphitheater for scheduled ranger-naturalist programs during the summer.

Natural Features: Located on a windswept bluff above the ocean beach; campground vegetation consists of short to medium height trees and leafy bushes which provide a fairly good windbreak; several inviting beaches are accessible from here; elevation 50'.

Season, Fees & Phone: Open all year; $7.00; 14 day limit; Olympic National Park Headquarters, Port Angeles, (206) 452-4501.

Camp Notes: Most of the campsites are well-sheltered from oceanside weather; those that aren't have the advantage of good ocean views. The beaches in the Kalaloch (*Klay*-lock) area are varied in their nomenclature and points of interest. Some have proper nouns for names, like Ruby Beach; most are merely numbered: Beach 2, Beach 3, Beach 6, and so on. Each beach has its own special appeal: Ruby beach is adorned with spires of stone called "seastacks"; steep, colorful cliffs rise above Beach 6; the shoreline north of Beach 4 is noted for its tidepools.

Washington 4

WILLOUGHBY CREEK & MINNIE PETERSON
Washington Department of Natural Resources

Location: Western Washington on the west side of the Olympic Peninsula southeast of Forks.

Access: From U.S. Highway 101 at milepost 178 +.5 (13 miles south of Forks, 21 miles north of Kalaloch), turn east onto Hoh Valley Road (paved, winding and bumpy); travel easterly for 3.6 miles, then turn south (right) into Willoughby Creek; or continue easterly on Hoh River Road for another mile, then turn north (left) into Minnie Peterson.

Facilities: 3 campsites in Willoughby Creek, 6 sites in Minnie Peterson; sites are small, reasonably level, with nominal to fair separation; parking pads are gravel, mostly short straight-ins; small to medium-sized areas for tents; fire rings; some firewood is available for gathering in the vicinity, but may be wet; water at a hand pump in Minnie Peterson, no drinking water in Willoughby Creek; gravel driveways; camper supplies at a small store, 2 miles east on Hoh Valley Road; adequate supplies and services are available in Forks.

Activities & Attractions: Hoh Rain Forest visitor center in Olympic National Park, 15 miles east; fishing.

Natural Features: Located along the banks of the Hoh River in a valley below the west slopes of the Olympic Mountains; moderately dense rain forest vegetation predominates in and around the campgrounds; small creeks flow through or past the camping areas; elevation 300'.

Season, Fees & Phone: Open all year; no fee (subject to change); 5 day limit; Washington Department of Natural Resources Office, Forks, (206) 374-6131.

Camp Notes: If it's a midsummer afternoon, you're heading toward the national park campground at Hoh, and a campsite is available in one of these two simple spots, you may want to consider staying here for the night. Hoh's campground is justifiably popular, and the occasion might be one of those where "a vault along the road is worth two restrooms in the rain forest". This area was the home of pioneers Oscar and Minnie Peterson, who carved a homestead out of the wilderness and lived in relative isolation until a road was built along the Hoh in 1932.

Washington 5

HOH
Olympic National Park

Location: Western Washington on the west side of the Olympic Peninsula east/southeast of Forks.

Access: From U.S. Highway 101 at milepost 178 +.5 (13 miles south of Forks, 21 miles north of Kalaloch), turn east onto Hoh Valley Road (paved, winding); travel easterly for 19 miles to the campground; (allow a minimum of 45 minutes for the trip).

Facilities: 95 campsites in 3 loops; most sites are generously sized, level, and well spaced; parking pads are paved, short to medium-length straight-ins, plus some medium to long pull-throughs; most units offer good tent-pitching opportunities; fireplaces; b-y-o firewood from outside the park; water at central faucets; restrooms; holding tank disposal station; paved driveways; ranger station; nearest supplies (very limited) at a small store, 12 miles west on Hoh Valley Road; adequate supplies and services are available in Forks.

Activities & Attractions: Visitor center; 2 self-guided nature trails; paved mini-trail; hiking trail along the river; amphitheater for evening campfire programs during the summer; day use area.

Natural Features: Located on a moderately forested flat on the Hoh River deep in the Olympic Mountains; a number of campsites are along the edge of the riverbank; the Hoh Rain Forest, with its incomparable variety of flora and fauna, encircles the campground; elevation 600'.

Season, Fees & Phone: Open all year, with limited services in winter; $7.00; 14 day limit; Hoh Ranger Station/Visitor Center (206) 374-6925.

Camp Notes: Hoh is so truly unique that it's worth just about any amount of time and effort you need to get here. Spend a day or two listening to the river and silently walking the rain forest trails, and you'll remember the experience for a lifetime.

Washington 6

BOGACHIEL
Bogachiel State Park

Location: Western Washington on the west side of the Olympic Peninsula south of Forks.

Access: From U.S. Highway 101 at milepost 186 (5.5 miles south of Forks, 0.4 mile northwest of the Bogachiel River bridge), turn south/west into the park. (Note that the normally north-south highway runs in an east-west line as it passes the park, so according to the compass, technically you turn south off the west side of 101 into the park.)

Facilities: 41 campsites; (a hike-bike site is also available); sites are small to medium-sized, essentially level, with nominal to fair separation; parking pads are gravel, mostly short to medium-length straight-ins; 2 kitchen shelters; fireplaces; firewood is available for gathering in the vicinity, but is likely to be wet, so b-y-o is recommended; water at faucets throughout; restrooms with showers; holding tank disposal station; paved driveways; adequate supplies and services are available in Forks.

Activities & Attractions: The Bogachiel is a renowned steelhead fishery (with both winter and summer runs); boating, floating, drifting; boat launch; nature trail; day use area.

Natural Features: Located on the north/east bank of the wide, swift and deep Bogachiel River in the western foothills of the Olympic Mountains; dense rain forest dominates the region, but the park is in a slightly more open forest setting; elevation 200'.

Season, Fees & Phone: Open all year; please see Appendix for standard Washington state park fees; 10 day limit; park office (206) 374-6356.

Camp Notes: The camp area is wedged between the highway, the bridge and the river. One rule-of-thumb for classifying a region as 'rain forest' is an annual rainfall of more than 100 inches. This area exceeds that benchmark with about a third more liquid. All of that precip helps to produce the stunning rain forest on this side of the peninsula.

MORA
Olympic National Park

Location: Western Washington on the west side of the Olympic Peninsula west of Forks.

Access: From U.S Highway 101 at milepost 193 +.2 (2 miles north of Forks, 9 miles south of Sappho), turn west-southwest onto LaPush Road and drive 8.4 miles to the Quilliute Prairie Fire Department building; turn west (right) onto Mora Road, and continue for 3.3 miles to the campground.

Facilities: 90 campsites in 5 loops; sites are medium-sized, level, with fair separation; parking pads are paved, of assorted lengths and types; adequate space for medium to large tents in most sites; fireplaces; b-y-o firewood; water at central faucets; restrooms; holding tank disposal station; paved driveways; groceries, gas, laundromat and showers at the intersection of LaPush & Mora Roads, 3.3 miles east; adequate supplies and services are available in Forks.

Activities & Attractions: Ocean beaches 1.5 miles west, with trails that lead north and south along the coast; riverside campfire circle for evening nature programs; fishing.

Natural Features: Located on the north bank of the swift, deep Quilliute River; very dense rain forest with lots of ferns and twiggy hardwoods; cloudy/rainy throughout the year, but somewhat less in summer than during other seasons; elevation 100'.

Season, Fees & Phone: Open all year; $7.00; 14 day limit; Olympic National Park Headquarters, Port Angeles, (206) 452-4501.

Camp Notes: Mora Campground is located in the narrow coastal section of Olympic National Park. There is a very quiet, (some might say somber) atmosphere associated with this area. Several of the most scenic beaches in the Park are near here. There are some particularly nice sites on the bank of the Quilliute River.

BEAR CREEK
Washington Department of Natural Resources

Location: Western Washington on the north side of the Olympic Peninsula northeast of Forks.

Access: From U.S. Highway 101 at milepost 206, (15 miles northeast of Forks, 46 miles west of Port Angeles), turn south into the campground.

Facilities: 10 campsites; most sites are medium to large, quite level, and well-spaced; parking pads are gravel, and vary from short to long; majority of the campsites are OK for tents, but better for vehicle camping; fire rings; plenty of firewood is available for gathering, but it may be wet; water at a hand pump; vault facilities; oiled gravel driveways; nearest supplies (limited) in Sappho, 4 miles west; adequate supplies and services are available in Forks.

Activities & Attractions: Soleduck River trails; fishing.

Natural Features: Located on a high bank above the wide, deep Soleduck River; the campground is moderately forested but without a substantial amount of low-level vegetation; lots of moss-covered trees and rocks; Bear Creek enters the Soleduck from the north at this point; elevation 500'.

Season, Fees & Phone: Open all year; no fee (subject to change); 5 day limit; Washington Department of Natural Resources Office, Forks, (206) 374-6131.

Camp Notes: The campground is situated at the site of an old logging camp used as a base of operations to cut spruce for airplanes during World War I. Although it's a bit close to the highway, it is convenient-- and the price is right. This area has also been known as the Albin Wahlgren recreation area.

KLAHOWYA
Olympic National Forest

Location: Western Washington on the north side of the Olympic Peninsula northeast of Forks.

Access: From U.S. Highway 101 at milepost 211 +.9 (20 miles northeast of Forks, 41 miles west of Port Angeles), turn north onto a campground access road and continue for 0.3 mile to the campground.

Facilities: 48 campsites in two loops; most units are spacious, level, and moderately spaced; parking pads are mostly medium-length straight-ins, plus a few pull-offs; many sites, including a couple of walk-ins, are right on the river's edge; fireplaces; firewood is available for gathering, but may be wet; water at several faucets; vault facilities; gravel driveways; nearest supplies (limited) in Sappho, 10 miles west, or Fairholm, 8 miles east; adequate supplies in Forks; complete supplies and services are available in Port Angeles.

Activities & Attractions: Pioneers' Path Nature Trail meanders through the forest within the campground, with signs along the trail that tell of man's past influence on this area; fishing.

Natural Features: Located on the north bank of the Soleduck River in a narrow, steep-sided 'corridor' in a moderately dense rain forest with lots of hanging moss on the trees; cool and moist most of the year; elevation 800'.

Season, Fees & Phone: Open all year, with limited services in winter; $7.00; 14 day limit; Soleduck Ranger District, Forks, (206) 374-6522.

Camp Notes: This strikingly beautiful campground exhibits the somber, almost moody atmosphere typical of rain forest camps. Even on cloudless days not much sun filters through the giant trees. You may hear a little highway noise, but most of it is dampened (no pun intended) by the lush vegetation.

Washington 10

SOLEDUCK
Olympic National Park

Location: Western Washington on the Olympic Peninsula southwest of Port Angeles.

Access: From U.S. Highway 101 at milepost 219 +.3 (2 miles west of Fairholm, 34 miles west of Port Angeles, 27 miles east of Forks), turn southwest onto Soleduck Road (paved) and head southwest then southeast for 11 miles (past the ranger station, the hot springs resort, and resort campground); turn westerly (right) into the camp loops.

Facilities: 80 campsites in 2 loops; sites are small to small+. with nominal to fair separation; parking pads are gravel, mostly short to medium-length straight-ins; adequate space for medium to large tents; fireplaces; firewood is available for gathering in the vicinity; water at central faucets; restrooms; holding tank disposal station; paved driveways; ranger station; camper supplies at the resort (in summer); adequate supplies in Forks; nearest source of complete supplies and services is Port Angeles.

Activities & Attractions: Several miles of hiking trails along the river, to Soleduck Falls, and up to Mink Lake and Deer Lake; (a helpful day hike trail guide handout is available from the ranger station); nature walks and campfire programs scheduled during the summer.

Natural Features: Located in dense forest along the north-east bank of the Soleduck River in the Soleduck Valley; campground vegetation consists of tall conifers and some hardwoods; closely bordered by the densely forested north slopes of the Olympic Mountains; elevation 1700'.

Season, Fees & Phone: Open all year, with limited services October to April; possible closures due to snow; $7.00; 14 day limit; Olympic National Park Headquarters, Port Angeles, (206) 452-4501.

Camp Notes: "Soleduck" is a corruption of *Sol-Duc*, an Indian phrase meaning "sparkling water". Since the 1880's, when the Indians first revealed their whereabouts to Whites, the local mineral springs have had a far-reaching reputation for their healing powers. In the early 1900's, an elaborate health spa was operated here. The private resort adjacent to park campground is a downscale version of the original facility.

Washington 11

FAIRHOLM
Olympic National Park

Location: Western Washington on the north side of the Olympic Peninsula west of Port Angeles.

Access: From U.S Highway 101 at milepost 220 +.9 at Fairholm (26 miles west of Port Angeles, 33 miles east of Forks), turn north onto the paved campground access road and proceed 0.3 mile to the campground.

Facilities: 87 campsites in three loops, including 16 walk-in sites just above the lake shore; most sites are small+, quite sloped, with nominal to fair separation; parking pads are gravel, mostly short to medium-length straight-ins; small to medium-sized tent areas; fireplaces; b-y-o firewood; water at central faucets; restrooms; holding tank disposal station; paved driveways; small store and gas station on the highway near the campground turnoff; adequate supplies in Forks, complete supplies and services are available in Port Angeles.

Activities & Attractions: Self-guiding 0.75 mile nature trail; other trails lead through the campground loops and down to the lake; designated swimming area; boat launch and docks; fishing.

Natural Features: Located on a moderately steep hillside at the west end of Crescent Lake; dense conifer and hardwood forest, plus enough low-level brush in the campground for some campsite separation; the entire area is surrounded by densely forested mountains; elevation 600'.

Season, Fees & Phone: Open all year; $7.00; 14 day limit; Olympic National Park Hq, Port Angeles, (206) 452-4501.

Camp Notes: Crescent Lake is perhaps the most picturesque of the easily accessible lakes on the Peninsula. There are some truly spectacular mountain vistas in this area. Many campers consider the walk-ins to be the best campsites.

Washington 12

ELWHA
Olympic National Park

Location: Western Washington on the north side of the Olympic Peninsula west of Port Angeles.

Access: From U.S. Highway 101 at milepost 239 +.5 (at the east end of the Elwha River bridge, 9 miles west of Port Angeles), turn south onto Elwha Valley Road (paved); proceed 3.1 miles to the campground entrance on the east (left) side of the road.

Facilities: 41 campsites, including 7 walk-ins; most sites are very level and of average size for a park service campground, with minimal separation; parking pads are paved, mostly short to medium straight-ins, plus a few pull-throughs; excellent tent-pitching opportunities for small to medium sized tents; fireplaces; b-y-o firewood; water at several faucets; central restrooms; shelter with a large stone fireplace; paved driveways; ranger station 1 mile south; limited supplies (and showers) at a resort on the main highway; complete supplies and services are available in Port Angeles.

Activities & Attractions: Elwha Campground Trail, a 0.7 mile loop; nearby amphitheater for scheduled ranger-naturalist programs in the summer; fishing.

Natural Features: Located on a wooded flat in the Elwha River Valley; Elwha River is 200 yards west of the campground; moderately dense conifer and hardwood forest (in slightly more open forest than many other campgrounds in the Olympics); el. 400'.

Season, Fees & Phone: Open all year; $7.00; 14 day limit; Olympic National Park Headquarters, Port Angeles, (206) 452-4501.

Camp Notes: Although this campground is very popular in the summer, it's nearly deserted in winter. That's unfortunate, since this valley can be enjoyed year 'round. Bring your rain gear.

Washington 13

ALTAIRE
Olympic National Park

Location: Western Washington on the north side of the Olympic Peninsula west of Port Angeles.

Access: From U.S Highway 101 at milepost 239 +.5 (at the east end of the Elwha River bridge, 9 miles west of Port Angeles), turn south onto the Elwha Valley Road (paved); travel south for 4.5 miles (0.5 mile past the Elwha Ranger Station) to the campground access road; turn west (right), go down a steep paved road 0.1 mile to the campground.

Facilities: 32 campsites; sites are small+ to medium-sized, level, with nominal separation; parking pads are paved, most units have straight-ins, some have pull-throughs; good tent-pitching possibilities; fireplaces; b-y-o firewood; water at several faucets; restrooms; spacious shelter with a large stone fireplace; paved driveways; nearest supplies (and showers) at a resort on the main highway; complete supplies and services are available in Port Angeles.

Activities & Attractions: Whiskey Bend Trail leads off from the ranger station; scenic drive to the south on the Elwha Valley Road; fishing.

Natural Features: Located on a small flat on the bank of the swiftly flowing Elwha River; fairly dense conifer and hardwood forest, but little ground-level vegetation; high, heavily timbered hills on either side of the river; typically quite damp/wet; elevation 400'.

Season, Fees & Phone: May to October; $7.00; 14 day limit; Olympic National Park Headquarters, Port Angeles, (206) 452-4501.

Camp Notes: This is really a pretty nice little campground: very level, somewhat off the beaten path, with the sound of the rushing river for background music.

Washington 14

HEART O' THE HILLS
Olympic National Park

Location: Western Washington on the north side of the Olympic Peninsula south of Port Angeles.

Access: From U.S. Highway 101 in midtown Port Angeles, turn south onto South Race Street (street signs will indicate that this is the way to Hurricane Ridge); travel south for 6.3 miles to the park entrance station and the campground just beyond, on the east (left) side of the road. (Note that the last several miles of the access road are steep and winding.)

Facilities: 105 campsites in 5 loops; overall, the camp units are small+ to medium-sized, with nominal to fair separation; parking pads are paved, short to medium-length straight-ins or pull-offs, which will probably require additional leveling; adequate space for medium-sized tents; fireplaces; b-y-o firewood; water at central faucets; restrooms; paved driveways; complete supplies and services are available in Port Angeles.

Activities & Attractions: Visitor centers at park headquarters in Port Angeles and at Hurricane Ridge; several trailheads nearby; amphitheater for scheduled ranger-naturalist programs.

Natural Features: Located in dense conifer forest on the north slope of the Olympic Mountains; some head-high vegetation provides additional campsite separation; wide, deep valleys and sharply defined mountains are in the vicinity; elevation 1800'.

Season, Fees & Phone: Open all year; $7.00; 14 day limit; Olympic National Park Headquarters, Port Angeles, (206) 452-4501.

Camp Notes: As the name implies, this is hilly country. While Heart O' The Hills may be crowded during the summer months, staying here provides you with access to some of the finest scenery in the park, the most notable of which is found at Hurricane Ridge, 13 miles south. If you manage to get here during clear weather, you won't soon forget the astounding vistas which can be enjoyed throughout this region.

Washington 15

SALT CREEK
Clallam County Recreation Area

Location: Western Washington on the north edge of the Olympic Peninsula west of Port Angeles.

Access: From Washington State Highway 112 at milepost 53 +.9 (11 miles west of Port Angeles), turn north onto Camp Hayden Road; proceed 3.5 miles to the recreation area entrance.

Facilities: 80 campsites in two sections: the first consists of 48 closely spaced rv sites in three parallel rows; the second group of sites would be preferable for tenters, since the location affords substantially more protection from the elements than the first (see below); additional leveling is needed at many sites; fire rings; firewood is usually for sale, or b-y-o; restrooms with showers; nearest supplies (limited) at a small store at the intersection of Highway 112 and Camp Hayden Road; complete supplies and services are available in Port Angles.

Activities & Attractions: Large children's play area; foot trails to viewpoints and to the beach; abandoned harbor defense bunkers.

Natural Features: Located on a high bluff near Tongue Point above the Strait of Juan de Fuca; one area is located on an open grassy, slightly sloping flat surrounded by a conifer and hardwood forest; a second area is situated on a forested point just to the west of the first section; typically very windy; elevation 200'.

Season, Fees & Phone: Open all year; $7.00 for Clallam County residents, $9.00 for non-county residents; Clallam County Parks & Recreation Department, Port Angeles, (206) 452-7831, ext. 291.

Camp Notes: Although the facilities are adequate and reasonably priced, the big attraction here is the view--wow! On a clear day you can see Puget Sound far to the east, and the southern tip of Vancouver Island to the north.

DUNGENESS
Clallam County Recreation Area

Location: Western Washington on the north edge of the Olympic Peninsula east of Port Angeles.

Access: From U.S. Highway 101 at milepost 260 (4 miles west of Sequim, 11 miles east of Port Angeles), turn north onto Kitchen-Dick Lane; continue for 3.3 miles to a point where the road curves east (right) and becomes Lotzgessel Road; proceed 0.2 mile east on Lotzgessel Road to Voice of America Road; turn north (left) onto VoA Road (watch for the large "Dungeness Recreation Area" sign) and continue for a final 0.6 mile to the recreation area.

Facilities: 90 campsites; most sites are fairly good-sized, level, with quite a bit of privacy; parking pads are gravel, primarily long straight-ins, plus some large pull-throughs; nice, grassy tent spots; fire rings; firewood is usually for sale, or b-y-o; water at central faucets; restrooms; paved driveways; adequate+ supplies and services are available in Sequim.

Activities & Attractions: Trails from near the campground to Dungeness Spit; beachcombing; clamming; children's play area; hunting October to January.

Natural Features: Located in a large pine grove on a bluff above 7-mile-long Dungeness Spit, the country's largest natural sand hook; the area abounds in marine wildlife; windy, but not as wet as most of the peninsula; elevation 100'.

Season, Fees & Phone: February to October; $7.00 for Clallam County residents, $9.00 for non-residents; Clallam County Parks & Recreation Department, Port Angeles, (206) 452-7831, ext. 291.

Camp Notes: Some of the most sweeping panoramas of the Olympic Peninsula region are available here: The Olympic Mountains, in full view to the south; Vancouver Island to the north; the Strait of Juan de Fuca to the west; Puget Sound to the east.

SEQUIM BAY
Sequim Bay State Park

Location: Western Washington on the northeast corner of Olympic Peninsula east of Port Angeles.

Access: From U.S. Highway 101 at milepost 269 +.1 (5 miles southeast of Sequim, 13 miles northwest of Discovery Bay), turn north into the park.

Facilities: 86 campsites, including 26 with full hookups, in 2 loops; (3 hike-bike/primitive sites are also available); sites in the upper loop are primarily for large vehicles, with paved, level, pull-through parking pads; lower loop has smaller sites with better separation, and short straight-in parking pads which may need additional leveling; small to medium-sized, but nice, tent spots; fireplaces; b-y-o firewood; water at several faucets; restrooms with showers; paved driveways; adequate+ supplies and services are available in Sequim.

Activities & Attractions: Boating; boat launch, moorage buoys and floats; fishing; swimming beach; scuba diving; nature trails; playground; large, open, grass recreation areas; day use area with shelters.

Natural Features: Located on the forested shore of Sequim Bay in the 'rain shadow' of the Olympic Mountains; campsites receive medium to moderately dense shade/shelter from tall conifers; sea level.

Season, Fees & Phone: Open all year; please see Appendix for standard Washington state park fees; 10 day limit; park office (206) 683-4235.

Camp Notes: Because of the 'rain shadow' effect of the Olympic Mountains, considerably less rain falls here than in the rest of the Olympic Peninsula--only 10-15 inches of annual precipitation, versus rain measured with a log-scaling pole elsewhere. Because of its mild, dry climate, the Sequim Bay area is occasionally termed the 'Banana Belt of the Pacific Northwest'. Lest you get your hopes too high, however, we should point out that the area does get a good share of cloudy, cool weather. This isn't Palm Springs.

FALLS VIEW
Olympic National Forest

Location: Western Washington on the east side of the Olympic Peninsula north of Shelton.

Access: From U.S. Highway 101 at milepost 298 + .3 (4 miles south of Quilcene, 8 miles north of Brinnon), turn west into the campground.

Facilities: 38 campsites in 2 loops; sites are average to large, with good to excellent separation; parking pads are paved, short to short+ straight-ins; most pads will require some additional leveling; ample room for medium-sized, possibly large tents; terraced arrangement for tables; fireplaces; firewood is available for gathering near the campground; water at several faucets; vault facilities; paved driveways; limited to adequate supplies and services are available in Quilcene.

Activities & Attractions: Falls View/Canyon Trail (length 1000') to a falls on the Big Quilcene River; Falls View Loop Trail (length 300'); day use area; 4-wheel drive trails lead east to 2800' Mt. Walker and west toward the Buckhorn Wilderness.

Natural Features: Located on the densely forested west slope in the Quilcene Range of the Olympic Mountains; the Big Quilcene River flows through a deep canyon here; waterfall nearby on the river; Buckhorn Wilderness is to the west; elevation 500'.

Season, Fees & Phone: May to September; $6.00; 14 day limit; Quilcene Ranger District (206) 765-3368.

Camp Notes: Nice-looking campsites, good mountain views. The drive along Highway 101 to Falls View is first class! In this section, the highway leaves the coast and meanders between a sheer forested bluff and a pleasant valley. Falls View, and neighboring Rainbow, are unlike all other campgrounds in the area because they're situated several miles inland from the shore of Hood Canal. In addition to the forest camps along this stretch of highway, there's also a campground in a small Jefferson County park right along the highway in Quilcene.

Washington 19

RAINBOW
Olympic National Forest

Location: Western Washington on the east side of the Olympic Peninsula north of Shelton.

Access: From U.S. Highway 101 at milepost 299 +.7 (5 miles south of Quilcene, 7 miles north of Brinnon), turn west into the campground.

Facilities: 9 campsites; (the campground may be used by groups, by reservation); sites are small, with fairly good to very good separation; parking pads are gravel, short to medium-length straight-ins; most pads will require a little to a lot of additional leveling; small tent areas; fireplaces; firewood is available for gathering in the vicinity; water at a central faucet; vault facilities; gravel driveway; gas and groceries in Quilcene; nearest sources of adequate supplies and services are Sequim and Shelton.

Activities & Attractions: Rainbow Canyon Trail.

Natural Features: Located on a slope on the edge of a deep, forested canyon in the lower foothills of the Olympic Mountains; campground vegetation consists of dense, tall conifers and hardwoods; elev. 700'.

Season, Fees & Phone: April to October; no fee for individual site use (fee for group use); availablity of sites to individual campers is on a first-come, first-served basis, subject to prior reservations by groups; 14 day limit; Quilcene Ranger District (206) 765-3368.

Camp Notes: In addition to this snug, nine-site deal and the other two forest camps (Falls View and Seal Rock) along the main highway around the Olympics, there are much more remote campgrounds deep in the heart of the peninsula's great river valleys. From near U.S. 101 milepost 306, take the Dosewallips River Road northwest for 12 miles (paved for several miles, then gravel) for 12 miles to Elkhorn Campground. Or from U.S. 101 milepost 310, travel northwest on the paved Duckabush River Road for 6 miles to Collins Campground. And you can reach Hamma Hamma and Lena Creek Campgrounds from U.S. 101 milepost 317 +.9, then heading northwest up the paved Hamma Hamma River Road for 6 miles and 8 miles, respectively. All of these small camps are on the edge of The Brothers Wilderness, under 800' of elevation in deep forest, and have drinking water, vaults, short or medium-length parking pads, a nominal fee, and offer stream fishing for a campground diversion. If you're looking for a day trip from a camp along the highway, any of the river routes would present you with lots of fine scenery.

Washington 20

SEAL ROCK
Olympic National Forest

Location: Western Washington on the east side of the Olympic Peninsula north of Shelton.

Access: From U.S. Highway 101 at milepost 305 +.4 (10 miles south of Quilcene, 2 miles north of Brinnon), turn east then immediately north and follow the paved access road for 0.2 mile to the campground.

Facilities: 41 campsites in 3 tiers; sites are small to medium-sized, with nominal to fairly good separation; parking pads are hardened gravel, mostly short to medium-length straight-ins or pull-offs; additional leveling may be necessary; tent spots are fairly clear of underbrush and adequate for medium-sized tents; some sites have framed-and-gravelled tent pads; fireplaces; some firewood is available for gathering on nearby forest lands (none in the campground area), so b-y-o is recommended; water at several faucets; restrooms; paved driveways are narrow, with limited space for large vehicles to maneuver; gas and groceries in Quilcene; nearest sources of adequate supplies and services are Sequim and Shelton.

Activities & Attractions: Self-guided nature trail; steep trails to the beach; designated swimming area; day use area; beachcombing, clamming and crabbing; boating; boat launch; fishing.

Natural Features: Located on a forested hillside overlooking Dabob Bay and Hood Canal on Puget Sound; fairly dense vegetation in the campground consists of tall conifers, hardwoods, bushes and ferns; rocky beach; Olympic Mountains rise to the west; elevation 50'.

Season, Fees & Phone: April to October; $7.00 to $9.00; 14 day limit; Quilcene Ranger District (206) 765-3368.

Camp Notes: Indians lived at Seal Rock as long as 700 years ago, and the short interpretive trail explains how they used local resources. The campground is on a sheltered bay with good to great views through the trees from virtually all sites. The drive along U.S. 101 in this region is superscenic--between the Bay to the east and the Olympics to the west.

Washington 21

DOSEWALLIPS
Dosewallips State Park

Location: Western Washington on the east side of the Olympic Peninsula north of Shelton.

Access: From U.S. Highway 101 at milepost 307 (0.3 mile south of the Dosewallips River Bridge, 11 miles south of Quilcene, 25 miles north of Hoodsport), turn west onto the campground access road and proceed northwesterly for 0.35 mile to the campground entrance station, then swing right, into the campground. (Note: a section of the campground is on the east side of the highway, and is accessible from the main campground via a driveway which passes under the highway bridge spanning the river; bridge clearance is only 10 feet.)

Facilities: 127 campsites, including 40 with full hookups; (2 hike-bike sites and a group camp are also available); sites are small to medium-sized, generally level, with minimal to fair separation; parking pads are gravel or paved, short to long straight-ins; most sites have excellent tent-pitching opportunities; fireplaces; b-y-o firewood is recommended; water at several faucets; restrooms with showers; paved driveways; gas and groceries in Quilcene.

Activities & Attractions: Beach access; clamming; oyster gathering; a trail connects both sections of the park; day use area.

Natural Features: Located on large, grassy, semi-open flats ringed by dense forest; campsites receive light to medium shade/shelter from large conifers and some hardwoods; the Dosewallips River flows along the northeast corner of the park and into Hood Canal at this point; the Olympic Mountains rise to the west; sea level.

Season, Fees & Phone: Open all year; please see Appendix for standard Washington state park fees; 10 day limit; park office (206) 796-4415.

Camp Notes: Views toward the Olympic Mountains from certain vantage points in the campground are quite good. (However, other vantage points around here will give you a clear shot of clear-cut mountainsides.) In addition, some of the campsites on the east side of the highway are riverside. The fairly mild climate here draws campers year-round.

Washington 22

LAKE CUSHMAN
Lake Cushman State Park

Location: Western Washington on the east side of the Olympic Peninsula north of Shelton.

Access: From U.S. Highway 101 at milepost 331 +.7 (on the north edge of the community of Hoodsport, 15 miles north of Shelton), turn west onto Lake Cushman Road (paved) and travel northwest then north for 7.2 miles; turn west (left) into the main campground; or continue north for another 0.7 mile; turn west (left) onto a paved access road and go southwest for 0.7 mile to the upper campground.

Facilities: 51 campsites, including 30 with full hookups, in the main camp; (2 hike-bike sites are also available); 29 campsites in the upper camp; (a reservable group camp in the upper area is also available); sites are small to medium-sized, with minimal to very good separation; parking pads are paved, medium-length straight-ins or long pull-throughs; many pads in the upper section will require some additional leveling; medium to large tent spots; water at several faucets; restrooms with showers; holding tank disposal station; paved driveways; gas and groceries+ in Hoodsport.

Activities & Attractions: Boating; boat launch; fishing, mainly for kokanee salmon, rainbow and cutthroat trout; 4 miles of hiking trails; swimming beach.

Natural Features: Located near the northeast shore of Lake Cushman in the eastern foothills of the Olympic Mountains; main area is on a gently rolling flat, upper area is on a moderate slope; surrounded by a dense forest of tall conifers, hardwoods, ferns and other plants and bushes; elevation 750'.

Season, Fees & Phone: Open all year, but limited to weekends and holidays during the winter; please see Appendix for standard Washington state park fees; park office (206) 877-5491 or (206) 877-5665 or (206) 877-5361.

Camp Notes: Be sure to check out the upper camp loop. The upper sites although not as near to the lake as are those in the main loop, are slightly larger and offer a little more privacy. Subjectively, they are in a somewhat nicer forest environment, too. The upper camp is also a better choice if you're a hiker, since most of the park's trails are accessible from that area.

Washington 23

BIG CREEK
Olympic National Forest

Location: Western Washington on the east side of the Olympic Peninsula north of Shelton.

Access: From U.S. Highway 101 at milepost 331 +.7 (on the north edge of the community of Hoodsport, 15 miles north of Shelton), turn west onto Lake Cushman Road (paved) and travel northwest then north for 9.3 miles to a "T" intersection; turn left onto Forest Road 24, go 200 yards, then turn right into the campground; get onto the one-way driveway and keep going until you reach the first sites about a quarter mile around the three-quarter-mile loop.

Facilities: 24 campsites; sites are small+, with very good to excellent separation; parking pads are gravel, mostly short+ to medium-length straight-ins or pull-offs, plus several long pull-throughs; some additional leveling will be needed in most sites; small to medium-sized tent areas, generally sloped; fireplaces; firewood is available for gathering (may be wet); water at hand pumps; vault facilities; gravel driveways; gas and groceries+ in Hoodsport.

Activities & Attractions: Big Creek Loop Trail; boating, boat launch, fishing for kokanee, rainbow and cutthroat trout on Lake Cushman, 5 miles south.

Natural Features: Located on hilly terrain on the east slope of the Olympic Mountains; campground vegetation consists of extremely dense, slender, tall conifers and equally dense undercover; elev. 900'.

Season, Fees & Phone: April to October; $7.00; 14 day limit; Hood Canal Ranger District, Hoodsport, (206) 877-5254.

Camp Notes: In the middle segment of the nine miles of road that lead to Big Creek Campground, the way becomes steep and twisty for a couple of miles. If you want to burn-in the piston rings and wear-in the hides on your new 'vette (or whatever), this is the place you'll do it. Continuing on Forest Road 24 past the turnoff to Big Creek for another seven miles will get you to Staircase Campground, just inside the boundary of Olympic National Park. Staircase has 59 small campsites with piped water and restrooms in a densely forested, hilly setting at an elevation of 800'. Sitting at the camp table or in an rv here in Big Creek, you wouldn't see anybody or anything else except your camp appliances and whatever is six inches into the foliage. The campground's water supply comes from the Big Creek Well. The hole that's bored into the foothills of the Olympics is more than 120 feet deep, so keep pumping!

Washington 24

POTLATCH
Potlatch State Park

Location: Western Washington on the east side of the Olympic Peninsula north of Shelton.

Access: From U.S. Highway 101 at milepost 335 + 100 yards (3 miles south of Hoodsport, 2 miles north of the junction of U.S. 101 and Washington State Highway 106), turn west into the campground.

Facilities: 35 campsites, including 18 with full hookups; (a pair of hike-bike sites are also available); sites are very small to small+, with minimal to nominal separation; parking pads are gravel, medium-length straight-ins or long pull-throughs; some pads might require a touch of additional leveling; b-y-o firewood; water at several faucets; restrooms with showers; holding tank disposal station; paved driveways; gas and groceries+ in Hoodsport; adequate supplies and services are available in Shelton.

Activities & Attractions: Sandy beach with bathhouse; playground; boating; fishing; clamming, crabbing, oystering, shrimping; hiking and jeep trails lead westward toward Olympic National Park; day use area.

Natural Features: Located along and near the shore of Annas Bay on Hood Canal, a major arm of Puget Sound; campground is on slightly hilly terrain just across the highway from the shore; campsites are very well shaded/sheltered by large hardwoods and conifers; a small stream passes the south edge of the campground; the Olympic Mountains rise to the west; sea level.

Season, Fees & Phone: Open all year; please see Appendix for standard Washington state park fees; 10 day limit; park office (206) 877-5361.

Camp Notes: A *potlatch* is a Northwest Indian get-together, and this beautiful area was a traditional festival site. Reportedly, it is still used for Native gatherings in modern times. Because of its convenient, highwayside location and scenic value, this small park isn't one of Washington's better-kept secrets. (Park signs specifically recommend that you lock your valuables out of site when camping here.)

Washington 25

SCHAFER
Schafer State Park

Location: Western Washington on the south side of the Olympic Peninsula west of Olympia.

Access: From U.S Highway 12 at milepost 14 +.8 (5 miles west of Elma, 5 miles east of Montesano), turn north onto a paved road at the "Schafer State Park" sign; continue north and east for 9.1 miles along the East Fork of the Satsop River; turn southwest (right) into the campground.

Facilities: 47 campsites, including 6 with partial hookups; (hike-bike sites are also available); sites are small+ to medium-sized, basically level, with nominal to fair separation; parking pads are gravel/earth, and vary from short to long; large tent spaces; fireplaces; b-y-o firewood is recommended; water at several faucets; restrooms; holding tank disposal station; paved driveways; adequate supplies and services are available in Montesano and Elma.

Activities & Attractions: Fishing (reportedly best in fall for salmon, winter for steelhead, summer for sea-run cutthroat); hiking trails; small playground; horseshoe pits; volleyball court; day use area with shelters.

Natural Features: Located on a forested flat along the East Fork of the Satsop River south of the Olympic Mountains; a rain forest atmosphere is created by tall, moss-covered hardwoods and a carpet of ferns and tiny plants; elevation 300'.

Season, Fees & Phone: Open all year, but limited to weekends and holidays during the winter; please see Appendix for standard Washington state park fees; 10 day limit; park office (206) 482-3852.

Camp Notes: The park land originally was owned by a prominent logging industry family. The picnics they arranged for family, friends and employees in the early 1900's reportedly were real humdingers. True to tradition, the park is still a popular spot for group gatherings.

Washington 26

LAKE SYLVIA
Lake Sylvia State Park

Location: Western Washington on the south side of the Olympic Peninsula west of Olympia.

Access: From U.S. Highway 12 near milepost 10+.5, take the Montesano exit into midtown Montesano; travel west on Pioneer Avenue to Third Street; turn north onto Third Street and proceed northerly on a rather steep, winding, paved road for 1.5 miles to the park entrance; the campground is 0.2 mile ahead.

Facilities: 35 campsites; (hike-bike sites and a reservable group camp are also available); most sites are small to small+, with nominal to fair separation; parking pads are gravel, short to medium-length straight-ins; medium-sized, grassy tent areas; fireplaces; firewood is usually for sale, or b-y-o; water at faucets throughout; restrooms with showers; holding tank disposal station; paved driveways; some groceries are available at the park concession in summer; adequate supplies and services are available in Montesano.

Activities & Attractions: Swimming; motorless boating; hiking trail; playground; fishing for bass and stocked trout; day use area with shelter.

Natural Features: Located on a point of land on the east shore of 30-acre Lake Sylvia; park vegetation consists of tall hardwoods, conifers and underbrush; bordered by forested hills; elevation 200'.

Season, Fees & Phone: Open all year, with limited services October to April; please see Appendix for standard Washington state park fees; 10 day limit; park office (206) 249-3621.

Camp Notes: Lake Sylvia was built as a mill pond for the sawmill which used to stand here. After the mill lost its profitability in the 1930's, the property was given to the city of Montesano, which in turn transferred it to the state.

Washington 27

OCEAN CITY
Ocean City State Park

Location: Western Washington at the southwest corner of the Olympic Peninsula west of Aberdeen-Hoquiam.

Access: From the junction of Washington State Highways 109 and 115 (16 miles west of Hoquiam), travel south for 1 mile on Highway 115; turn west into the park.

Facilities: 178 campsites, including 29 with full hookups, in 3 loops: (3 hike-bike/primitive sites and a small group camp are also available); 130 standard sites (located in 2 loops which flank the entrance station) are small to medium-sized, level, with minimal to nominal separation; most parking pads are short to medium-length straight-ins; large, grassy areas ideal for tent-pitching; 48 hookup units (in a third loop west of the entrance station) are small to small+, level, with nominal to fair separation; parking pads are paved, medium to long, straight-ins or pull-throughs; fireplaces; b-y-o firewood; water at faucets; restrooms with showers; holding tank disposal station; paved driveways; limited supplies are available in Ocean City, 2 miles north, or Ocean Shores, 2 miles south.

Activities & Attractions: Beachcombing; fishing (boat or surf fishing on the ocean, freshwater fishing southeast of the park on Duck Lake); clamming and crabbing; short hiking trails; Ocean Shores Environmental Interpretive Center, near the south end of Ocean Shores, has exhibits and programs which focus on the history, wildlife and land use of Point Brown; day use area.

Natural Features: Located on a fairly level stretch of Pacific Ocean coastline on Point Brown; standard camp loops have large conifers which provide light to medium shelter/shade; hookup loop is a little more open, with a beach view from some sites; expansive ocean beach; typically breezy; sea level.

Season, Fees & Phone: Open all year; please see Appendix for standard Washington state park fees; 10 day limit; park office (206) 289-3553.

Camp Notes: Another state park on this stretch of the coast is Pacific Beach SP, in the burg of Pacific Beach, a few miles north of Ocean City. The park is operated by a concessionaire and it has nearly 140 unsheltered campsites (a few with hookups) packed together along the edge of an open beach.

Washington 28

TWIN HARBORS
Twin Harbors State Park

Location: Southwest Washington south of Westport.

Access: From the junction of Washington State Highway 105 and the Highway 105 Spur into Westport (2 miles south of Westport): there are several park entrances to the west, south and east of the intersection. (Note: If you glance at a highway map, you'll see that Highway 105 makes a 90° bend at this junction; campground entrances are located south of the east-west segment of the highway, and both east and west of the north-south segment; you'll need to check-in at the campground office near the hookup section on the southeast quadrant of the junction.)

Facilities: 332 campsites, including 49 with full hookups, in several sections on both sides of the highway: (a reservable group camp is also available); the largest area, on the east side of the highway in a grove of tall trees, has small to medium-sized, level sites with medium-length, parking pads; a second major area is on the west side of the highway along the beach; sites are small, with minimal to fair separation; full hookup units are located in a third section on the southeast corner of the intersection in an open, "parking lot" arrangement; fireplaces; firewood is usually for sale, driftwood may be gathered, b-y-o is suggested; water at faucets; restrooms with showers in each section; holding tank disposal station; adequate supplies and services are available in Westport.

Activities & Attractions: Beach trails; Shifting Sands Nature Trail (guide booklet available); playground; beachcombing (best in winter); limited clamming; access to the well-known charter fishing fleet of Westport.

Natural Features: Located along or near a long, windswept ocean beach; beach campsites are located in dunes covered with tall grass, and are minimally to lightly shaded/sheltered by bushy pines and shrubs; the sites in the large section on the east side of the highway afford substantially more protection from the wind (and the sun, when it shines) than those on the beach; hookup sites are lightly to moderately sheltered from sun and wind; sea level.

Season, Fees & Phone: Open all year; please see Appendix for standard Washington state park fees; 10 day limit; campsite reservations recommended for summer weekends, please see Appendix; park office (206) 268-9717 or (206) 268-9565.

Camp Notes: Twin Harbors takes it name from the two anchorages--Grays Harbor to the north and Willapa Bay to the South--which flank this area. The campground is very heavily used, especially on weekends--and it shows its experiences none too gracefully.

Washington 29

GRAYLAND BEACH
Grayland Beach State Park

Location: Southwest Washington south of Westport.

Access: From Washington State Highway 105 at milepost 25 +.7 at the south edge of the community of Grayland (6 miles south of Westport), turn west onto County Line Road and proceed 0.1 mile; turn south (left) to the campground entrance station; the campground is 0.25 mile south and west of the entrance.

Facilities: 60 campsites with full hookups in 6 'pods'; (hike-bike sites are also available); sites are small, level, with nominal to good separation; parking pads are paved, medium-length straight-ins; small to medium-sized, grassy tent spots; fireplaces; firewood is usually for sale, or b-y-o; restrooms with showers; paved driveways; limited supplies and services are available in Grayland.

Activities & Attractions: Trail to the beach from the campground; beachcombing (best in winter).

Natural Features: Located a few hundred yards from the sea, but without an ocean view; campground vegetation consists of small sections of mown grass, and bushy pines and shrubs which provide light to medium shade and generally good wind-shelter; sea level.

Season, Fees & Phone: Open all year; please see Appendix for standard Washington state park fees; phone c/o Twin Harbors State Park (206) 268-9717 or (206) 268-9565.

Camp Notes: This campground was designed primarily with the recreational vehicle camper in mind, but even if you don't need the hookup, it would still provide you with the best camp in this vicinity.

Washington 30

FORT CANBY
Fort Canby State Park

Location: Southwest Washington west of Illwaco.

Access: From U.S. Highway 101 in midtown Illwaco at the corner of First Street and Spruce Street, head west on Spruce Street (Fort Canby Road) and out of town on a winding, hilly road for 3.4 miles to a 4-way intersection; turn northwest (right) to the campground entrance; campsites are in several sections within 2 miles of the entrance.

Facilities: 250 campsites, including 60 with full hookups; sites are small to small+ in size, essentially level, with fair to very good separation; parking pads are paved, short to medium-length, mostly straight-ins; adequate space for medium to large tents; b-y-o firewood is recommended; water at several faucets; restrooms with showers; holding tank disposal station; paved driveways; camper supplies at the park concession; limited+ to adequate supplies and services are available in Illwaco.

Activities & Attractions: Lewis and Clark Interpretive Center (open daily during the summer, and weekends by appointment during the winter); swimming or wading in a small cove on Waikiki Beach (really); Cape Disappointment Lighthouse, the oldest West Coast lighthouse still in operation; four hiking trails; good beachcombing in winter; boat launch; fishing; day use areas.

Natural Features: Located on more than 1700 acres along the Pacific Ocean at the mouth of the Columbia River; campsites receive light to moderately dense shade/shelter from medium-high shrubbery, bushy pines, and some large hardwoods; sea level.

Season, Fees & Phone: Open all year; please see Appendix for standard Washington state park fees; 10 day limit; campsite reservations recommended for anytime during the summer, please see Appendix; park office (206) 642-3078 or (206) 642-3029.

Camp Notes: Fort Canby was operated as a Columbia River defense post from the 1870's to the end of World War II. The interpretive center features exhibits about frontier foods, early medicine, trade goods, and information about Lewis and Clark and the Corps of Discovery. Lewis and Clark spent most of their time on the Coast at their winter home at Fort Clatsop in Oregon. Fort Canby is large enough, though, and has enough items of interest, that you'll probably spend more time than Meriwether & William did on this side of the Columbia. If Fort Canby is all booked up when you desire to camp in this area, you might be able to find a campsite at Chinook Park (see info below).

Washington 31

CHINOOK
Pacific County Park

Location: Southwest corner of Washington east of Illwaco.

Access: From U.S. Highway 101 at milepost 3.8 (on the east edge of the town of Chinook, 3.5 miles west of the Columbia River bridge from Astoria, Oregon), turn south onto Chinook Park Road (paved) and go 0.1 mile to the park.

Facilities: Approximately 60 campsites, including some with partial hookups; sites are small to small+, level, with nominal separation; parking surfaces are grass, mostly medium to long straight-ins; large areas for tents; random parking on the grass for standard/tent sites; fire rings; b-y-o firewood; water at several faucets; restrooms with showers; paved driveways; gas and groceries+ in Chinook; limited+ to adequate supplies and services are available in Illwaco.

Activities & Attractions: Small boat launch area in the park (usable at high tide); large boat launch 1 mile west; boat fishing for salmon; bank fishing for perch and flounder; playground; Fort Columbia State Park, 1 mile east.

Natural Features: Located on a flat along the north bank of the Columbia River a few miles upriver of the Pacific Ocean; sites are lightly to moderately sheltered/shaded, mostly by hardwoods; bordered by dense vegetation and a rock sea wall; sea level.

Season, Fees & Phone: Open all year; $9.00 for a standard site, $11.50 for a hookup site; 14 day limit; park manager (206) 777-8442 or Pacific County Public Works Department, Long Beach, (206) 642-9300, ext. 273.

Camp Notes: Chinook serves as a simple fishing camp for hundreds of Columbia River anglers each year. If you're not a boater of fisherman and would like some diversion, pleasant surroundings and scenery, Fort Columbia could easily occupy a couple of hours. The nearby state park features the well-preserved buildings and grounds of a harbor defense post that dates back to the early 1900's.

Washington 32

MILLERSYLVANIA
Millersylvania State Park

Location: Western Washington south of Olympia.

Access: From Interstate 5 Exit 95 for Maytown/Little Rock (12 miles south of Olympia, 11 miles north of Centralia), drive east on Maytown Road SW for 2.5 miles; at a "T" intersection, turn north (left) onto Tilley Road and proceed 0.7 mile; turn west (left) into the park; continue ahead (northwest, then curving southwest) for 0.3 mile to the campground.

Facilities: 187 campsites, including 52 with partial hookups; sites are small to medium-sized, essentially level, with minimal to fairly good separation; parking pads are gravel, mostly short to medium-length straight-ins; ample space for a large tent in most sites; fire rings; firewood is usually for sale, or b-y-o; water at several faucets; restrooms with showers; kitchen shelter; holding tank disposal station; paved driveways; camper supplies at a small local store; complete supplies and services are available in the Tumwater-Olympia area.

Activities & Attractions: Swimming beaches with swim platforms; playgrounds; several hiking trails; jogging and fitness trails; sports field; limited boating (5 mph); boat launch; fishing; day use areas with shelters.

Natural Features: Located on a forested flat; park vegetation consists of very tall conifers which provide moderate to dense shelter/shade for campsites, plus sections of mown grass, and some hardwoods, bushes and ferns; Deep Lake and Spruce Creek are the park's water features; elevation 100'.

Season, Fees & Phone: Open all year; please see Appendix for standard Washington state park fees; 10 day limit; park office (206) 753-1519.

Camp Notes: Millersylvania's name was coined from the three members of the *Miller* family who donated this *sylvan* (forested) location for the park. The CCC lent a hand in constructing some of the facilities in the 1930's and 1940's.

Washington 33

RAINBOW FALLS
Rainbow Falls State Park

Location: Southwest Washington west of Centralia-Chehalis.

Access: From Washington State Highway 6 at a point 15.8 miles west of Interstate 5 Exit 77 in Chehalis and 35 miles east of Raymond, turn north and drive across a bridge into the park.

Facilities: 47 campsites; (3 hike-bike/primitive sites are also available); sites are small to small+, basically level, with nominal to fair separation; parking pads are gravel or paved, mostly short to medium-length straight-ins; most units will accommodate medium to large tents; fireplaces; b-y-o firewood; water at several faucets; restrooms with showers; kitchen shelter; holding tank disposal station; paved driveways; gas and groceries in Doty, 1 mile west; complete supplies and services are available in Chehalis-Centralia.

Activities & Attractions: Fishing on the Chehalis River; playground and large lawn for recreational activities in the interior of the park; nature trails; hiking trails; suspension bridge over the river; day use area with shelter.

Natural Features: Located in the Chehalis River Valley north of the Willapa Hills; the park is engulfed in a rain forest atmosphere with tall conifers, hanging moss, and luxuriant ferns on a thick carpet of conifer needles; elevation 250'.

Season, Fees & Phone: Open all year; please see Appendix for standard Washington state park fees; 10 day limit; park office (206) 291-3767.

Camp Notes: Portions of Rainbow Falls State Park were constructed years ago by the CCC. There are a number of structures here which are characteristic of that era.

Washington 34

LEWIS AND CLARK
Lewis and Clark State Park

Location: Western Washington south of Centralia-Chehalis.

Access: From U.S. Highway 12 at milepost 69 +.2 in the hamlet of Marys Corner (2.6 miles east of Interstate 5 Exit 68, 18 miles west of Mossyrock), turn south onto Jackson Highway and proceed 1.7 miles; turn west (right) into the park; continue past the day use area for 0.15 mile to the campground.

Facilities: 25 campsites in 2 loops; (a reservable small group camp is also available); sites are small to small+, with fair to very good separation; parking pads are gravel, mostly short+ to medium+ straight-ins; additional leveling may be required on most pads; medium to large tent spots, generally somewhat sloped; fireplaces; b-y-o firewood is recommended; kitchen shelter; water at several faucets; restrooms; paved driveways; gas and groceries in Marys Corner; complete supplies and services are available in Centralia-Chehalis, 12 miles north.

Activities & Attractions: Interpretive trails (a trail guide pamphlet is available); several miles of hiking only or hiking/equestrian trails; equestrian parking and horse-handling area; amphitheater; playground; day use area with shelters.

Natural Features: Located on a hillside in the Cowlitz River Valley; campsites are generally well-shaded/sheltered by tall conifers and some hardwoods; elevation 300'.

Season, Fees & Phone: Open all year; please see Appendix for standard Washington state park fees; 10 day limit; park office (206) 864-2643.

Camp Notes: The secluded little camping area is just a few yards from a picturesque creek and a tiny waterfall. This region originally was the home of the Cowlitz Indians, for whom the major river and its valley are named. Perhaps the park would have been better-named for the Cowlitz, since Lewis and Clark never made it this far north.

MAYFIELD LAKE
Lewis County Park

Location: Western Washington southeast of Centralia-Chehalis.

Access: From U.S. Highway 12 at milepost 83 + .6 (17 miles east of Interstate 5 Exit 68, 2.5 miles west of Mossyrock, 15 miles west of Morton), turn northwest onto Beach Road; travel 1 mile to the park entrance, then turn right into the campground.

Facilities: 54 campsites in 2 loops; sites are small+ to medium+, with fair separation; parking pads are gravel, and some are roomy enough to accommodate large rv's; a little additional leveling may be necessary; tent spots vary in size and levelness; fireplaces; b-y-o firewood is recommended; water at several faucets; restrooms with showers; holding tank disposal station; paved driveways; minimal supplies at a small store on Highway 12; gas and groceries in Silver Creek, 3 miles west; limited supplies and services are available in Mossyrock.

Activities & Attractions: Boating; boat launch; fishing; designated swimming area with sandy beach; playground; hiking trails; dam tours; nearby White Pass skilift operates during summers for sightseeing.

Natural Features: Located on Mayfield Lake, a reservoir formed by Mayfield Dam on the Cowlitz River; sites are situated in an open, grassy area or near tall trees; some sites are on a bluff overlooking the lake while others are right on the lakeshore; bordered by forested hills; Mount St. Helens National Volcanic Monument is to the southeast; Mount Rainier is located to the northeast; elevation 450'.

Season, Fees & Phone: May to September; $9.00 for a site, $5.00 reservation fee; 10 day limit; for reservations, write Mayfield Lake Park, 180 Beach Road, Mossyrock, WA 98564; park office (may be a recorded message), (206) 985-2364.

Camp Notes: Mayfield Lake is 13 miles long, and the treeline on the surrounding hillsides dips right down to meet the lake's 33 miles of shoreline. The park offers some of the better camping and recreational opportunities in this part of Washington.

IKE KINSWA
Ike Kinswa State Park

Location: Southwest Washington southeast of Centralia-Chehalis.

Access: From U.S. Highway 12 (eastbound) at milepost 80 + .3 in Silver Creek (14 miles east of Interstate 5 Exit 68, 7 miles west of Mossyrock), turn north onto Silver Creek Road (paved) and travel northeast for 1.9 miles to a fork; bear (right) onto Harmony Road and continue northeast for 2.2 miles (across the Tilton River bridge) to a 4-way intersection; turn south (right) for 0.1 mile to the campground.

Alternate Access: From U.S 12 (westbound) at milepost 86 + .9 in Mossyrock, (10 miles west of Morton), turn north onto Harmony Road and proceed north and west for 3.8 miles to the 4-way intersection and continue as above.

Facilities: 101 campsites, including 41 with full hookups, in 3 loops; sites are medium to large, most are essentially level, with fairly good to very good separation; parking pads are paved/packed gravel, medium-length straight-ins or medium to long pull-throughs; adequate space for large tents; fireplaces; firewood is usually for sale, or b-y-o; water at hookup sites and at several faucets; restrooms with showers; holding tank disposal station; paved driveways; gas and groceries and limited services in the Silver Creek-Mossyrock metro area.

Activities & Attractions: Swimming beach with bathhouse; 6 miles of hiking trails; playground; boating; boat launch (at the west end of the Tilton River bridge); fishing.

Natural Features: Located along or near the north shore of Mayfield Lake; park vegetation consists primarily of dense, tall hardwoods and conifers, ferns and other dense undergrowth; the campground is on a point on the north shore between the Cowlitz River and Tilton River inlets; the lake is bordered by high, densely forested hills and mountains; park area is 454 acres; elevation 450'.

Season, Fees & Phone: Open all year; please see Appendix for standard Washington state park fees; 10 day limit; park office (206) 983-3402.

Camp Notes: Camping is the principal reason for coming to this park and, barring unforeseen circumstances, you couldn't go wrong in just about any campsite. Only a few campsites enjoy glimpses of the lake, but trails lead from the campground through the dense forest to the lake's edge.

Washington 37

SEAQUEST
Seaquest State Park

Location: Southwest Washington north of Longview.

Access: From Washington State Highway 504 (Spirit Lake Highway) at milepost 5 +.6 (5.6 miles east of Interstate 5 Exit 49 at Castle Rock), turn north onto the park access road and proceed north/northwest for 0.2 mile to the park entrance; the campground loops are straight ahead or to the left. (Note: the park turnoff is on the opposite side of the highway from the east end of the parking lot for the Mount Saint Helens Visitor Center.)

Facilities: 92 campsites, including 16 with full hookups, in 3 loops; (hike-bike sites and a reservable group camp are also available); sites are small to medium-sized, with nominal to very good separation; most parking pads are gravel, short+ to medium+ straight-ins or medium to long pull-throughs; (sites in the full hookup loop are medium-length pull-throughs in a side-by-side, semi-parking lot arrangement); additional leveling may be necessary in many standard sites; adequate space for medium to large tents; fireplaces; b-y-o firewood; water at several faucets; restrooms with showers; holding tank disposal station; paved driveways; gas and groceries at several points along Highway 504; adequate supplies and services are available in Castle Rock.

Activities & Attractions: Hiking trails; short nature trail; playground, horseshoe pits and a ball field; volleyball court; boating, fishing and swimming at Silver Lake; adjacent Mount Saint Helens Visitor Center features displays explaining the famous volcanic peak's 1980 eruption; day use area with large shelter.

Natural Features: Located on 300 acres of level to hilly terrain, among a light to moderately dense mixture of tall conifers and hardwoods; day use area also has mown lawns trimmed with rail fences; Silver Lake is accessible across the highway to the south; Mount Saint Helens National Volcanic Monument is located 30 miles east; elevation 100'.

Season, Fees & Phone: Open all year; please see Appendix for standard Washington state park fees; 10 day limit; park office (206) 274-8633.

Camp Notes: The nicely landscaped day use area near the camp loops will provide you with a pleasant outdoor parlor for sitting, or a spacious family room for playing. The large Mount St. Helens visitor center across the road is a real bonus to a trip to Seaquest, particularly if you have youngsters. Besides a host of educational displays, there's also a walk-through model of a volcano, complete with special effects.

Washington 38

PARADISE POINT
Paradise Point State Park

Location: Southwest Washington north of Vancouver.

Access: From Interstate 5 Exit 16 (5 miles south of Woodland, 17 miles north of Vancouver), on the *east* side of I-5, turn north onto a frontage road (Paradise Point Park Road) and proceed 1 mile to the park entrance and the campground.

Facilities: 70 campsites in 2 loops; (9 primitive sites are also available); sites are small to small+, with minimal to fair separation; most parking pads are paved, short to medium-length straight-ins; tent spots tend to be either large and level or small and private; fireplaces; b-y-o firewood; water at several faucets; restrooms with showers; holding tank disposal station; paved driveways; adequate supplies and services are available in Woodland.

Activities & Attractions: Hiking trails; boating; boat launch; fishing; designated swimming beach on the riverbank.

Natural Features: Located along the East Fork of the Lewis River; one camp loop is on a somewhat open flat with manicured lawns and a rail fence bordering the driveway; the second loop is more forested and is situated on a hillside amid a mixture of hardwoods and conifers; bordered by forested hills; volcanic Mount Saint Helens can be seen from the park; elevation 100'.

Season, Fees & Phone: Open all year, with limited services October to April; please see Appendix for standard Washington state park fees; 10 day limit; park office (206) 263-2350.

Camp Notes: Before you stuff the sleeping bags into the pickup, or pack the sheets and pillow cases in the rv, there's one thing you should know about Paradise Point: Many of the campsites are within 50 yards of I-5. That said, it should also be noted that the grounds are well-landscaped, and a row of trees camouflages the four-lane to some degree. It *is* a handy, freewayside stop.

Washington 39

BATTLE GROUND LAKE
Battle Ground Lake State Park

Location: Southwest Washington north of Vancouver.

Access: From the junction of Washington State Highways 502 and 503 just west of the city of Battle Ground, drive east on Highway 502 (Main Street) for 0.8 mile into midtown Battle Ground; turn north (left) onto 142nd (Grace Street); drive 0.6 mile north and turn east (right) onto 229th (Heissen Road); drive east, then north, then west on Heissen Road for 2.3 miles to 249th; at the intersection just after the railroad tracks, jog a few yards south (left) then west (right) to the park entrance and the campground.

Facilities: 50 campsites, including 15 walk-in tent sites; (a horse camp and a group camp with 4 shelters are also available, by reservation); sites are small+ to medium-sized, with fair to fairly good separation; parking pads are paved, reasonably level, medium-length straight-ins or medium+ pull-throughs; fireplaces; b-y-o firewood; water at several faucets; restrooms with showers; holding tank disposal station; paved driveways; adequate supplies and services are available in Battle Ground.

Activities & Attractions: Fishing for stocked trout; limited boating; small boat launch; sandy swimming beach; nature trail; 5 miles of hiking trails; 5 miles of hiking/equestrian trails and roads; day use area with large shelter.

Natural Features: Located around the shore of 28-acre, spring-fed Battleground Lake in the western foothills of the Cascade Range; the lake's waters have collected in the *caldera* (basin) of an extinct volcano; (chunks of lava--called 'lava bombs'--have been found in the park where they landed after the volcano erupted); campground vegetation consists of tall conifers, hardwoods, ferns and shrubs; bordered by densely forested hills; elevation 100'.

Season, Fees & Phone: Open all year; please see Appendix for standard Washington state park fees; 10 day limit; park office (206) 687-4621.

Camp Notes: This is a really neat place! Nice campground, nice landscaping, nice lake. "Battle Ground" is actually a tongue-in-cheek name that sprung-up in the aftermath of an armed conflict that never happened. Back in 1855 an Army captain named Strong was sent from Fort Vancouver to capture a band of Klickitat Indians who had escaped from the fort. When he caught up with the escapees, the Indians talked the captain into letting them go long enough to bury their chief, who had met with a fatal accident. The Klickitats said that they would turn themselves in after the funeral. Soft-hearted Captain Strong said OK to this plan, and returned to the fort empty-handed. For his "bravery and courage" he was awarded a petticoat, and the area became known as "Strong's Battle Ground".

Washington
Puget Sound
Please refer to the Washington map in the Appendix

Washington 40

BOWMAN BAY
Deception Pass State Park

Location: Northwest Washington north of Oak Harbor.

Access: From Washington State Highway 20 at milepost 42 +.7 (0.6 mile north of the Deception Pass bridge, 10.5 miles north of Oak Harbor, 5 miles south of the junction of Highway 20 and the Highway 20 north spur to Anacortes), turn west onto Rosario Road; a few yards west of the highway, turn southwest (left) and proceed 0.5 mile to the campground.

Facilities: 16 campsites; sites are small, with minimal separation; parking pads are gravel or paved, medium to long straight-ins or pull-throughs; additional leveling may be required in some sites; small to medium-sized tent areas; fireplaces; b-y-o firewood; water at central faucets; restrooms; paved driveways; adequate+ supplies and services are available in Oak Harbor.

Activities & Attractions: Interpretive Center sketches the history of the Civilian Conservation Corps using anecdotes, photos and memorabilia of CCC workers; boating; boat launch; fishing pier; scuba diving area at nearby Rosario Beach; fly fishing with barbless hooks on Pass Lake; day use area with small shelters.

Natural Features: Located on hilly terrain on Fidalgo Island around the shore of Bowman Bay on the north side of Deception Pass; campsites receive light to medium shade/shelter from tall conifers; Pass Lake lies along the main highway, just northeast of the Bowman Bay turnoff; sea level.

Season, Fees & Phone: April to October; please see Appendix for standard Washington state park fees; 10 day limit; park office (206) 675-2417.

Camp Notes: Deception Pass was named by Captain George Vancouver in 1792. One historical account relates that as his ship approached the area and Vancouver saw the rapid flow of water through the channel between Fidalgo Island and Whidbey Island, the great Northwest explorer at first thought he had encountered a large inlet where a great river entered the sea. He soon discovered that the rapid flow of water was caused by tidal movement through the narrow gap between the two islands. Because he was deceived as to the nature of the place, Vancouver named it Deception Passage.

Washington 41

DECEPTION PASS
Deception Pass State Park

Location: Northwest Washington north of Oak Harbor.

Access: From Washington State Highway 20 at milepost 41 +.3 (0.5 mile south of the Deception Pass Bridge, 6.5 miles south of the junction of Highway 20 and the Highway 20 north spur to Anacortes, 9 miles north of Oak Harbor), turn west into the park entrance to a "Y" intersection; turn southwest (left) and proceed westerly for 0.6 mile, then turn north (right) into the campground.

Facilities: 230 campsites; (5 hike-bike sites and a reservable group camp are also available); sites are small to medium-sized, with nominal to good separation; parking pads are gravel, short to medium-length straight-ins or medium to long pull-throughs; most pads will require additional leveling; (the steepest pads are paved--probably so they won't be washed-away in a heavy rain); small to medium-sized tent spots; fireplaces; b-y-o firewood is recommended; water at several faucets; restrooms with showers; holding tank disposal station; paved driveways; adequate+ supplies and services are available in Oak Harbor.

Activities & Attractions: Swimming beach on Cranberry Lake; beachcombing; several miles of hiking trails; Deception Pass Nature Trail (guide pamphlet available); boating (electric or people-propelled on the lakes); boat launch; playground; fishing pier on Cranberry Lake; large day usea are with several shelters.

Natural Features: Located on forested, generally hilly terrain on the northwest corner of Whidbey Island; campsites are moderately shaded by tall conifers and well-sheltered by dense shrubbery; tall conifers tower over lush ferns and underbrush throughout much of the park; sea level.

Season, Fees & Phone: Open all year; please see Appendix for standard Washington state park fees; 10 day limit; park office (206) 675-2417.

Camp Notes: Your choice: freshwater or saltwater beaches within a few yards of your campsite. The huge campground is *very* much in demand during the summer. It might take you a while to pick your way through what might seem to be an unending maze of camp loop driveways.

Washington 42

FORT EBEY
Fort Ebey State Park

Location: Northwest Washington south of Oak Harbor.

Access: From Washington State Highway 20 at milepost 25 +.4 (3 miles north of Coupeville, 7 miles south of Oak Harbor), turn west onto Libbey Road and proceed 0.9 mile; turn south (left) onto Valley Drive for 0.6 mile, then turn west (right) into the park; continue ahead for 0.3 mile to a "T" intersection, and turn southerly (left) to the campground.

Facilities: 50 campsites in 2 loops; (3 hike-bike/primitive sites at Lake Pondilla are also available); sites are mostly medium-sized, with fair to very good separation; parking pads are gravel, medium to long straight-ins or pull-throughs; some parking pads may require a little additional leveling; fireplaces; b-y-o firewood is recommended; water at several faucets; restrooms with showers; paved driveways; adequate supplies and services are available in Oak Harbor and Coupeville.

Activities & Attractions: World War II harbor defense gun sites and bunker; fishing (saltwater, and also reportedly very good bass fishing in the lake); 3 miles of hiking trails; beachcombing on 3 miles of stoney beach; day use areas.

Natural Features: Located on Whidbey Island on a short bluff overlooking Admiralty Inlet of Puget Sound; campsites are moderately shaded by tall conifers towering over very dense shrubbery, ferns and other small plants around the sites; miniature Lake Pondilla is the park's freshwater feature; sea level.

Season, Fees & Phone: Open all year; please see Appendix for standard Washington state park fees; 10 day limit; park office (206) 678-4636.

Camp Notes: Fort Ebey's campsites are some of the best around here, and the beach is expansive enough to accommodate quite a few 'combers and strollers. It may often be cloudy here, but it doesn't rain very much. (In testimony to the scant rainfall, this is one of the few spots in Western Washington where prickly pear grows.)

Washington 43

FORT CASEY
Fort Casey State Park

Location: Northwest Washington south of Oak Harbor.

Access: From Washington State Highway 20 at the Keystone ferry terminal (3.4 miles west of the junction of State Highways 20 & 525 south of Coupeville), proceed northwest on Fort Casey Road for 0.45 mile; turn southwest (left) into the park entrance and proceed up the hill for 0.35 mile then turn east (left) onto the campground access road for 0.35 mile to the campground. (Note: if you're southbound to the park from Oak Harbor and Coupeville, you can save time, miles and fuel by taking a paved secondary road from Coupeville; from Highway 20 at milepost 21 +.9 in Coupeville, turn south onto South Main Street and proceed 0.3 mile through a small business district, then pick up Engle Road and continue traveling south for another 2.8 miles until you merge with Fort Casey Road; continue south on Fort Casey Road for a final 0.5 mile to the park entrance.

Facilities: 35 campsites; most sites are small, level, with minimal to fair separation; parking pads are gravel, medium-length straight-ins or medium+ pull-throughs; small tent spaces on a grassy surface; fireplaces; b-y-o firewood; water at faucets; restrooms with showers; paved driveway; adequate supplies and services are available in Coupeville.

Activities & Attractions: Well-preserved coast artillery installation; visitor center features displays related to the history of the fort; self-guided walking tour (guide booklet available); hiking trails; access to 2 miles of beach; fishing; boat launch and scuba diving area nearby; day use area.

Natural Features: Located below a bluff/hill on the middle-west coast of Whidbey Island on Admiralty Inlet; the campground is at the base of the hill along an open shoreline on small Admiralty Bay, with vegetation that consists primarily of sparse grass, bushes and a few small conifers; a rocky beach skirts the shoreside campsites; sea level to 100'.

Season, Fees & Phone: Open all year; please see Appendix for standard Washington state park fees; 10 day limit; park office (206) 678-4519.

Camp Notes: Many campsites have reasonably good saltwater views; but the viewpoints from the shore batteries and from the lighthouse along the edge of the bluff above the camp area are excellent. The campground is only a few yards across the bay from the ferry terminal. If you like to take an afternoon snooze, plan your nap around the ferry schedule--the arrival and departure 'toots' from the boat's whistle could provide you with a startling awakening.

Washington 44

SOUTH WHIDBEY
South Whidbey State Park

Location: Northwest Washington south of Oak Harbor.

Access: From Washington State Highway 525 (southbound) at a point 5 miles south of the junction of State Highways 535 & 20 and 5 miles north of Freeland, head west and south on Smuggler's Cove Road for 4 miles; turn west (right) into the park. **Alternate Access:** From Washington State Highway 525 (northbound) in Freeland, turn west onto Bush Point Road and proceed west and north, then pick up Smuggler's Cove Road and continue north for a total of 7 miles to the park.

Facilities: 54 campsites; (a group camp is also available); sites are small to medium-sized, level, with nominal to good separation; parking pads are gravel, short to medium-length, mostly straight-ins; medium to large tent areas; fireplaces; b-y-o firewood; water at several faucets; restrooms with showers; holding tank disposal station; paved or gravel driveways; limited supplies and services are available in Freeland, 8 miles southeast.

Activities & Attractions: Boating (nearest public boat launch is 2 miles south at Bush Point); swimming; scuba diving; clamming and crabbing; fishing (particularly good for salmon in late summer); nature trails; trails to the beach; amphitheater for scheduled evening programs; day use area with shelter.

Natural Features: Located on a forested bluff on the west coast of Whidbey Island; vegetation consists of a variety of old growth tall conifers, and a dense undercover of small hardwoods, ferns and bushes; sandy beach; elevation 150'.

Season, Fees & Phone: Open all year, (weekends and holidays only during the winter); please see Appendix for standard Washington state park fees; 10 day limit; park office (206) 321-4559.

Camp Notes: Access to this park is through a corridor of dense vegetation. From the beach and from a number of campsites there is a captivating view of the Olympic Mountains to the west across Puget Sound.

Washington 45

FORT WORDEN
Fort Worden State Park

Location: Western Washington at the northeast corner of the Olympic Peninsula north of Port Townsend.

Access: From Washington State Highway 20 (Sims Way) at the west edge of the downtown area in Port Townsend (0.5 mile west of the ferry terminal) turn north onto Kearney Street and continue for 0.4 mile to a "T" intersection; turn east (right) onto Blaine Street for 0.15 mile; turn north (left) onto Cherry Street and follow Cherry Street for 1.2 miles to another "T"; jog east (right) onto W Street for 0.05 mile, then north (left) into the park; from here, head toward the northeast corner of the large parade ground on your choice of streets, then northerly along the edgewater road for a final mile to the campground.

Facilities: 50 campsites with full hookups; sites are small to medium-sized, level, with minimal separation; parking pads are paved, medium to long straight-ins or pull-throughs; large, grassy tent spots; fireplaces; b-y-o firewood; water at sites; restrooms with showers; paved driveways; adequate supplies and services are available in Port Townsend.

Activities & Attractions: National Historic Landmark District with renovated 1900 military buildings; renovated pavilion in the former balloon hanger; interpretive center; Coast Artillery Museum; boating; boat launch, dock and moorage buoys; beach access; 6 miles of hiking trails; playground; tennis courts; underwater park; day use area.

Natural Features: Located on the beach at Point Wilson; campground is on an open, grassy flat between a forested hillside to the west and a beach on Admiralty Inlet; sweeping view across Admiralty Inlet toward Whidbey Island from the camp area; sea level.

Season, Fees & Phone: Open all year; please see Appendix for standard Washington state park fees; park office (206) 385-4730.

Camp Notes: If you take the ferry from Whidbey Island to Port Townsend (as do many visitors), the park will be in full view off the starboard side of the vessel. Look for a long, forested hill with a large "notch" or "saddle" to the north of Port Townsend; the huge parade ground, officers row, barracks and numerous other buildings are situated within the notch. The campground is below and north of the notch at beach level.

Washington 46

OLD FORT TOWNSEND
Old Fort Townsend State Park

Location: Western Washington at the northeast corner of the Olympic Peninsula south of Port Townsend.

Access: From Washington State Highway 20 at milepost 8 +.3 (4 miles south of Port Townsend, 8 miles north of the junction of Highway 20 and U.S. Highway 101 near Discovery Bay), turn east onto Old Fort Townsend Road and proceed 1.4 miles to the park and the campground.

Facilities: 40 campsites in 2 loops; (a reservable group camp is also available); upper loop sites are small, with fair to good separation, with hard-surfaced, short to medium-length straight-in parking pads, plus a few medium-length pull-throughs; lower section sites are very small, with paved, short to medium-length, tolerably level, pull-through parking pads in a parallel row, and nil separation; small to medium-sized tent spots throughout; fireplaces or barbecue grills; restrooms with showers; holding tank disposal station; paved driveways; adequate supplies and services are available in Port Townsend.

Activities & Attractions: Several hiking trails; nature trail; historic walk; sports field; limited beach access; moorage buoys; day use area with shelters.

Natural Features: Located on a slope above a 150-foot cliff above Port Townsend Bay; upper campsites are on a steep slope in a dense conifer forest, lower campsites are on a small, grassy flat with very light to medium shade; some views of Admiralty Inlet, Puget Sound and the Cascade Range from the park area; elevation 200'.

Season, Fees & Phone: April to October; please see Appendix for standard Washington state park fees; 10 day limit; phone c/o Fort Worden State Park (206) 385-4730.

Camp Notes: Old Fort Townsend is the grandaddy of the forts in this area. Its construction in the late 1850's pre-dates the others by nearly 40 years. One additional local item: strictly speaking, Port Townsend and its nearby state parks are actually on a small northeast extension of the Olympic Peninsula known as the Quimper Peninsula. You might occasionally run across that nomenclature on a map.

Washington 47

FORT FLAGLER
Fort Flagler State Park

Location: Western Washington at the northeast corner of the Olympic Peninsula south of Port Townsend.

Access: From Washington State Highway 20 south of Port Townsend or Washington State Highway 104 northwest of the Hood Canal Bridge, follow the signs on local roads to the community of Port Hadlock (also called just 'Hadlock'); from midtown Port Hadlock at the corner of Irondale Road and Oak Bay Road, proceed easterly on Oak Bay Road for 0.9 mile; turn northeasterly (left) onto Flagler Road (watch for signs to Marrowstone Island and Fort Flagler), and travel on this winding road northeast, then southeast, then northerly (through the hamlet of Nordland) for a total of 8.4 miles to a 4-way intersection (0.5 mile inside the park boundary); turn left to the campground entrance station; continue for 1 mile past the entrance station to the upper camp area, or another 0.2 mile to the beach and lower camp loops.

(Note: The abbreviated directions from the main highways are given because there are at least a half-dozen ways of getting to Port Hadlock, all of which are on paved secondary roads. Your choice of route will depend upon which highway you're approaching on and from which direction you're arriving.)

Facilities: 116 campsites in 3 loops; (hike-bike sites and a group camp are also available); sites are small to medium-sized, with minimal to fair separation in the lower loops, and fair to fairly good separation in the upper loop; parking pads are gravel, short to medium-length straight-ins or medium to long pull-throughs; some pads will require a little additional leveling, especially in the upper loop; many good to excellent tent spots in the lower loops; fireplaces; b-y-o firewood is suggested; water at several faucets; restrooms with showers; holding tank disposal station; paved driveways; camper supplies at the park concession; adequate supplies and services are available in Port Hadlock.

Activities & Attractions: Self-guided tours of Fort Flagler; Roots of a Forest Interpretive Trail; hiking trails; beach access; boating; boat launches, dock, and moorage buoys; fishing; clamming; playground.

Natural Features: Located at the northern tip of Marrowstone Island in Puget Sound; campsites 1-47 are on a forested hillside with some scenic views through the trees; sites 48-96 are along the treeline near the beach; sites 97-116 are on an open, grass flat along the beach; great views of Admiralty Inlet and Whidbey Island from the park; sea level to 100'.

Season, Fees & Phone: Open all year; please see Appendix for standard Washington state park fees; 10 day limit; campsite reservations recommended for anytime during the summer, well in advance for weekends, please see Appendix; park office (206) 385-1259.

Camp Notes: The upper and lower camp loops are so dissimilar, it's difficult to realize that they're in the same park. Of the triad of defense posts set up in the 1890's to guard the entrance to Puget Sound (also see Fort Worden and Fort Casey), Fort Flagler has, subjectively, the best camping opportunities. Although the east side of the Puget Sound region gets a lot of precipitation, Fort Flagler is in the "rain shadow" of the Olympic Mountains and consequently the rainfall here is measured not in feet but in inches--an average of only 17 inches a year.

Washington 48

KITSAP MEMORIAL
Kitsap Memorial State Park

Location: Western Washington north of Bremerton.

Access: From Washington State Highway 3 at milepost 57 (3 miles south of Port Gamble, 4 miles north of the junction of State Highways 3 & 305 near Poulsbo), turn west onto the park access road and proceed 0.3 mile, then turn north (right) and go through the day use parking lot to the campground.

Facilities: 43 campsites in two sections; (5 hike-bike/primitive sites and a small group camp are also available); sites 1 through 19 are parallel to each other in a single line on the east side of the camping area; the remainder of the camp units are in a loop on the north side; sites are small to small+, level, with nil to nominal separation; parking surfaces are gravel, short to medium-length straight-ins; most sites can accommodate a medium-sized tent; kitchen shelter; fireplaces; b-y-o firewood; water at several faucets; restrooms with showers; holding tank disposal station; paved driveways; limited supplies in Port Gamble; adequate+ supplies and services are available in the Poulsbo area, 6 miles south.

Activities & Attractions: Beach trail; beachcombing; clamming; fishing; sports field; playground; museums in Port Gamble; day use area with shelters.

Natural Features: Located on a bluff above Hood Canal (a major inlet on Puget Sound); shade/shelter for the camp loop is provided by tall conifers, plus shrubbery between the sites; pasture adjacent to the park; a wide variety of clams, oysters, geoduck and octopus inhabit the nearby waters; the Olympic Mountains lie to the west; sea level.

Season, Fees & Phone: Open all year; please see Appendix for standard Washington state park fees; 10 day limit; park office (206) 779-3205.

Camp Notes: As seen from the park, the Olympic Mountains, a few miles to the west, seem to rise right out of Hood Canal. Beachcombing along the park's 1000' of saltwater frontage can be highly rewarding, particularly during the winter months.

Washington 49

FAY-BAINBRIDGE
Fay-Bainbridge State Park

Location: Western Washington north of Bremerton.

Access: From Washington State Highway 305 at milepost 4 +.3 (4 miles north of Winslow, 8 miles south of Poulsbo), turn east onto NE East Day Road; proceed 1.4 miles to a "T" intersection; turn north (left) onto Sunrise Drive NE, and travel 1.6 miles; turn east (right) into the park; continue on the park roadway past the bell and the primitive tent camping area, then down the hill to the main campground.

Facilities: 26 campsites with water hookups; (10 hike-bike/primitive sites with a small shelter are also available); sites are small, level, with minimal to nominal separation; parking pads are gravel, short+ straight-ins; ample space for large tents; fireplaces; b-y-o firewood; water at faucets; restrooms with showers; holding tank disposal station; paved driveways; nearest supplies (limited) in Winslow; adequate+ supplies and services are available in the Poulsbo area.

Activities & Attractions: Beachcombing; clamming; playground; boating; boat launch and moorage buoys; Old Port Madison bell is on display near the park entrance; Suquamish Museum and Tribal Center nearby; day use area with shelter.

Natural Features: Located along an open beach on Puget Sound (main camping area) and on a grassy, forested hill overlooking the Sound (primitive sites); beach camp has some trees planted between many sites; views across Puget sound to the east and north; driftwood-strewn, sand/pebble, 1400' beach; sea level to 100'.

Season, Fees & Phone: Open all year; please see Appendix for standard Washington state park fees; 10 day limit; park office (206) 842-3931.

Camp Notes: The primitive camping area might serve as a convenient stop for cyclists touring the West Sound, although some tenters might find the hillside sites to be a little too sloped. (Well, they *are* well-drained!)

Washington 50

SCENIC BEACH
Scenic Beach State Park

Location: Western Washington northwest of Bremerton.

Access: From Washington State Highway 3 at milepost 43 +.5 (the Newberry Hill Exit, 8 miles north of Bremerton), travel west on Newberry Hill Road for 3 miles to a "T" intersection; turn north (right) and follow the road 5 miles in a long sweeping 180 degree curve to Seabeck (you'll now be headed south); at a point 0.1 mile south of the Seabeck elementary school, turn west onto Scenic Beach Road and proceed 1.5 miles to the park entrance.

Facilities: 50 campsites in two loops; (2 hike-bike/primitive sites are also available); most sites are medium to large, with fair to excellent separation; parking pads are medium+ to very long, packed/oiled gravel, pull-throughs or straight-ins; a little additional leveling may be required in some sites; adequate level space for large tents in most sites; fireplaces; b-y-o firewood; water at several faucets; restrooms with showers; holding tank disposal station; paved driveways; gas and groceries in Seabeck; complete supplies and services are available in Bremerton.

Activities & Attractions: Trails through the forest and down to the beach; beachcombing; swimming area; fishing; boating; public boat launch at Misery Point, 1 mile north; playgrounds; day use area with shelter.

Natural Features: Located on the Kitsap Peninsula above the east shore of Hood Canal, a major arm of Puget Sound; campground is on a densely forested hillside a few hundred yards from the 1600' beach; elevation 100'.

Season, Fees & Phone: Open all year, but limited to weekends and holidays October to April; please see Appendix for standard Washington state park fees; 10 day limit; park office (206) 831-5079.

Camp Notes: Many tables in the campground are installed on the hillside above the parking spots, with steps for easy accessibility, so campers in those sites get a slightly elevated view of their richly forested surroundings. It gets a little busy on summer weekends, so you may enjoy it more in spring or fall. (To be honest about it, the park can be pretty nice in winter too.) Fabulous views of the Olympic Mountains from the beach!

Washington 51

ILLAHEE
Illahee State Park

Location: Western Washington northeast of Bremerton.

Access: From midtown Bremerton at the junction of Washington State Highways 303 and 304 (near the ferry terminal), travel north on Highway 303 for 2.1 miles to its junction with State Highway 306 (Sylvan Way); turn east (right) onto Highway 306 and proceed 1.5 miles, then turn north (left) into the park entrance and the campground.

Facilities: 25 campsites; (8 hike-bike/primitive sites are also available); sites are small to medium-sized, with fair to good separation; parking pads are paved, medium-length straight-ins or pull-throughs; most spaces will probably require a little additional leveling; fairly good spots for medium-sized tents; fireplaces; b-y-o firewood; water at faucets throughout; restrooms with showers; holding tank disposal station; paved driveways; complete supplies and services are available in Bremerton.

Activities & Attractions: Beachcombing; clamming and crabbing; hiking trails; fishing; boat launch with a 350' dock and moorage buoys; playground; sports field; Puget Sound Naval Shipyard and Shipyard Museum in Bremerton; day use area with shelters.

Natural Features: Located along the beach and on a gently rolling hillside on Port Orchard Bay, at the junction of 3 major arteries of Puget Sound: Port Orchard Bay, Sinclair Inlet and Rich Passage; vegetation consists primarily of tall conifers, some hardwoods and ferns; rail fences throughout the grounds enhance the natural landscaping; elevation 100'.

Season, Fees & Phone: Open all year; please see Appendix for standard Washington state park fees; 10 day limit; park office (206) 478-6460.

Camp Notes: A pair of 5"/50 guns from the battleship U.S.S. West Virginia stand guard at the park entrance, acknowledging, to some extent, the importance of the Navy's influence in Bremerton. The shipyard here was the principal reason for the establishment of the gauntlet of coastal artillery forts which line the inlets and passages of Puget Sound between the Strait of Juan de Fuca and the yard. (See Fort Worden State Park, et.al.)

Washington 52

MANCHESTER
Manchester State Park

Location: Western Washington east of Bremerton.

Access: From Washington State Highway 160 at milepost 7 +.5 (4.5 miles east of Port Orchard, 3 miles northwest of Southworth), turn north onto Colchester Drive; travel north 1.7 miles to East Main Street in

Manchester; turn west (left) onto East Main, go 1 block, then jog north (right) onto Beach Drive East; proceed 1.9 miles to East Hilldale Road; turn right onto East Hilldale, and continue for 0.3 mile to the park entrance and the campground.

Facilities: 50 campsites in 2 loops; (3 hike-bike/primitive sites are also available); most sites are medium-sized, essentially level, with fair to good separation; parking pads are paved or packed gravel, medium-length straight-ins or long pull-throughs; medium to large tent areas; fireplaces; b-y-o firewood; water at faucets throughout; restrooms with showers; holding tank disposal station; paved driveways; limited supplies in Manchester; adequate supplies and services are available in Port Orchard.

Activities & Attractions: Wide, paved pathways along the beach; swimming beach; volleyball court; interpretive trail; early twentieth century military structures; fishing; scuba diving/snorkeling; day use area with shelters.

Natural Features: Located on a forested bluff above Rich Passage in Puget Sound; vegetation consists of several varieties of conifers, hardwoods, and ferns which provide medium to dense shade/shelter for most campsites; (a large supply of poison oak is also available); a small creek flows through the center of the campground; elevation 100'.

Season, Fees & Phone: Open all year, (available on weekends and holidays only, October to April); please see Appendix for standard Washington state park fees; 10 day limit; park office (206) 871-4065.

Camp Notes: One of the drawing points of this campground is its easy accessibility from the Seattle-Tacoma area: Less than an hour from Seattle by ferry, or via highway from Tacoma. Even if the trip is a little longer from your local home or last night's camp, this somewhat secluded spot on the Sound is still worth the time spent getting here.

Washington 53

BELFAIR
Belfair State Park

Location: Western Washington southwest of Bremerton.

Access: From the junction of Washington State Highways 3 and 300 in Belfair (10 miles southwest of Bremerton), drive southwest on Highway 300 for 3.1 miles; turn south (left) into the park, go a few yards, then turn right to the campground entrance station and the campground.

Facilities: 184 campsites, including 47 with full hookups, in 3 loops; sites are very small to medium-sized, essentially level, with minimal to fairly good separation; parking pads are gravel, short to medium+ straight-ins or pull-throughs; tent areas vary from small to large; fireplaces; b-y-o firewood is recommended; water at several faucets; restrooms with showers; holding tank disposal station; paved driveways; adequate supplies and services are available in Belfair.

Activities & Attractions: Swimming lagoon; sports field; volleyball court; beachcombing; crabbing, clamming, oystering; fishing; playground; day use area.

Natural Features: Located along the shore of Hood Canal, a major arm/inlet of Puget Sound; one camp loop is on a large, semi-open, grassy, Soundside flat; most campsites are in a dense forest of very tall conifers, ferns and a considerable amount of undercover; the loop closest to Hood Canal is more open and includes some lawn areas; Little Mission Creek drifts past the camp loops; sea level.

Season, Fees & Phone: Open all year; please see Appendix for standard Washington state park fees; 10 day limit; campsite reservations suggested for anytime during summer, please see Appendix; park office (206) 478-4625.

Camp Notes: The campground has a distinctive dual personality. The shoreside camp loop, with its sections of mown grass dotted with hardwoods and evergreens, bears little resemblance to the two large camp loops deep in the tall timber. The park is noted for its tideflats, and for the shellfishing and bird viewing opportunities along its 2000' of shoreline.

Washington 54

TWANOH
Twanoh State Park

Location: Western Washington northeast of Shelton.

Access: From Washington State Highway 106 at milepost 12 +.3 (8 miles southwest of Belfair, 12 miles northeast of the junction of Highway 106 and U.S. Highway 101 north of Shelton), turn south then east for 0.05 mile to the campground.

Facilities: 46 campsites, including 8 with full hookups and 8 walk-in sites; (a reservable group camp is also available); sites are small, with minimal to nominal separation; parking pads are paved, mostly short to medium-length straight-ins, plus a few pull-throughs; many pads will require additional leveling; adequate space for large tents in most sites; fireplaces; b-y-o firewood is recommended; water at several faucets; restrooms with showers; paved driveway; snacks at the park concession; adequate supplies and services are available in Belfair.

Activities & Attractions: Large, gravel swimming beach (nearly 600' long); wading pool; 2-mile loop hiking trail; playground; tennis court; boating; boat launches, dock and mooring buoys; fishing; day use area with shelters.

Natural Features: Located on a forested slope several hundred yards south of the south shore of Hood Canal, a major arm of Puget Sound; campsites receive very light to medium shade/shelter from tall conifers and some hardwoods on a surface of mown grass; a small stream flows past the west edge of the campground; bordered by dense forest; the Olympic Mountains rise about 20 miles to the west; sea level.

Season, Fees & Phone: April to October; please see Appendix for standard Washington state park fees; 10 day limit; park office (206) 275-2222.

Camp Notes: *Twanoh* is a derivative of the name of the *Twana* Indians, a local tribe who are more commonly called the *Skokomish*. The park originally was a logging site, then a private resort before it finally became the popular public park it is today. Twanoh is located in one of the more scenic areas along Hood Canal. An extensively developed residential and resort area stretches for miles in either direction along Highway 106.

JARRELL COVE
Jarrell Cove State Park

Location: Western Washington northeast of Shelton.

Access: From Washington State Highway 3 at milepost 10 +.7 (8 miles northeast of Shelton, 9 miles southwest of Allyn), turn south onto Pickering Road and proceed 2.7 miles; continue easterly on East Harstene Bridge Road across the Harstene Island Bridge for 0.6 mile to a "T" intersection; turn north (left) onto North Island Drive and travel north and east for 3.5 miles; turn north (left, at the bottom of a hill) onto Wingert Road (gravel) and proceed 0.5 mile; turn westerly (left) onto the paved park access road for a final 0.2 mile to the campground.

Facilities: Approximately 15 campsites; sites are small, basically level to slightly sloped, with minimal to fair separation; parking and tent surfaces are grass, in more or less a park-'em-and-pitch-'em-near-a-table-and-fireplace ("random") arrangement; b-y-o firewood is recommended; water at several faucets; restrooms with showers; adequate+ supplies and services are available in Shelton.

Activities & Attractions: 2 boat docks and moorage buoys can accommodate roughly 20 to 30 boats; short trails from the camp area to the boat docks; 1-mile hiking trail; fishing; day use areas with small shelters.

Natural Features: Located on the mid-north side of Harstene Island on a shelf above Jarrell Cove on Puget Sound; campsites are very lightly to moderately shaded/sheltered, by hardwoods and conifers; bordered by dense forest; elevation 50'.

Season, Fees & Phone: Open all year; please see Appendix for standard Washington state park fees; 10 day limit; park office (206) 426-9226.

Camp Notes: Although many visitors arrive by boat and spend a night or two, a lot of people drive in to camp. The small camp area is especially good for tenters, but it's not uncommon to find a camper who's hauled a trailer in here.

PENROSE POINT
Penrose Point State Park

Location: Western Washington west of Tacoma.

Access: From Washington State Highway 302 at milepost 11 +.3 in Key Center (9 miles southwest of the Purdy/Shelton Exit on State Highway 16, 11 miles southeast of the junction of State Highways 302 and 3 south of Belfair), travel southerly on Key Peninsula Highway for 6.2 miles (through Lakebay); turn easterly (left) onto Delano Road and proceed 1.2 miles, then turn north (left) onto 158th Avenue for a final 0.3 mile to the park entrance; continue ahead for 0.3 mile, then turn left into the campground.

Facilities: 83 campsites in a complex loop; (2 hike-bike/primitive sites and a group camp are also available); sites are small, with fair to good separation; parking pads are gravel or paved, mostly short to short+ straight-ins, plus a few medium-length pull-throughs; many pads will require a little additional leveling; adequate space for medium to large tents in most sites; kitchen shelters; fireplaces; b-y-o firewood; water at several faucets; restrooms with showers; holding tank disposal station; paved driveways; gas and groceries+ in Lakebay.

Activities & Attractions: Beachcombing; clamming; swimming beach; 2.5 miles of hiking trails; A Touch of Nature Interpretive Trail (guide pamphlet available); boating; boat launch, 120' dock, moorage buoys; fishing; day use area.

Natural Features: Located on Key Peninsula along Carr Inlet near the south end of Puget Sound; campground vegetation consists of dense stands of tall conifers, hardwoods, ferns, and other dense ground cover; the campground is within a few minutes' walk of the shore; park area includes 2 miles of waterfront along and adjacent to Mayo Cove; sea level.

Season, Fees & Phone: Open all year; please see Appendix for standard Washington state park fees; 10 day limit; park office (206) 884-2514.

Camp Notes: Penrose Point's location, 8 miles off numbered highways, enhances its appeal as a getaway place that's reasonably easy to get away to under most circumstances. Suggestion: Bring a sharp navigator who can simultaneously read the Access instructions, follow the faint lines on the highway map, and watch for road signs. Keeping a compass and a flashlight handy might be a good idea, too. Finding this campground on a rainy night in January, though, can be a challenge. (We know.)

Washington 57

KOPACHUCK
Kopachuck State Park

Location: Western Washington west of Tacoma.

Access: From Washington State Highway 16 (a 4-lane divided highway) at the Gig Harbor City Center Exit near milepost 12 (4 miles northwest of the Tacoma Narrows bridge), turn southwest onto Wollochet Drive NW for 0.4 mile, then west (right) on Hunt Street NW for 0.2 mile, then north (right again) on 45th Avenue NW (Skansie Street) for 1 mile; turn west (left) onto Rosedale Street NW and travel 2.4 miles; turn southwest (left) onto Ray Nash Drive NW for 0.7 mile, then pick up Kopachuck Drive and continue southwest for 1.7 miles to the end of Kopachuck Drive; angle south (an easy left) onto Artondale Drive for another 0.1 mile; turn west (right) into the park and proceed 0.2 mile to the campground.

(Note: You should be able to follow a locally signed route on this grand tour through residential neighborhoods to the park; the above directions can then serve as a backup in case a critical "Kopachuck State Park--thataway" sign is missing.)

Facilities: 41 campsites; (a group camp is also available); sites are small+ to medium-sized, reasonably level, with good to excellent separation; parking pads are gravel/paved, short to medium-length straight-ins; some pads will require a little additional leveling; adequate space for medium to large tents; fireplaces; b-y-o firewood; water at several faucets; restrooms with showers; holding tank disposal station; paved driveways; adequate supplies and services are available in Gig Harbor.

Activities & Attractions: Beachcombing; underwater scuba park; boating; moorage buoys; (nearest public boat launch is near the community of Arletta, 3 miles by land, 4 if by sea around Green Point); day use area with shelter.

Natural Features: Located on a slope above the west shore of Henderson Bay, a major arm of Puget Sound, at the head of Carr Inlet, a small, secondary bay; campground park vegetation consists of light to medium-dense, towering conifers, plus hardwoods, dense bushes and ferns; elevation 100'.

Season, Fees & Phone: Open all year; please see Appendix for standard Washington state park fees; 10 day limit; park office (206) 265-3606.

Camp Notes: Even if there were no campground, a trip to the park could be justified on the basis of your being able to enjoy a walk among the giants in this fern-carpeted forest by the bay. *Kopachuck* is from an Indian phrase *kopa-chuck*, which simply means "at the water".

Washington 58

SALTWATER
Saltwater State Park

Location: Western Washington between Seattle and Tacoma.

Access: From Interstate 5 Exit 149 for Des Moines (midway between Seattle and Tacoma), turn west onto Washington State Highway 516 and travel 1 mile to the junction of State Highways 516 and 509; turn south onto Highway 509 and proceed 1.4 miles; turn west into the park entrance, then south, and go down a hill, then easterly through the parking lot and under the highway bridge to the campground.

Facilities: 50 campsites in two sections; (2 hike-bike/primitive sites and a small group camp are also available); sites are small to medium-sized, with minimal to fair separation; parking pads are gravel, short to medium+ straight-ins or long pull-throughs; some pads will require a little additional leveling; adequate space for medium to large tents; fireplaces; b-y-o firewood; water at several faucets; restrooms with showers; holding tank disposal station; paved driveways; complete supplies and services are available in Des Moines.

Activities & Attractions: Foot trails; scuba diving; limited clamming; playground; volleyball court; large day use area with shelters.

Natural Features: Located in wooded McSorley's Gulch, a few hundred yards east of Puget Sound's Poverty Bay; a creek crossed by a footbridge flows along the south edge of the campground; closely bordered by densely wooded hills and bluffs; elevation 50'.

Season, Fees & Phone: Open all year; please see Appendix for standard Washington state park fees; 10 day limit; park office (206) 764-4128.

Camp Notes: Perhaps the more desirable sites are those in the section higher-up in the gulch to the east of the pull-through area. You may develops some misgivings about camping here when you see the "Lock Your Valuables. . ." signs and the amount of local traffic that passes across the highway bridge overhead, or in and out of the large day use parking lot. However, this is the closest public campground to Seattle and thus may be useful to many campers.

Washington 59

DASH POINT
Dash Point State Park

Location: Western Washington north of Tacoma.

Access: From Washington State Highway 509 at milepost 8 +.3 (8 miles north of Interstate 5 exit 133 at Tacoma, 6 miles west of the junction of State Highways 509 & 99 near Federal Way), turn south (i.e., right, if approaching from Tacoma) into the main campground. (Note that the highway lies in an east-west direction at this point.)

Facilities: 136 campsites, including 28 with partial hookups, in two sections; (2 hike-bike/primitive sites and a reservable group camp are also available); sites are small to medium-sized, generally well-leveled, with nominal to fair separation; parking pads are hard surfaced, short to long, straight-ins or pull-throughs; adequate space for medium to large tents; water at several points; fireplaces; b-y-o firewood; restrooms with showers; disposal station; paved driveways; closest complete shopping is in Federal Way.

Activities & Attractions: 6 miles of hiking trails, including beach access trails; swimming beach; playground; day use area.

Natural Features: Located on a bluff above Puget Sound in a heavily wooded area, with a dense mixture of tall hardwoods and conifers over a very thick carpet of ferns; elevation 200'.

Season, Fees & Phone: Open all year; please see Appendix for standard Washington state park fees; 10 day limit; park office (206) 593-2206.

Camp Notes: Dash Point is on the outskirts of one of the Northwest's major cities, so the park is predictably busy, spring through fall. The campground is a favorite 'motel' for travelers visiting relatives and friends in the city. The hookup loop of the campground is closer to the highway than the standard district, but the hookup sites are also a little nicer.

Washington
Northwest
Please refer to the Washington map in the Appendix

Washington 60

CAMANO ISLAND
Camano Island State Park

Location: Western Washington northwest of Everett.

Access: From Interstate 5 Exit 212 for Stanwood/Camano Island (17 miles north of Everett, 15 miles south of Mount Vernon), head west on Washington State Highway 532 for 9.5 miles to a fork; take the south (left) fork, continuing on Highway 532, which then becomes East Camano Drive and follow this road for 5.7 miles to another fork; continue southwesterly (i.e., straight ahead, on the right fork) onto Elger Bay Road for 1.9 miles; turn west (right) onto West Camano Drive and proceed 1.7 miles, then turn southerly (left) onto Park Drive for 0.9 mile into the park and a final fork (just past the park office); take the left fork for 0.7 mile to the camping areas.

Facilities: 87 campsites; (a large group camp is also available); sites are small or large, with fair to very good separation; parking pads are gravel, short straight-ins or medium to long pull-throughs; additional leveling will be required in some sites; medium to large, acceptably level tent areas; fireplaces; firewood is usually for sale, or b-y-o; water at central faucets; restrooms with showers; holding tank disposal station; paved driveways; gas and groceries at a local store; adequate supplies and services are available in Stanwood, 14 miles northeast.

Activities & Attractions: Hiking trails; Al Emerson Nature Trail (a guide pamphlet is available); boating; boat launch; swimming beach; amphitheater; day use areas, shelter.

Natural Features: Located on a short hill/bluff above the middle-west shore of Camano Island on Saratoga Passage, north of Puget Sound; vegetation consists of a dense blanket of ferns and bushes topped by tall conifers; some of the Doug firs here are more than 600 years old; the Olympic Mountains are in view to the southwest; elevation 50'.

Season, Fees & Phone: Open all year; please see Appendix for standard Washington state park fees; 10 day limit; park office (206) 387-3031 or (206) 387-2575.

Camp Notes: A big attraction is the park's 6700' of shoreline, all of it within a couple-minutes' walk of any campsite. The island was named for a relatively obscure Spanish explorer, Jacinto Camano. Whether or not Camano and his crew camped here is uncertain.

Washington 61

WENBERG
Wenberg State Park

Location: Northwest Washington north of Everett.

Access: From Interstate 5 Exit 206 for Lakewood and Smoky Point (10 miles north of Everett, 21 miles south of Mount Vernon), travel westerly on 172nd Street NE/Lakewood Road (through the whistle stop of Lakewood) for 2.2 miles to a 3-way intersection; continue west (right) on Lakewood Road for another 2.5 miles; turn south (left) onto East Lake Goodwin Road and proceed 1.4 miles; turn west (right) into the park; continue west for a final 0.2 mile to the campground.

Facilities: 75 campsites, including 10 with partial hookups, in 3 loops; sites are small, with minimal to fair separation; parking pads are gravel, short to medium-length straight-ins (medium-length pull-throughs for hookups); many pads will require some additional leveling; fireplaces; b-y-o firewood; water at several faucets; restrooms with showers; holding tank disposal station; paved driveways; minimal supplies are available in the park; groceries in Lakewood, 5 miles east.

Activities & Attractions: Boating; boat launch and docks; fishing (periodically stocked with rainbow trout); swimming beach; short, paved, foot trails; playground; day use area with bathhouse and shelters.

Natural Features: Located above the shore of 545-acre Lake Goodwin; some campsites are on a fairly open grassy area, others are well-shaded/sheltered by tall conifers and hardwoods, plus light to medium dense underbrush; elevation 100'.

Season, Fees & Phone: Open all year; please see Appendix for standard Washington state park fees; 10 day limit; park office (206) 652-7417.

Camp Notes: Paved walkways lead from the campground area down to some fine picnicking/sitting spots along and above the lake shore. The immediate surroundings and the view are excellent.

Washington 62

BIRCH BAY
Birch Bay State Park

Location: Northwest Washington northwest of Bellingham.

Access: From Interstate 5 Exit 266 for Custer/Grandview Road (3 miles north of Ferndale, 11 miles south of Blaine), travel west on Grandview Road for 7 miles (to the first side road past the refinery); turn north (right) onto Jackson Road and proceed 0.8 mile; turn west (left) onto Helwig Road and go 0.6 mile to the park entrance station; the camp areas are left or right, just beyond the entrance. (Note: if you're southbound from British Columbia, you could take Blaine Road south out of Blaine or take I-5 Exit 270, then follow the signs on a zig-zag route along the back roads to the park; but overall, using the principal route is the most economical from a time-and-fuel standpoint.)

Facilities: 167 campsites, including 20 with partial hookups; sites are small to small+, level, with nil to fair separation; parking pads are gravel, short to medium-length straight-ins, plus a few long pull-throughs; adequate space for a medium to large tent in most sites; fireplaces; b-y-o firewood; water at several faucets; restrooms with showers; holding tank disposal station; paved driveways; limited+ supplies and services are available in the city of Birch Bay, 5 miles north.

Activities & Attractions: Beachcombing; clamming and crabbing; swimming; Terrell Marsh Nature Trail, a half-mile loop which winds through a 40-acre freshwater marsh; (a guide pamphlet for the marsh trail is available); day use area with shelters.

Natural Features: Located at the south end of Birch Bay, east of the Strait of Georgia; park vegetation consists of tall conifers, hardwoods and a moderate amount of underbrush, which provide light to moderately dense shade/shelter for virtually all campsites; about a mile of seashore is included within the park; sea level.

Season, Fees & Phone: Open all year; please see Appendix for standard Washington state park fees; 10 day limit; (patrolled day and night); park office (206) 371-2800.

Camp Notes: You can catch glimpses of the shore through the trees from some campsites. The camp loops are just above high tide level, so it's an easy walk from anywhere in the place through the treeline and across the creek to the beach. Reportedly, about a million people a year visit the park. Birch Bay's clientele seems to be typically composed of roughly equal numbers of Yanks and Canucks, so if you want to become pals with someone from another country, this is the place to do it.

Washington 63

LARRABEE
Larrabee State Park

Location: Northwest Washington south of Bellingham.

Access: From Interstate 5 (northbound), Exit 231 in Burlington, travel northwest on Washington State Highway 11 for 14 miles; turn west (left) into the park. Alternate **Access:** From Interstate 5 (southbound), Exit 250 (4 miles south of Bellingham), turn west onto Highway 11 and proceed west then south for 7 miles to the park entrance and the campground.

Facilities: 87 campsites, including 26 with full hookups; (3 hike-bike/primitive sites and a group camp are also available); sites are small to medium-sized, with nominal separation; parking pads are paved or gravel, mostly short to medium+ straight-ins; (longer pads are designated for trailers); many pads may require additional leveling; fireplaces; b-y-o firewood is recommended; water at several faucets; restrooms with showers; holding tank disposal station; paved driveway; complete supplies and services are available in Bellingham.

Activities & Attractions: 8 miles of hiking trails; (a shoreline guide pamphlet is available); swimming area; playground; fishing; boating; boat launch; day use area with shelters.

Natural Features: Located on a forested, hilly terrain along and above the shore of Samish Bay; there is a view of Puget Sound from some campsites; the camping area has a mown lawn with huge trees, ferns and shrubbery; elevation 100'.

Season, Fees & Phone: Open all year; please see Appendix for standard Washington state park fees; 10 day limit; park office (206) 676-2093.

Camp Notes: The scenic drive along Highway 11 (the highway is locally known as Chuckanut Drive) is quite fascinating. It follows the shore and at times passes through a tunnel of lush, green vegetation. There are some excellent views of the San Juan Islands from the park.

Washington 64

BAY VIEW
Bay View State Park

Location: Northwest Washington northwest of Mount Vernon.

Access: From Washington State Highway 20, at milepost 53 +.3 (7 miles west of Interstate 5, 5 miles east of the junction of Highway 20 and the Highway 20 north spur to Anacortes), turn north onto Bay

View-Edison Road and travel north for 3.5 miles; at the north edge of the small community of Bay View, turn east (right) onto the park access road and go 0.1 mile to the campground.

Facilities: 68 campsites, including 9 with full hookups, in 3 loops; (a group camp is also available); sites are generally level, vary in size from tiny to large, with minimal to excellent separation; most parking pads are gravel, short to medium-length straight-ins, plus a few pull-throughs; tent space varies from nil to large; fireplaces; b-y-o firewood; water at several faucets; restrooms with showers, supplemented by vault facilities; paved driveways; gas and groceries at several points along Highway 20; nearly complete supplies and services are available in Anacortes.

Activities & Attractions: Beachcombing; a short trail leads from the campground down to the 1300' beach; Padilla Bay Shore Trail, Padilla Bay Reserve and Interpretive Center nearby; day use area with shelter.

Natural Features: Located on a short hilltop above Padilla Bay; one camp loop is in a forested area which encircles a grassy infield; a second loop is set within a forested area; a third section, with hookups, sits on a grassy, lightly sheltered shelf overlooking the bay; elevation 50'.

Season, Fees & Phone: Open all year; please see Appendix for standard Washington state park fees; 10 day limit; park office (206) 757-0227.

Camp Notes: Looking northwest across the bay from here you can see the hilly San Juan Islands rising a few miles away; to the southwest is a bayside plain; and directly to the west are the refineries rising above the bay several miles from here over in Anacortes. For camping, there's quite a variety of sites to select from. A few of the campsites are among the smallest anywhere--there's enough room for a subcompact station wagon (with the tailgate closed), the table and a flicker of a fire--but the privacy factor is good.

MORAN
Moran State Park

Location: Northwest Washington southwest of Bellingham.

Access: From the Washington State ferry terminal at Anacortes, take the ferry to Orcas Island; from the Orcas ferry terminal, turn west (*left*) for 0.1 mile, then head northerly on Horseshoe Highway for 8 miles to and through the small community of Eastsound; continue southeasterly on Horseshoe Highway for another 3.5 miles to the park entrance; continue ahead for 0.1 mile to North End camp, 0.5 mile to Midway camp, 1.1 mile to South End camp, 1.3 mile to the primitive camp, or 2.5 miles to Mountain Lake camp.

Facilities: 136 campsites in four areas--North End, Midway (Cascade Lake), South End (Cascade Lake), and Mountain Lake; (a dozen hike-bike/primitive sites are also available in a fifth area along the road between the two lakes); sites are small to medium-sized, with nominal for fairly good separation; parking pads are mostly short to medium-length straight-ins, plus a few medium+ pull-throughs; tent space varies from small to large; fireplaces; b-y-o firewood; water at several faucets; restrooms with showers; holding tank disposal station; groceries in Eastsound and near the ferry landing; adequate+ supplies and services are available in Anacortes.

Activities & Attractions: 30 miles of hiking opportunities on more than a dozen trails (a guide pamphlet is available); swimming, sandy beach, limited lake boating (no gas motors), boat launch, windsurfing and fishing on Cascade Lake; stone CCC-built tower at the summit of Mount Constitution; day use area with shelters.

Natural Features: Located on and around Mount Constitution, at 2409' the highest point in the San Juan Islands, and smaller Mount Picket; vegetation consists of a conifer forest with dense undercover, plus some open grassy fields; 5 lakes, including sizeable Cascade Lake and Mountain Lake, plus much smaller Summit Lake and Twin Lakes, are within the park; campground elevations 400' to 1100'.

Season, Fees & Phone: Open all year; please see Appendix for standard Washington state park fees; 10 day limit; campsite reservations recommended for weekends and holidays, please see Appendix; park office (206) 376-2326.

Camp Notes: This park's remoteness, it's abundance of fine scenery, it's varied activities--and, if nothing else, the ferry schedule--will frustrate your attempts to just pack it all in on a quick day-trip from the mainland. Besides, one of the great advantages of being a camper is your mobility, self-sufficiency, and flexibility when in need of accommodations in remote or high-tourist areas such as the San Juans. No need to buy into a stuffy motel or a (gasp!) bed-and-breakfast arrangement.

SPENCER SPIT
Spencer Spit State Park

Location: Northwest Washington southwest of Bellingham.

Access: From the Washington State ferry terminal at Anacortes, take the ferry to Lopez Island; from the Lopez ferry terminal, head south on Ferry Road for 1 mile then east and south on Port Stanley Road for 2 miles; turn east onto Bakerview Road for a final 0.8 mile to the park.

Facilities: 25 campsites; (20 primitive sites, 2 of them with Adirondak shelters, are also available); sites are small to medium-sized, with nominal to fair separation; parking pads are gravel, short straight-ins or medium+ pull-throughs; medium to large areas for tents; fireplaces; b-y-o firewood is recommended; water at faucets; restrooms; holding tank disposal station; gas and groceries in Lopez Village, on the west side of the island; adequate+ supplies and services are available in Anacortes.

Activities & Attractions: Beachcombing; swimming/wading; generally good clamming; hiking trails; mooring buoys; day use area with shelter.

Natural Features: Located on a low, wooded hill/bluff and along the beach on the northeast side of Lopez Island, south of Swifts Bay; vegetation consists principally of tall conifers, hardwoods and brush; a long, triangular sand spit juts into Lopez Sound and extends almost to neighboring Frost Island; (the shoreside end of the spit holds a sizeable, triangular, salt marsh lagoon); park area includes a mile of beach; elevation 100'.

Season, Fees & Phone: Open all year; please see Appendix for standard Washington state park fees; 10 day limit; park office (206) 468-2251.

Camp Notes: Spencer Spit is an excellent destination for cyclist-campers--Lopez is the most-level of all the San Juan Islands. The passage just offshore of the park is usually busy with a good assortment of small and large craft, so if you're a boat-watcher, you'll always have something to be occupied with while camping at this outpost.

DOUGLAS FIR
Mt. Baker-Snoqualmie National Forest

Location: Northwest Washington northeast of Bellingham.

Access: From Washington State Highway 542 at a point 2.5 miles east of the community of Glacier, turn north (left) into the campground.

Facilities: 30 campsites in 2 loops; sites are average or better in size, level, and well separated; parking pads are gravel, mostly short to medium-length straight-ins; some excellent tent spots on a soft forest floor; fireplaces; firewood is usually available for gathering; water at hand pumps; vault facilities; paved or gravel driveways; limited supplies in Maple Falls, 10 miles west of Glacier on Highway 542.

Activities & Attractions: Stream fishing; Horseshoe Bend hiking trail begins south across the highway; an extensive network of hiking trails is located in the Mount Baker area; nearby Kulshan Ridge provides an excellent view of Mount Baker.

Natural Features: The Nooksack River flows alongside the lower loop of the campground; the upper loop is on a forested knoll; all sites are surrounded by dense rain forest-like vegetation--lush ferns cover the soft pine-needle forest floor, moss grows on rocks and trees and hangs from the tree limbs; the extinct volcano, Mount Baker, rises to almost 11,000' about 10 miles south; campground elevation 1000'.

Season, Fees & Phone: May to September; $10.00; 10 day limit; may be operated by concessionaire; Mount Baker Ranger District, Sedro Wooley, (206) 856-5700.

Camp Notes: The surrounding rain forest vegetation here, between the Nooksack River to the south and a rock-faced bluff to the north, creates a serene atmosphere in this campground. The river can be seen or heard from virtually all sites. Nice place. Douglas Fir is the first of the campgrounds you'll encounter as you travel east on this one-way-in/same-way-out highway in the Mount Baker-Mount Shuksan region. The other, Silver Fir, 11 miles east of Douglas Fir, has 19 sites and comparable facilities. There is a 1000' spread in elevation between Douglas Fir and Silver Fir near the upper (east) end of the highway, and the availability dates vary accordingly.

ROCKPORT
Rockport State Park

Location: Northwest Washington northeast of Mount Vernon.

Access: From Washington State Highway 20 at milepost 96 +.4 (7 miles east of Concrete, 1 mile west of Rockport), turn north into the park and continue for 0.15 mile to the campground.

Facilities: 58 campsites, including 50 with full hookups and 8 walk-in tent sites; (a group camp area is also available); most hookup sites are large, with good to very good separation; parking pads are paved, long straight-ins or pull-throughs; most pads will require additional leveling; large, acceptably level tent spots; 4 Adirondak shelters in the tent loop (extra charge); fireplaces; b-y-o firewood; water at faucets throughout; restrooms with showers; holding tank disposal station; paved driveways; gas and groceries in Rockport; limited supplies and services are available in Concrete; adequate+ supplies and services are available in Sedro Wooley.

Activities & Attractions: 5 hiking trails, including a handicapped accessible Skagit View Trail; fishing; small day use area.

Natural Features: Located on sloping terrain in the Skagit River Valley; the river is about a third of a mile south of the park; campground vegetation consists of medium-dense to dense, very tall conifers and hardwoods over a forest floor of ferns, brush and small plants; flanked by high, densely forested mountains; elevation 250'.

Season, Fees & Phone: March to November; please see Appendix for standard Washington state park fees; 10 day limit; park office (206) 853-8461.

Camp Notes: Rockport has the first or last public campground, depending upon you're direction of travel, along the superscenic North Cascades Highway. It's also the best campground on or near the route. (However, anyone who favors sunshine and open space might prefer to camp at Pearrygin Lake SP near the east end of the highway). If you're planning to take a loop tour of the North Cascades and have some discretion as to whether you drive the Highway east-to-west or west-to-east, consider the latter as the preferred direction of travel. The drive seems more spectacular, and the anticipation heightened, by starting out at sea level and, after a couple-hundred miles of peaks and ridges and forests and lakes and streams and waterfalls, finally exiting onto the high drylands of Central Washington.

GOODELL CREEK
Ross Lake National Recreation Area

Location: Northwest Washington east of Mount Vernon.

Access: From Washington State Highway 20 at milepost 119 +.4 (0.5 mile west of Newhalem, 13 miles east of Marblemount), turn south, then immediately east (left) onto a paved campground access road, proceed 0.2 mile, then swing right, into the campground.

Facilities: 22 campsites; (group camps are also available, in separate areas nearby); sites are small to small+, level, with fair to good separation; parking pads are gravel, short to short+ straight-ins; medium-sized tent areas; fireplaces; firewood is available for gathering in the vicinity; water at central faucets; vault facilities; paved driveway; groceries in Newhalem, gas and groceries+ in Marblemount.

Activities & Attractions: Raft launch; fishing.

Natural Features: Located on a streamside flat at the confluence of the Skagit River and Goodell Creek in a valley in the western foothills of the Cascade Range; campground vegetation consists of dense hardwoods, scattered tall conifers and dense bushery; bordered by densely forested hills and mountains; North Cascades National Park lies north and south of here; elevation 600'.

Season, Fees & Phone: Available all year, subject to weather conditions, with limited services October to May; $6.00; 14 day limit; Ross Lake NRA Hq, Sedro Wolley, (206) 856-5700.

Camp Notes: One of the Pacific Northwest's principal streams, the Skagit River is wide and fairly deep, and was navigable in the old days. Goodell Creek Campground is used as a launch point for rafters in modern times. Prepare for rain.

NEWHALEM CREEK
Ross Lake National Recreation Area

Location: Northwest Washington east of Mount Vernon.

Access: From Washington State Highway 20 at milepost 119 +.9 on the west edge of the hamlet of Newhalem (13 miles east of Marblemount, 38 miles west of Rainy Pass), turn south onto a paved access road, cross the narrow river bridge, and proceed 0.1 mile to the ranger/check-in station; just beyond the station, turn right or left to the camp loops.

Facilities: 116 campsites in 4 loops, plus 13 walk-in sites; sites are small to medium-sized, level, with fairly good to very good separation; parking pads are paved, mostly medium-length straight-ins, plus some long pull-throughs; enough space for small to medium-sized tents in most sites; fireplaces; firewood is available for gathering in the vicinity, (b-y-o dry kindling); water at central faucets; restrooms; disposal station; paved driveways; groceries in Newhalem, gas and groceries+ in Marblemount.

Activities & Attractions: Nature trail; hiking trails; amphitheater for scheduled nature talks and children's programs; large public playground and day use area in Newhalem; visitor center and museum at the local hydroelectric plant.

Natural Features: Located on flats near the confluence of the Skagit River and Newhalem Creek on the west slope of the Cascade Range; campground vegetation consists of very dense, tall conifers and low shrubbery; bordered by forested hills and mountains; elevation 600'.

Season, Fees & Phone: May to October; $8.00; 14 day limit; Ross Lake NRA Headquarters, Sedro Wolley, (206) 856-5700.

Camp Notes: Like its much smaller sister camp, Goodell Creek, Newhalem Creek has a subdued, streamside environment, rather than a busy lakeside location, as you might expect in a national recreation area named for a major lake. Good views in most directions from in and around camp. Newhalem itself is a Seattle City Light 'company town' with a highwayside park that's quite a showplace, particularly for a small, remote location like this one. Midtown is just a couple-tenths of a mile from the campground.

COLONIAL CREEK
Ross Lake National Recreation Area

Location: North-central Washington between Winthrop and Newhalem.

Access: From Washington State Highway 20 at milepost 130 +.2 (0.2 mile west of the Colonial Creek bridge and 0.2 mile east of the Diablo Lake crossing, 20 miles east of Newhalem, 63 miles west of Winthrop), turn south or north into the 2 respective sections of the campground.

Facilities: 164 campsites in 2 sections; most sites are small+ to medium-sized, with fair to fairly good separation; parking pads are gravel, short to medium-length straight-ins or pull-throughs; some sites may require additional leveling; many small, private tent spots; a few walk-in tent sites; fireplaces; b-y-o firewood is recommended; water at several faucets; restrooms; holding tank disposal station; paved driveways; nearest reliable sources of supplies and services are Newhalem, and Marblemount, 20 and 40 miles west, respectively.

Activities & Attractions: Boating and related water sports on Diablo Lake and Thunder Creek; self-guided nature trail; Thunder Creek Hiking Trail; evening interpretive programs in summer; Diablo Lake is at the southern tip of expansive Ross Lake National Recreation Area.

Natural Features: Located on a forested hillside near the south end of Diablo Lake; very tall conifers, hardwoods, and varying amounts of underbrush provide good separation; tall peaks of the Cascades tower over the lake and the campground; elev. 1200'.

Season, Fees & Phone: May to November; $8.00; 14 day limit; Ross Lake NRA Hq, Sedro Wolley, (206) 856-5700.

Camp Notes: This campground tends to fill early due to its location right beside the lake and on the highway. A few lakefront sites provide for tentside mooring of boats. Some sites may be a bit close to the highway or to a neighboring camper, but the dense vegetation helps to subdue extraneous noise. Of the trio of Ross Lake NRA campgrounds along Highway 20 (also see Newhalem Creek and Goodell Creek) only Colonial Creek is on a lake, and it's not actually on Ross Lake. The North Cascades Highway--Highway 20--passes through a corridor earmarked for easy public recreational access and very limited commercial development. The highway, which bisects North Cascades National Park, remained unpaved over Rainy Pass until the latter part of the Twentieth Century. The parklands have been set aside as a wilderness area.

Washington 72

WALLACE FALLS
Wallace Falls State Park

Location: Northwest Washington southeast of Everett.

Access: From U.S. Highway 2 at milepost 27 +.9 in the community of Gold Bar, turn north onto 1st Street and proceed 0.4 mile; turn easterly (right) onto May Creek Road and go 0.7 mile; bear northeast (left) onto Ley Road for 0.35 mile, then turn north (left) into the park.

Facilities: 6 park n' walk tent sites; sites are very small, level, with minimal separation; parking in the adjacent lot; enough space for small to medium-sized tents; fireplaces; some firewood is available for gathering in the vicinity; drinking water and restrooms nearby; gas and groceries in Gold Bar and other neighboring towns.

Activities & Attractions: Hiking trails, hiker's choice: along the Woody Trail, a standard foot trail all the way to Wallace Falls viewpoints and the valley overlooks, or part of the way via an old railroad grade, then a link-up with the trail; 3 miles max via the standard trail, 4 miles max via the railroad/trail option; (maps and mileage information are posted at the trailhead near the parking lot); day use area.

Natural Features: Located in the western foothills of the Cascade Range in the Skykomish River Valley; campground vegetation consists of dense, tall conifers and hardwoods; Wallace Falls on the Wallace River takes a 265' spill down the mountain; campground elevation 300'.

Season, Fees & Phone: Open all year, with limited services October to April; please see Appendix for standard Washington state park fees; 10 day limit; park office (206) 793-0420.

Camp Notes: Although they're right off a fairly busy day use area and trailhead parking lot, the little campsites here are really pleasant spots in their own right. (Nighttime access to the lot is restricted, so things should settle down after dark.) If you're a hiker, as are many tent campers, you'll like this place. It's a 2-mile hike to the first of four viewpoints along the trail to Wallace Falls. One of the viewpoints offers a positively spectacular panorama of the Skykomish River Valley. A rail fence at the edge of the viewpoint gives you something to grab if you swoon and teeter a bit from the exhilarating spectacle that unfolds a thousand feet below the soles of your well-worn waffle-stompers.

Washington 73

MONEY CREEK
Mt. Baker-Snoqualmie National Forest

Location: Western Washington east of Everett.

Access: From U.S. Highway 2 at milepost 45 +.9 (4 miles west of Skykomish, 9 miles east of the national forest boundary, 17 miles east of Gold Bar), turn south onto a paved access road, cross a river bridge, then turn left or right into the campground. (Note: The campground turnoff is about 100 yards west of a short highway tunnel, so if you're westbound, it'll come up rather quickly after you emerge from the tube.)

Facilities: 24 campsites in 2 loops; sites are small to small+, level, with fair to good separation; parking pads are gravel or paved, short to medium-length, mostly straight-ins or pull-offs, and a few are extra wide; some excellent, medium-sized tent areas are located among the trees; fireplaces; firewood is available for gathering in the vicinity; water at several faucets; vault facilities; waste water receptacles; paved driveways; gas and groceries in Skykomish and Gold Bar.

Activities & Attractions: Foot trails in the campground; stream fishing; sandy river beach; small picnic area.

Natural Features: Located on a streamside flat in the Skykomish River Valley on the west slope of the Cascade Range; Money Creek flows into the South Fork of the Skykomish River here amid a very dense mixture of hardwoods and conifers; many sites, especially in the east loop, are situated right along the riverbank; elevation 900'.

Season, Fees & Phone: May to October; $7.00; 14 day limit; Skykomish Ranger District (206) 677-2414.

Camp Notes: The drive along U.S. 2 through the deep green Skykomish River Valley is in itself worth the trip. Because Money Creek is close to the metropolitan area and easy to find, it's very popular. Taking into account the dense foliage and streamside location, this camp might be best in cooler or breezier weather. You might also want to check the AMTRACK schedules and then adjust your nap and nighttime rest periods accordingly. (Chugga-chugga, rumble-rumble, honk-honk.) Terrific Cascade views from near the campground.

Washington 74

BECKLER RIVER
Mt. Baker-Snoqualmie National Forest

Location: Western Washington east of Everett.

Access: From U.S. Highway 2 at milepost 49 +.5 in Skykomish (21 miles east of Gold Bar, 15 miles west of Stevens Pass) turn north (a sharp right for westbound traffic) onto Beckler River Road/Forest Road 65 (paved) and proceed 1.3 miles; turn west (left) into the campground.

Facilities: 27 campsites in a string and a loop; sites are small to small+, level, with fair to good separation; parking pads are paved, mostly short to medium-length straight-ins, plus a half-dozen long pull-throughs; ample space for tents; fireplaces; firewood is available for gathering; water at a hand pump; vault facilities; paved driveways; gas and groceries in Skykomish and Gold Bar.

Activities & Attractions: Fishing; small picnic area.

Natural Features: Located on a flat along the east bank of the Beckler River in the Skykomish River Valley; sites are deeply shaded by large hardwoods and conifers; the Cascade Range rises to the east; elevation 900'.

Season, Fees & Phone: May to October; $7.00; 14 day limit; Skykomish Ranger District (206) 677-2414.

Camp Notes: The Beckler River is a good stream with a cobble bottom that looks like it should hold some nice fish. Simple as it is, overall this is one of the best forest camps along Highway 2.

Washington 75

TINKHAM
Mt. Baker-Snoqualmie National Forest

Location: Western Washington east/southeast of Seattle.

Access: From Interstate 90 Exit 42 for Tinkham Road (12 miles east of North Bend, 40 miles east of Seattle, 10 miles west of Snoqualmie Pass summit), go to the south side of the Interstate, then continue south/southeast on Tinkham Road/Forest Road 55 (first paved, then gravel) for 1.6 miles, then turn left and go about 100 yards to the campground. (Note: Intermittent, seasonal streams and rivulets may cross the access road, so if your small craft lacks freeboard, you might want to check the speed and depth of the current before plunging through; Tinkham Road parallels the south side of I-90 between Exits 42 and 47; if you're westbound on the freeway, you could save a mile, but probably not much time or fuel, by getting off at Exit 47, then traveling Tinkham Road for 4 miles to the campground.)

Facilities: 47 campsites, including several double units, in 3 loops; sites are small to medium+, with fair to very good separation; parking pads are gravel, mostly short to medium-length straight-ins or pull-throughs; many pads will require a little additional leveling; enough space for a small to medium-sized tent in most sites, (medium+, if you install it on the parking pad); fireplaces; firewood is available for gathering (may be wet); water at a hand pump; vault facilities; gravel driveways; pack-it-in/pack-it-out trash system; gas and snacks at Snoqualmie Pass; adequate supplies and services are available in North Bend.

Activities & Attractions: McClellan Butte Trail; picnic grounds and trail to Franklin Falls in Asahel Curtis Recreation area, 5 miles east.

Natural Features: Located along a good-sized creek in a very dense forest of large hardwoods, some tall timber, ferns and bushes on the west slope of the Cascade Range; elevation 2100'.

Season, Fees & Phone: May to October; $8.00 for a single site, $14.00 for a double site; 14 day limit; North Bend Ranger District (206) 888-1421.

Camp Notes: Some of the sites are so densely enshrouded in foliage and so dark, it's almost like camping in a big refrigerator shipping box. Many sites are narrow, but they go waaaay back into the trees. Forget the tent and tarp. If it rains, a dome of arched hardwoods will shed the drips. (Well, almost!) For many of the campsites, just enough of the forest was chiseled out to hold the pad, tent space and table. Very private. Spending more than a weekend in one of these cozy nooks might test an average camper's tolerance toward claustrophobic tendencies, but it would be an interesting experience. And all of this is just off a major transcontinental highway and only 40 miles from the Puget Sound gigalopolis.

Washington 76

DENNY CREEK
Mt. Baker-Snoqualmie National Forest

Location: Western Washington east/southeast of Seattle.

Access: From Interstate 90 Exit 47 for Denny Creek Road and Tinkham Road (17 miles east of North Bend, 45 miles east of Seattle, 5 miles west of Snoqualmie Pass summit), go to the north/west side of the freeway to a "T", then turn easterly onto Denny Creek Road/Forest Road 58 (paved) for 0.3 mile; turn northerly (left) continuing on Denny Creek Road (narrow, paved) for 2.1 miles, then turn left into the campground.

Facilities: 33 campsites, including several double units, in a complex loop; (a group site is also available, by reservation); sites are medium to large, reasonably level, with fair to good separation; parking pads are paved, medium-length straight-ins or medium+ pull-throughs; medium to large tent spots, including many large, framed-and-gravelled tent pads; fireplaces; firewood is available for gathering (may be wet); water at a hand pump; vault facilities; paved driveways; pack-it-in/pack-it-out trash system; gas and snacks at Snoqualmie Pass; adequate supplies and services are available in North Bend.

Activities & Attractions: Footbridge across a side stream; trail to Franklin Falls and picnic grounds in Asahel Curtis Recreation area, 2 miles southwest.

Natural Features: Located on forested, terraced terrain high on the west slope of the Cascade Range along Denny Creek; local vegetation consists of very dense, very tall conifers over a thick undercover of bushes and ferns; several streamside sites; elevation 2700'.

Season, Fees & Phone: May to October; $8.00 for a single site, $14.00 for a double site; 14 day limit; North Bend Ranger District (206) 888-1421.

Camp Notes: Even when the sun is high on a cloudless day (rare), you might be tempted to turn your headlights on as you approach the campground through the super dense tunnel of vegetation that engulfs the access road. Interesting touches of landscaping are evident throughout the campground. Even old, decaying, moss-shrouded logs add natural interest and beauty to this place. Considering the high elevation and very high winter precipitation levels, the campground isn't in a 'rain forest' as much as it is in a 'snow forest' environment. There's still a generous quantity of liquid precip here during the camping season, though. If you left your raingear at home, you could use one of the incredibly huge leaves of certain local plants for a bumbershoot.

Washington 77

CRYSTAL SPRINGS
Wenatchee National Forest

Location: West-central Washington northwest of Ellensburg.

Access: From Interstate 90 Exit 62 for Lake Kachess and Stampede Pass (24 miles west of Cle Elum, 10 miles east of the summit of Snoqualmie Pass), from the south side of the freeway, proceed westerly on Forest Road 54 (paved) for 0.5 mile to the campground.

Facilities: 20 campsites, including a few double sites, in a loop and a string; sites are small to medium-sized, with fair to excellent separation; parking pads are gravel, primarily short straight-ins, plus a few long pull-throughs; some pads may require a little additional leveling; medium to large tent areas; fire rings; firewood is available for gathering; water at faucets throughout; vault facilities; gravel/dirt driveway; limited+ supplies in Cle Elum; complete supplies and services are available in Ellensburg.

Activities & Attractions: Picnic shelter; boating and fishing at Lake Kachess, 5 miles northeast (see separate information); Keechelus Lake, 2 miles west, has limited water activities, depending upon lake level.

Natural Features: Located on a forested flat in a valley in the Cascade Range; sites are very densely sheltered/shaded by tall conifers and underbrush; a sizeable stream flows past the campground; bordered by forested mountains; elevation 2500'.

Season, Fees & Phone: May to October; $6.00 for a single site, $12.00 for a double site; 14 day limit; Cle Elum Ranger District (509) 674-4411.

Camp Notes: Because of the dense vegetation, quite a few of the sites are quite private, even though they're a bit small and closely spaced. According to maps, the wide, deep, clear stream which passes the campground is the Yakima River just downstream of its headwaters, Keechelus Lake. Because of extremely fluctuating lake levels, tree stumps, clear-clipped mountainsides, and the wide swath cut by I-90, Keechelus Lake isn't one of the most scenic bodies of water in Washington State. In contrast, Crystal Springs is kind of a neat little spot.

Washington 78

KACHESS
Wenatchee National Forest

Location: West-central Washington northwest of Ellensburg.

Access: From Interstate 90 Exit 62 for Lake Kachess and Stampede Pass (24 miles west of Cle Elum, 10 miles east of the summit of Snoqualmie Pass), from the north side of the freeway head northeast on Forest Road 49 (paved) for 5.1 miles to a "T" intersection; swing easterly (right) for a few yards to the campground entrance; continue easterly for 0.1 mile to another "T", then turn right to sites 1-23, or turn left to the main campground.

Facilities: 183 campsites, including a number of double sites, in 6 loops; sites are small+ to medium+, basically level, with fair to very good separation; parking pads are packed gravel, mostly short+ to medium-length straight-ins, plus a couple-dozen long pull-throughs; a few pads might require a bit of additional leveling; medium to large areas for tents; fire rings or fireplaces; plenty of firewood is available for gathering in the surrounding area; water at several faucets; restrooms, plus supplemental vaults; paved driveways; limited+ supplies in Cle Elum; complete supplies and services are available in Ellensburg.

Activities & Attractions: Boating; sailing; boat launches; fishing for kokanee salmon and rainbow trout; designated swimming areas; Lakeshore Trail and Big Trees self-guided nature trail; several other hiking trails and forest roads lead into the mountains; large day use area.

Natural Features: Located on a slightly rolling flat on the west shores of Lake Kachess and Little Lake Kachess; sites generally are very well sheltered/shaded by tall conifers and brushwork; small streams tumble down over the rocks through several camp loops; Lake Kachess is a 4500-acre impoundment on the Kachess River and its tributaries; bordered by the densely forested mountains of the east slope of the Cascade Range; elevation 2300'.

Season, Fees & Phone: Available all year, subject to weather and road conditions, with limited services in winter; principal season is May to October; $9.00; 14 day limit; Cle Elum Ranger District (509) 674-4411.

Camp Notes: You'll find few, if any, forest camps in the Cascades that are larger or better-equipped than this one. If you're looking for a two-family site, you might want to consider getting a pair of adjacent single units instead. Many of the 'doubles' aren't much bigger than the 'singles'. Little Lake Kachess is a secondary body of water at the north tip of the main Lake Kachess. The lakes are connected by a 'narrows' offshore of the campground. The name of the lakes and their attendant campground are locally pronounced *Katcheez*. By the end of summer, the level of the principal lake may be drawn down as much as 60 feet for irrigation.

Washington 79

LAKE EASTON
Lake Easton State Park

Location: West-central Washington west of Ellensburg.

Access: From Interstate 90 Exit 70 for Lake Easton (15 miles west of Cle Elum, 18 miles east of Snoqualmie Pass), follow the frontage road on the south side of the Interstate easterly for 0.5 mile; turn south (right) into the park entrance; continue ahead for 0.1 mile to the standard camping area; turn northwest (right) and proceed 1 mile to the hookup camp.

Facilities: 145 campsites in two sections; the primary area consists of 100 standard sites; campsites here are mostly small to medium-sized, reasonably level, with nominal to fairly good separation; parking pads are packed gravel, short to medium-length straight-ins, plus a few pull-throughs; water at several faucets; the hookup section contains 45 level, full-hookup units; about half of the hookup pads are pull-throughs, the balance are straight-ins; restrooms with showers; fireplaces; firewood is usually for sale, or b-y-o; holding tank disposal station; paved driveways; gas and groceries in Easton; limited+ supplies and services are available in Cle Elum.

Activities & Attractions: Swimming beach; fishing for several varieties of trout; boating; boat launch; hiking trails; playground; day use area.

Natural Features: Located on the densely forested north shore of Lake Easton, a 250-acre irrigation reservoir; the primary camping area is situated near the east end of the lake; the hookup units are located on a hilltop at the west end of the lake; tall, timbered mountains are visible in most directions; elevation 2200'.

Season, Fees & Phone: April to October; please see Appendix for standard Washington state park fees; 10 day limit; park office (509) 656-2230.

Camp Notes: If you come to Lake Easton, and you're an individual who is readily troubled by logging scars, it might be a good idea to concentrate on your activity--camping, walking, jogging, boating, fishing, or whatever--and avoid looking at the nearby mountainsides. Another local state park, Iron Horse SP, consists of 25 miles of former railroad right-of-way between the towns of Easton and Thorp. The old RR bed is now called the John Wayne Pioneer Trail. Lake Easton campers looking for a long stroll in unforested surroundings on level terrain might find that it suits their needs.

Washington 80

WISH-POOSH
Wenatchee National Forest

Location: West-central Washington west of Ellensburg.

Access: From Interstate 90 Exit 80 for Roslyn/Salmon La Sac (28 miles west of Ellensburg, 9 miles east of Easton), travel north on a local paved connecting road for 2.9 miles to Roslyn; turn northwest (left) onto Washington State Highway 903 and proceed 7.7 miles; turn southwest (left) onto the paved recreation area access road for a few yards, then swing left into the campground; (Note: Highway 903 officially ends after you've traveled 6 miles, but just continue beyond that point on the paved road for the remaining 1.7 miles of the total 7.7 miles to the campground.)

Facilities: 39 campsites, including several 2-family units; sites are small to medium-sized, with good to excellent separation; parking pads are gravel, short to medium-length straight-ins; a little additional leveling will be needed in some sites; small to large tent areas; fire rings or barbecue grills; firewood is available for gathering in the area; water at several faucets; restrooms; waste water receptacles; paved driveways; gas and groceries+ are available in Roslyn; limited+ supplies and services are available in Cle Elum.

Activities & Attractions: Boating; boat launch nearby; fishing; day use area nearby.

Natural Features: Located on a slightly sloping, forested flat several hundred yards from the north-east shore of Cle Elum Lake, a reservoir on the Cle Elum River; sites are well-shaded/sheltered by tall conifers, ferns and a considerable amount of brush; the lake is bordered by high, forested mountains; elevation 2200'.

Season, Fees & Phone: May to October; $9.00 for a standard site; $18.00 for a 2-family unit; 14 day limit; Cle Elum Ranger District (509) 674-4411.

Camp Notes: Lots of privacy, "modern" facilities, a big lake, and 15 minutes from the Interstate. Need more be said?

Washington 81

KANASKAT-PALMER
Kanasket-Palmer State Park

Location: Western Washington east of Auburn.

Access: From the junction of Washington State Highways 169 & 516 in the community of Summit (3 miles south of Maple Valley, 3 miles north of Black Diamond), head east on SE Kent-Kangley Road for 3.4 miles to a "Y" intersection; bear southeast (right) onto SE Retreat-Kanaskat Road and proceed 3.1 miles; turn west (right) onto Cumberland-Kanaskat Road and go west/southwest for 1.8 miles, then turn north (right) into the park; continue ahead for 0.6 miles to a 3-way intersection; turn east (right) into the campground.

Alternate Access: From Washington State Highway 410 at milepost 25 +.7 on the east edge of Enumclaw, turn north onto Farman Road (284th Avenue SE, which shortly becomes Veazie-Cumberland Road) and travel 9 miles (to a point 3.8 miles beyond Nolte State Park); turn west (left) onto Cumberland-Kanaskat Road and continue as above. (The primary access is the better one if you're approaching from Seattle and other points north; the access through Enumclaw is better from the South Sound--and a little less convoluted.)

Facilities: 50 campsites, including 19 with electrical hookups; (4 primitive sites and a group camp with shelters are also available); sites are small+ to medium-sized, with fairly good to excellent separation; parking pads are gravel or paved, medium to long straight-ins or medium+ to long pull-throughs; a little additional leveling will be needed in some sites; medium to large tent areas; fireplaces; firewood is usually for sale, or b-y-o; water at several faucets; restrooms with showers; holding tank disposal station; paved driveways; nearest reliable sources of supplies and services are Summit (limited+) and Enumclaw (adequate+).

Activities & Attractions: Kayaking and rafting; 3 designated put-in/take-out points (trails lead down to the river from the parking lots); hiking trails meander throughout the park and along the riverbank; day use areas with shelters.

Natural Features: Located on the inside of a large, squared bend in the Green River; most of the campground is densely forested with tall hardwoods, conifers, plus very dense low-level vegetation; elevation 700'.

Season, Fees & Phone: Open all year; please see Appendix for standard Washington state park fees; 10 day limit; park office (206) 886-0148.

Camp Notes: Many campers here are river-runners looking for an opportunity to tackle part or all of the 14-mile stretch of the Green River between here and Flaming Geyser State Park. Generally speaking, late September is the prime time for that, but it's recommended that you be up to the task of handling Class IV water. River-running aside, a lot of people camp here just to enjoy the river and the forest and to catch a few glimpses of the action on the Green.

Washington

Southwest

Please refer to the Washington map in the Appendix

Washington 82

DALLES
Mt. Baker-Snoqualmie National Forest

Location: Southwest Washington northeast of Mount Rainier National Park.

Access: From Washington State Highway 410 at milepost 50 +.4 (7 miles north of the Mount Rainier National Park boundary, 26 miles southeast of Enumclaw), jog west onto a paved access road for a few yards, then turn north (right) into the campground.

Facilities: 45 campsites; sites are small to medium-sized, basically level, with fair to very good separation; parking pads are oiled, packed gravel, short to medium-length straight-ins; some very good, small to medium-sized tent spots, especially in the more open sites; fireplaces or fire rings; some firewood is available for gathering in the vicinity, b-y-o to be sure; water at several faucets; vault facilities; paved driveways; camper supplies in Greenwater, 8 miles north; adequate+ supplies and services are available in Enumclaw.

Activities & Attractions: Short, self-guided nature trail at the north end of the campground leads to an old Douglas fir tree that's 235' high, over 9 feet in diameter and is more than 700 years old; Dalles River Trail; day use area with large picnic shelter; possible fishing; Sunrise Visitor Center is located nearby in Mount Rainier National Park.

Natural Features: Located between the highway and the White River, at the river's confluence with Minnehaha Creek; most sites are surrounded by towering evergreens and some hardwoods, but a few are in a relatively open forest setting; closely bordered by the forested hills and mountains of the Cascade Range; the boundary of Mount Rainier National Park is 8 miles south; Norse Peak Wilderness Area lies just to the east; elevation 2200'.

Season, Fees & Phone: May to September; $8.00; 14 day limit; may be operated by concessionaire; White River Ranger District, Enumclaw, (206) 825-6585.

Camp Notes: There are some excellent campsites here in the shadow of the ol' Doug fir that towers over this spot. You can't help but be awed (or at the very least, very impressed) by this forest giant. The drive along Highway 410 through this forested country reveals a number of first-rate views of perpetually snow-clad Mount Rainier. Some printed sources refer to this campground as "The Dalles", meaning "The Narrows", referring to the slim, mountain corridor which the river and the highway pass through in this section.

SILVER SPRINGS
Mt. Baker-Snoqualmie National Forest

Location: Southwest Washington northeast of Mount Rainier National Park.

Access: From Washington State Highway 410 at milepost 56 +.5 (0.35 mile north of the Silver Creek Guard Station, 1 mile north of the Mount Rainier National Park boundary, 33 miles southeast of Enumclaw), turn west into the campground.

Facilities: 56 campsites; sites are small to medium-sized, with fair to good separation; parking pads are packed gravel, level, mostly medium-length straight-ins; many good tent spots; fireplaces or fire rings; gathering of firewood on national forest lands prior to arrival is suggested; water at several faucets; vault facilities; paved driveway; camper supplies in Greenwater, 14 miles north; adequate+ supplies and services are available in Enumclaw.

Activities & Attractions: Hiking trails lead off toward Mount Rainier and Norse Peak Wilderness; footbridge across the stream; fishing; day use areas with large and small shelters.

Natural Features: Located on a rolling, forested flat or on sloped terrain along Silver Creek, where it flows into the White River, in the Cascade Range; a few sites are close to the highway but the tall, thick trees and fairly heavy underbrush provide a good sound barrier; some sites are right on the riverbank; bordered by steep, forested mountains; Mount Rainier National Park is 1 mile south; Norse Peak Wilderness Area is to the east; elevation 2800'.

Season, Fees & Phone: May to September; $8.00; 14 day limit; may be operated by concessionaire; White River Ranger District, Enumclaw, (206) 825-6585.

Camp Notes: Silver Springs is the closest campground to this corner of Mount Rainier National Park. The setting, along the east bank of glacier-fed White River, is a nice spot for a highwayside campground--especially since it's within 2 hours' drive of the metropolitan area. Under certain runoff conditions, though, the origin of the White River's name manifests itself. The stream's name comes not from the whitecaps and foamy riffles on the surface of its crystal clear waters, but from the milky white pigmentation of the glacial silt it carries over its gravelly banks and bottom. Well, any port in a water-lovers storm . . .

WHITE RIVER
Mount Rainier National Park

Location: Southwest Washington in northeast Mount Rainier National Park.

Access: From Washington State Highway 410 (Mather Memorial Parkway) at milepost 62 +.2 (4.5 miles north of Cayuse Pass summit, 39 miles southeast of Enumclaw), turn west onto a paved park road toward the national park's White River Entrance and Sunrise Point; travel 5.2 miles to a fork in the road; take the left fork and continue for another 2.5 miles to the campground.

Facilities: 115 campsites in 4 loops; most sites are average in size and fairly well separated; parking pads are gravel, medium-length straight-ins or pull-offs; some pads will require additional leveling; some excellent tent-pitching opportunities; fireplaces; b-y-o firewood; water at several faucets; restrooms; paved driveways; camper supplies are available at Sunrise Point.

Activities & Attractions: Amphitheater for ranger-naturalist campfire programs on summer weekends; trailhead for Glacier Basin located at the west end of the campground; Sunrise Point Visitor Center located several miles north.

Natural Features: Located on a forested slope along the White River, which flows down from the heights of Mount Rainier; moderately dense vegetation consists of conifers, bushes and ferns over a somewhat rocky forest floor; nearby Sunrise Point offers a magnificent view of Mount Rainier; elevation 4400'.

Season, Fees & Phone: July to September; $8.00; 14 day limit; park headquarters (206) 569-2211.

Camp Notes: Mount Rainier National Park offers visitors a chance to commune with nature at its best. Subalpine meadows bloom with a myriad of flowers near the edge of acres of tenacious glaciers. White River Campground is at one of the closest drive-in points to the great dormant volcano which the Indians called *Tahoma*, simply "The Mountain".

OHANAPECOSH
Mount Rainier National Park

Location: Southwest Washington in the southeast corner of Mount Rainier National Park.

Access: From Washington State Highway 123 at milepost 3 +.7 (1.5 miles south of the junction of Highway 123 & Stevens Canyon Road, 2 miles north of the national park-national forest boundary, 3.7 miles north of the junction of Highway 123 & U.S. Highway 12 northeast of Packwood), turn west onto a paved access road; go a few yards to a fork, then bear right and proceed 0.3 mile down to the campground.

Facilities: 220 campsites, including some walk-in sites, in several loops; campsites are generally small to small+, and closely spaced; parking pads are packed gravel, short to scant medium-length straight-ins; many pads may require additional leveling; a few sites will accommodate medium-sized rv's; many excellent tent spots; fireplaces; b-y-o firewood; restrooms; water at several faucets; holding tank disposal station; paved driveways; limited supplies and services are available in Packwood.

Activities & Attractions: Ohanapecosh Visitor Center offers historical information, plus exhibits about local animal life and vegetation; amphitheater for scheduled campfire programs in summer; self-guided and naturalist-guided walks to Silver Falls, Hot Springs, Laughing Water and Grove of the Patriarchs.

Natural Features: Located on hilly terrain in a densely forested valley along the glacier-fed Ohanapecosh River; Ohanapecosh Hot Springs is accessible by foot trail 0.1 mile east; campsite settings vary considerably: some sites are moderately forested, others have a few tall trees and no underbrush; some sites are situated on small knolls while others are on a creek's edge; elevation 1900'.

Season, Fees & Phone: May to October; $9.00; 14 day limit; park headquarters (206) 569-2211.

Camp Notes: Superscenic hikes, bikes and drives are important features of this park. Mount Rainier, at 14,410 feet, towers over the rest of the park and solicits spectacular views from numerous hiking trails and roadside pullouts.

LA WIS WIS
Gifford Pinchot National Forest

Location: Southwest Washington near the southeast corner of Mount Rainier National Park.

Access: From U.S. Highway 12 at milepost 138 (7 miles northeast of Packwood, 1 mile southwest of the junction of U.S. 12 and Washington State Highway 123), turn north (i.e., left if approaching from Packwood) onto a paved, but steep and twisty, access road; continue for 0.6 mile down to the campground.

Facilities: 101 campsites in 5 main loops plus 23 more in a "Hatchery" rv loop and a few walk-in tent sites; sites are average or better in size, mostly level, and fairly well separated; parking pads are paved, primarily very short to medium-length straight-ins; A Loop has longer pads; Hatchery Loop has paved, pull-off parking; fairly level, small to large tent spots; fireplaces or fire rings; some firewood is usually available for gathering in the area; water at several faucets; centrally located restrooms, plus auxiliary vault facilities; paved driveways; limited+ supplies and services are available in Packwood.

Activities & Attractions: Fishing; Blue Hole Trail; day use area and picnic shelter; the surrounding forested region has many trails--including one for exploring an old growth forest; Ohanapecosh Visitor Center is nearby in Mount Rainier National Park.

Natural Features: Located in the Cascade Range in the narrow Ohanapecosh River Valley near the confluence of the Ohanapecosh and Cowlitz Rivers; rain forest-like vegetation predominates in this area; Mount Rainier National Park is 4 miles north; elevation 1400'.

Season, Fees & Phone: May to September; $7.00 for a standard site, $8.00 for a 'premium' site (along the riverbank), $10.00 for a multiple site; 14 day limit; Packwood Ranger District (206) 494-5515.

Camp Notes: La Wis Wis is located in a lush forest of fir, hemlock and cedar, above a soft carpet of ferns and moss. The narrow valley between the Ohanapecosh and Cowlitz Rivers is a really lovely setting for a mountain campground. Being able to camp in places like La Wis Wis can be measurably credited to Gifford Pinchot, first Chief of the Forest Service. Pinchot spearheaded the establishment of the national forest system back in the 1890's and early 1900's when national conservation policy was as inflammatory a topic as it is today. As a member of both the Theodore Roosevelt and William H. Taft administrations, Pinchot was involved in some of the most controversial national issues of the early Twentieth Century. A conservational conflict over the sale of public lands in Wyoming, Montana and Alaska erupted between Pinchot and Taft's Secretary of the Interior Richard Bollinger, who supported the sell-off. Taft's mishandling of the affair eventually contributed to his political downfall. The fiasco inflicted enough embarrassment on the Republican Party that, in the 1910 elections, the Democrats won control of the U.S. House of Representatives for the first time in nearly two decades. Pinchot later was elected Governor of Pennsylvania.

Washington 87

COUGAR ROCK
Mount Rainier National Park

Location: Southwest Washington in the southwest quadrant of Mount Rainier National Park.

Access: From Paradise Road at a point 2.3 miles northeast of Longmire and 26 miles west of the junction of Paradise Road & State Highway 123 northeast of Packwood), turn north-west into the campground. (Note: Paradise Road-Stevens Canyon Road is the main east-west route through the southern section of the national park; it links Washington State Highway 706 at the southwest corner of the park with State Highway 123 at the southeast corner of the park.)

Facilities: 200 campsites in 6 loops; sites are generally small to small+, with nominal to fair separation; parking pads are gravel, mostly short to medium-length straight-ins, although about one-fourth are longer pull-throughs; some pads may require additional leveling; excellent tent-pitching opportunities; fireplaces; b-y-o firewood; water at faucets; restrooms; holding tank disposal station; paved driveways; camper supplies in Longmire.

Activities & Attractions: Wonderland Hiking Trail; Carter Falls; amphitheater for campfire programs; ranger-directed naturalist programs for children on summer weekends; Paradise Visitor Center and Viewpoint located a few miles east; Longmire also has a visitor center and museum.

Natural Features: Located in the Cascade Range on the south slope of Mount Rainier; the Paradise River flows into the Nisqually River at Cougar Rock; vegetation in the campground is predominantly tall conifers covered with hanging moss, plus a considerable quantity of ferns and underbrush; elevation 3200'.

Season, Fees & Phone: June to October; $7.00; 14 day limit; park headquarters (206) 569-2211.

Camp Notes: This campground is located in a rain forest-like atmosphere created by the moist maritime air flowing upward across the west slopes of Mount Rainier. The drive along Paradise Road offers some truly *great* scenic views. If you're westbound on this route from Highway 123 to Cougar Rock and the other camps in the park's southwest quadrant (Longmire and Sunshine Point, below), allow *at least* a couple of hours for the winding, hilly trip.

Washington 88

SUNSHINE POINT
Mount Rainier National Park

Location: Southwest Washington in the southwest quadrant of Mount Rainier National Park.

Access: From Paradise Road at a point 0.2 mile east of the Nisqually Entrance Station and 6 miles west of Longmire, turn south into the campground.

Facilities: 18 campsites; sites are small to medium-sized, level, with minimal to nominal separation; parking pads are gravel, mostly short to medium-length straight-ins; medium to large areas for tents; fireplaces; b-y-o firewood; water at faucets; vault facilities; paved driveways; minimal supplies in Longmire, limited supplies and services are available in Ashford, 7 miles west.

Activities & Attractions: Very large visitor center at Paradise; museum in Longmire; fishing and hiking.

Natural Features: Located on a large flat along the Nisqually River; campsites are either in the open right along the riverbank, or just at the forest's edge; vegetation consists primarily of some tall grass and medium-dense, tall conifers; Mount Rainier, visible to the north, is a glacier-clad 14,000' dormant volcano surrounded by lush rain forests and alpine meadows; the Nisqually River, parented by the glaciers of Rainier, flows west past Sunshine Point on its way to Puget Sound; elevation 2000'.

Season, Fees & Phone: Open all year with limited services in winter; $6.00; 14 day limit; park headquarters (206) 569-2211.

Camp Notes: Sunshine Point is distinctively different from the other campgrounds in Mount Rainier National Park. Its climatic conditions allow for year-round camping, whereas most other camping areas are snowed-in for much of the year. If you want to see the sight of your life (it indeed may lengthen your years), do whatever it takes to spend time at the Paradise Visitor Center on a clear day. The captivating view of *The Mountain* through the visitor center's walls of glass and from the observation decks is nothing short of absolutely astounding. Period.

ALDER LAKE
City of Tacoma Park

Location: Southwest Washington west of Mount Rainier National Park.

Access: From Washington State Highway 7 at a point 31 miles south of Tacoma and 19 miles west of the Nisqually Entrance to Mount Rainier National Park, turn south into the park.

Facilities: 78 campsites, including 25 with partial hookups, and 37 with full hookups, in the main camp area; plus 19 campsites, inclding some with partial hookups, in a less-developed "overflow area"; main area sites are medium-sized, with fair to fairly good separation; parking pads are paved, long straight-ins or pull-throughs; some pads may require additional leveling; overflow sites have gravel pads; some nice tent spots; fire rings or fireplaces; b-y-o firewood is recommended; water at hookup sites and at central faucets; restrooms with showers in the main camp, vault facilities in the overflow area; paved driveways in the main area, gravel driveway in the overflow unit; limited supplies and services are available in Alder and La Grande.

Activities & Attractions: Boating; boat launch; fishing; Mount Rainier National Park has fabulous scenery, a visitor center at Paradise Point, and museum at Longmire.

Natural Features: Located on a point of land above the north-east shore of Alder Lake; most campsites are shaded/sheltered by a mixture of conifers and hardwoods, other sites are in open areas; Alder Lake is a reservoir created by Alder Dam on the Nisqually River as a source of water for the city of Tacoma; forested slopes surround the lake; elevation 1100'.

Season, Fees & Phone: Open all year; principal season is April to October, with limited services in winter; $9.00 for a standard site, $12.00 for a partial hook-up site, $13.00 for a full hookup site; 10 day limit; park office (206) 569-2778.

Camp Notes: Alder Lake Campground is in a prime location: within 30 miles of the Tacoma urban area, and 20 miles from a world-renowned national park. The lake environment and the recreational facility here are quite good. The main campground is some distance above the lake and most sites lack lake views, so some campers opt for the "overflow" area. This campground might serve well as an attractive alternative to the campgrounds in Mount Rainier National Park.

IRON CREEK
Gifford Pinchot National Forest

Location: Southwest Washington northeast of Mount St. Helens National Volcanic Monument.

Access: From U.S. Highway 12 at milepost 115 in Randle (16 miles west of Packwood, 17 miles east of Morton), head south on Cispus Road/Forest Road 23 (paved) for 1 mile to a fork; take the right fork onto Forest Road 25 (paved) and continue southerly for another 8.6 miles; turn northeast (left) onto a paved access road into the campground. (Notes: Bear left at a fork just south of the Cispus River Bridge to continue on Road 25--from there it's still 1 more mile to the campground access road; total mileage from U.S. 12 to the campground is 9.6 miles).

Facilities: 98 campsites, including some double-occupancy units, in 4 loops; sites are small+ to medium-sized, with fairly good to excellent separation; parking pads are paved, short+ to long straight-ins; a touch of additional leveling may be needed in some sites; ample room for tents in most sites; fire rings; firewood is available for gathering; water at central faucets; vault facilities; paved driveways; limited+ supplies and services are available in Randle.

Activities & Attractions: Fishing; short trails lead down to the river; Big Trees Nature Trail; small amphitheater for campfire interpretive programs on summer weekends; small picnic area; scores of hiking trails and forest roads in the area, including Forest Road 99 to the Spirit Lake area just below Mount St. Helens; small visitor information center, 4 miles north on Forest Road 25 at mile 4 +.7 (open during midsummer).

Natural Features: Located on gently rolling, sloping terrain above the confluence of the Cispus River and Iron Creek in the foothills of the west slope of the Cascade Range; sites receive medium to moderately dense shade/shelter from lofty conifers and abundant undercover; the active volcano, Mount St. Helens, rises to a foreshortened 8400', 18 miles southwest; campground elevation 1100'.

Season, Fees & Phone: May to November; $7.00 for a single site, $10.00 for a double unit; 14 day limit; Randle Ranger District (206) 497-7565.

Camp Notes: Standing in the middle of an Iron Creek campsite and gazing skyward through the forest is like having a view from the lower deck of a 200-foot silo of light, air and space. Each site, in a nice-sized clearing encircled by towering trees, has its own natural cathedral ceiling, so to speak. A small camper could stand under a giant fern and stay dry in a downpour in this forest. Whoever picked the location and designed the campground knew what they were doing. Except for the wind through the tall timber, the only breaks in the nighttime tranquility might be the occasional screeches of speedy birds from air bases in the region. It's not a big deal, but it can be momentarily startling when the aluminum avians pass close overhead at 11:00 p.m. while your consciousness is drifting into the cosmos. (Especially when you're in a tent. Ed.)

Many campers use this as a jumpoff spot for exploring the Mount St. Helens area. If Iron Creek has the "no vacancy" neon shining brightly when you arrive on a really pleasant summer Saturday, you may be able to find a site at Tower Rock Campground, up the Cispus River on Forest Road 76, 7 miles east of Iron Creek. The only other local camps are North Fork and Blue Lake Creek, 14 miles and 18 miles east, respectively, by forest roads from Iron Creek. Campground hosts at Iron Creek or the attendant at the information center on Forest Road 25 can provide you with straightforward routes to follow to any of those camps.

Washington 91

LODGEPOLE
Snoqualmie/Wenatchee National Forests

Location: West-central Washington northwest of Yakima.

Access: From Washington State Highway 410 at milepost 76 +.8 (7 miles east of Chinook Pass, 11 miles east of the junction of State Highways 410 & 123, 44 miles northwest of Naches), turn north into the campground.

Facilities: 33 campsites in 2 loops; sites are small to medium-sized, with nominal to fairly good separation; parking pads are paved or gravel, short to medium-length straight-ins, plus a number of medium-length pull-throughs; some pads will require additional leveling; tent space varies from small to large; fireplaces or fire rings; firewood is available for gathering; water at a hand pump; vault facilities; paved driveways; gas and camper supplies in Cliffdell, near milepost 96; limited+ supplies and services are available in Naches.

Activities & Attractions: Hiking trails; fishing.

Natural Features: Located on a gently rolling flat along the American River on the east slope of the Cascade Range; vegetation consists of moderately dense lodgepole pines, a few aspens and some bushy undercover; bordered by densely forested mountains; elevation 3500'.

Season, Fees & Phone: May to October; $5.00; 14 day limit; Naches Ranger District (509) 653-2205.

Camp Notes: Lodgepole has several nice riverside sites. (One site is almost under a highway bridge which spans the river; if you're a troll, you can take that one.)

Washington 92

PLEASANT VALLEY
Snoqualmie/Wenatchee National Forests

Location: West-central Washington northwest of Yakima.

Access: From Washington State Highway 410 at milepost 80 +.3 (11 miles east of Chinook Pass, 15 miles east of the junction of State Highways 410 & 123, 40 miles northwest of Naches), turn south onto an oiled gravel access road and proceed 0.1 mile to the campground.

Facilities: 17 campsites in 2 loops; sites are medium+ to very large, with fair to very good separation; parking pads are gravel/dirt, mostly medium to very long straight-ins; a few pads may require additional leveling; large, mostly level areas for tents; fire rings or fireplaces; firewood is available for gathering; firewood is available for gathering; water at a hand pump; vault facilities; gravel/dirt driveways; gas and camper supplies in Cliffdell, near milepost 96; limited+ supplies and services are available in Naches.

Activities & Attractions: Kettle Creek Trail; footbridge across the stream; trout fishing; picnic shelter; small day use area.

Natural Features: Located on a slightly rolling flat along the bank of the American River in Pleasant Valley in the Cascade Range; campground vegetation consists of dense, very tall conifers and dense undergrowth, adjacent to a meadow; Norse Peak Wilderness lies to the north, William O. Douglas Wilderness (named for the late conservationist and U.S. Supreme Court Justice) lies to the south; elevation 3300'.

Season, Fees & Phone: May to October; $5.00; 14 day limit; Naches Ranger District (509) 653-2205.

Camp Notes: The large shelter could definitely come in handy on the not-infrequent rainy days around here. It comes complete with a good-sized, chimneyed barbecue grill--just the appliance you might need to help conquer rainy day appetites.

Washington 93

HELLS CROSSING
Snoqualmie/Wenatchee National Forests

Location: West-central Washington northwest of Yakima.

Access: From Washington State Highway 410 at milepost 83 +.5 (14 miles east of Chinook Pass, 18 miles east of the junction of State Highways 410 & 123, 37 miles northwest of Naches), turn north into the camp loops; (campsites are located in 2 loops east and west of a highway bridge).

Facilities: 18 campsites in 2 loops; sites are medium to quite large, essentially level, with good to excellent separation; parking pads are gravel, medium to long straight-ins; large tent spots; fire rings or fireplaces; firewood is available for gathering; water at a hand pump; vault facilities; gravel driveway; gas and camper supplies in Cliffdell, near milepost 96; limited+ supplies and services are available in Naches.

Activities & Attractions: Hiking trails; trout fishing.

Natural Features: Located on streamside flats along the American River; sites are sheltered/shaded by a moderately dense forest of tall conifers and underbrush; bordered by the densely forested mountains of the Cascade Range; elevation 3300'.

Season, Fees & Phone: May to October; $5.00; 14 day limit; Naches Ranger District (509) 653-2205.

Camp Notes: The campsites are situated along both banks of the wide, deep, swift river, and there are a number of good streamside sites. You might want to check the east loop first. It seems to have a bit more riverfront real estate and, subjectively, might be a touch nicer than the west section. Another nearby area which you might see on a map, Pine Needle Campground, 2 miles east of Hells Crossing, is a highwayside group camp available by reservation only.

Washington 94

AMERICAN FORKS & CEDAR SPRINGS
Snoqualmie/Wenatchee National Forests

Location: West-central Washington northwest of Yakima.

Access: From Washington State Highway 410 at milepost 88 +.5 (19 miles east of Chinook Pass, 23 miles east of the junction of State Highways 410 & 123, 32 miles northwest of Naches), turn south onto Bumping River Road (paved) and proceed 0.1 mile, then turn east (left) into American Forks; or continue southwest on Bumping River Road for an additional 0.45 mile, then hang a left into Cedar Springs.

Facilities: 16 campsites in American Forks and 15 sites in Cedar Springs; sites are generally large (a few are huge), reasonably level, with good separation in Cedar Springs and good to excellent separation in American Forks; parking pads are gravel, mostly medium-length straight-ins; large tent spaces; fire rings or fireplaces; firewood is available for gathering; water at hand pumps; vault facilities; paved driveways; gas and camper supplies at Goose Prairie, 3 miles southwest on Bumping River Road; limited+ supplies and services are available in Naches.

Activities & Attractions: Trout fishing; large picnic shelter.

Natural Features: Located at the confluence of the American River and the Bumping River in a medium-dense forest of conifers and underbrush; bordered by forested mountains; elevation 2800'.

Season, Fees & Phone: May to October; $5.00; 14 day limit; Naches Ranger District (509) 653-2205.

Camp Notes: About half of the sites at American Forks are along the south riverbank, but all sites are within a couple-minutes' stroll to the stream. Cedar Springs seems to be the more popular of the pair, possibly because more of its sites are closer to the river. Both campgrounds are tied together by an internal connecting road. So if you take a tour of the sites in American Forks and don't find something to your liking, just continue south on the gravel driveway into Cedar Springs.

Washington 95

SODA SPRINGS
Snoqualmie/Wenatchee National Forests

Location: West-central Washington northwest of Yakima.

Access: From Washington State Highway 410 at milepost 88 +.5 (19 miles east of Chinook Pass, 23 miles east of the junction of State Highways 410 & 123, 32 miles northwest of Naches), turn south onto Bumping River Road (paved) and travel southwest for 5 miles; turn easterly (left) into the campground.

Facilities: 26 campsites in 2 loops connected by a string; sites are small to medium-sized, reasonably level, with fair to good separation; parking pads are gravel, medium-length straight-ins; large tent areas; fireplaces; firewood is available for gathering; water at a hand pump; vault facilities; gravel driveways; gas and camper supplies at Goose Prairie, 3 miles southwest on Bumping River Road; limited+ supplies and services are available in Naches.

Activities & Attractions: Fishing; trail; foot bridge; picnic shelters.

Natural Features: Located on a rolling flat along the bank of the Bumping River in the Cascade Range; campground vegetation consists of light to medium-dense conifers and some undercover; flanked by forested hills and ridges; elevation 3100'.

Season, Fees & Phone: May to October; $5.00; 14 day limit; Naches Ranger District (509) 653-2205.

Camp Notes: Probably 80 percent of the campsites here are riverside, making this one of the more populated places in this area. A surprisingly large number of tent campers stay here and in the other 'grounds in this region.

Washington 96

COUGAR FLAT
Snoqualmie/Wenatchee National Forests

Location: West-central Washington northwest of Yakima.

Access: From Washington State Highway 410 at milepost 88 +.5 (19 miles east of Chinook Pass, 23 miles east of the junction of State Highways 410 & 123, 32 miles northwest of Naches), turn south onto Bumping River Road and proceed 6 miles; turn westerly (right) into the campground.

Facilities: 12 campsites; sites are medium to large, level or nearly so, and somewhat closely spaced but with very good visual separation; parking pads are gravel, short+ to medium-length straight-ins; plenty of tent space; fireplaces; firewood is available for gathering in the vicinity; water at a hand pump; vault facilities; gravel driveway; gas and camper supplies at Goose Prairie, 2 miles southwest on Bumping River Road; limited+ supplies and services are available in Naches.

Activities & Attractions: Fishing.

Natural Features: Located on a gently rolling flat along the bank of the Bumping River; sites receive medium shelter/shade from tall conifers and head-high brush; closely bordered by forested hills, ridges and mountains that rise to 6600'; campground elevation 3100'.

Season, Fees & Phone: May to October; $5.00; 14 day limit; Naches Ranger District (509) 653-2205.

Camp Notes: The tall timber towers about 150' above Cougar Flat, or so it seems. Like many other campgrounds in this region, about half of Cougar Flat's sites are riverside. But there's something pleasantly attractive about this little camp that makes it distinctive. Maybe you can figure out what it is.

Washington 97

BUMPING DAM
Snoqualmie/Wenatchee National Forests

Location: West-central Washington northwest of Yakima.

Access: From Washington State Highway 410 at milepost 88 +.5 (19 miles east of Chinook Pass, 23 miles east of the junction of State Highways 410 & 123, 32 miles northwest of Naches), turn south onto Bumping River Road (paved) and travel 10.5 miles to a point at the south end of the dam; turn northwesterly (right) onto a sandy gravel road, drive across the dam for 0.6 mile, then turn right and go down into the campground.

Facilities: 20 campsites; sites are small to medium-sized, generally level, with fair separation; parking pads are gravel/dirt, mostly short to medium-length straight-ins; adequate space for tents; fireplaces; some firewood is available for gathering; water at a hand pump; vault facilities; gravel/dirt driveway; pack-it-in/pack-it-out trash system; gas and camper supplies at Goose Prairie, 2 miles northwest on Bumping River Road.

Activities & Attractions: Stream and lake fishing.

Natural Features: Located on a short, forested shelf above the Bumping River just downstream of Bumping Dam; sites are lightly sheltered/shaded by conifers and a small amount of ground cover; some sites are riverside; elevation 3400'.

Season, Fees & Phone: May to October; $5.00; 14 day limit; Naches Ranger District (509) 653-2205.

Camp Notes: Bumping Dam itself was constructed nearly a century ago (1909-10) as one of the earliest Bureau of Reclamation projects in the state. The reservoir it created provides water for the Yakima Valley. The campground below the dam hasn't been here quite that long. Another small camping area downstream of the dam, Bumping Crossing, is less than a few tenths of a mile northwest of here, also off the west side of Bumping River Road. The area has roughly a dozen campsites, vaults, and serves mostly as a rustic fishing camp with a rock-bottom rental price.

Washington 98

BUMPING LAKE
Snoqualmie/Wenatchee National Forests

Location: West-central Washington northwest of Yakima.

Access: From Washington State Highway 410 at milepost 88 +.5 (19 miles east of Chinook Pass, 23 miles east of the junction of State Highways 410 & 123, 32 miles northwest of Naches), turn south onto Bumping River Road (paved) and head southwest for 11.5 miles to the end of the pavement just beyond the south end of the dam; continue on gravel for an additional 0.3 mile, then turn southeasterly (left) onto a gravel campground access road for a final 0.2 mile to the campground.

Facilities: 39 campsites in a string and a loop; sites are medium to large+, with fair to very good separation; parking pads are gravel/dirt, medium to long straight-ins; perhaps a third of the pads may require a bit of additional leveling; large tent spaces; fire rings; firewood is available for gathering; water at a hand pump; vault facilities; waste water receptacles; gravel/dirt driveways; gas and camper supplies at Goose Prairie, 3 miles northwest on Bumping River Road; limited+ supplies and services are available in Naches.

Activities & Attractions: Boating; boat launch nearby; fishing.

Natural Features: Located on rolling or hilly terrain near a small bay on the southeast shore of Bumping Lake, a reservoir which impounds the Bumping River and about a dozen of its tributaries; sites are sheltered/shaded by medium-dense conifers and low-level vegetation; maximum depth of the lake is about 35'; the lake is encircled by forested mountains; elevation 3400'.

Season, Fees & Phone: May to October; $6.00; 14 day limit; Naches Ranger District (509) 653-2205.

Camp Notes: Many of the sites are tucked into forested pockets, contributing to the privacy factor in this popular camp. The majority of campers bring a boat. Although it's not truly a lakeshore campground, you can catch good lake views, or at least good glimpses, of the small bay through the trees from some of the campsites. An island enhances an area that already holds plenty of interest. Lots of nice mountain scenery.

Washington 99

INDIAN FLAT
Snoqualmie/Wenatchee National Forests

Location: West-central Washington northwest of Yakima.

Access: From Washington State Highway 410 at milepost 89 +.4 (20 miles east of Chinook Pass, 24 miles east of the junction of State Highways 410 & 123, 31 miles northwest of Naches), turn south onto a gravel access road and proceed easterly (parallel to the highway) for 0.4 mile to the campground.

Facilities: 9 campsites; sites are medium to large, with fair to very good separation; parking pads are gravel, medium-length straight-ins; tent areas are quite spacious; fireplaces; firewood is available for gathering; water at a hand pump; vault facilities; gravel driveway; gas and camper supplies in Cliffdell, near milepost 96; limited+ supplies and services are available in Naches.

Activities & Attractions: Fishing.

Natural Features: Located on a flat along the bank of the American River; campground vegetation consists of medium-dense conifers, with moderate to dense underbrush; bordered by forested hills and mountains; elevation 2800'.

Season, Fees & Phone: May to October; $5.00; 14 day limit; Naches Ranger District (509) 653-2205.

Camp Notes: A large, rocky, forested island splits the big, swift stream just offshore of the campground. Indian Flat's sites may grab a bit more sunshine than those in many other camps around here.

Washington 100

LITTLE NACHES
Snoqualmie/Wenatchee National Forests

Location: West-central Washington northwest of Yakima.

Access: From Washington State Highway 410 at milepost 92 +.1 (23 miles east of Chinook Pass, 27 miles east of the junction of State Highways 410 & 123, 29 miles northwest of Naches), turn north onto Forest Road 19 (paved) and proceed 0.1 mile, then turn westerly (left) into the campground.

Facilities: 16 campsites; sites are small to medium-sized, level, with nominal separation; parking pads are gravel, medium-length straight-ins; adequate space for tents; fireplaces; firewood is available for gathering in the vicinity; water at a hand pump; vault facilities; gravel driveway; gas and camper supplies in Cliffdell, near milepost 96; limited+ supplies and services are available in Naches.

Activities & Attractions: Fishing.

Natural Features: Located on a flat along the Little Naches River; some sites are very lightly sheltered/shaded by tall conifers, others are in more open areas; bordered by forested hills and mountains; elevation 2700'.

Season, Fees & Phone: May to October; $5.00; 14 day limit; Naches Ranger District (509) 653-2205.

Camp Notes: Riverside sites? Yep, a bunch of 'em. The campground lies a few yards upstream of the confluence of the Little Naches and American Rivers. From that point on flows the main stream of the Naches River. (The traditional pronunciation of the river's name is somewhat like *Natcheez*, with a hard *e*, unlike the softer *e* of Natchez, Mississippi.)

Washington 101

KANER FLAT
Snoqualmie/Wenatchee National Forests

Location: West-central Washington northwest of Yakima.

Access: From Washington State Highway 410 at milepost 92 +.1 (23 miles east of Chinook Pass, 27 miles east of the junction of State Highways 410 & 123, 29 miles northwest of Naches), turn north onto Forest Road 19 (paved) and proceed 2.3 miles, then turn east (right) into the campground.

Facilities: 40 campsites; sites are medium to large, essentially level, with fair to good separation; parking pads are paved, short to medium-length straight-ins or long pull-throughs; large, grassy areas for tents; fireplaces; firewood is available for gathering in the vicinity; water at a hand pump; vault facilities; paved driveways; gas and camper supplies in Cliffdell, near milepost 96; limited+ supplies and services are available in Naches.

Activities & Attractions: Trout fishing.

Natural Features: Located in a small valley near the Little Naches River; vegetation consists of light to medium-dense, tall pines, plus some wildflower-flecked meadow areas; bordered by forested hills; elevation 2700'.

Season, Fees & Phone: May to October; $5.00; 14 day limit; Naches Ranger District (509) 653-2205.

Camp Notes: Nice environment here, even though the campground is on the opposite side of the road from the river. There's a good balance of sunshine and shade in and around the camp. Some of the sites in the 'tent' section are quite well sheltered. Riverbank walking is fairly easy--not much brush-busting is necessary. Another campground in the immediate vicinity: Continue on FR 19 for a couple of tenths of a mile past Kaner Flat to Crow Creek, a riverside spot with about a dozen sites, vaults, but no drinking water.

SAWMILL FLAT
Snoqualmie/Wenatchee National Forests

Location: West-central Washington northwest of Yakima.

Access: From Washington State Highway 410 at milepost 93 +.4 (24 miles east of Chinook Pass, 28 miles east of the junction of State Highways 410 & 123, 27 miles northwest of Naches), turn west (i.e., right if arriving from Chinook Pass), into the campground.

Facilities: 24 campsites, including several park 'n walk units; sites are medium-sized, level, with fair to good separation; parking pads are paved, short to medium-length straight-ins or long pull-throughs; medium to large areas for tents; fire rings; firewood is available for gathering in the vicinity; water at a hand pump; vault facilities; paved driveway; gas and camper supplies in Cliffdell, near milepost 96; limited+ supplies and services are available in Naches.

Activities & Attractions: Boulder Cave National Recreation Trail access, 2 miles southeast; possible rafting in season; trout fishing; picnic shelter.

Natural Features: Located in a forested canyon on a flat along the bank of the Naches River; sites are lightly to moderately shaded/sheltered by tall conifers and waist-high brush; elevation 2600'.

Season, Fees & Phone: May to October; $5.00; 14 day limit; Naches Ranger District (509) 653-2205.

Camp Notes: From Sawmill Flat you can see Halfway Flat Campground, on the opposite riverbank, "but you can't get there from here". Halfway Flat is most easily accessed by turning south off the highway at milepost 91 +.5, two miles northwest of Sawmill Flat. Go across the river bridge, then turn easterly (left) and follow Forest Road 1704 east and south for 1.4 miles down to the small, simple campground with vaults but no drinking water. The campsites are scattered along the riverbank, against a forested slope.

COTTONWOOD
Snoqualmie/Wenatchee National Forests

Location: West-central Washington northwest of Yakima.

Access: From Washington State Highway 410 at milepost 99 +.4 (31 miles east of Chinook Pass, 35 miles east of the junction of State Highways 410 & 123, 21 miles northwest of Naches), turn west (i.e., right if arriving from Chinook Pass), into the campground.

Facilities: 16 campsites; sites are small to small+, level, with fair to good separation; parking pads are gravel, mostly short to medium-length straight-ins; medium-sized tent areas; fire rings or fireplaces; firewood is available for gathering; water at a hand pump; vault facilities; paved driveway; gas and camper supplies in Cliffdell, near milepost 96; limited+ supplies and services are available in Naches.

Activities & Attractions: Boulder Cave National Recreation Trail access, 4 miles northwest; possible rafting in season; trout fishing.

Natural Features: Located on a wooded flat along the bank of the Naches River; sites are moderately shaded/sheltered by tall timber, hardwoods and dense, medium-high vegetation; elevation 2300'.

Season, Fees & Phone: May to October; $5.00; 14 day limit; Naches Ranger District (509) 653-2205.

Camp Notes: Cottonwood owes much of its popularity to about a dozen riverside sites, plus its location as the first or last of the many campgrounds (depending upon your direction of travel) along this highway. Its relatively low elevation also makes it the first and last camp available during the seasonal cycle. There's still plenty of timber in the area, but the climate is decidedly drier, with more 'open' patches on the adjacent slopes than in most of the other campgrounds. Indeed, the Wenatchee National Forest boundary is just southeast of here at mile 100. A few miles further east, the terrain widens into the semi-arid Yakima Valley.

INDIAN CREEK
Snoqualmie/Wenatchee National Forests

Location: South-central Washington between Mount Rainier National Park and Yakima.

Access: From U.S. Highway 12 at milepost 159 +.4 (9 miles east of White Pass, 26 miles west of the junction of U.S. 12 & Washington State Highway 410 near Naches), turn south into the campground.

Facilities: 43 campsites; sites are medium to large, level, with fair to very good separation; parking pads are gravel, medium to long straight-ins; some large, level tent spots; fireplaces or fire rings; firewood is available for gathering in the area; water at faucets throughout; vault facilities; camper supplies at a small store on the north shore of Rimrock Lake; limited+ supplies and services are available in Naches.

Activities & Attractions: Boating; fishing; public boat launch located at the east end of Rimrock Lake; White Pass Recreation Area is 8 miles west; Mount Rainier National Park is 30 miles west.

Natural Features: Located on a large, timbered flat in the Cascade Range at the west end of Rimrock Lake, a beautiful mountain lake formed by a dam across the Tieton River about 5 miles east; high timbered ridges encircle the lake; some sites offer views of the lake through the trees; sites are separated by lofty conifers and a little underbrush; elevation 2900'.

Season, Fees & Phone: End of May to mid-September; $7.00; 14 day limit; Naches Ranger District (509) 653-2205.

Camp Notes: All the sites in this campground are level and nicely sheltered. The lake is accessible from the campground area, but lake views are limited because of the vegetation. The level of the lake varies considerably from one season to another. Indian Creek is one of the nicest campgrounds along this highway. For an off-highway campground, you might want to take a look at Clear Lake Campground, near the east shore of the lake of the same name. From U.S. 12 a mile west of Indian Creek, go southwest on Forest Road 12 for 1.3 miles, then south for 0.9 mile along the east shore road to the campground. Clear Lake's two-dozen campsites are served by vault facilities, but no drinking water or fee. A short segment of the Tieton River links Clear Lake with much larger Rimrock Lake about a half-mile downstream of Clear Lake Campground.

Washington 105

HAUSE CREEK
Snoqualmie/Wenatchee National Forests

Location: South-central Washington between Mount Rainier National Park and Yakima.

Access: From U.S. Highway 12 at milepost 169 (16.5 miles west of the junction of U.S. 12 & Washington State Highway 410 near Naches, 18 miles east of White Pass), turn south into the campground.

Facilities: 41 campsites in 3 loops; site size is average or better, tolerably level, with fairly good separation; parking pads are gravel, short to medium-length straight-ins; a few pads may require additional leveling; most sites have good tent spots; fireplaces; firewood is available for gathering in the area; water at several faucets; restrooms, supplemented by vault facilities; minimal supplies and gas at a small store 4 miles east; limited+ supplies and services are available in Naches.

Activities & Attractions: Trout fishing; foot trails and 4-wheel drive trails lead up into the surrounding densely forested mountains; superscenic drive along Highway 12 and up through White Pass.

Natural Features: Located along the Tieton River on the east slope of the Cascades; 2 loops are situated along the river and a third loop is on a forested bluff slightly above it (and closer to the highway); tall timber surrounds some sites, other sites are on a fairly open riverbank, still others are along a brushy creekbed; closely bordered by forested hills; elevation 2700'.

Season, Fees & Phone: End of May to mid-November; $7.00; 14 day limit; Naches Ranger District (509) 653-2205.

Camp Notes: The Tieton River flows swiftly by, at this point, and on toward the east. The drive along Highway 12 through here and up over White Pass offers some of the best scenery in this part of the state.

Washington 106

WILLOWS
Snoqualmie/Wenatchee National Forests

Location: South-central Washington between Mount Rainier National Park and Yakima.

Access: From U.S. Highway 12 at milepost 170 +.3 (15 miles west of the junction of U.S. 12 & Washington State Highway 410 near Naches, 20 miles east of White Pass), turn south into the campground.

Facilities: 16 campsites; sites are average-sized, fairly level, with nominal to very good separation; parking pads are gravel, mostly short to medium-length straight-ins; most tent spots are level and medium-sized; fireplaces; some firewood is available for gathering in the area; water at a hand pump;

vault facilities; gravel driveway; limited supplies and gas at a small store 3 miles east; limited+ supplies and services are available in Naches.

Activities & Attractions: Fishing on the river; foot trails and 4-wheel drive roads lead from near here up into the surrounding mountains.

Natural Features: Located in the steep-walled Tieton River Canyon on the east slope of the Cascade Range, where a small creek flows into the Tieton River; sites are situated on 2 levels: a number of sites are right along the riverbank, others are positioned a few feet above, on a small rise; predominant vegetation is tall conifers, hardwoods, and some brush in the creekbed; elevation 2700'.

Season, Fees & Phone: End of May to mid-September; $5.00; 14 day limit; Naches Ranger District (509) 653-2205.

Camp Notes: Though some of the sites are within 100 yards of the highway, there are other sites located farther from the road right along the swift Tieton River. Signs indicate that the stream level is subject to sudden fluctuations.

Washington 107

WINDY POINT
Snoqualmie/Wenatchee National Forests

Location: South-central Washington between Mount Rainier National Park and Yakima.

Access: From U.S. Highway 12 at milepost 177 +.5 (8 miles west of the junction of U.S. 12 & Washington State Highway 410 near Naches, 27 miles east of White Pass), turn south into the campground.

Facilities: 12 campsites; sites are average-sized, level, with fairly good separation; parking pads are gravel straight-ins, including several long enough to accommodate large rv's; medium-sized tent spots; fireplaces; some firewood is available for gathering in the area; water at a hand pump; vault facilities; limited+ supplies in Naches; complete supplies and services are available in Yakima, 25 miles east.

Activities & Attractions: Stream fishing; nearby mountain trails for hikers and 4-wheel-drive vehicles; the Oak Creek Game Range, located 6 miles east, is available for recreational activities and wildlife observation.

Natural Features: Located on the lower east slope of the Cascade Range along the north bank of the Tieton River; sheer canyon walls rise sharply across the river to the south, and rocky bluffs are an important part of the scenic landscape to the north; some sites are very open, and others are well-sheltered; vegetation in the camping area consists of tall conifers and hardwoods bordering an open meadow; elevation 2600'.

Season, Fees & Phone: April to November; $5.00; 14 day limit; Naches Ranger District (509) 653-2205.

Camp Notes: Most sites offer an attractive view, northward, of fluted canyon walls. A low rail fence along the northern edge of the camping area adds a congenial touch. All of the foregoing campgrounds along State Highway 410 and U.S. Highway 12 east of the Cascade Crest are located within the historical boundaries of Snoqualmie National Forest, but are managed by Wenatchee National Forest.

Washington 108

BEACON ROCK
Beacon Rock State Park

Location: Southern Washington border east of Vancouver.

Access: From Washington State Highway 14 near milepost 35 (5 miles west of North Bonneville, 35 miles east of Vancouver), turn north/east and drive up a steep winding paved road, for 1 mile to the campground.

Facilities: 33 campsites; (a group camp is also available); sites are small to medium-sized, with nominal to fairly good separation; parking pads are packed/oiled gravel, mostly short to medium+ straight-ins; some pads may require additional leveling; small to medium-sized tent areas; fireplaces; b-y-o firewood is recommended; water at several faucets; restrooms with showers; holding tank disposal station; paved driveway; limited to adequate supplies are available in Cascade Locks, Oregon, 6 miles east.

Activities & Attractions: Hiking or climbing to the top of Beacon Rock (registration mandatory, guide pamphlet available); 7.5 miles of hiking trails to Rodney Falls, Hardy Falls and Hamilton Mountain; playground; boating; boat launch and dock; Bonneville Dam Visitor Center, 4 miles east; day use area with shelter.

Natural Features: Located on densely forested hills in the Columbia Gorge above the Columbia River; Campground vegetation consists of very dense, tall hardwoods, conifers and undercover; Beacon Rock sits on the north bank of the Columbia River, directly opposite the park entrance; elevation 400'.

Season, Fees & Phone: April to October; please see Appendix for standard Washington state park fees; 10 day limit; park office (509) 427-8265.

Camp Notes: Beacon Rock, at 848', is the world's second-largest monolith, and is what remains of the core of a volcano. The Rock marked the beginning of tidewater for early settlers. The steep trail to the summit of the Rock has handrails along most of the route. It goes without saying that the view from the top is excellent.

Washington 109

HORSETHIEF LAKE
Horsethief Lake State Park

Location: South-central Washington along the Columbia River northeast of The Dalles, Oregon.

Access: From the junction of Washington State Highway 14 and U.S. Highway 197 north of The Dalles, Oregon (take Exit 87 if you're traveling Interstate 84), drive east on Highway 14 for 1.6 miles; turn south onto the park access road and continue for 1 mile to the park.

Facilities: 12 campsites; (2 hike-bike/primitive sites are also available); sites are very small, level, arranged in a parallel row, with zero separation; parking pads are gravel, short+ straight-ins; adequate space for small tents; fireplaces; b-y-o firewood; water at faucets; restrooms; holding tank disposal station; complete supplies and services are available in The Dalles, 6 miles south/west.

Activities & Attractions: Boating; windsurfing; boat launch on Horsethief Lake and on the Columbia River; swimming in the lake; trails; Indian rock art can be seen just to the west of the park entrance; visitor tours at The Dalles Dam.

Natural Features: Located on the west shore of 90-acre Horsethief Lake, a small secondary impoundment on the Columbia River; vegetation consists of mown lawns dotted with hardwoods and also rows of hardwoods which provide minimal to light shade for campsites; high, dry bluffs and monument-type rock formations, including Horsethief Butte, border the area; elevation 150'.

Season, Fees & Phone: April to October; please see Appendix for standard Washington state park fees; 10 day limit; phone c/o Maryhill State Park.

Camp Notes: Horsethief Lake is operated as a satellite area of Maryhill State Park. It might provide you with a lower-cost and less-crowded alternative to the excellent campground at Maryhill. Horsethief Lake SP is bordered by 7500' of Columbia River frontage.

Washington 110

MARYHILL
Maryhill State Park

Location: South-central Washington along the Columbia River south of Goldendale.

Access: From U.S. Highway 97 at the north end of the Columbia River bridge (1.2 miles north of Interstate 84 Exit 104 in Oregon, 0.5 mile south of the junction of U.S. 97 and Washington State Highway 14 south of Goldendale), turn east into the park entrance and proceed 0.5 mile to the campground.

Facilities: 50 campsites with full hookups; (3 hike-bike/primitive sites are also available); sites are medium-sized, level, with minimal separation; parking pads are packed gravel, medium to long straight-ins or pull-throughs; ample space for large tents; windbreaks for many sites; fireplaces; b-y-o firewood; water at sites and at several faucets; restrooms with showers; holding tank disposal station; paved driveways; nearest supplies (gas, groceries, cafes) are on the Oregon side of the river; adequate supplies and services are available in Goldendale.

Activities & Attractions: Swimming beach; boating; windsurfing; boat launch, docks and moorage buoys; old railroad locomotive and coal tender on display in the park; Maryhill Museum of Fine Arts, 3 miles west; Stonehenge replica, 2 miles east, is visible from the park; large day use area with shelters and bathhouse.

Natural Features: Located on a large flat on the north bank of the Columbia River a dozen miles upstream (east) of The Dalles Dam and just downstream of John Day Dam; campsites are lightly shaded by large hardwoods on mown and watered lawns; range grass and sage surround the park; high, fluted rock bluffs rise directly north of the park; typically windy; elevation 150'.

Season, Fees & Phone: Open all year; please see Appendix for standard Washington state park fees; 10 day limit; park office (509) 773-5007 or (509) 773-4957.

Camp Notes: This is a fine campground, especially for rv campers. It's as flat as a ping-pong table and has all the necessities. If there isn't enough elbow room for you in the spacious camping area, just take a stroll through the adjacent, expansive, nicely landscaped day use grounds. Nearly a mile of the Columbia River forms the southern edge of the park. (This section of the dammed Columbia is also known as Lake Celilo.) One minor drawback that should be mentioned: An occasional freight train rumbles past the campground just north of the park boundary. Looming high above the park on the upper edge of the bluff is the full-size Stonhenge replica built by Early-Twentieth Century railroad magnate, J. J. Hill. The mysterious, millenia-old edifice on the moors of England is now thought to have been an observatory of sorts which ancient Britons used to predict or commemorate solar or lunar eclipses. The duplicate structure on the windswept bluff above Maryhill was built by Hill as a World War I memorial.

Washington 111

BROOKS MEMORIAL
Brooks Memorial State Park

Location: South-central Washington north of Goldendale.

Access: From U.S. Highway 97 at milepost 24 +.6 (12 miles north of Goldendale, 3 miles south of the summit of Satus Pass), turn west onto the park access road for 0.2 mile to the campground.

Facilities: 45 campsites, including 23 with full hookups, in two sections; (2 hike-bike/primitive sites and a group camp are also available); sites are generally small, with minimal to fair separation; parking pads are gravel, short to medium-length straight-ins; most pads will probably require some additional leveling; small to medium-sized areas for tents; fireplaces; b-y-o firewood; water at several faucets; restrooms with showers; holding tank disposal station; kitchen shelter; gravel driveways; adequate supplies and services are available in Goldendale.

Activities & Attractions: 9 miles of hiking trails; fishing in streams; Goldendale Observatory State Park nearby.

Natural Features: Located in the Simcoe Mountains along the banks of the Little Klickitat River and its tributaries; vegetation consists mostly of light to medium dense conifers and hardwoods, and some grassy fields/meadows; elevation 3000'.

Season, Fees & Phone: April to November; please see Appendix for standard Washington state park fees; 10 day limit; park office (509) 773-4611 or (509) 773-5382.

Camp Notes: This park is oriented toward natural activities: hiking, wildlife observation, stargazing. The latter is particularly rewarding in the high, dry atmosphere here. Goldendale Observatory State Park, perched atop a forested hill just north of Goldendale, offers the largest telescope in the country available for public viewing.

Washington
Northeast
Please refer to the Washington map in the Appendix

Washington 112

LONE FIR
Okanogan National Forest

Location: North-central Washington between Winthrop and Newhalem.

Access: From Washington State Highway 20 at milepost 168 +.4 (24 miles west of Winthrop, 49 miles east of Newhalem), turn southeast into the campground.

Facilities: 27 campsites; sites are a bit small but quite well separated; parking pads are gravel, short to medium-length straight-ins or pull-throughs; many pads may require additional leveling; some secluded tent spots have been carved out of the dense vegetation; fireplaces; firewood is available for gathering in the vicinity; water at several faucets; vault facilities; gravel driveway; adequate supplies and services are available in Winthrop.

Activities & Attractions: A principal activity is hiking in the Cascades: Cutthroat Lake Trailhead is 1 mile west and the Pacific Crest Trail is accessible from near milepost 157 +.7 on Highway 20; stream fishing; the superscenic North Cascades Highway continues west from here over 5483' Washington Pass.

Natural Features: Located on the east slopes of the North Cascades; tiny Pine Creek joins Early Winters Creek at this point; sites are surrounded by dense forest with tall conifers and considerable underbrush; elevation 5000'.

Season, Fees & Phone: June to September; $6.00; 14 day limit; Winthrop Ranger District (509) 996-2266.

Camp Notes: This is a high-altitude campground with a relatively short season. Near here are great views of several landmarks, including those with inspiring names like The Needles to the north, Silver Star Mountain to the east, and Liberty Bell Mountain to the west.

Washington 113

KLIPCHUCK
Okanogan National Forest

Location: North-central Washington between Winthrop and Newhalem.

Access: From Washington State Highway 20 at milepost 175 +.1 (18 miles west of Winthrop, 55 miles east of Newhalem), turn northwest onto a paved access road; continue for 1.3 miles to the campground.

Facilities: 46 campsites; sites are average-sized, with excellent separation; parking pads are gravel, short to medium-length straight-ins; some additional leveling will probably be required; small to medium-sized tents can be tucked into small nooks among the trees; stairs lead from parking pads to some table and tent areas; fireplaces; some firewood is available for gathering in the vicinity; water at several faucets; restrooms; paved driveway; adequate supplies and services are available in Winthrop.

Activities & Attractions: Stream fishing; hiking on several mountain trails, including those to Cedar Falls and Rattlesnake Creek, which ultimately join the Pacific Crest Trail; the drive across the North Cascades Highway from here toward Newhalem offers magnificent mountain scenery.

Natural Features: Located on a forested hillside in a narrow valley along Early Winters Creek; vegetation consists of dense stands of conifers and hardwoods, with considerable grass and underbrush; high, timbered ridges flank the valley; peaks of the North Cascades rise just to the west; elevation 4300'.

Season, Fees & Phone: May to September; $6.00; 14 day limit; Winthrop Ranger District (509) 996-2266.

Camp Notes: A conscientious attempt was made in this campground to provide the most level sites possible, considering the steep terrain. The dense vegetation provides excellent privacy and a peaceful environment.

Washington 114

EARLY WINTERS
Okanogan National Forest

Location: North-central Washington between Winthrop and Newhalem.

Access: From Washington State Highway 20 at milepost 177 +.7 (16 miles west of Winthrop, 58 miles east of Newhalem), turn left or right at the east end of the Early Winters Creek Bridge; (campsites are located on both sides of the highway.)

Facilities: 7 sites on the north and 7 sites on the south side of the highway; sites are small to average in size, with fair separation; parking pads are gravel, short to medium-length straight-ins; additional leveling may be necessary in some sites; medium-sized tent areas; fireplaces; firewood is available for gathering in the vicinity; water at several faucets; vault facilities; gravel driveways; adequate supplies and services are available in Winthrop, 16 miles east.

Activities & Attractions: Stream fishing; Cedar Creek Trailhead is 3 miles west; superscenic drive along the North Cascades Highway, over Washington Pass, past North Cascades National Park.

Natural Features: Located in a valley bordered by high rocky ridges on the east slope of the Cascade Range; Early Winters Creek joins the waters of the Methow River a few yards to the east; terrain along the river is level but a bit rocky; medium-sized conifers and moderate underbrush provide some shelter and separation for the campsites, many of which are creekside; elevation 4200'.

Season, Fees & Phone: May to September; $6.00; 14 day limit; Winthrop Ranger District (509) 996-2266.

Camp Notes: This is a good base-of-operations camp for exploration of the inviting mountain areas to the west. Many sites are so close to the creek that most highway noise would be moderated by the sound of the rushing water. Early Winters Creek is one of the main tributaries of the Methow River, and the highway hugs the swift creek from the summit of Washington Pass to the Methow-Early Winters confluence near here.

Washington 115

PEARRYGIN LAKE
Pearrygin Lake State Park

Location: North-central Washington north of Winthrop.

Access: From Washington State Highway 20 (Riverside Avenue) at milepost 192 +.9 in midtown Winthrop, turn north onto Bluff Street and proceed 1.5 miles; turn east (right) onto the state park access road and continue for 1.7 miles, then turn southwest (right again) into the park entrance; go another 1.3 miles to the campground.

Facilities: 83 campsites, including 27 with water hookups and 30 with full hookups; (3 hike-bike/primitive sites are also available); sites are small to medium-sized, with minimal to nominal separation, (some lakeside sites are well separated); most parking pads are gravel, medium to long straight-ins or pull-throughs; large, fairly level, grassy tent spots; fireplaces; b-y-o firewood; water at several faucets; restrooms with showers; holding tank disposal station; paved driveways; adequate supplies and services are available in Winthrop.

Activities & Attractions: Boating; boat launch and docks; windsurfing; designated swimming area; fishing; day use area.

Natural Features: Located on the north shore of Pearrygin Lake in the Methow Valley in the eastern foothills of the Cascade Range; the park has large sections of watered and mown lawns dotted with hardwoods which provide very light to light-medium shade for campsites; sandy swimming beach; sage-and-grass covered, partially wooded hills surround the lake; elevation 1900'.

Season, Fees & Phone: April to November; please see Appendix for standard Washington state park fees; 10 day limit; campsite reservations especially recommended for weekends, please see Appendix; park office (509) 996-2370.

Camp Notes: At Pearrygin Lake, some lucky lakeside campers can tie up their boats within a few feet of their tents. There's an outstanding view up the valley toward the rugged peaks of the Cascade Mountains. The park is near the eastern terminus of the superscenic North Cascades Highway.

Washington 116

LOUP LOUP
Okanogan National Forest

Location: North-central Washington between Twisp and Okanogan.

Access: From Washington State Highway 20 at milepost 214 +.7 (12 miles east of Twisp, 18 miles west of Okanogan), turn north onto Forest Road 42 (paved); proceed 0.5 mile north and west; turn north (right, still on Road 42) and continue for another 0.6 mile, then turn west (left) into the campground.

Facilities: 27 campsites in 2 tiered loops; sites are generally quite large, level, with good separation; parking pads are gravel straight-ins or pull-throughs, some spacious enough for large rv's; most tent areas are large and level; fireplaces; ample firewood is available for gathering; water at several faucets; vault facilities; gravel driveways; limited supplies and services are available in Twisp.

Activities & Attractions: Nearby opportunities for backcountry exploration; Road 42 leads north to Conconully State Park and Reservoir; Loup Loup Winter Sports Area is close by.

Natural Features: Located in the foothills of the Cascades, between steep, forested slopes east and west; moderately dense vegetation in the campground's main loop consists of tall conifers with hanging moss; the lower 5 units, along the creek, have tall grass and typical creekside brush; elevation 4000'.

Season, Fees & Phone: May to September; $5.00; 14 day limit; Twisp Ranger District (509) 997-2131.

Camp Notes: This is a super stop, near a main highway, for a traveler seeking forest tranquility; a secluded camp with lots of elbow room. The larger loop is close to the road, but the lower, smaller loop is further away, down along a creek. Which would you choose? Another nearby forest campground, JR, is located near highway milepost 214. It has 7 small sites right along Highway 20. If you're westbound on the North Cascades Highway, consider getting a few extra gallons of fuel and rounding-out your larder in one of the 'river' cities (Brewster, Chelan, Okanogan, Omak, Wenatchee) or at the very latest, Winthrop. It's slim pickins' along the 130-some miles between Winthrop and Sedro Wooley at the other end.

Washington 117

LEADER LAKE
Washington Department of Natural Resources

Location: North-central Washington between Twisp and Okanogan.

Access: From Washington State Highway 20 at milepost 224 + .3 (9 miles west of Okanogan, 22 miles east of Twisp), turn northeast onto a paved single-lane road; continue on this twisty road for 0.4 mile to the campground.

Facilities: 16 campsites; sites vary in size, with nominal to fair separation; parking areas are gravel/dirt, small to very large, some are straight-ins, some are pull-throughs, and some are however-you-can-manage; most parking areas will require additional leveling; a few sites have framed-and-leveled tent pads; fireplaces; b-y-o firewood is recommended; no drinking water; vault facilities; pack-it-in/pack-it-out trash removal system; gravel driveways; adequate supplies and services are available in Okanogan.

Activities & Attractions: Boating; fishing; paved boat ramp; Conconully State Park and Reservoir are accessible from here by traveling north on some back roads.

Natural Features: Located in a small basin surrounding a picturesque mountain lake on the lower east slope of the Cascades; all sites are on a rocky hillside along the lakeshore; vegetation varies from medium-dense timber to just a few sparse bushes; moderately forested hills surround the area; a small stream flows into the lake near its southwest corner; elevation 2900'.

Season, Fees & Phone: Available all year, subject to weather and road conditions; principal season is April to November; no fee (subject to change); 5 day limit; Washington Department of Natural Resources Northeast Region Office, Colville, (509) 684-7474.

Camp Notes: This campground is quite popular, even with its limited facilities. The scenery is exceptionally pleasant, and virtually all sites have a lake view. A companion Department of Natural Resources campground, Rock Creek, is located off Highway 20 at milepost 223, and 4 miles north on a gravel road.

Washington 118

CONCONULLY
Conconully State Park

Location: North-central Washington north of Omak.

Access: From Washington State Highway 20 in midtown Okanogan at the corner of 2nd Avenue South and Pine Street (by the big clock), turn north onto Pine Street and wind out of town on Pine, then 6th Avenue North and finally onto Okanogan-Conconully Road for a total of 19 miles to a 3-way intersection on the south end of the community of Conconully; turn west (left) onto a park access road for 100 yards; turn south (left) into the main campground; or continue west for another 0.2 mile to the hookup section.

Alternate Access: From U.S Highway 97 at milepost 299 + .1 in Riverside (8 miles north of Omak, 15 miles south of Tonasket), turn southwest onto Riverside Cutoff (paved) and travel 5.3 miles to a "T" intersection; turn northwest (right) onto Okanogan-Conconully Road and proceed 10.4 miles to Conconully and continue as above.

Facilities: 75 campsites, including 10 with water hookups; (6 primitive sites are also available); sites are small, basically level, with nil to minimal separation; parking surfaces in most sites are grass, any length you need, straight-ins; (hookups have medium-length pull-throughs); plenty of space for tents; fireplaces; b-y-o firewood; water at several faucets; restrooms with showers, plus supplementary vault facilities; holding tank disposal station; paved or gravel driveways; gas and groceries in Conconully; adequate supplies and services are available in Okanogan and Omak.

Activities & Attractions: Fishing; boating; boat launch; swimming area; cross-country skiing; snowmobiling.

Natural Features: Located on a large, grassy flat on the north shore of Conconully Reservoir in a small valley in the eastern foothills of the Cascade Range; campsites are lightly shaded by large hardwoods and conifers; surrounded by moderately forested mountains; park area is 80 acres, including 5400' of lakeshore; elevation 2300'.

Season, Fees & Phone: Open all year, with limited services November to April; please see Appendix for standard Washington state park fees; 10 day limit; park office (509) 826-2108.

Camp Notes: Nothin' fancy here, but there's plenty of grass to roam around on, and adequate shade too. There's a good possibility that, when you're running late on a summer holiday weekend, you'll find a camp spot here when the state parks and forest camps closer to the main drags are filled.

Washington 119

ALTA LAKE
Alta Lake State Park

Location: North-central Washington north of Wenatchee.

Access: From Washington State Highway 153 at milepost 1 +.7 (1.7 miles west of the junction of Highway 153 & U.S. Highway 97 near Pateros, 10 miles southeast of Methow), turn south onto a paved local road and proceed 2 miles to the park; campsites are in several sections along both sides of the park road within a half-mile of the entrance.

Facilities: 200 campsites, including 16 with partial hookups, in 4 loops; (a group camp is also available, by reservation); sites along the lakeshore are small, with nil to nominal separation; sites across the roadway above the lake tend to be slightly larger and a bit better separated; most parking spaces/pads are gravel, short to medium-length straight-ins (pull-throughs for hookups) which will require additional leveling; small to medium-sized, generally sloped tent spots; fireplaces; a limited amount of firewood is available for gathering in the vicinity, b-y-o is suggested; water at several faucets; restrooms with showers; holding tank disposal station; paved driveways; gas and groceries+ in Pateros, 4 miles northeast; adequate supplies and services are available in Brewster, 9 miles northeast.

Activities & Attractions: Swimming beach; boating; boat launch; fishing (the lake is stocked annually); hiking trail; cross-country skiing and snowmobiling in the vicinity.

Natural Features: Located in the eastern foothills of the Cascade Range on the northwest shore of Alta Lake; most campsites are on a slope above the lake and are very lightly to moderately shaded by tall conifers on a surface of sparse natural grass; one camp section is on a gently sloping, open flat; bordered by rocky, partly forested hills and low mountains; lake area is 180 acres; elevation 1200'.

Season, Fees & Phone: Open all year, with limited services in winter; please see Appendix for standard Washington state park fees; 10 day limit; park office (509) 923-2473.

Camp Notes: The rugged, barren rock mountains which form the valley or basin that holds the lake were carved by glacial activity and closely resemble those usually found at much higher altitudes. Plan to get here early for a summer weekend camp spot.

Washington 120

LAKE CHELAN
Lake Chelan State Park

Location: West-central Washington north of Wenatchee.

Access: From U.S Highway 97 at milepost 230 +.4 (4 miles west/southwest of the city of Chelan, 19 miles north of Entiat), turn west/northwest onto South Shore Drive and travel 5.9 miles; turn north (right), then immediately right again to the park entrance station; just past the entrance, swing an easy left for 0.1 mile to a 4-way intersection; turn left or right to the camping areas.

Facilities: 144 campsites, including 17 with full hookups, and about 30 park 'n u-haul sites; sites are tiny to small, with zero to nominal separation; parking pads/spots are gravel, very short to short+, straight-ins or curbside; most pads will probably require additional leveling; small to large, sloped tent areas (smallest in the u-haul/walk-down sites); fireplaces; b-y-o firewood; water faucets throughout; restrooms with showers; holding tank disposal station; paved driveways; camper supplies at the concession stand; adequate supplies and services are available in Chelan.

Activities & Attractions: Swimming beach; sports field; playground; boating; boat launch; docks; ski floats; day use area.

Natural Features: Located on a slope along and above the south shore of Lake Chelan; vegetation consists of medium to tall hardwoods, conifers and bushes which provide light to medium shade/shelter for most campsites, and some open mown, grassy areas; the lake is closely flanked by grassy, sagey, rocky hills and mountains lightly trimmed with trees; park area includes 6500' of lakeshore property; elevation 1100'.

Season, Fees & Phone: April to November; please see Appendix for standard Washington state park fees; 10 day limit; park office (509) 687-3710.

Camp Notes: Although the scenery at the upper end of sinuous Lake Chelan might resemble the fjords of northern Europe, the southeast end looks more like the Mediterranean. Likewise, on a summer weekend, the park's campground resembles its Southern Continental counterparts--fender-to-fender, tent peg-to-tent peg. Another local state park campground that is more remote, though probably not much less populated, is Twenty-Five Mile Creek. To get there, just keep heading northwest on the lake road past Lake Chelan SP for another 10 miles to milepost 16, then turn north into the recreation area. Twenty-Five Mile Creek has 85 campsites, 33 of them with full hookups, packed onto a slope in a small draw/coulee, plus a boat ramp and docks. Bring your jet skis.

Washington 121

NASON CREEK
Wenatchee National Forest

Location: West-central Washington north of Leavenworth.

Access: From the junction of U.S. Highway 2 and Washington State Highway 207 (at U.S. 2 milepost 84 +.7, 15 miles north of Leavenworth, 20 miles east of Stevens Pass), drive north on Highway 207 for 3.5 miles; turn west (left) onto a paved access road (Forest Road 6607) and go 50 yards, then turn left or right into the campground.

Facilities: 68 campsites in 3 loops; sites vary from small to quite large, reasonably level, with fair to very good separation; parking pads are paved, short to medium-length straight-ins or very long pull-throughs; many sites will accommodate large tents; fire rings; some firewood is available for gathering in the vicinity; water at several faucets; restrooms; waste water receptacles; paved driveways; camper supplies at a small store nearby; adequate supplies and services are available in Leavenworth.

Activities & Attractions: Trout fishing on the creek; boating, fishing and swimming on Lake Wenatchee, 1 mile northwest.

Natural Features: Located in a fairly open conifer forest along the banks of Nason Creek, on the east slope of the Cascade Range; many of the campsites are creekside; forested mountains completely encircle this area; Lake Wenatchee is less than a mile west; elevation 1900'.

Season, Fees & Phone: May to October; $8.00; 14 day limit; Lake Wenatchee Ranger District (509) 763-3103.

Camp Notes: Nason Creek is a very likable campground in itself, but having Lake Wenatchee and all its attractions close at hand is a solid bonus. This campground is also a good alternative to the one at the state park. Campsites at Nason Creek are superior to the park's in most ways. The nearby burg of Leavenworth attracts a lot of tourists. The town's architectural motif and commercial theme are 100 percent Bavarian gingerbread.

Washington 122

LAKE WENATCHEE
Lake Wenatchee State Park

Location: West-central Washington northwest of Wenatchee.

Access: From the junction of U.S. Highway 2 and Washington State Highway 207 (at U.S. 2 milepost 84 +.7, 15 miles north of Leavenworth, 20 miles east of Stevens Pass), drive north on Highway 207 for 3.5 miles; turn west (left) onto a paved access road (Forest Road 6607) and proceed 0.8 mile (past Nason Creek national forest camp) to the south unit; or continue north/northwest on Highway 207 for an additional mile, then turn south (left) into the north unit and proceed 0.3 mile to the north campground.

Facilities: *South unit*: 100 campsites; (a reservable group camp is also available); sites are generally small, sloped, with minimal to fair separation; parking pads are gravel, most are short to medium-length straight-ins; medium to large tent areas. *North unit*: 97 campsites; sites are small+ to medium-sized, most are marginally level, with nominal to fairly good separation; parking pads are gravel, medium-length straight-ins or long pull-throughs; large tent areas. *Both units*: fireplaces; some firewood is available for gathering on nearby national forest land, b-y-o to be sure; water at several faucets; restrooms with showers; holding tank disposal station; paved driveways; gas and camper supplies at a nearby store; adequate supplies and services are available in Leavenworth.

Activities & Attractions: Boating; boat launch; fishing; sandy swimming beach; several short hiking trails in the park, plus miles of national forest trails in the area; several miles of groomed cross-country ski trails; playgrounds; amphitheater.

Natural Features: Located on the north and south shores of glacier-fed Lake Wenatchee; campground vegetation consists of medium-dense, tall conifers and moderate underbrush; the lake is 5.5 miles long, averages about a mile across, with an average depth of 200'; the Wenatchee River flows out of the lake through the middle of the park; bordered by the heavily-timbered mountains of the Cascade Range; elevation 1900'.

Season, Fees & Phone: Open all year, with limited services October to April; please see Appendix for standard Washington state park fees; 10 day limit; park office (509) 763-3101.

Camp Notes: Because of its scenic superiority, Lake Wenatchee has always been a favorite spot for summer visits, but it is becoming one of the more popular spots for snow camping in the state as well. In a typical year, the park has a continuous snow cover of 3-4 feet. Since the park is right off a state highway, and only a few miles from a major trans-state route, it is usually readily accessible in winter. (Winter may indeed be a better time than summer to visit the lake--the area is famous for its mosquitos, and the park has an ongoing mosquito control program.) Lake Wenatchee has one of only two sockeye salmon populations in the Columbia Basin. The salmon 'run' usually takes place in mid-August, but not every year.

Washington 123

GLACIER VIEW
Wenatchee National Forest

Location: West-central Washington north of Leavenworth.

Access: From the junction of U.S. Highway 2 and Washington State Highway 207 (at U.S. 2 milepost 84 +.7, 15 miles north of Leavenworth, 20 miles east of Stevens Pass), travel north on Highway 207 for 3.5 miles; turn west (left) onto a paved access road (Forest Road 6607) and head northwesterly (past Nason Creek Campground and the turnoff to Lake Wenatchee State Park) for 5 miles along the south shore of the lake to the end of the road and the campground.

Facilities: 21 campsites, including 7 standard sites which can accommodate rv's, and 14 park 'n walk units; sites are small to medium-sized, with good separation; standard sites have gravel, medium-length straight-ins which might require a bit of additional leveling; adequate level space for tents in the park n' walk units; roadside parking above the sites for park n' walk units; fire rings; firewood is available for gathering in the vicinity; spring water (availability subject to change, b-y-o to be sure); vault facilities; gravel driveway; camper supplies in the state park; adequate supplies and services are available in Leavenworth.

Activities & Attractions: Windsurfing; boating; boat launch; fishing.

Natural Features: Located on the southwest shore of Lake Wenatchee in the Cascade Range; sites are moderately shaded/sheltered by tall conifers and some undercover; bordered by forested mountains; elevation 1800'.

Season, Fees & Phone: May to October; $6.00; 14 day limit; Lake Wenatchee Ranger District (509) 763-3103.

Camp Notes: If your style of camping is a little bit "different" (that is not to say you're an "odd" camper), Glacier View may be of interest to you. Its sites afford more privacy than other camps on or near the lake, and it's popular with windsurfers. Glacier View's tent sites are the only lakeshore campsites on Lake Wenatchee. Another campground in this region for "different" campers is Goose Creek, constructed specifically for campers with motorized trail bikes (but not three or four-wheeled orv's). To get there, instead of turning off Highway 207 toward Glacier View, continue northerly for a mile on '207, then pick up Forest Road 62. Drive northeast for three miles (past Fish Lake), then turn southeast onto Forest Road 6100 for a final mile to the campground. Goose Creek's 20 sites and their parking pads come in two basic sizes and are priced accordingly. Drinking water and vaults are provided. Trails lead off from the creekside campground and connect to an extensive network of marked trails and roads throughout a sizeable section of the forest.

Washington 124

TUMWATER
Wenatchee National Forest

Location: West-central Washington northwest of Wenatchee.

Access: From U.S. Highway 2 at milepost 90 +.4 (11 miles northwest of Leavenworth, 7 miles south of Coles Corner and just north of a highway bridge over the Wenatchee River), turn east off the highway (i.e., right if approaching from Leavenworth), then turn right or left into the campground.

Facilities: 80 campsites, including 60 in one main loop, plus 20 more sites in a spur to the west along Chiwaukum Creek; (a group camp with shelter is also available, by reservation); sites are small to

74

small+, with good to excellent separation; parking pads are paved, short to medium-length straight-ins; a bit of additional leveling may be needed in many sites; small to medium-sized tent spots; fire rings; firewood is available for gathering; water at several faucets; restrooms; holding tank disposal station; paved driveways; adequate supplies and services are available in Leavenworth.

Activities & Attractions: Fishing on the creek and river; a hiking trail winds from the campground, through the bushes, along the river and creek, then back to the campground; trailhead to Alpine Lakes Wilderness nearby.

Natural Features: Located on a gently rolling, streamside flat in Tumwater Canyon on the east slope of the Cascade Range; Chiwaukum Creek flows into the Wenatchee River at this point; all sites are sheltered and separated by tall hardwoods, dense, high bushes, and a stand of tall conifers; some campsites are right along the creek; Alpine Lakes Wilderness lies to the west; Tumwater Botanical area is located to the south; elevation 2000'.

Season, Fees & Phone: May to November; $7.00; 14 day limit; Leavenworth Ranger District (509) 782-1413.

Camp Notes: Highway 2 passes through a narrow canyon in this section, and there's just enough room for the road and the river. The campground is inside an isosceles triangle bordered by the highway, the river, and the creek. This is a brilliantly colorful camp in autumn. The Wenatchee River is a good, wide stream with deep pools along this segment. It's a favorite spot of fishermen. If you'd like a streamside campground closer to city services, Wenatchee River Chelan County Park has room for 50 or more campers, drinking water, restrooms, and reasonable fees. It's located off the south side of Highway 2 near milepost 115 +.5, midway between Cashmere and Wenatchee. There's plenty of grass, and light to medium shade courtesy of a long row of big cottonwoods along the river. It's a popular spot with rv'rs.

SWAUK
Wenatchee National Forest

Location: West-central Washington north of Ellensburg.

Access: From U.S. Highway 97 at milepost 159 +.8 (4 miles south-west of Swauk Pass, 20 miles northeast of Cle Elum), turn south (i.e., right if approaching from Ellensburg), then immediately east onto an access road which parallels the highway; continue for 0.2 mile (past the day use area) to the campground.

Facilities: 23 campsites; most sites are medium-sized, with reasonable separation; parking pads are gravel, well leveled (considering the terrain), medium-length straight-ins; good tent sites in grassy areas among the trees; fireplaces; some firewood is available for gathering; no drinking water; restrooms, plus auxiliary vaults; gravel driveways; limited supplies at a store/cafe, 6 miles south on Highway 97; limited+ supplies and services are available in Cle Elum.

Activities & Attractions: Stream fishing; Sculpture Rock Trail leads from south of the creek (across a small wooden footbridge); day use area includes a sports field, children's play area, kitchen shelters and a large fireplace for group use.

Natural Features: Located in a narrow valley in the Wenatchee Mountains; the campground is situated in a moderately dense conifer forest; Swauk Creek tumbles right past many of the sites on its way toward the Yakima River; closely flanked by forested slopes; elevation 3900'.

Season, Fees & Phone: Mid-April to November; no fee (subject to change); 14 day limit; Cle Elum Ranger District (509) 674-4411.

Camp Notes: Two other highwayside campgrounds are north of Swauk along this route, Tronsen, near mile 165, and Bonanza, near mile 169 may have limited availability. Tronsen's old growth spruce trees have developed a natural 'root rot' and the campground is being rehabilitated. (Leavenworth Ranger District at 509-782-1413 can give you current info on the status of these two camps.) For a daytime diversion from Swauk, you might explore the local mountain scenery along the old Blewett Pass Road. Access is from near milepost 158, two miles southwest of this campground, off the west side of U.S. 97. The old road is steep and snakey, but paved. Plan a one-way-in/same way out excursion. Check locally about road and traffic conditions so you don't encounter any surprises and have to say at the end of the day "I blew it".

MINERAL SPRINGS
Wenatchee National Forest

Location: West-central Washington north of Ellensburg.

Access: From U.S. Highway 97 at milepost 156 +.1 (8 miles southwest of Swauk Pass, 16 miles northeast of Cle Elum), turn west and cross a small bridge into the campground.

Facilities: 12 campsites in 2 loops; sites are average or better in size, and fairly well separated; parking pads are gravel, mostly level, pull-offs or straight-ins of varying lengths; some very nice tent spots; fireplaces; firewood is available for gathering in the vicinity; water at faucets; vault facilities; gravel driveways; camper supplies at a resort and cafe across the highway; limited+ supplies and services are available in Cle Elum.

Activities & Attractions: Stream fishing; foot trails; 4-wheel drive trails in the vicinity; popular winter sports area (Nordic skiing and snowmobiling).

Natural Features: Located on a shelf 100 feet above the creek and highway, in a narrow valley (or canyon) on the east slope of the Cascade Range; sites are in an open forest with tall conifers and light underbrush; a terraced, timbered hillside rises behind the campground to the west; a similar hillside forms the east wall of the valley; Medicine Creek flows from the west into Swauk Creek here; elevation 3700'.

Season, Fees & Phone: May to December; $6.00; generally available in winter for camper parking, without water or fee; 14 day limit; Cle Elum Ranger District (509) 674-4411.

Camp Notes: Mineral Springs is one of relatively few forest campgrounds in the Cascades which might be available for winter use. This isn't the tropics, so if you do plan to stop here anytime between November and April, be sure to bring chains and a big shovel in case a sudden overnight storm dumps a couple of feet of snow on your camper. Fortunately, it's only a few yards from the camp loops to the highway and most of the way is downhill.

LINCOLN ROCK
Lincoln Rock State Park

Location: Central Washington north of Wenatchee.

Access: From U.S. Highway 2/Washington State Highway 151 at U.S. 2 milepost 132 +.5 (on the east bank of the Columbia River, 9 miles north of East Wenatchee, 7 miles south of the Orondo junction) turn west onto the access road, then angle northwest and proceed 0.3 mile to the park entrance and a "Y" intersection; turn west (left) to the campground.

Facilities: 94 campsites, including 35 with partial hookups and 32 with full hookups, in 3 loops; most sites are small+ to medium-sized, tolerably level, with minimal to nominal separation; parking pads are paved, medium to medium+ straight-ins or long pull-throughs; adequate space for large tents; fireplaces; b-y-o firewood; water at hookup sites and at several additional faucets; restrooms with showers; holding tank disposal station; paved driveways; gas and groceries along the highway; complete supplies and services are available in Wenatchee, 10 miles south.

Activities & Attractions: Swimming beach; sports fields; tennis, volleyball, and basketball courts; walk/bike trails; boating; boat launch and docks; fishing; amphitheater for interpretive programs; playground; cross-country skiing; large day use area with shelters.

Natural Features: Located on a large flat along the east bank of the Columbia River (Lake Entiat) just north of Rocky Reach Dam; campground vegetation consists of watered and mown lawns dotted with planted trees; campsites are unshaded to lightly shaded/sheltered; the river is flanked by barren hills and bluffs; forested peaks of the Cascade Range are visible beyond the bluffs to the west; open and breezy; elevation 700'.

Season, Fees & Phone: Open all year; please see Appendix for standard Washington state park fees; 10 day limit; campsite reservations suggested for anytime during the summer, please see Appendix; park office (509) 884-8702.

Camp Notes: A lot of residents of rainy Pugetopolis seek relief from its drizzle and gloom in this locale's sunny, semi-arid climate. The park could be described as having a "country club" environment, with its manicured landscaping, tennis courts, and soccer field. "Lincoln Rock" is a prominent geological feature which is said to resemble the countenance of said president. From your campsite, look across the river to the rocky bluffs rising from the west bank and see if you can make it out.

DAROGA
Daroga State Park

Location: Central Washington north of Wenatchee.

Access: From Washington State Highway 151 at milepost 219 +.6 (on the east bank of the Columbia River, 6 miles north of the Orondo junction, 21 miles south of Chelan,) turn northwest onto the park access road and proceed 0.1 mile to the park entrance; continue ahead for 0.6 mile to the campground.

Facilities: 25 campsites with partial hookups; (a primitive camp area is also available); sites are small+, with minimal separation; parking pads are paved, medium to long straight-ins or long pull-throughs; most pads will require additional leveling; adequate space for large tents; fireplaces; b-y-o firewood; water at sites; restrooms with showers; holding tank disposal station; paved driveways; adequate supplies and services are available in Chelan.

Activities & Attractions: Swimming beach; sports fields; tennis courts; volleyball courts; basketball courts; boating; boat launch and docks; fishing; ("no kite flying", see Notes below); day use area with shelters.

Natural Features: Located on hilly terrain above the east bank of the Columbia River (the Lake Entiat segment); park vegetation consists of large areas of watered and mown lawns dotted with hardwoods, plus rows of tall poplars; the river is closely bordered by sparsely vegetated, rocky hills and bluffs; typically breezy; elevation 700'.

Season, Fees & Phone: April to October; please see Appendix for standard Washington state park fees; 10 day limit; phone c/o Lincoln Rock State Park.

Camp Notes: According to official sources, Chelan County Public Utility District purchased the orchard that formerly was planted here in order to erect the massive, megavolt power line supports which loom over the park and dominate the landscape. The PUD then built the park and leased the place to the state. Daroga is a satellite unit of Lincoln Rock, which is also a leased park. Lincoln Rock, however, lacks the brightly painted power towers which decorate Daroga. As long as you ignore the power lines swaying high above your sheet metal rv or your aluminum-poled pup tent, you'll have a very pleasant time here.

BRIDGEPORT
Bridgeport State Park

Location: Central Washington east of Bridgeport.

Access: From Washington State Highway 17 at milepost 136 +.3 (0.1 mile north of the Columbia River bridge, 2 miles northeast of Bridgeport, 7 miles south of the junction of Highway 17 & U.S. Highway 97 east of Brewster), turn east onto a paved access road and proceed 2.6 miles (past Chief Joseph Dam) to the park; once inside the entrance, swing northeast (left) for 0.2 mile to the campground.

Facilities: 30 campsites, including 20 with partial hookups; (a reservable group camp is also available); sites are small+ to medium-sized, with nominal to fair separation; parking pads are paved short to medium-length straight-ins or long pull-throughs; a few pads may require a little additional leveling; adequate space for large tents; fireplaces; b-y-o firewood; water at several faucets; restrooms with showers; holding tank disposal station; paved driveways; limited+ supplies and services are available in Bridgeport.

Activities & Attractions: Swimming beach; boating; boat launch and dock; fishing; playground; golf course adjacent; day use area.

Natural Features: Located on a gentle slope on the north shore of Rufus Woods Lake, formed on the Columbia River by Chief Joseph Dam; the campground is in a sheltered hollow a short distance above the shore; campsites receive very light to light-medium shade from a variety of large hardwoods and some evergreens on a watered and mown grass surface; the lake/river is bordered by very high, dry, grass-and-sage-covered bluffs and hills; elevation 1000'.

Season, Fees & Phone: April to November; please see Appendix for standard Washington state park fees; 10 day limit; park office (509) 686-7231 or (509) 923-2473.

Camp Notes: The beach is a walk-in area, accessible on a paved walkway from the campground. That arrangement may seem a little inconvenient if you have a beach umbrella, a big picnic lunch and a fully iced cooler to haul back and forth from your campsite; otherwise the distance from any motor traffic (except for boats) provides an excellent atmosphere for a day's worth of quiet enjoyment on the shore.

SPRING CANYON
Coulee Dam National Recreation Area

Location: North-central Washington southeast of Grand Coulee.

Access: From Washington State Highway 174 at milepost 24 +.2 (3 miles east of Grand Coulee, 20 miles west of Wilbur), turn north onto a paved access road; continue for 1.2 miles and turn west (left) into the campground.

Facilities: 78 campsites, including 66 for rv's; rv sites are very small, with short+ straight-ins in a reasonably level, paved parking lot arrangement; ramadas (sunshades) with 10' of clearance for about 2-dozen rv sites; tent sites have short to medium-length gravel parking pads and large, mostly sloped, tent spaces; (using the somewhat leveled parking pad for a free-standing tent may be advisable); additional, paved parking for tenters; fireplaces; b-y-o firewood; water at central faucets; restrooms; holding tank disposal station; paved driveways; adequate supplies are available in Grand Coulee.

Activities & Attractions: Bunchgrass Prairie Nature Trail; interpretive programs scheduled during the summer; playground; swimming beach, boat launch and dock nearby; fishing; within view of Grand Coulee Dam; visitor center at the dam has auto tour information.

Natural Features: Located on a sage-and-grass slope overlooking Franklin D. Roosevelt Lake, created on the Columbia River by Grand Coulee Dam; campsites receive very light to light shade from large hardwoods on areas of watered-and-mown grass; typically breezy; bordered by dry hills and bluffs; elevation 1500'.

Season, Fees & Phone: Memorial Day to Labor Day; $8.00; 14 day limit; Coulee Dam NRA Headquarters, Grand Coulee, (509) 633-9441.

Camp Notes: Rv'ers have one of the most unusual setups to be found in a public campground, anywhere. The sunshades are in rows that resemble carports in an econo condo complex. Unconventional, but cheap and reasonably effective. Anything that sheds the blazing summer sun is welcome. The campground is within view of the massive hydroelectric powerhouse at 'Grand Cooler', but there's no juice here to run an rv's a/c. (Not even from a current bush. Ed.) Also very welcome is the big swimming beach with its nicely landscaped grounds. The camping area provides a great view of the lake and the surrounding countryside. All things considered, Spring Canyon is one of the nicer campgrounds in semi-arid Central Washington.

STEAMBOAT ROCK
Steamboat Rock State Park

Location: Central Washington southeast of Coulee Dam.

Access: From Washington State Highway 155 at milepost 15 +.6 (10 miles southwest of the city of Grand Coulee, 18 miles northeast of Coulee City), turn west onto a paved park access road; travel west then north for 2 miles to the park entrance; continue ahead for 0.2 mile to the first camp area or an additional 0.4 mile to the second camp area.

Facilities: 105 campsites, including 100 with full hookups, in 2 clusters; sites are small, level, with minimal separation; parking pads are paved, medium-length straight-ins; adequate space for a large tent, only on the tent pad in each site; fireplaces; b-y-o firewood; restrooms with showers; paved driveways; gas and groceries in Electric City, adequate supplies and services are available in Grand Coulee.

Activities & Attractions: Swimming area; boating; boat launch and dock; fishing; nature trail; hiking trail to the top of the Rock; playground; large day use area.

Natural Features: Located along the west shore of Banks Lake in the great, canyon-like Grand Coulee; campsites receive minimal to medium shade/shelter from large hardwoods on mown lawns; high, rocky, sheer-walled bluffs flank the lake east and west; Steamboat Rock, a colossal, 700-foot high, treeless butte rises just west of the park; elevation 1500'.

Season, Fees & Phone: April to November; please see Appendix for standard Washington state park fees; 10 day limit; campsite reservations recommended for anytime during the summer, please see Appendix; park office (509) 633-1304.

Camp Notes: The campground might remind you of one of those lush and plush Sunbelt or South Coast resort camps--small sites, big trees, acres of lawns, etc. For completely different surroundings, take the foot trail to the top of Steamboat Rock. There are striking views of Grand Coulee (the geological feature, that is, not the dam or the town of the same name). You can also wander across the top of the Rock's square mile of area. The country around Grand Coulee is unlike any other region in the Northwest.

SUN LAKES
Sun Lakes State Park

Location: Central Washington southwest of Coulee City.

Access: From Washington State Highway 17 at a point 17 miles north of Soap Lake and 4 miles south of the junction of Highway 17 & U.S. Highway 2, turn east and follow a winding, paved access road for 1 mile (past a private campground) to the park entrance; turn east (left) into the campground.

Facilities: 190 campsites, including 18 with full hookups; (a reservable group camp is also available); sites are small, level, with minimal separation; most parking areas are short to medium-length pull-offs; large tent spaces; fireplaces; b-y-o firewood; water at several faucets; restrooms with showers; holding tank disposal station; paved driveways; camper supplies at a small store nearby; adequate supplies and services are available in Coulee City, 6 miles north.

Activities & Attractions: Boating; boat launch; trout fishing; swimming on a well-protected cove; playground; nature trail; day use area with shelter.

Natural Features: Located on a grassy flat at the base of steep, rocky walls deep in Grand Coulee; large hardwoods provide light to medium shade for most campsites; Mirror Lake, Park Lake, Dry Falls Lake, Deep Lake and other small lakes collectively are called Sun Lakes; elevation 1200'.

Season, Fees & Phone: Open all year; please see Appendix for standard Washington state park fees; 10 day limit; park office (509) 632-5583.

Camp Notes: Four thousand acres is a lot of park, even for Central Washington. If the slim campsite spacing is a bit snug for your preferences, you'll find plenty of room to stretch your legs and fingertips in the park's nicely landscaped day use areas. Another state park unit in the vicinity merits your consideration for a visit. Dry Falls Interpretive Center is located off the east side of Highway 17 just north of the Sun Lakes access road. It has exhibits describing the formation of an ancient waterfall, which, if active today, would make Niagara look like an overflowing rain gutter. A large picture window overlooks the 400-foot high, three-and-a-half mile wide precipice over which plunged billions of gallons of water per minute. The Sun Lakes don't contain quite that much liquid in modern times.

OSOYOOS LAKE
Osoyoos Lake State Park

Location: North-central Washington near the U.S.-Canadian border.

Access: From U.S. Highway 97 at milepost 332 +.7 (0.7 mile north of Oroville, 4 miles south of the international border), turn east into the park and the campground.

Facilities: 80 campsites; (6 hike-bike/primitive sites are also available); sites are small to medium-sized, level, with minimal separation; parking pads are gravel, mostly medium-length straight-ins; excellent tent-pitching possibilities; fireplaces; b-y-o firewood; water at several faucets; restrooms with showers; holding tank disposal station; paved driveways; adequate supplies and services are available in Oroville.

Activities & Attractions: Boating; boat launch and dock; sandy swimming beach; day use area with shelter.

Natural Features: Located on a large, grassy flat along the south shore of Osoyoos Lake in the Okanogan Valley; campsites receive minimal to light shade from large hardwoods on a grassy surface; adjacent marsh area is home for a variety of wildlife; dry hills and high mountains flank this very fertile valley; lake area is 5700 acres, about half of it in Canada; elevation 900'.

Season, Fees & Phone: Open all year, principal season is April to November; please see Appendix for standard Washington state park fees; 10 day limit; park office (509) 476-3321.

Camp Notes: The Okanogan Valley is renowned for its mild climate, long growing season, and delicious fruits and vegetables (grown and sold at roadside stands on both sides of the border). Boating campers may be pleased to know that, at a few lakeside campsites, their vessel can be moored right at their site. Since the north end of the lake is in Canada, many boaters take the opportunity to motor or sail across the border. Don't forget to check-in with Customs.

BONAPARTE LAKE
Okanogan National Forest

Location: Northeast Washington west of Republic.

Access: From Washington State Highway 20 at milepost 282 +.2 (20 miles east of Tonasket, 20 miles west of Republic), turn north onto Forest Road 396 (paved); travel northerly for 5.9 miles, then turn west (left) into the campground.

Facilities: 24 campsites in 2 loops; sites are medium-sized, with fair separation; level parking pads are gravel, short to medium-length, straight-ins or pull-throughs; good tent spots; fireplaces; some firewood is available for gathering in the vicinity; water at central faucets; restrooms, plus auxiliary vaults; waste water receptacles for gray water; hard-surfaced driveways; limited supplies are available in Republic and Tonasket.

Activities & Attractions: Boating; boat launch; fishing; foot trail from the west end of the campground; day use area along the shore; many sites have lake views through the trees.

Natural Features: Located on the forested south shore of Bonaparte Lake; tall conifers tower over the campsites, with only a little underbrush and second growth to separate the sites; the lake is bordered by steep-sided, rocky, timbered mountains that rise to 7200'; elevation 4000'.

Season, Fees & Phone: May to October; $7.00 for a single unit, $10.00-$15.00 for a multiple unit; 14 day limit; Tonasket Ranger District (509) 486-2186.

Camp Notes: This is a really nice campground for any part of the country, but here in mostly dry eastern Washington, it's a very pleasant surprise! And this picturesque, tree-ringed lake is just a half dozen miles from the main highway, to boot. If you just need a quick enroute camp for the night, another nearby forest campground, Sweat Creek, is located east of here at milepost 293 +.5 on Highway 20. Sweat Creek has 7 sites, a hand pump and vault facilities on a forested, highwayside flat.

CURLEW LAKE
Curlew Lake State Park

Location: Northeast Washington north of Republic.

Access: From Washington State Highway 21 at milepost 144 +.3 (6 miles north of Republic, 20 miles south of the U.S.-Canadian border), turn west onto a paved access road and proceed southwesterly for 0.7 mile to the park; turn north (right) into the main camp area, or continue southerly for another 0.1 mile to the lakeside camp area.

Facilities: 72 campsites, including 18 with full hookups and a number of park 'n walk sites, in the main area, plus 10 additional sites in the lakeside area; (5 hike-bike/ primitive sites are also available); sites are very small to medium-sized, with minimal separation; parking pads are gravel, mostly short to medium-length straight-ins; adequate space for large tents in most sites, but may be sloped; fireplaces; b-y-o firewood; water at several faucets; restrooms with showers; holding tank disposal station; paved/packed gravel driveways; adequate supplies and services are available in Republic.

Activities & Attractions: Boating; fishing; boat launch and dock; sand and grass swimming beach.

Natural Features: Located on a tree-dotted, grassy, rolling hillside above the east shore of Curlew Lake; park grounds are mown and watered; conifers and hardwoods provide limited shade for some campsites; bordered by rolling, grassy hills and forested mountains; elevation 2300'.

Season, Fees & Phone: April to November; please see Appendix for standard Washington state park fees; 10 day limit; park office (509) 775-3592.

Camp Notes: You might consider scouting both the lakeside and main camping areas if you're planning to spend the night here, since each has its own distinctive qualities. The lake, which is a half-mile wide and 5 miles long, has a reputation for being a good producer of both bass and 'bows.

SHERMAN PASS
Colville National Forest

Location: Northeast Washington between Republic and Kettle Falls.

Access: From Washington State Highway 20 at milepost 320 +.4 (17 miles east of Republic, 25 miles west of Kettle Falls) turn north onto a narrow gravel road; after 100 yards take the left fork and continue west for a few more yards into the campground.

Facilities: 9 campsites; units are small and quite close together, although some separation is provided by trees and bushes; parking pads are gravel, short or short+ straight-ins or pull-offs; additional leveling may be necessary; some secluded tent areas are squeezed in among the trees; fireplaces; firewood is usually available for gathering in the area; water at a hand pump; vault facilities; gravel driveway; adequate supplies and services are available in Republic and Kettle Falls.

Activities & Attractions: Sweeping vistas through the trees from some of the sites, and even better, unobstructed views from the nearby picnic area and scenic viewpoint; Overlook Trail (300 yards); Kettle Crest Trailhead is a few hundred yards west of the campground.

Natural Features: Located in the Kettle River Range just 1 mile east of Sherman Pass; a moderately dense stand of conifers shelters the campsites on a pine-needle forest floor; moderately dense forest covers the surrounding mountains; elevation 5100'.

Season, Fees & Phone: May to September; no fee; 14 day limit; Kettle Falls Ranger District (509) 738-6111.

Camp Notes: This is a neat group of campsites perched on a hilltop above timbered ridges. Though the highway is quite near many of the sites, this is a great wayside for hikers and highway travelers. Can't ask for a better facility for the price!

Washington 137

CANYON CREEK
Colville National Forest

Location: Northeast Washington west of Kettle Falls.

Access: From Washington State Highway 20 at milepost 334 +.3 (12 miles west of Kettle Falls, 15 miles east of Sherman Pass, 31 miles east of Republic), turn south onto a campground access road and proceed 0.2 mile to the campground.

Facilities: 12 campsites; sites are medium to large, with very good separation; parking pads are gravel, medium to long straight-ins; some nice, cleared and leveled tent sites; fireplaces; firewood is available for gathering in the area; water at a hand pump; vault facilities; pack-it-in/pack-it-out trash removal system; gravel driveway; adequate supplies and services are available in Kettle Falls.

Activities & Attractions: Log Flume Interpretive Trail (handicapped access), 1 mile east off Highway 20; the starting point for the Bangs Mountain self-guiding auto tour is also at the Log Flume Trailhead; fishing on Sherman Creek; reportedly excellent fishing at Trout Lake, 7.5 miles north on a gravel road; Coulee Dam National Recreation Area, only a few miles to the east, has boat ramps and docks, fishing and swimming.

Natural Features: Located in a fairly dense forest at the base of Bangs Mountain; the campground is built on a bit of a hill, but the sites have been quite well-leveled considering the slope; Canyon Creek and Sherman Creek are swiftly flowing small streams that pass within a couple-hundred yards of the campsites; the Columbia River (Franklin D. Roosevelt Lake) is 6 miles east; elevation 2200'.

Season, Fees & Phone: May to September; no fee (subject to change); 14 day limit; Kettle Falls Ranger District (509) 738-6111.

Camp Notes: This is a well-planned and nicely constructed campground with plenty of elbow room. It should seldom be crowded, and is a great buy!

Washington 138

HAAG COVE
Coulee Dam National Recreation Area

Location: Northeast Washington west of Kettle Falls.

Access: From Washington State Highway 20 at milepost 338 (8 miles southwest of Kettle Falls, 19 miles east of Sherman Pass, 35 miles east of Republic), turn south onto Inchelium Road and travel 2.1 miles to a paved access road; turn east (left), and continue for 1 mile to the campground.

Facilities: 12 campsites strung out along a grassy riverbank; sites are small, with minimal separation; parking pads are gravel, short to medium-length straight-ins or pull-offs; most pads need additional leveling; good tent-pitching opportunities on or near the beach; fireplaces or barbecue grills; firewood may be available in the vicinity at times, but b-y-o is recommended; water at a hand pump; vault facilities; gravel driveway; adequate supplies and services are available in Kettle Falls.

Activities & Attractions: Boating; fishing; boat launch and dock; sandy beach with a small play area for children.

Natural Features: Located on the west shore of Franklin D. Roosevelt Lake, formed by Coulee Dam on the Columbia River; sites are on a pine-dotted grassy slope along a sandy beach; forested ridges are visible across the lake/river to the east; Sherman Creek Wildlife Recreation Area boundary is just north of the campground; elevation 1300'.

Season, Fees & Phone: Open all year, subject to weather conditions; no fee; 14 day limit; Coulee Dam NRA Headquarters, Grand Coulee, (509) 633-9441.

Camp Notes: This is a small, rough, but very popular camping facility. It's the only campground in this region that's right on the west bank of the Columbia River (Roosevelt Lake, whatever).

Washington 139

KETTLE RIVER
Coulee Dam National Recreation Area

Location: Northeast Washington northwest of Kettle Falls.

Access: From U.S. Highway 395 at milepost 247 +.9 in the burg of Boyds (10 miles northwest of Kettle Falls, 20 miles south of the Canadian border), turn east, cross the RR tracks and take the left fork *down* the hill; continue for 0.8 mile east on a gravel access road to the campground.

Facilities: 12 campsites; sites are large, level, with virtually no separation; parking pads are gravel, straight-ins or pull-offs, long enough to accommodate medium-sized rv's; some large, level tent sites on a pine needle forest floor; fireplaces; firewood is scarce, so b-y-o is recommended; water at a hand pump; vault facilities; gravel driveway; adequate supplies and services are available in Kettle Falls.

Activities & Attractions: Fishing on the Kettle River; boating on nearby Franklin D. Roosevelt Lake; a boat dock is located here, at Kettle River, but the nearest boat ramps are at the Kettle Falls and Marcus Island recreation sites.

Natural Features: Located on a short grassy bluff overlooking the Kettle River; tall, light timber with virtually no underbrush shades/shelters the campsites; the campground is skirted by meadowland; the Kettle River enters the Columbia River about 3 miles downstream of this point; distant mountain views from most sites; elevation 1300'.

Season, Fees & Phone: Open all year, subject to weather conditions; no fee; 14 day limit; Coulee Dam NRA Headquarters, Grand Coulee, (509) 633-9441.

Camp Notes: This is actually a nice stop, especially for Highway 395 travelers who prefer a campground not quite so close to the mainstream of the recreation area's traffic. It tends to be much less-frequented than Haag Cove (above). Because of the impounding effect of the Columbia River, the Kettle's 'backed-up' waters are placid off this bank.

Washington 140

EVANS
Coulee Dam National Recreation Area

Location: Northeast Washington north of Kettle Falls.

Access: From Washington State Highway 25 at a point 10.2 miles north of Kettle Falls and 30 miles south of the U.S.-Canada border, turn west onto a paved access road and proceed 0.1 mile to the campground.

Facilities: 56 campsites; sites are small+, level, with nominal separation; parking pads are paved, mostly short straight-ins, plus some pull-throughs; many good tent spots; fireplaces; b-y-o firewood; water at faucets throughout; restrooms; freshwater-rinse showers; holding tank disposal station; paved driveways; gas and groceries nearby on Highway 25; adequate supplies and services are available in Kettle Falls.

Activities & Attractions: Boating; boat launch; fishing for a wide variety of freshwater species (trolling is reportedly the most productive method); designated swimming area with swim platform; nice sandy beach; children's play area; amphitheater for scheduled ranger-naturalist programs.

Natural Features: Located on an open grassy/sandy flat on the east shore of Franklin D. Roosevelt Lake, a major impoundment on the Columbia River; campsites are very lightly to lightly shaded by tall conifers; bordered by a small meadow; grass and evergreen-covered hills and high ridges border the lake; typically quite windy; elevation 1300'.

Season, Fees & Phone: Open all year, with limited services, October to May; $8.00; (no fee in winter); 14 day limit; Coulee Dam NRA Headquarters, Grand Coulee, (509) 633-9441.

Camp Notes: This very attractive, albeit well-used, campground affords tremendous views of the countryside. Definitely recommended, especially for weekday camping.

Washington 141

MARCUS ISLAND
Coulee Dam National Recreation Area

Location: Northeast Washington north of Kettle Falls.

Access: From Washington State Highway 25 at a point 5.6 miles north of Kettle Falls and 35 miles south of the U.S.-Canada border, turn west onto a paved road which leads 0.5 mile to the river level, doubles back around to the east for 0.5 mile, then crosses a short causeway northward into the campground.

Facilities: 20 campsites; sites are small to medium in size, level, with minimal to fairly good separation; parking pads are paved, mostly short straight-ins, plus a few pull-throughs; most sites have adequate space for tents; fireplaces; b-y-o firewood is recommended; water at a hand pump; vault facilities; paved driveways; adequate supplies and services are available in Kettle Falls.

Activities & Attractions: Fishing for a variety of fresh water species including walleye, trout, salmon and sturgeon; trolling is probably the most effective means of taking fish; good boat launch and dock adjacent to the campground.

Natural Features: Located on a small island along the east shore of 150-mile-long Franklin D. Roosevelt Lake (part of the Columbia River system); campground vegetation consists of medium-dense moderately tall pine, plus tall grass; high grass and timber-covered mountains parallel the river; moderately dry climate; elevation 1300'.

Season, Fees & Phone: Open all year, subject to weather conditions, with limited services October to May; $8.00; (no fee in winter); 14 day limit; Coulee Dam NRA Headquarters, Grand Coulee, (509) 633-9441.

Camp Notes: All campsites are near the water's edge. A few sites at the tip of the point offer sweeping views of the local landscape. Skinny-dipping Canucks seem to favor the placid waters of the adjoining cove for refreshing midnight plunges.

Washington 142

KETTLE FALLS
Coulee Dam National Recreation Area

Location: Northeast Washington just west of Kettle Falls.

Access: From Washington State Highway 20 at the east end of the Columbia River bridge 3 miles west of Kettle Falls, turn south onto a paved two-lane road which parallels the river; follow this road for 1.8 miles to the ranger station and the campground. **Alternate Access:** From Washington State Highway 25 at a point 0.5 mile south of the junction of Highways 20 and 25, turn west at a sign indicating "Recreation Area 3 Miles"; follow this paved road for the specified distance to the campground.

Facilities: 76 campsites in 3 loops; most sites are of average size, level, with nominal to fair separation; parking pads are mostly short straight-ins, some are medium-length pull-throughs; excellent tent-pitching opportunities; fireplaces; firewood is a bit scarce in the immediate vicinity, so b-y-o is recommended; water at faucets throughout; restrooms with camper service sinks; holding tank disposal station near the ranger station; paved driveways; adequate supplies and services are available in Kettle Falls, 5 miles northeast.

Activities & Attractions: Super-nice picnic area with playground and swimming beach 0.2 mile south of the campground; fishing; marina nearby.

Natural Features: Located on a gently rolling flat along the east shore of Franklin D. Roosevelt Lake (actually the impounded Columbia River); campground vegetation consists of moderately dense timber with little ground-level vegetation except tall grass; the lake is flanked by forested hills; elevation 1300'.

Season, Fees & Phone: Open all year, with limited services October to May; $8.00; (no fee in winter); 14 day limit; Coulee Dam NRA Headquarters, Grand Coulee, (509) 633-9441.

Camp Notes: This is an agreeably pleasant, sheltered campground. It's usually quite busy on midsummer weekends, but definitely worth considering due to its good facilities and proximity to the community of Kettle Falls. On major holiday weekends, all camps along the lake play to a standing-room-only crowd.

Washington 143

GIFFORD
Coulee Dam National Recreation Area

Location: Northeast Washington south of Kettle Falls.

Access: From Washington State Highway 25 at milepost 56 +.4 (1.5 miles south of the hamlet of Gifford, 14 miles north of the community of Hunters), turn west onto a paved access road which leads 0.1 mile down to the campground.

Facilities: 42 campsites; sites are medium-sized, with nominal separation; parking pads are gravel straight-ins or pull-throughs which may require a little additional leveling; a few walk-in sites are in a little cove at the south end of the grounds; fireplaces; very little firewood is available for gathering, so b-y-o is recommended; water at faucets; restrooms; holding tank disposal station; paved driveways; gas and groceries in Gifford.

Activities & Attractions: Boating; boat launch and docks; rock jetty; fishing for more than 30 species, including walleye (the number one game fish in the lake), rainbow trout, perch and kokanee.

Natural Features: Located on the east shore of Franklin D. Roosevelt Lake; most camp spots are right on the edge of the lake and/or have a lake view; campground vegetation consists of medium height pines and tall grass with a thick carpet of pine needles; usually quite windy; sites are fairly well sheltered, except for those closest to the lake shore; elevation 1300'.

Season, Fees & Phone: Open all year, with limited services October to May; $8.00; (no fee in winter); 14 day limit; Coulee Dam NRA Headquarters, Grand Coulee, (509) 633-9441.

Camp Notes: Camping in this very 'open' atmosphere provides you with excellent views north and south along the lake. The walk-in sites are a couple of the nicest you'll find in this part of the state. If you're a boater, there are lots of little coves and sandy beaches nearby for you to explore.

Washington 144

HUNTERS
Coulee Dam National Recreation Area

Location: Northeast Washington south of Kettle Falls.

Access: From Washington State Highway 25 at milepost 42 +.3 in the small community of Hunters (37 miles south of Kettle Falls, 42 miles north of Davenport), turn west at the "Hunters Campground" sign onto a paved access road and proceed 0.8 mile to the campground.

Facilities: 52 campsites, including some double-occupancy units; sites are medium to large, well leveled, with minimal separation; parking pads are gravel, mostly medium or medium+ pull-throughs; adequate space for large tents; several walk-in sites on the beach; fireplaces; very little firewood is available for gathering, so b-y-o is recommended; water at central faucets; restrooms with naturally cool and refreshing showers; holding tank disposal station; paved driveways; limited supplies and services are available in Hunters.

Activities & Attractions: Boating; boat launch and docks; rock jetty; fishing; designated swimming area; picnic area with barbecue grills; playground; Hunters community fair held annually in late August.

Natural Features: Located on the east shore of Franklin D. Roosevelt Lake on the Columbia River; campground vegetation consists of medium-dense conifers and a little undergrowth; sandy beach; interesting, heavily eroded bluffs are opposite the campground on the west shore of the lake; better-protected from the elements than other camping areas near here; elevation 1300'.

Season, Fees & Phone: Open all year, with limited services October to May; $8.00; (no fee in winter); 14 day limit; Coulee Dam NRA Headquarters, Grand Coulee, (509) 633-9441.

Camp Notes: This is terrific country around here! In summer, its colors are rich green and gold and blue and brown. All sites have some sort of a lake view, and many are on or near the lake shore. The walk-in sites, in particular, have a super view.

FORT SPOKANE
Coulee Dam National Recreation Area

Location: Northeast Washington north of Davenport.

Access: From Washington State Highway 25 at milepost 23 +.1 (23 miles north of Davenport, 19 miles south of Hunters), turn east into the campground.

Facilities: 62 campsites, including quite a few double-occupancy units, in several large loops; virtually all sites are quite spacious, level, with nominal separation; parking pads are paved pull-throughs; plenty of space for tents; fireplaces; b-y-o firewood; water at faucets throughout; restrooms; holding tank disposal station; paved driveways; limited supplies in Hunters; adequate supplies and services are available in Davenport.

Activities & Attractions: Visitor center and ranger station 0.2 mile south of the campground; self guiding tours around the well-maintained remnants of Fort Spokane; amphitheater on the bank of the Spokane River for planned ranger-naturalist programs; fishing; boat launch.

Natural Features: Located at the confluence of the Columbia and Spokane Rivers; light to medium-dense very tall pines shelter the campsites; ground cover consists of some shrubbery, but mostly pine needles and grass; the Spokane River is within easy walking distance of all campsites; elevation 1300'.

Season, Fees & Phone: Open all year, with limited services October to May; $8.00; (no fee in winter); 14 day limit; Coulee Dam NRA Headquarters, Grand Coulee, (509) 633-9441.

Camp Notes: Fort Spokane is a very popular place, but is it *nice*! There's a pleasant open-air feeling here. Most sites are equally well suited for tent or vehicle camping. They really did a good job on this park. The drive down Highway 25 from the north passes through some of the most impressive scenery in this sparsely settled region.

MILLPOND
Colville National Forest

Location: Northeast corner of Washington east of Metaline Falls.

Access: From Washington State Highway 31 at milepost 16 +.4 (1.5 miles north of Metaline Falls, 11 miles south of the Canadian border), turn east onto Sullivan Lake Road (Forest Road 9345, paved); travel easterly, for 3.7 miles; turn southwest (right) onto a gravel access road leading 0.2 mile down into the campground.

Facilities: 11 campsites; sites are average-sized, level, with good separation; parking pads are gravel, medium-length straight-ins; some large, level tent spots; fireplaces; firewood is available for gathering in the area; water at a hand pump; vault facilities; gravel driveways; limited supplies and services are available in Metaline Falls.

Activities & Attractions: Limited boating; Hand-launch boat area; fishing; sand and grass beach; several foot trails in the area; Crawford State Park's limestone cave, located 12 miles north of Metaline Falls, is available for tours during the summer months.

Natural Features: Located in a heavily forested creek valley; a considerable amount of vegetation provides very good separation and shelter for most of the sites; a small pond is near the west end of the campground; tall, forested peaks surround the immediate area; elevation 2500'.

Season, Fees & Phone: May to October; $6.00; 14 day limit; Sullivan Lake Ranger District (509) 446-7500.

Camp Notes: This is a small, basic, but really neat campground. It's located toward the northern edge of the popular Sullivan Lake Recreation Area.

SULLIVAN LAKE
Colville National Forest

Location: Northeast corner of Washington east of Metaline Falls.

Access: From Washington State Highway 31 at milepost 16 +.4 (1.5 miles north of Metaline Falls, 11 miles south of the Canadian border) turn east onto Sullivan Lake Road (Forest Road 9345); travel east, then south for 4.7 miles; turn east (left) onto Forest Road 22 and proceed 0.4 mile, then turn south (right) onto a gravel access road for a final 0.3 mile to the campground. **Alternate Access:** From Washington State Highway 31 at milepost 3 +.1 (at the south edge of the town of Ione) turn east onto Elizabeth Street, which becomes Sullivan Lake Road and Forest Road 9345 (paved); travel east and north for 12.5 miles to Forest Road 22 and continue as above. (Note: The first Access is the shortest and most direct route from the main highway, and the preferred route for southbound travelers on Washington 31; the Alternate Access is a 'backdoor' approach and works very well for northbound travelers, and it is especially scenic.)

Facilities: 34 campsites in 2 sections (locally termed West and East); sites are fairly good-sized, level, with fair separation; parking pads are gravel, medium to long straight-ins; many large, level spots for tents; fireplaces; firewood is available for gathering in the area; water at several faucets; vault facilities; disposal station; gravel driveways; limited supplies and services are available in Metaline Falls.

Activities & Attractions: Boating; boat launch; fishing; designated swimming area; a foot trail leads south along the east shore of the lake for 4.1 miles to Noisy Creek Campground; benches along the shore line and a Sullivan Lake Viewpoint provide lake-watching opportunities; a grass airstrip makes fly-in camping possible.

Natural Features: Located near the north shore of glacially formed Sullivan Lake; tall conifers are the predominant vegetation, and the campsites are fairly well-cleared of underbrush; the lake is 3.5 miles long and up to 275' deep; encircled by forested hills and mountains; elevation 2600'.

Season, Fees & Phone: May to October; $7.00; 14 day limit; Sullivan Lake Ranger District (509) 446-7500.

Camp Notes: The relaxed atmosphere of this campground is due in part to its distance from population concentrations. The sight of this alluring mountain lake surrounded by pristine forested hills is, in itself, worth the trip.

Washington 148

NOISY CREEK
Colville National Forest

Location: Northeast corner of Washington northeast of Ione.

Access: From Washington State Highway 31 at milepost 3 +.1 (at the south edge of the town of Ione) turn east onto Elizabeth Street, which becomes Sullivan Lake Road and Forest Road 9345 (paved); travel east and north for 8.2 miles; turn east (right) and continue for 0.1 mile on gravel to a fork in the road; take the left fork for a final 0.3 mile to the campground.

Facilities: 19 campsites in 2 tiered loops; (an adjacent overflow camp area is also available); sites are small to medium-sized, with fair to good separation; parking pads are gravel and may require additional leveling; some sites are designated for tents or small vehicles; tent spots are mostly small and sloped; fireplaces; firewood is available for gathering; water at several faucets; vault facilities; narrow, one-way, gravel driveway; limited supplies and services are available in Ione.

Activities & Attractions: Fishing; designated swimming beach; boating; boat launch; a foot trail leads north along the lake shore for 4.1 miles to Sullivan Lake Campground.

Natural Features: Located on the south shore of glacially formed Sullivan Lake; Noisy Creek tumbles past many of the sites on its way to the lake; moderately dense, tall conifers, hardwoods, and very little underbrush provide shade/shelter for the sites; towering, forested peaks cover most of the region; elevation 2600'.

Season, Fees & Phone: May to October; $7.00 for a standard site, $9.00 for a "preferred" (lakeside) site; 14 day limit; Sullivan Lake Ranger District (509) 446-7500.

Camp Notes: This campground--on the shore of a beautiful mountain lake, along a rushing stream, and some distance off the mainstream--is a particularly popular place with Spokaners, (Spokanites? Spokanians?), but little used by campers from outside the region. Mountainous, evergreen-cloaked, and sparsely populated, Washington's remote northeast corner is one of the state's unheralded scenic sanctuaries.

Washington 149

EDGEWATER
Colville National Forest

Location: Northeast corner of Washington northeast of Ione.

Access: From Washington State Highway 31 at milepost 3 +.1 (at the south edge of the community of Ione), turn east onto Elizabeth Street and proceed 0.5 mile east across the Pend Oreille River bridge; turn north (left) onto Forest Road 3669 (gravel) and proceed 2 miles; turn west (left) onto a gravel access road and continue for 0.5 mile to the campground.

Facilities: 23 campsites; sites are medium to large, level with good separation; parking pads are gravel/grass, medium to long straight-ins; large, level tent spots; fireplaces; some firewood is available for gathering in the area; water at faucets; pack-it-in/pack-it-out trash removal system; vault facilities; gravel driveway; limited supplies and services are available in Ione.

Activities & Attractions: Fishing; boating; boat launch, (not always accessible due to fluctuations in the river level); day use area; Box Canyon Dam spans the river just to the north.

Natural Features: Located on the east bank of the Pend Oreille River; sites are on a flat above river level in a fairly dense conifer forest; access is through private farmland; the Selkirk Mountains rise above 7000' to the east and west; campground elevation 2100'.

Season, Fees & Phone: May to October; no fee (subject to change); 14 day limit; Sullivan Lake Ranger District (509) 446-7500.

Camp Notes: The campground has some pretty nice sites, and is easily accessible from a main highway and a small community. It appears this facility is only rarely used to its full potential.

Washington 150

GILLETTE & LAKE GILLETTE
Colville National Forest

Location: Northeast Washington east of Colville.

Access: From Washington State Highway 20 at milepost 379 +.1 (11 miles southwest of Tiger, 25 miles northeast of Colville), turn east (i.e., left if approaching from Tiger) at the "Lake Thomas/Lake Gillette" sign; follow a paved access road for 0.5 mile; Lake Gillette Campground is on the north (left) side of the access road, and Gillette Campground is 100 yards farther on the south side of the road; (note that Highway 20 follows a north-south line in this section).

Facilities: 30 campsites in Gillette; 14 campsites, including several multiple units, in Lake Gillette; sites are fairly large, level, and well spaced; parking pads are gravel, and some can accommodate large rv's; excellent tent spots in most sites; fireplaces and/or barbecue grills; firewood is available for gathering in the vicinity; water at several faucets; restrooms, plus auxiliary vaults; holding tank disposal station in Gillette; central kitchen shelter; paved driveways; nearest reliable source of adequate supplies and services is Colville.

Activities & Attractions: "Springboard" and "Rufus" self guided nature trails lead off from the east end of Gillette; sand and gravel beach; boating; boat launch and dock; fishing for rainbow and cutthroat trout; ampthitheater; good berry-picking for currants, huckleberries and gooseberries in July and August.

Natural Features: Located on or near the southeast corner of Lake Gillette in the Selkirk Mountains; tall thin conifers, tall grass and a thick carpet of conifer needles make up the principal vegetation in the camping areas; campsites are near the lake, but most do not have lake views; elevation 3300'.

Season, Fees & Phone: May to October; $7.00 for a Gillette site; $8.00 for a standard site or $11.00 for multiple-family unit at Lake Gillette; 14 day limit; Colville Ranger District (509) 684-4557.

Camp Notes: Gillette campground is considered by many to be the best of the several camping areas in this vicinity. However, it is a little busier and less private than Lake Gillette (which is also known as the "Beach" unit), or nearby Lake Thomas. A chain of eight glacial lakes and their several attendant campgrounds along this highway are part of the Little Pend Oreille recreation area.

Washington 151

LAKE THOMAS
Colville National Forest

Location: Northeast Washington east of Colville.

Access: From Washington State Highway 20 at milepost 379 +.1 (25 miles northeast of Colville, 11 miles southwest of Tiger), turn east (i.e., left if approaching from Tiger) at the "Lake Thomas/Lake Gillette" sign onto a paved access road; drive 1.2 miles easterly (past the campgrounds near Lake Gillette) to Lake Thomas.

Facilities: 15 campsites; sites are small to medium-sized, with fair separation; small, paved parking aprons; not recommended for trailers but suitable for smaller camping vehicles; many units have large, level, framed and gravelled tent pads; several walk-in tent sites; fireplaces, plus some barbecue grills; firewood is available for gathering in the vicinity; water at faucets throughout; vault facilities; narrow, paved, one-way driveway; nearest reliable source of adequate supplies and services is Colville.

Activities & Attractions: Trout fishing; boating; windsurfing; hiking trails in the area.

Natural Features: Located on a somewhat steep hillside amid dense, mature conifers mixed with some second growth and low brush; the campground is surrounded by moderately tall, heavily-timbered mountains; Lake Thomas is the largest of several lakes in the vicinity; elevation 3300'.

Season, Fees & Phone: May to October; $6.00; 14 day limit; Colville Ranger District (509) 684-4557.

Camp Notes: A number of campsites have good views of the lake, since the campground is located right along and above the south shore. Lake Thomas Campground is markedly different from nearby Gillette and Lake Gillette Campgrounds (see separate description). Another small, nearby camp is Lake Leo, above the north shore of the tiny lake of the same name. Lake Leo's basic, eight-site camp is a couple-hundred yards south of the main highway, 3.5 miles northeast of the turnoff to Lakes Gillette and Thomas.

Washington 152

PIONEER PARK
Colville National Forest

Location: Northeast Washington east of Newport.

Access: From U.S. Highway 2 at the east end of the Pend Oreille River Bridge at the Washington-Idaho border (1 mile east of Newport, Washington, 6 miles west of Priest River, Idaho), turn north onto a paved road at the "Pioneer Park Campground" sign; proceed north 2.3 miles to the campground entrance on the west side of the road.

Facilities: 14 campsites; sites are quite large and well separated; parking pads are short to medium-length, paved/gravel straight-ins; some additional leveling will probably be needed; the campground is a little hilly, but is still suitable for tents; fireplaces; some firewood is available for gathering nearby; water at faucets; vault facilities; paved/oiled gravel driveways; adequate+ supplies and services are available in Newport.

Activities & Attractions: Trails from the campground to the river; fishing; boat launch (gravel with concrete traction strips).

Natural Features: Located on the moderately forested, east bank of the wide, deep Pend Oreille (pronounced Pond-oh-*ray*) River; this region is generally mountainous, quite densely forested and sparsely populated; elevation 2100'.

Season, Fees & Phone: May to October; $7.00; 14 day limit; Newport Ranger District (509) 447-3129.

Camp Notes: One of the appeals of Pioneer Park is its proximity to the services available in Newport. The campground appears to be in Idaho, but it is actually just inside the Washington State Line, although there is no formal indication of that fact along the access road.

Washington 153

BALD KNOB
Mount Spokane State Park

Location: Northeast Washington northeast of Spokane.

Access: From the junction of U.S Highway 2 and Washington State Highway 206 at a point 10.4 miles north of Interstate 90 Exit 281 in downtown Spokane, head northeast on Highway 206 for 15.4 miles to the park entrance; continue upward on the paved park road for 4.4 miles to the campground. **Alternate Access:** From Interstate 90 Exit 287 for Argonne Road and Millwood on the east end of Spokane, travel north on Argonne Road for 8.5 miles to pick up Highway 206, then turn northeast (right) and follow Highway 206 for 12.9 miles to the park.

(Note: Argonne Road begins as a 4-lane boulevard then becomes 2-lane and curves a couple of times, but if you just keep heading northerly you'll run into Highway 206; via either of the above routes, allow plenty of time to get up to the park because the curves begin at about milepost 8 on Highway 206; the road inside the park is very steep and twisty; getting up the mountain isn't so much of a bother as getting back down; bring a drag chute and a replacement set of brake pads for the return trip. Keep 'em cool.)

Facilities: 9 campsites; (a group camp and a horse camp are also available); sites are very small, most are sloped, with minimal to nominal separation; parking spaces have an earth/gravel surface and are very small; enough space for a small tent; fireplaces; b-y-o firewood; water at a central faucet; restrooms; gravel/earth driveway; nearest supplies and services (complete) are in Spokane.

Activities & Attractions: Several miles of hiking and equestrian trails; horse-handling areas; Vista House, a CCC-built stone building at the summit of the mountain.

Natural Features: Located on the upper slopes of Mount Spokane; campground vegetation consists mainly of scattered, tall conifers; elevation 4500'.

Season, Fees & Phone: Principal season is April to November, with limited services in winter; please see Appendix for standard Washington state park fees; 10 day limit; park office (509) 456-4169 or (509) 238-6845.

Camp Notes: Mount Spokane is a good place to retreat on those summer nights when the heat sears the soles of your tennies and it's steamy enough to wilt your permed curls in the camp down at Riverside SP. With the right motor vehicle and equipment, the campground is accessible during part of the winter, too. (There's a major ski area on the mountaintop about 1500' above the campground, so that should tell you something about the weather up here.) Summer or winter, the pleasant drive along Highway 206 and the spectacular views from the campground area once you manage to get up here are quite good. (Reading through the Access and Facilities info might make you wonder if it's really worth the time, fuel and effort to camp here, though.)

RIVERSIDE
Riverside State Park

Location: Eastern Washington on the northwest corner of Spokane.

Access: From the junction of U.S Highways 2/95 & Washington State Highway 291 on the north side of Spokane (4.5 miles north of Interstate 90 Exit 281, 1.6 miles south of the merge point of U.S. 2 & 95 north of the city), turn west onto State Highway 291 (Francis Avenue) and proceed 3.7 miles west then northwest to Rifle Club Road; turn southwest (left) onto Gun Club Road for 0.4 mile to Aubrey White Parkway; from this point, turn southeast (left) onto Aubrey White Parkway and proceed 1 mile to the campground.

Alternate Access: If you're inbound on I-90, you could take Exit 280, then north on Walnut Street across the Maple Street Bridge for 1.4 miles, then west on Maxwell for 0.3 mile; turn northwest onto Petit Drive and follow the river for 2.5 miles (Petit soon becomes Downriver Drive) to a fork; take the left fork for another 2 miles, then turn southwest (left) into the campground.

Facilities: 101 campsites; (2 hike-bike/primitive sites and 2 large group camps are also available); most sites are small, reasonably level, with minimal to nominal separation; parking pads are gravel, short to medium-length straight-ins; small to medium-sized tent spots; fire rings; b-y-o firewood; water at several faucets; restrooms with showers; kitchen shelter; paved driveways; complete supplies and services are available within 3 miles in Spokane.

Activities & Attractions: 32 miles of hiking and equestrian trails; off-road vehicle (orv) area; nature trail; jogging trail; boating/floating and fishing on the river; cross-country skiing and sledding; large day use areas with shelters.

Natural Features: Located in a valley along the banks of the Spokane River; vegetation consists principally of tall conifers, some hardwoods and brush; timbered hillsides flank the river; park property includes 8 miles of riverbank; elevation 1900'.

Season, Fees & Phone: Open all year; please see Appendix for standard Washington state park fees; 10 day limit; park office (509) 456-3964.

Camp Notes: Riverside has one of only three metropolitan public campgrounds in the Pacific Northwest. (The others are near Seattle and Tacoma.) Another unusual feature is its large orv area--one of the few in Northwest parks. For a more tranquil outdoor experience, you can visit another nearby state park property, the Little Spokane Natural Area. A six-mile hiking trail follows the bank of the Little Spokane River, and there are put-in/take-out spots for canoers and kayakers.

Washington 155

YAKIMA SPORTSMAN
Yakima Sportsman State Park

Location: South-central Washington east of Yakima.

Access: From Interstate 82 Exit 34 (3 miles southeast of Yakima), travel east on Washington State Highway 24 for 0.8 mile; turn north (left) onto Keyes Road and continue for 1 mile; turn west (left) onto Gun Club Road and proceed 0.3 mile to the park; the campground is toward the south end of the park.

Facilities: 64 campsites, including 36 with full hookups; (2 hike-bike/primitive sites are also available); sites are small to medium-sized, level, with nominal separation; parking pads are paved or gravel, medium to long straight-ins or pull-throughs, some are spacious enough for very large vehicles; excellent tent-pitching opportunities; fireplaces; b-y-o firewood; water at hookups and at several faucets; restrooms with showers; holding tank disposal station; paved driveways; complete supplies and services are available in Yakima.

Activities & Attractions: Fishing on the river; fishing on the stocked ponds (limited to children); nice playground; birding (nearly 12 dozen species have been identified in the area, plus the resident gaggle of geese); fishing; canoeing and rafting; day use area with shelters.

Natural Features: Located on a large, grassy flat along the east bank of the Yakima River; some campsites receive light to medium shade from large hardwoods and a few conifers; one group of campsites is on an open grassy area; 5 small ponds and lakes and a small stream (Blue Slough Creek) are within the park; the park is bordered by orchards and bunchgrass plains; Yakima Ridge lies to the north and the Rattlesnake Hills to the south; the park includes a total of 3 miles of water frontage on the river, stream and ponds; elevation 1100'.

Season, Fees & Phone: Open all year, with limited services October to April; please see Appendix for standard Washington state park fees; 10 day limit; park office (509) 575-2774.

Camp Notes: The park was originally established in 1940 when the Yakima Sportsman's Association purchased the land as a means of providing an area near the city which would promote better management of natural resources. Thanks to the Yakima Valley's semi-arid climate it gets pretty warm during the summer (daytime highs are typically in the dry 90's), so the nicely shaded camp spots offer a welcome respite from the more or less continuous sunshine. (B-y-o shade or a/c in case you get one of the sunnier campsites.)

Washington 156

WANAPUM
Ginkgo/Wanapum State Park

Location: Central Washington east of Ellensburg.

Access: From Interstate 90 Exit 136 for Vantage (28 miles east of Ellensburg, 40 miles west of Moses Lake), turn south onto a paved local road and drive 2.7 miles; turn east (left) onto the park access road and continue for 0.3 mile to the campground.

Facilities: 50 campsites with full hookups, in 2 loops; sites are fairly large, level or nearly so, with nominal separation; parking pads are packed/oiled gravel straight-ins or pull-through's, spacious enough to accommodate very large rv's; plenty of space for tents; fireplaces; b-y-o firewood; water at sites and at several faucets; restrooms with showers; paved driveways; gas and groceries in Vantage, 3 miles north; complete supplies and services are available in Ellensburg.

Activities & Attractions: Boating; boat launch and dock; a trail leads from the campground down to the river; swimming beach; fishing; Ginkgo Petrified Forest Interpretive Center and nature trail north of Vantage.

Natural Features: Located on a shelf overlooking the west bank of the Columbia River; campground vegetation consists of expansive sections of mown grass dotted with hardwoods and some evergreens, and bordered by rows of poplars planted as a windbreak; campsites receive minimal to light shade;

tremendous views of the Columbia River to the east, north and south; bordered by high, rocky, treeless bluffs which flank the river; elevation 600'.

Season, Fees & Phone: Open all year; please see Appendix for standard Washington state park fees; 10 day limit; park office (509) 856-2700.

Camp Notes: Considering the surrounding terrain--rocky, sage-covered bluffs, hills and flatlands--the park is a great stop for Central Washington travelers. The seemingly ceaseless wind funnels down through the deep, semi-arid valley, so you can usually count on some air movement for summer cooling. And even when the leaves are off the trees and the grass is golden instead of green, this actually makes a good, temperate, winter stop as well.

Washington 157

POTHOLES
Potholes State Park

Location: Central Washington south of Moses Lake.

Access: From Interstate 90 Exit 164 for Dodson Road, (15 miles west of Moses Lake), head south on Dodson Road for 9.9 miles to a 4-way intersection at the north base of a long line of hills; turn east (left) onto Frenchman Hills Road and proceed east, then south, for 4.8 miles to a "T" intersection; turn east (left) onto O'Sullivan Dam Road and travel 5.8 miles; turn north (left) onto the park access road and proceed 0.25 mile to the park entrance; continue ahead for 0.1 mile, then turn left and proceed 0.5 mile to the hookup camp; or continue north for 0.4 mile to the standard camp loop.

Alternate Access: From Interstate 90 (westbound), Exit 179 for Moses Lake/Othello, travel south on Washington State Highway 17 for 9.5 miles; turn west (right) onto O'Sullivan Dam Road and proceed 12 miles to a point 0.1 mile past the settlement on the west end of O'Sullivan Dam; turn north (right) onto the park access road and continue as above. **Alternate Alternate Access:** From Washington State Highway 26 at milepost 25 +.3 (8 miles east of Royal City, 15 miles west of Othello), turn north onto Road A-SE and proceed 12.8 miles north and east to the park access road and continue as above. (Note: All roads are paved; unless you're approaching from the south, e.g., the Tri-Cities, the first Access given above is probably your best bet from the standpoint of efficiently using miles and minutes.)

Facilities: 126 campsites, including 60 with full hookups; sites are small+ to medium-sized, with minimal to fair separation; parking pads are short, gravel straight-ins for standard sites, paved, level, medium+ straight-ins for hookup sites; ample space for large tents in most sites; fireplaces; b-y-o firewood; water at hookup sites and at central faucets; restrooms with showers; holding tank disposal station; paved driveways in the hookup camp, gravel driveways in the tent camp; gas and groceries in the settlement just east of the park.

Activities & Attractions: Boating; boat launches; fishing for trout, bass, perch, crappie, bluegill, walleye; day use area.

Natural Features: Located on gently sloping terrain near the southwest shore of Potholes Reservoir; hookup camp has watered and mown grass and rows of tall hardwoods which provide minimal to light shade and fairly good wind shelter; standard/tent sites have high brush for some wind shelter, b-y-o shade; bordered by sage plains and a miles-long line of hills along the southern boundary of this locale; elevation 1000'.

Season, Fees & Phone: Open all year; please see Appendix for standard Washington state park fees; 10 day limit; park office (509) 765-7271.

Camp Notes: 'Potholes' are hundreds of pock marks in the sand dunes which have filled with water as a result of the raising of the water table following construction of the dam. This region, with its sage plains and seasonally strange odors might remind you of the Salton Sea country in the Southern California desert. However, the hookup camp is far better than anything at the Salton Sea. But the po' folks in the standard/tent camp don't have it so good. If you're a tent/van/pickup camper, it probably would be worth digging deep down into the pockets of your faded jeans for the extra couple of bucks needed to pay the rent on a hookup site. Bring along a coffee maker or a hotplate or a fan so you can use the power post for something, anyway.

Washington 158

CROW BUTTE
Crow Butte State Park

Location: South-central Washington along the Columbia River southwest of Kennewick.

Access: From Washington State Highway 14 at milepost 155 (26 miles west of the junction of Highway 14 & Interstate 82, 54 miles east of the junction of Highway 14 & U.S. 97), turn north and follow the paved access road as it loops around to the east, passes under Highway 14, and continues south across a causeway to the park entrance 1 mile from the highway; continue for another 1.2 miles to the campground.

Facilities: 50 campsites with full hookups; (2 hike-bike/primitive sites and a group camp are also available); sites are small to medium-sized, reasonably level, with minimal separation; parking pads are paved, long straight-ins or pull-throughs; large, gravel tent pads (no tents on the grass); windbreaks for some sites; barbecue grills; b-y-o firewood; water at sites and at several faucets; restrooms with showers; holding tank disposal station; paved driveway; supplies are scarce along Route 14: fill up with gas and groceries before venturing onto this stretch of road.

Activities & Attractions: Large, sand/pebble swimming beach; boating; boat launch, docks and moorage buoys; fishing; hiking trails, including a trail to the top of Crow Butte; day use area with shelters.

Natural Features: Located at the base of 671' Crow Butte, on an island in Lake Umatilla on the Columbia River; vegetation consists principally of mown lawns, and hardwoods which provide limited shade for campsites; barren hills and bluffs surround the campground; the area around the perimeter of the park is posted as rattlesnake territory; elevation 300'.

Season, Fees & Phone: Open all year (may be limited to weekends and holidays, November to March); please see Appendix for standard Washington state park fees; 10 day limit; park office (509) 875-2644.

Camp Notes: Far out! That's probably the most concise description for this place. It certainly is an unexpected oasis in this rather desolate, semi-arid country. All campsites have an excellent view of the lake and surrounding terrain.

Washington 159

PLYMOUTH
Lake Umatilla/Corps of Engineers Park

Location: Southern Washington border south of Kennewick.

Access: From Washington State Highway 14 at a point 2 miles west of the Plymouth/Highway 14 Exit on Interstate 82 and 12 miles east of the junction of State Highways 14 & 221 near Paterson, turn south onto a local paved road; continue southerly through the community of Plymouth to Christy Road; turn west onto Christy Road for 0.1 mile to the park entrance; turn south (left) and immediately east into the campground.

Facilities: 32 campsites with partial hookups; sites are small, level, with minimal separation; parking pads are paved, mostly long pull-throughs; ample space for tents on gravel pads or on the grass; fireplaces; b-y-o firewood; restrooms with showers; holding tank disposal station; paved driveways; limited+ supplies and services are available across the river in Umatilla, Oregon.

Activities & Attractions: Boating; boat launch; designated swimming area; fishing for smallmouth bass, walleye, sturgeon; large day use area nearby; McNary Dam Visitor Center is located across the Columbia River, in Oregon.

Natural Features: Located on the north bank of the Columbia River/Lake Umatilla just west of McNary Dam; vegetation in the campground consists mainly of tall hardwoods, bushes and mown grass; dry, rocky ridges parallel the river on the north and south; the campground is just onshore of Lake Umatilla, created by John Day Dam nearly 100 miles downriver of this point; elevation 300'.

Season, Fees & Phone: May to October, with limited pre- and post- season availability; $12.00; 14 day limit; Corps of Engineers John Day Project Office, The Dalles, OR, (503) 296-1181.

Camp Notes: Plymouth Park is a patch of fertility in this otherwise dry region of southern Washington. Trees and shrubs have been planted to provide each site with a small measure of separation from the driveway and neighboring campers. Broad vistas of the river and surrounding area are available from this riverside park.

Washington 160

HOOD
Lake Sacajawea/Corps of Engineers Park

Location: Southeast Washington southeast of Pasco.

Access: From Washington State Highway 124 at a point 0.2 mile east of the junction of Highway 124 and U.S. 12/395 (3 miles southeast of Pasco), turn north onto a paved park access road and proceed 0.3 mile to the campground.

Facilities: 69 campsites with electrical hookups; sites are medium to large, with minimal to fair separation; parking pads are paved, medium to long, and most are fairly level; good, grassy tent spots; fireplaces or barbecue grills; b-y-o firewood; water at several faucets; restrooms with showers; holding tank disposal station; paved driveways; complete supplies and services are available in the Tri-Cities area (Richland-Pasco-Kennewick).

Activities & Attractions: Foot trails; playground; an adjacent day use area, on a level sheltered riverbank, has picnic shelters, barbecue grills, playground, boat ramp and swimming beach; interpretive center at nearby Sacajawea State Park; Juniper Dunes Wilderness Area is located 10 miles north off Highway 395.

Natural Features: Located on the south bank of the Snake River at its confluence with the Columbia River; the camping area is on a low, grassy hill dotted with large hardwoods; dry bluffs rise across the lake; elevation 400'.

Season, Fees & Phone: April to October; $11.00 for a site, $5.00 for overflow camping; 14 day limit; Corps of Engineers Ice Harbor Dam Project Office, Pasco, (509) 547-7781.

Camp Notes: Hood Park offers an amiable camping facility very close to the Tri-Cities urban area. From an engineering standpoint, the campsites here overlook the Snake River Arm of Lake Wallula, formed by McNary Dam on the Columbia River 50 miles downstream. The entire Columbia-Snake River System has been dammed for flood-control and irrigation purposes. Hood Park is the last camp on the Snake River, at the point where the Snake loses the last traces of its own identity.

Washington 161

CHARBONNEAU
Lake Sacajawea/Corps of Engineers Park

Location: Southeast Washington east of Pasco.

Access: From Washington State Highway 124 at milepost 8 +.5 (10 miles east of Pasco, 38 miles west of Waitsburg), turn north onto Sun Harbor Drive; drive 1.7 miles north to the park entrance and a fork; take the right fork for 0.5 mile to the camping area.

Facilities: 54 campsites, including 36 with electrical hookups and 18 with full hookups; hookups; sites are medium-sized, with minimal separation; parking pads are paved, fairly level, some are long enough for large rv's; grassy tent areas, many of them on a slight slope; fireplaces and/or barbecue grills; b-y-o firewood; water at several faucets; restrooms with showers; holding tank disposal station; paved driveways; limited supplies at a nearby marina, complete supplies and services are available in the Tri-Cities area.

Activities & Attractions: Boating; fishing; swimming; large day use area, adjacent, with tall hardwoods and picnic shelters; playground; Ice Harbor Dam Visitor Center is located 2 miles west.

Natural Features: Located just east of Ice Harbor Dam which forms Lake Sacajawea on the Snake River; campsites are all on a hilltop overlooking the water and a natural jetty which protrudes into the lake; some hardwoods dot the manicured lawn, but the camping area is still quite exposed to sun and wind; most sites have views of the lake and bluffs on the opposite shore; elevation 500'.

Season, Fees & Phone: Open all year, with limited services November to March; $11.00 for an electrical hookup site, $12.00 for a full hookup site, $5.00 for overflow camping; 14 day limit; Corps of Engineers Ice Harbor Dam Project Office, Pasco, (509) 547-7781.

Camp Notes: Situated on a breezy hill overlooking the Snake River, this campground offers vast views of the countryside in all directions. The park is named for Pierre Charbonneau, the French-Canadian member of the Lewis and Clark Expedition and husband of Sacajawea, the Shoshone person who guided the group through Montana and Idaho.

Washington 162

FISHHOOK
Lake Sacajawea/Corps of Engineers Park

Location: Southeast Washington east of Pasco.

Access: From Washington State Highway 124 at milepost 16 (18 miles east of Pasco, 30 miles west of Waitsburg), turn north onto Page Road; drive 4.5 miles on this paved road (past the park entrance and day use area) to the campground.

Facilities: 76 campsites, including 35 tents-only sites and 41 sites with partial hookups, in one long loop; sites are medium-sized, with nominal separation; parking pads are paved and well leveled, considering the terrain; pads are generally medium-length straight-ins, but a few are pull-throughs long enough for very large rv's; large tent spots; barbecue grills and/or fireplaces; b-y-o firewood; water at central faucets; restrooms with showers; holding tank disposal station; paved driveways; complete supplies and services are available in the Richland-Pasco-Kennewick area.

Activities & Attractions: Boating; boat launch; fishing for steelhead, salmon, bass and catfish; swimming; large day use area with beach, picnic facilities and playground; hiking in adjacent wildlife habitat.

Natural Features: Located on a grassy hillside on the south shore of Lake Sacajawea above Ice Harbor Dam; the dam spans the Snake River to form the lake; park lawns are watered and mown, and dotted with large hardwoods and conifers; rolling, sage-covered hillsides surround the park; dry bluffs border the river; elevation 500'.

Season, Fees & Phone: April to late-September; $9.00 for a tent site, $11.50 for a partial hookup site; 14 day limit; Corps of Engineers Ice Harbor Dam Project Office, Pasco, (509) 547-7781.

Camp Notes: Ice Harbor Dam and subsequent irrigation projects have created a welcome recreational refuge here at Fishhook Park. The grassy hillsides, manicured lawns, boat launch and swimming beach stand in distinct contrast to the surrounding sage-and-orchard covered slopes. A railroad line runs along the edge of the park, so be prepared for possible periodic breaks in the tranquil routine here.

Washington 163

PALOUSE FALLS
Palouse Falls State Park

Location: Southeast Washington north of Walla Walla.

Access: From Washington State Highway 261 at milepost 20 +.6 (15 miles south of Washtucna, 21 miles north of the junction of Highway 261 with U.S. 12), turn east onto a fairly good, wide, gravel road and proceed 2.4 miles to the park.

Facilities: 6 campsites; tents may be pitched on the grass, vehicle campers can park in the main gravel parking area; fireplaces; b-y-o firewood; water at faucets; vault facilities; pack-it-in/pack-it-out system of trash removal; limited supplies are available at Washtucna, 15 miles north.

Activities & Attractions: Falls and canyon viewpoints.

Natural Features: Located on a small, mown grass hill above the rugged Palouse River Canyon; picturesque Palouse Falls drops 190 feet into a deep pool on the opposite side of the canyon from the park; sage and range grass hills comprise most of the surrounding semi-arid terrain; shade trees in the campground; elevation 800'.

Season, Fees & Phone: Open all year, subject to weather conditions; please see Appendix for standard Washington state park fees; 10 day limit; phone c/o Lyons Ferry State Park.

Camp Notes: From here there are terrific views of Palouse Falls as well as the main part of Palouse Canyon to the south. This is a pleasant little spot which usually doesn't see a lot of camping activity. It's a popular place for weekend day-trippers who spend a little time looking at the strikingly beautiful falls pouring over the barren rock walls of the canyon, and then move on.

Washington 164

LYONS FERRY
Lyons Ferry State Park

Location: Southeast Washington north of Walla Walla.

Access: From Washington State Highway 261 at milepost 15 +.4 (15 miles north of the junction of Highway 261 and U.S. Highway 12, 15 miles south of the junction of State Highways 261 and 260 near Washtucna), turn east into the park; continue through the day use area, then turn westerly and pass under the highway bridge into the campground.

Facilities: 50 campsites; (2 hike-bike/primitive sites are also available); sites are small, acceptably level, with minimal to nominal separation; parking pads are gravel, medium-length straight-ins, plus a number of long pull-throughs; adequate space for large tents in most sites; fireplaces; b-y-o firewood; water at faucets throughout; restrooms with showers; holding tank disposal station; paved driveways; camper supplies at a marina across the river; gas and groceries+ are available in Washtucna.

Activities & Attractions: Boating; boat launch and dock; fishing; swimming area with a 400' grassy beach; hiking trail to an overlook; old Lyons Ferry is permanently moored at the north end of the day use area.

Natural Features: Located on a lightly shaded sage flat in a canyon at the confluence of the Palouse and Snake Rivers; high, dry, rocky bluffs and buttes flank the river; elevation 500'.

Season, Fees & Phone: Open all year; please see Appendix for standard Washington state park fees; 10 day limit; park office (509) 646-3252.

Camp Notes: This is rugged, sparsely populated country around here, but nonetheless very interesting in its semi-desolation. The beautifully landscaped and maintained day use area is a big bonus for campers. And the park *usually* isn't very crowded.

Washington 165

CENTRAL FERRY
Central Ferry State Park

Location: Southeast Washington northeast of Walla Walla.

Access: From Washington State Highway 127 at milepost 10 +.1 (just north of the Snake River Bridge, 10 miles north of Dodge, 17 miles south of the junction of State Highways 127 & 26 near Dusty), turn west onto a paved park access road; proceed 0.8 mile to the campground.

Facilities: 60 campsites with full hookups, in 6 loops; (2 hike-bike/primitive sites are also available); sites are small+ to medium-sized, level, with nominal separation; parking pads are paved, medium to long straight-ins; ample space for large tents; windbreaks for most sites; fireplaces; b-y-o firewood; water at sites and at central faucets; restrooms with showers; holding tank disposal station; gas and camper supplies at a small store, 3 miles south; limited+ supplies and services are available in Pomeroy, 17 miles southeast.

Activities & Attractions: Swimming; boating; boat launch and docks; fishing (said to be good for bass and catfish); hiking; day use area with shelters.

Natural Features: Located on a large flat on the north shore of Lake Bryan, a 10,000-acre reservoir on the Snake River; landscaping consists of watered and mown lawns, and a variety of hardwoods and conifers which provide very light to light shade for campsites; high bluffs border the river; elevation 600'.

Season, Fees & Phone: Open all year; please see Appendix for standard Washington state park fees; 10 day limit; park office (509) 549-3551 or (509) 549-3678.

Camp Notes: Central Ferry is another of the dozen or more very nice oasis places on the drylands east of the Cascades. (Considering how many thousands of square miles in Central and Southeast Washington are in the semi-arid climatic category, it sometimes makes you wonder how they coined the state motto "The Evergreen State". Ed.)

Washington 166

LEWIS AND CLARK TRAIL
Lewis and Clark Trail State Park

Location: Southeast Washington north of Walla Walla.

Access: From U.S. Highway 12 at milepost 362 (5 miles west of Dayton, 4.5 miles east of Waitsburg), turn north into the campground.

Facilities: 30 campsites; (4 hike-bike/primitive sites and a group camp are also available); most sites are small to medium-sized, level, with fair to excellent separation; parking pads are gravel/earth, medium-length straight-ins; small to medium-sized tent areas; fireplaces; b-y-o firewood; water at several faucets; restrooms with showers; holding tank disposal station; paved driveways; limited+ supplies and services are available in Dayton and Waitsburg.

Activities & Attractions: Self-guiding three-quarter mile nature trail with the theme "Food, Fuel and Medicine"; (a good guide pamphlet is available); 1 mile of hiking trails; sports field; amphitheater for summer campfire programs.

Natural Features: Located along and near the south bank of the Touchet River; campsites are generally well-shaded/sheltered and some are tucked into their own little alcoves of hardwoods and some conifers and lots of underbrush; bordered by grassy, rolling hills and agricultural land; elevation 1000'.

Season, Fees & Phone: Open all year, with limited services October to April; please see Appendix for standard Washington state park fees; 10 day limit; park office (509) 337-6457.

Camp Notes: The Lewis and Clark Expedition traveled through this valley in May of 1806, thus the name for the park. The setting for this campground is really a surprise, considering the comparatively barren hillsides of the surrounding terrain. The dense vegetation along the river, particularly around some of the campsites, might remind you of parks much closer to the Coast.

Washington 167

FORT WALLA WALLA
Walla Walla City Park

Location: South-central Washington in Walla Walla.

Access: From Washington State Highway 125 at the southwest corner of Walla Walla (on the west side of the highway opposite the fairgrounds and the Plaza Shopping Center), turn west onto Dalles-Military Road (also called just "Military Road"); continue west/southwest for 0.8 mile to the park. (You can't miss it--a pair of large cannons flank the entrance!)

Facilities: Approximately 30 campsites, some with partial hookups; sites are generally medium-sized, level, with very little separation; parking pads are gravel, and spacious enough to accommodate larger vehicles; lots of large, grassy tent-pitching spots; fire rings; b-y-o firewood; water at several faucets; restrooms with showers; holding tank disposal station; gravel driveways; complete supplies and services are available within 1 mile in Walla Walla.

Activities & Attractions: Old Fort Walla Walla Museum, just to the north of the campground, can be reached via a foot bridge across the creek; county fair held in late August.

Natural Features: Located on watered and mown grass lawns ringed by tall hardwoods; a little creek separates the campground and a day use area; rv sites have somewhat less shelter/shade than tent units; bordered by hilly plains and cropland; elevation 800'.

Season, Fees & Phone: Open all year; principal season is May September; limited services and reduced fees remainder of the year; $8.50 for a standard site, $11.00 for a partial-hookup site; more than 4 people per site, $1.00 each; 7 day limit in season; reservations accepted by mail (call the office for a reservation form); park office (509) 527-3770.

Camp Notes: This is a nicely landscaped and maintained park, somewhat superior to many other municipal campgrounds. Its proximity to all the services of Walla Walla will be considered an advantage by many campers. The adjacent museum is excellent.

Washington 168

CHIEF TIMOTHY
Chief Timothy State Park

Location: Southeast corner of Washington west of Clarkston.

Access: From U.S. Highway 12 at milepost 425 +.9 (8 miles west of Clarkston, 21 miles east of Pomeroy), turn north, proceed across the causeway to the park; turn east (right) and go 0.1 mile to the campground.

Facilities: 66 campsites, including 33 with full hookups and 16 park 'n walk tent sites; sites are medium-sized, with minimal separation; most parking pads are paved, level, long pull-throughs; excellent, grassy tent sites; fireplaces; firewood is usually for sale, or b-y-o; water at hookups and at several faucets; restrooms with showers; holding tank disposal station; paved driveways; complete supplies and services are available in the Lewiston-Clarkston area.

Activities & Attractions: Boating; boat launch and docks; really nice playground ("Tot Lot"); pebble and sand swimming beach; interpretive center; day use area.

Natural Features: Located on an island in Lower Granite Lake, an impoundment on the Snake River; planted pines and hardwoods on watered and mown lawns provide very light to light-medium shade; bordered by high, rocky hills and bluffs; elevation 700'.

Season, Fees & Phone: Open all year; please see Appendix for standard Washington state park fees; 10 day limit; park office (509) 758-9580.

Camp Notes: All campsites have quite a spectacular view. In summer, the park stands in rich green contrast to the rugged, nearly treeless bluffs which border the river. The campground stretches for nearly a half mile along the south shore of the island. Several docks are located along the island's shore line, so you can tie-up to within arm's length of your campsite.

FIELDS SPRING
Fields Spring State Park

Location: Southeast corner of Washington south of Clarkston.

Access: From Washington State Highway 129 at milepost 14 (0.5 mile south of Rattlesnake Summit, 26 miles south of Clarkston, 56 miles north of Enterprise, Oregon), turn east onto the paved park access road, and proceed 0.6 mile to the park; continue for 0.1 mile past the day use area to the campground.

Facilities: 20 campsites; sites are small to medium-sized, with minimal separation; parking pads are gravel, fairly level, mostly straight-ins, plus several long pull-throughs; small to medium-sized tent areas; (probably a little more suitable for vehicle camping than for tents); fireplaces; some firewood may be available for gathering near the park, b-y-o is recommended; water at faucets; restrooms with showers; holding tank disposal station; paved driveways; gas and groceries in Anatone, 3.5 miles north; complete supplies and services are available in the Lewiston-Clarkston area, 26 miles north.

Activities & Attractions: 1 mile hiking trail to the summit of Puffer Butte; nature trail; cross-country skiing, sledding; small day use area with shelters.

Natural Features: Located on moderately timbered, hilly terrain on the east slope of the Blue Mountains high above the Grande Ronde River; about half of the camp spots are somewhat sheltered/shaded by tall conifers, the remainder are in the open; moderately to heavily forested hills and low mountains lie in the surrounding area; more precipitation here than elsewhere in the region; elevation 3900'.

Season, Fees & Phone: Open all year, with limited services October to April; please see Appendix for standard Washington state park fees; 10 day limit; park office (509) 256-3332.

Camp Notes: If you prefer campgrounds with a natural appeal (versus those with the planted, groomed, and paved look) this place should please you very much. There's a breathtaking (quite literally) steep, winding, 10 mile drive through the 3000-foot deep Grande Ronde Canyon on State Highway 129 just south of the park. Should you approach from that direction, allow *plenty* of time for the trip. If the numerous steep curves don't slow you down, the super scenery certainly will.

Oregon

Public Campgrounds

The Oregon map is located in the Appendix.

Oregon 1

FORT STEVENS
Fort Stevens State Park

Location: Northwest corner of Oregon southwest of Astoria.

Access: From U.S. Highway 101 (southbound) at milepost 6 + .4 (on the northeast edge of the city of Warrenton near the south end of the bridge/causeway which crosses Youngs Bay, 5 miles southwest of Astoria), turn west onto East Harbor Drive; proceed toward midtown Warrenton, then pick up North Main Avenue and continue generally northwesterly (toward the community of Hammond) as North Main curves and becomes NW Warrenton Drive, and finally Pacific Drive for a total of 4.4 miles from U.S. 101; at the intersection of Pacific Drive and Ridge Road; turn south (left) onto Ridge Road and proceed 1 mile, then turn west (right) for 0.2 mile to campground.

Alternate Access: From U.S. 101 (northbound) at milepost 9 + .2 on the north edge of the Camp Rilea Military Reservation, turn west, then immediately north and proceed (on what should be a well-signed route to the park) northwesterly on Ridge Road for a total of 4.6 miles to the campground entrance, on the west (left) side of the road. (Note: From a distance, the above instructions may seem a bit fuzzy; but once you arrive in the area and find the highway turnoff points at their appropriate mileposts, the routes should become clear to you.)

Facilities: 605 campsites, including 130 with partial hookups and 213 with full hookups, in 15 loops; (8 small group tent camps are also available); sites are generally small, level, with minimal to fair separation; parking pads are paved, short to medium-length straight-ins or medium to long pull-throughs; medium to large tent areas; water at sites and at several faucets in each loop; restrooms with showers; paved driveways; adequate+ supplies and services are available in the Warrenton/Hammond area.

Activities & Attractions: Fort Stevens Historical Center features self-guided tours of the shore batteries which defended the mouth of the Columbia River for nearly 100 years, and a museum with military items and interpretive exhibits; several miles of ocean beach; 7 miles of paved bicycle trails; 5 miles of hiking trails; wreck of the Peter Iredale, a sailing ship which ran aground in 1906; swimming areas, fishing for trout and perch, and limited (10 mph) boating on Coffenbury Lake; fishing at the South Jetty on the northwest tip of the park; large day use areas.

Natural Features: Located on a peninsula near the Pacific Ocean at the mouth of the Columbia River; campground vegetation consists of dense stands of hardwoods, conifers and shrubbery; remaining sections of the park consist mostly of grass-covered dunes and miles of beach; small Coffenbury Lake is adjacent to the campground; sea level.

Season, Fees & Phone: Open all year; please see Appendix for standard Oregon state park fees; 10 day limit; park office (503) 861-1671.

Camp Notes: Detailed park maps are displayed at several points in order to help you get your bearings once you arrive. They'll come in handy. Fort Stevens' 4000 acres place it at the top of the list as the roomiest Oregon state park, and its 600+ campsites make it the third-largest public campground in the West. Among the historical exhibits is Battery Russell, a shore gun emplacement which was shelled by a Japanese sub in WWII. It is the only installation on the U.S. mainland to have been attacked by a foreign power since the War of 1812.

Oregon 2

SADDLE MOUNTAIN
Saddle Mountain State Park

Location: Northwest Oregon southeast of Seaside.

Access: From U.S. Highway 26 at milepost 10 + .15 (10 miles southeast of the junction of U.S. 26 & U.S. 101 south of Seaside, 11 miles northwest of Elsie) turn north onto the paved park access road and proceed 7.1 miles to the park and the campground.

Facilities: 10 park n' walk tent sites scattered about the hillside; sites are small+ to medium+, with minimal to good separation; medium to large, generally level, space for tents; fireplaces; ample firewood is available for gathering along the access road, but may be wet; water at several faucets; restrooms; parking in a paved lot; gas and groceries are available in Elsie.

Activities & Attractions: 4-mile hiking trail to the summit of Saddle Mountain.

Natural Features: Located near the base of 3283' Saddle Mountain in the Coast Range; park vegetation consists of tall conifers and hardwoods, and some underbrush which provide adequate shelter/shade for campsites; elevation 1650'.

Season, Fees & Phone: Open all year, subject to weather conditions; please see Appendix for standard Oregon state park fees; 10 day limit; phone c/o Fort Stevens State Park (503) 861-1671.

Camp Notes: Many, perhaps a majority, of visitors come here to take the trail up Saddle Mountain. The trail isn't the West's best for a casual hiker: much of the route to the summit is steep and precarious. A good hiker's efforts, however, will be rewarded with compelling views of Northwest Oregon, Southwest Washington and the Pacific Ocean.

Oregon 3

OSWALD WEST
Oswald West State Park

Location: Northern Oregon Coast north of Manzanita.

Access: From U.S. Highway 101 at milepost 39 +.3 (4 miles north of Manzanita, 10 miles south of Cannon Beach) turn west off the highway into the campground parking lot.

Facilities: 36 walk-in tent campsites, accessible via a somewhat steep, paved, 0.3-mile trail from the parking lot; (hand carts are available to help pack equipment up and down the trail); adequate space for medium to large tents; water at several faucets; restrooms; limited supplies and services are available in Manzanita.

Activities & Attractions: Trail to the beach (approximately 0.7 mile) from the campground; Oregon Coast Trail extends north and south from here for a total of 64 miles along the Pacific Ocean; good views of the Cape Falcon area from the beach.

Natural Features: Located in a coastal rain forest near the Pacific Ocean; Sand Creek flows along the north side of the campground; sea level.

Season, Fees & Phone: April to October; please see Appendix for standard Oregon state park fees; 10 day limit; park office (503) 368-5153.

Camp Notes: The park's major recreational item of interest is its strikingly beautiful and unique campground, and the hiking trails provide plenty of exploring opportunities on the beach. "Os West" (named for an Oregon governor of the early 1900's), was one of the first parks developed in the state. Neat place.

Oregon 4

NEHALEM BAY
Nehalem Bay State Park

Location: Northern Oregon Coast north of Tillamook.

Access: From U.S. Highway 101 at milepost 43 +.9 at the south edge of the community of Manzanita (25 miles north of Tillamook, 23 miles south of Seaside), turn south onto Necarney City Road and proceed 0.25 mile to a fork; turn west (right) and continue west, then south, for 1.7 miles to the park entrance; the campground is to the right.

Facilities: 292 campsites with partial hookups, in 6 loops; sites are small to small+, level, with nominal to fairly good separation; parking pads are paved, short to medium+ straight-ins; medium to large, grassy tent spots; special areas for hiker-biker and equestrian camping; fire rings; firewood is usually for sale, or b-y-o; water at each site; several restrooms with showers; holding tank disposal station; paved driveways; limited supplies and services are available in Manzanita and Nehalem.

Activities & Attractions: Short trails (some paved) up and over the dunes to the beach from the camp areas; bike trails; equestrian trails; beachcombing; very good crabbing, clamming, fishing on the bay; boat launch; recreational/meeting hall; 2400' paved airstrip.

Natural Features: Located on 4-mile-long Nehalem Bay Spit, a long, slender, fairly level peninsula which forms the ocean-side landmass of long, narrow Nehalem Bay; campsites are lightly shaded and fairly well wind-sheltered by small to medium-height, pines and shrubs; a grass-covered dune separates the camp areas from the beach which extends the full length of the spit; high, forested coastal mountains nearly surround the bay; sea level.

Season, Fees & Phone: April to November; please see Appendix for standard Oregon state park fees; 10 day limit; park office (503) 368-5943.

Camp Notes: There are some excellent Coast Range views from the park, particularly from certain camp loops. If you're planning on camping, you might check out Loops D, E, and F for a bit more privacy and better views.

Oregon 5

BARVIEW JETTY
Tillamook County Park

Location: Northern Oregon Coast north of Tillamook.

Access: From U.S. Highway 101 at milepost 53 +.7 in the hamlet of Barview (2 miles north of Garibaldi, 3 miles south of Rockaway), turn west onto Cedar Avenue, cross the railroad tracks and proceed 0.15 mile, then turn north (right) into the campground.

Facilities: 156 campsites, including 31 sites with full hookups, in 2 sections; the standard campsites are in a sand/grass loop, and most sites will accommodate tents; sand/gravel parking pads; the hookup area is in somewhat of a 'parking lot' arrangement; fire rings; b-y-o firewood; water at several faucets; restrooms with showers; holding tank disposal station; paved driveways; limited supplies in Garibaldi and Rockaway; adequate+ supplies and services are available in Tillamook, 11 miles south.

Activities & Attractions: Beachcombing; fishing; large sandy children's play area.

Natural Features: Located on a long, windswept flat at the north end of Tillamook Bay, near an ocean beach; a rock jetty extends several hundred yards into the ocean; lots of tall conifers plus smaller hardwoods shelter most of the campground; the hookup area is more open, but has trees every few sites; a few sites are close to the beach; sea level.

Season, Fees & Phone: Open all year; $7.00 for a standard site, $10.00 for a full-hookup site; 14 day limit; Tillamook County Parks, Garibaldi, (503) 322-3477.

Camp Notes: Just south of the park are good views of Tillamook Bay. This campground, which stretches for about a half mile along the shore, looks a lot like a typical Coastal Oregon state park. The facilities are perhaps a little more rustic, however. For about the same amount of money, you might consider Nehalem Bay State Park, a dozen miles north.

Oregon 6

KILCHIS
Tillamook County Park

Location: Northern Oregon coastal area northeast of Tillamook.

Access: From U.S. Highway 101 at milepost 63 +.1 (3 miles north of Tillamook, 2 miles south of Bay City), turn east/southeast onto Alderbrook Road (paved) and proceed 1 mile to a "T" intersection; turn easterly onto Kilchis River Road (paved) and continue for 4 miles to the the campground.

Facilities: 30 campsites in 1 large loop; sites are small to medium-sized, level, with minimal to fair separation; most sites have grass/dirt/gravel parking pads and large grassy tent spots; fire rings; some firewood is available for gathering, b-y-o is suggested; water at several faucets; restrooms; paved driveway; adequate+ supplies and services are available in Tillamook.

Activities & Attractions: Huge recreation area in the center of the park/campground: facilities include volleyball courts, horseshoe pits, and a large children's playground.

Natural Features: Located in a deep, narrow valley on a large flat overlooking the Kilchis River; campsites are situated around the heavily wooded perimeter of the park, and encircle a large, open recreation area; vegetation consists primarily of tall conifers and maple, plus other low-level hardwoods; the campground is several miles inland from the ocean; elevation 150'.

Season, Fees & Phone: April to October; $6.00; 14 day limit; Tillamook County Parks, Garibaldi, (503) 322-3477.

Camp Notes: The environment here differs from most of the other campgrounds in the coastal area, since it isn't right on the sea, but rather is in the coastal mountains. Very popular with the locals, the campground is also a favorite spot of parents with children. The park is named after Chief Kilchis, a cooperative Indian leader who maintained the peace in the county during the early days of settlement.

CAPE LOOKOUT
Cape Lookout State Park

Location: Northern Oregon Coast southwest of Tillamook.

Access: From U.S. Highway 101 in midtown Tillamook, turn west onto Third Street and travel 1.8 miles to the west end of the Tillamook River Bridge and a fork; take the left fork and continue south/southwest along the river, up and over the mountain, past the turnoff to Netarts, where you'll pick up Cape Lookout Road (the Three Capes Scenic Route) and continue southwesterly along Netarts Bay for another 10.5 miles; turn west (right) into the park entrance; just beyond the entrance, turn north into the campground.

Facilities: 250 campsites, including 53 with full hookups; (4 group camp areas and a hiker-biker camp are also available); sites are generally small to small+, closely spaced and semi-private; parking pads are paved, mostly level, short to long straight-ins; no extra vehicles permitted in campsite; large grassy tent areas; fireplaces; firewood is usually for sale, or b-y-o; water at faucets throughout; restrooms with showers; waste water basins; holding tank disposal station; paved driveways; gas and groceries in Netarts, 5 miles north; adequate+ supplies and services are available in Tillamook.

Activities & Attractions: Short trails from the camp areas to the beach; nature trail; 7 miles of hiking trails in the area; recreational/meeting hall; amphitheater; day use areas, shelter.

Natural Features: Located in a moderately to heavily forested area made up mostly of tall conifers; excellent Pacific Ocean beach; the park is at the juncture of a rugged peninsula which extends nearly 2 miles into the sea, and a spit which serves as a natural, 5-mile-long 'breakwater' for Netarts Bay; bordered by heavily timbered hills and mountains; sea level.

Season, Fees & Phone: Open all year; please see Appendix for standard Oregon state park fees; 10 day limit; campsite reservations recommended for summer weekends and holidays, please see Appendix; park office (503) 842-3182 or (503) 842-4981.

Camp Notes: Cape Lookout is one of the most remote coastal parks--and looks the part. There's an outstanding roadside viewpoint of the cape, the spit, and the bay from the top of a hill a mile south of the park. If the popular campground here is filled when you arrive in the area, you may be able to get a spot at the large Siuslaw National Forest campground 8 miles south of here at Sandlake (see info below).

SAND BEACH
Siuslaw National Forest

Location: Northern Oregon Coast southwest of Tillamook.

Access: From U.S. Highway 101 at a point 11 miles south of Tillamook, 3.2 miles north of Beaver and 6 miles north of Hebo, turn west onto Sandlake Road/Tillamook County Road 871 (paved) and travel west then south for 5.5 miles to the community of Sandlake; turn west (right) onto County Road 872 (paved, might be signed for "Sandlake Park & Dunes") for 2.4 miles (there's a sharp left turn after the first mile) to the campground.

Facilities: 101 campsites; (camping for about 50 vehicles in each of 2 nearby paved parking lots, with drinking water and restrooms, is also available); sites are medium to large, level, with minimal to fairly good separation; parking pads are paved, medium to long straight-ins, most are extra wide; large tent areas; fire rings; b-y-o firewood; water at several faucets; restrooms; paved driveways; gas and camper supplies in Sandlake; adequate+ supplies and services are available in Tillamook.

Activities & Attractions: Dune riding/orv driving; (street-legal vehicles or registered orv's only); 600 acres of national forest dunes, plus 300 acres of adjacent state and county land are available for orv use; crabbing; day use area.

Natural Features: Located in an area of sand dunes on a point near the Pacific Ocean; sites are lightly shaded/sheltered by small pines, bushes and tall grass; Sand Lake is actually a small, shallow bay off the ocean; bordered by sand dunes, forested hills, bluffs, and mountains; sea level.

Season, Fees & Phone: May to October for standard campground; parking lot camping is open all year; $9.00 for a standard site, $6.00 for a parking lot site; extra $5.00 entry permit is required from the ranger station *prior* to summer holidays or holiday weekends (Memorial Day, Independence Day, Labor Day); (cost for camping is thus $5.00 for the entry permit good for the entire holiday period, plus the fee for each night's camping); 10 day limit; Hebo Ranger District (503) 392-3161.

Camp Notes: Sand Beach Campground is most-often used by orv pilots and their pit crews. It also presents a viable option to any camper who can't get a site at Cape Lookout State Park. A designated "Quiet Zone" helps prevent camper-to-camper confrontations. "Quiet" is a relative term on holiday weekends. From 2000 to 4000 recreationers pack this area on summer holidays. The Access (above) is the most direct route to Sand Beach from U.S. 101 for both northbound and southbound travelers. If you have the time, we suggest you take the well-signed Three Capes Scenic Route. The Three Capes byway can be picked up in midtown Tillamook for southbound travelers and from near milepost 91, 7 miles north of Neskowin, for northbound campers. On the way into or out of the campground, allow some time to stop at one or more of the viewpoints and tiny coastal communities along the way. They're virtually guaranteed to hold your attention for a while.

Oregon 9

HEBO LAKE
Siuslaw National Forest

Location: Northern Oregon coastal area south of Tillamook.

Access: From U.S. Highway 101 in midtown Hebo (near the national forest ranger station, 17 miles south of Tillamook), travel northeasterly then easterly on Forest Road 14 (paved, very steep and winding) for 5 miles, then turn south (right) into the campground.

Facilities: 16 campsites; sites are small to medium-sized, with good separation; parking pads are gravel, mostly medium-length straight-ins, plus a few pull-offs; many pads may require additional leveling; enough room for small to medium-sized tents; fire rings; firewood is available for gathering in the vicinity; water at several faucets; vault facilities; gravel driveway; gas and groceries in Hebo; adequate+ supplies and services are available in Tillamook.

Activities & Attractions: Fishing; hiking trail.

Natural Features: Located on the side of 3200' Mount Hebo near the shore of 3-acre Hebo Lake; vegetation consists of dense conifers and hardwoods; elevation 1700'.

Season, Fees & Phone: May to September; $6.00; 14 day limit; Hebo Ranger District (503) 392-3161.

Camp Notes: Fishing is said to be quite good shortly after the lake's periodic planting with trout, then fair at other times. The campground is most often used by residents of the Willamette Valley who come up to this forested, cool, often rainy spot to get away from the summer heat on the other side of the Coast Range.

Oregon 10

DEVIL'S LAKE
Devil's Lake State Park

Location: Central Oregon Coast in Lincoln City.

Access: From U.S. Highway 101 at milepost 114 + .7 in Lincoln City, turn east onto North 6th Drive and proceed 0.1 mile, then turn south into the campground.

Facilities: 100 campsites, including 32 with full hookups; sites are small to small+, essentially level, with nominal to fairly good separation; most parking pads are paved, short straight-ins; hookup units generally can accommodate larger rv's; medium-sized, grassy tent areas; hiker-biker camp near the entrance; fireplaces; firewood is usually for sale, or b-y-o; water at faucets throughout; waste water receptacles; restrooms with solar showers; adequate+ supplies and services are available in Lincoln City.

Activities & Attractions: Boating; boat launch and large dock facility nearby; fishing on the lake; wide, paved walkways from the campground to the lake; Pacific Ocean beach, within walking distance, across the main highway.

Natural Features: Located a few yards from Devil's Lake, a sizeable body of freshwater connected to the Pacific Ocean by what is locally promoted as "the world's shortest river"--the D River; moderately dense conifers and some hardwoods provide shelter within the campground; sea level.

Season, Fees & Phone: Mid-April to late October; please see Appendix for standard Oregon state park fees; reservations recommended for summer weekends and holidays, please see Appendix; park office (503) 994-2002.

Camp Notes: Lincoln City is the econocenter of what is locally called the "Twenty Miracle Miles". The town's popularity stems in large measure from its proximity to the 50 percent of Oregon's residents who live in the Portland area--and Devil's Lake is one of the most easily accessible of the Oregon coastal campgrounds from that metropolis.

Oregon 11

BEVERLY BEACH
Beverly Beach State Park

Location: Central Oregon Coast north of Newport.

Access: From U.S. Highway 101 at milepost 134 +.1 (7 miles north of Newport, 8 miles south of Depoe Bay), turn east onto the park access road and proceed 0.2 mile to the park entrance and the campground.

Facilities: 279 campsites, including 75 with partial hookups and 52 with full hookups, in 8 loops; (4 small group sites are also available); sites are small to small+, with nominal to fairly good separation; parking pads are paved, acceptably level, short to medium-length straight-ins; some partial-hookup sites have long, pull-through parking pads; framed tent pads in some sites; hiker-biker campsites; fireplaces or fire rings; firewood is usually for sale, or b-y-o; water at faucets throughout; restrooms with showers; waste water receptacles in several locations; holding tank disposal station; complete supplies and services are available in Newport.

Activities & Attractions: Trail to the beach; nature trail; whale watching in season; beachcombing, particularly good during the winter.

Natural Features: Located in a heavily forested area a short distance from the ocean; most campsites are very well sheltered/shaded; Spencer Creek flows past the campground to the ocean; a very long, wide beach is within walking distance; low hills form the eastern backdrop for the park; sea level.

Season, Fees & Phone: Open all year; please see Appendix for standard Oregon state park fees; 10 day limit; park office (503) 265-4560.

Camp Notes: In certain respects, it's curious that Beverly Beach is one of only a handful of state park camps which are open year 'round, since the coastline in the vicinity isn't quite as spectacular as it is near some other parks. Possibly the location is a factor in a different way: campers may consider its proximity to a city the size of Newport to be a highly positive element. (Maybe campers have discovered some choice places in Newport to hang around in during the winter storms which frequently hit the Coast.)

Oregon 12

SOUTH BEACH
South Beach State Park

Location: Central Oregon Coast south of Newport.

Access: From U.S. Highway 101 at milepost 143 +.3 just south of the Yaquina Bay bridge (2 miles south of Newport, 14 miles north of Waldport), turn west onto the park access road and proceed 0.25 mile to the day use areas; turn north (right) for 0.3 mile to the campground.

Facilities: 254 campsites, all with partial hookups, in 7 loops; sites are small to small+, level, with nominal to fair separation; parking pads are paved, medium to long, straight-ins; medium to large, grassy tent spots; hiker-biker camping area; fire rings; firewood is usually for sale, or b-y-o; water at each site; restrooms with showers in each loop; holding tank disposal station; paved driveways; limited supplies on U.S. 101 near the campground; complete supplies and services are available in Newport.

Activities & Attractions: Paved trails to the beach (0.25 mile to 0.75 mile) from the campground; Cooper Ridge Nature Trail; program area with 'natural' seating near the campground; fishing, clamming and crabbing are reportedly very good in and around Yaquina Bay; Oregon State University's Hatfield Marine Science Center, 1 mile north, open daily year 'round, has a museum with educational displays about the ocean.

Natural Features: Located along and near a long, wide, ocean beach; campsites are lightly to moderately shaded/sheltered by short to medium-height evergreens; large infields in some camp loops; sea level.

Season, Fees & Phone: April to October; please see Appendix for standard Oregon state park fees; 10 day limit; park office (503) 867-7451 or (503) 867-4715.

Camp Notes: It might be helpful to have a tarp or awning or even an umbrella when camping at South Beach. Natural protection from the elements is a bit scant in some loops.

BEACHSIDE
Beachside State Park

Location: Central Oregon Coast south of Waldport.

Access: From U.S. Highway 101 at milepost 159 +.3 (3 miles south of Waldport, 5 miles north of Yachats) turn west into the park; the day use area is to the north, the campground is to the south.

Facilities: 81 campsites, including 20 with partial hookups; sites are small to small+, essentially level, with nominal to fairly good separation; parking pads are paved, short to medium-length straight-ins; medium-sized, grassy tent spaces; fire rings; firewood is usually for sale, or b-y-o; water at faucets in several locations; restrooms with solar showers; waste water receptacles; paved driveways; adequate supplies and services are available in Waldport.

Activities & Attractions: Beachcombing; short trails to the beach; fishing, primarily on the Alsea River, 4 miles north, and on the Yachats River, 4 miles south; also clamming and crabbing on Alsea Bay and Yachats Bay.

Natural Features: Located along a Pacific Ocean beach; standard campsites are right along the main highway, hookup campsites are closest to the beach; dense, low to medium-height vegetation separates most of the campsites; lots of shade (if you should need it); large, open, grass-covered recreation areas; a low dune separates the campground from the beach proper; sea level.

Season, Fees & Phone: April to October; please see Appendix for standard Oregon state park fees and reservation information; 10 day limit; park office (503) 563-3220.

Camp Notes: When you come right down to it, there *isn't* a lot to *do* right here. But maybe this is the type of place where it's best just to untether your beach bum instincts. Then when your *amigos* back home ask about your trip to the beach, you can tell them it was a real bummer.

TILLICUM BEACH
Siuslaw National Forest

Location: Central Oregon Coast south of Waldport.

Access: From U.S. Highway 101 at milepost 160 + .5 (4 miles south of Waldport, 30 miles north of Florence), turn west into the campground.

Facilities: 57 campsites; sites are medium to medium+, with fair to excellent separation; most sites have paved, straight-in parking pads, a few have pull-throughs or pull-offs; many pads may require some additional leveling; adequate tent-pitching spots; fireplaces; b-y-o firewood; restrooms; paved driveways; adequate supplies and services are available in Waldport.

Activities & Attractions: Tremendous ocean views; beachcombing, particularly productive during the winter; amphitheater; Siuslaw National Forest Visitor Center at Cape Perpetua, 7 miles south.

Natural Features: Located on the side of a bluff at the ocean's edge; very dense high brush and a few tall conifers provide a significant amount of separation between most sites; a rail fence borders the campground on the ocean side; sea level.

Season, Fees & Phone: Open all year; $10.00; 10 day limit; Waldport Ranger District (503) 563-3211.

Camp Notes: This is about the only national forest campground in Oregon which provides campers with beachfront property. A few sites have a commanding view of the ocean, many are tucked-away in the thick shrubbery. Tip: It's usually best to avoid Tillicum Beach in summer; if you really want to camp here during the standard vacation season, you may have to arrive at dawn and wait for a camp spot to open up.

CAPE PERPETUA
Siuslaw National Forest

Location: Central Oregon Coast south of Waldport.

Access: From U.S. Highway 101 at milepost 167 + .3 (11 miles south of Waldport, 23 miles north of Florence), turn east onto the campground access road, then proceed 0.1 mile to the campground. (Note that the access road is just a few yards north of the Cape Perpetua Visitor Center.)

Facilities: 37 campsites; (a group area is also available); sites are mostly medium-sized, with nominal to good separation; parking pads are paved, vary considerably in length, but most are in the small to medium-length range; sites are basically level, but a bit of extra leveling may be required on some pads; many good tent spots; fireplaces; some firewood is available for gathering in the vicinity; water at faucets throughout; restrooms; holding tank disposal station; paved driveway; limited supplies in Yachats, 3 miles north; adequate supplies and services are available in Waldport.

Activities & Attractions: Within a short walk of fascinating tidal pools along the ocean shore; a nature trail leads off into the forest from the east end of the campground; small amphitheater; Cape Perpetua Visitor Center, has informative forestry exhibits and an ageless film, *Forces of Nature*, plus a newer production titled *A Discovery at the Edge*.

Natural Features: Located along Cape Creek in a long, narrow valley in a very lush coastal forest environment; nearly all campsites are creekside; the Pacific Ocean is located just to the west; elevation 50'.

Season, Fees & Phone: May to mid-September; $9.00; 10 day limit; Waldport Ranger District (503) 563-3211.

Camp Notes: The campground is certainly in a very attractive setting. But the tidal pools, with their variety of ocean life, and the Visitor Center, seem to be the main attractions here. Even if you're not planning on staying at the campground, Cape Perpetua is definitely worth a stop.

Oregon 16

ROCK CREEK
Siuslaw National Forest

Location: Central Oregon Coast north of Florence.

Access: From U.S. Highway 101 at milepost 174 + .2 (15 miles north of Florence, 18 miles south of Waldport), turn east onto a paved campground access road, and proceed 0.2 mile to the campground.

Facilities: 16 campsites; sites are medium-sized, with adequate separation; parking pads are paved, level, and fairly short but wide; fireplaces; firewood is available for gathering in the area; water at several faucets; restrooms; paved driveways; limited supplies in Yachats, 10 miles north; adequate supplies and services are available in Florence.

Activities & Attractions: Some really majestic oceanic scenery is just a short walk from any of the campsites--follow the creek to the beach.

Natural Features: Located along the bank of Rock Creek in a densely forested narrow valley; nearly all campsites are creekside; the campground setting stands in vivid contrast to the windswept ocean bluffs and beaches a few yards to the west; elevation 50'.

Season, Fees & Phone: May to mid-September; $9.00; 10 day limit; Waldport Ranger District (503) 563-3211.

Camp Notes: Although it is one of the smaller campgrounds on the Oregon Coast, and has limited facilities, Rock Creek is certainly worth considering for a stay. Many campers are attracted by the quiet forest atmosphere of this camp. Since it is located somewhat away from the main highway, there is less traffic noise here than in many other coastal campgrounds.

Oregon 17

CARL G. WASHBURNE
Carl G. Washburne State Park

Location: Central Oregon Coast north of Florence.

Access: From U.S. Highway 101 at milepost 176 (14 miles north of Florence, 12 miles south of Yachats), turn east into the campground.

Facilities: 66 campsites, including 58 with full hookups and 6 walk-in tent sites; sites are small to small+, with fair to good separation; parking pads are paved, short to medium-length straight-ins; a little additional leveling may be required in some sites; small to medium-sized tent areas; hiker-biker camp; hand carts for use in packing gear to walk-in sites; fireplaces; firewood is usually for sale, or b-y-o; water at most sites; restrooms with solar showers; waste water receptacles; paved, rather narrow driveways; limited supplies in Yachats; adequate supplies and services are available in Florence.

Activities & Attractions: China Creek Trail from the campground to the beach; also access to Valley Trail and Hobbit Trail; picturesque Heceta Head Lighthouse, 2 miles south.

Natural Features: Located on densely forested, hilly terrain; an expansive Pacific Ocean beach is just across the main highway; elevation 50'.

Season, Fees & Phone: Open all year; please see Appendix for standard Oregon state park fees; 10 day limit; park office (503) 547-3416.

Camp Notes: Washburne probably serves best as a place to set up a base camp from which you can explore this strip of coast. One of the most photogenic landmarks on the Pacific Coast, the lighthouse at Heceta Head, is located just two miles south. Another short side trip can be made to Darlingtonia State Wayside, 10 miles south. The wayside features hundreds of natural specimens, plus exhibits about the unique, insect-eating plant, *darlingtonia californica*.

Oregon 18

ALDER DUNE
Siuslaw National Forest

Location: Central Oregon Coast north of Florence.

Access: From U.S. Highway 101 at milepost 183 +.5 (7 miles north of Florence, 26 miles south of Waldport), turn west onto the paved campground access road, and proceed 0.2 mile to the campground.

Facilities: 39 campsites; most sites are large and quite private; parking pads are paved, long, straight-ins or pull-throughs; about half the pads will require some additional leveling; small to medium-sized tent areas; fireplaces; a minimal amount of firewood is available for gathering; water at faucets throughout; restrooms; paved driveways; camper supplies on the main highway, 1 mile south; adequate supplies and services are available in Florence.

Activities & Attractions: Several self-guiding nature trails; beach access trails; Oregon Dunes National Recreation Area is a few miles south of here; boating, boat ramp and fishing for trout, bass and perch at Sutton Lake, about 1 mile south; day use area.

Natural Features: Located in a lightly forested, hilly area, with some pines and tall hardwoods; several small ponds are within or near the campground; sand dunes; elevation 50'.

Season, Fees & Phone: May to late-September; $9.00; 10 day limit; Mapleton Ranger District (503) 268-4473.

Camp Notes: This campground is just far enough off the main highway so that it usually is relatively peaceful here. The design of the loops and facilities isn't typical of Forest Service campgrounds elsewhere. Rather nicely done.

Oregon 19

SUTTON
Siuslaw National Forest

Location: Central Oregon Coast north of Florence.

Access: From U.S. Highway 101 at milepost 185 + .4 (5 miles north of Florence, 28 miles south of Waldport), turn west onto a paved access road and proceed 0.8 mile to the campground.

Facilities: 80 campsites in 4 complex loops; (2 group camps are also available, by reservation only); most sites are medium to large, level, and well separated; most parking pads are paved, medium+ straight-ins, or long pull-throughs; ample space for tents; fireplaces; some firewood is available for gathering; water at faucets throughout; restrooms; paved driveways; adequate supplies and services are available in Florence.

Activities & Attractions: Trail to the beach (about 0.7 mile); nature trail, along which you can observe the insect-eating *darlingtonia* plant in its natural

Natural Features: Located in a heavily vegetated area near a Pacific Ocean beach; a creek flows past the north edge of the campground; elevation 50'.

Season, Fees & Phone: Open all year; $9.00; 10 day limit; Mapleton Ranger District (503) 268-4473.

Camp Notes: Sutton, also called Sutton Creek in some literature, doesn't seem to receive as much use as some of the other campgrounds in this area. If you prefer a spot which offers an opportunity to stay some distance away from the main highway, along with campsites that afford a substantial amount of privacy, this might be a good place to check. Sutton Lake is a pleasant spot to spend some time.

Oregon 20

JESSIE M. HONEYMAN
Jessie M. Honeyman State Park

Location: Central Oregon Coast south of Florence.

Access: From U.S. Highway 101 near milepost 193 (3 miles south of Florence, 18 miles north of Reedsport), turn west into the main park entrance; proceed 0.1 mile to a "Y" intersection; turn left toward the campground.

Facilities: 381 campsites, including 75 with partial hookups and 66 with full hookups; (hiker-biker campsites and a group camp are also available); sites are generally small to small+, with fair separation; parking pads are paved, reasonably level, short to medium-length straight-ins; tent space varies from small to large; fireplaces or fire rings; firewood is usually for sale, or b-y-o; restrooms with showers; paved driveways; holding tank disposal station; camper supplies at a concession; adequate supplies and services are available in Florence.

Activities & Attractions: Paved walkways to the dunes area; fishing; freshwater swimming beaches; fishing, boating and boat launches on the lakes; Siuslaw Pioneer Museum in Florence; expansive day use areas with large kitchen shelters.

Natural Features: Located a short distance inland from the coast in moderate to dense stands of tall conifers mixed with low-level hardwoods; portions of Cleawox and Woahink Lakes are within the park; bordered on the west by high sand dunes; the park is noted for its wild rhododendrons; elevation 50'.

Season, Fees & Phone: Open all year; please see Appendix for standard Oregon state park fees and reservation informaiton; park office (503) 997-3851 or (503) 997-3641.

Camp Notes: Unless you're an orv enthusiast, you may not think that staying in the heavily used campground is a true treat. (Considering that some of the dunes south of the park are almost 500-feet high, the camp's shortcomings may pale in insignificance in relation to the locally available adventures.) The large picnic shelters in the day use area are *very* welcome on rainy days, especially if you're a tent camper.

Oregon 21

LAGOON & WAXMYRTLE
Oregon Dunes National Recreation Area

Location: Central Oregon Coast south of Florence.

Access: From U.S. Highway 101 near milepost 198 (7 miles south of Florence, 14 miles north of Reedsport), turn west onto the (paved) campground access road, and proceed 0.8 mile to the campgrounds; Lagoon is to the north (right), Waxmyrtle is to the south (left).

Facilities: 40 campsites at Lagoon, 56 campsites at Waxmyrtle; sites are small+ to medium-sized, with fair separation; parking pads are paved; Lagoon has mostly straight-ins, Waxmyrtle has straight-ins and many pull-throughs; plenty of level tent space in most sites; fireplaces; some firewood is available for gathering; water at several faucets; restrooms; paved driveways; adequate supplies and services are available in Florence.

Activities & Attractions: These campgrounds serve as a staging area for off road vehicle (orv) enthusiasts; "River of No Return" nature trail leads off from Lagoon; "Stagecoach" nature trail starts at Waxmyrtle; amphitheater in Lagoon.

Natural Features: Located on opposite sides of the Siltcoos River, in a semi-open forest setting with a substantial amount of lower-level vegetation; Waxmyrtle is somewhat more open than Lagoon; beaches 1 mile west are barren, wide, windswept and dune-covered; elevation 50'.

Season, Fees & Phone: Open all year, with either Lagoon or Waxmyrtle open in winter; $9.00; 10 day limit; Oregon Dunes National Recreation Area Headquarters, Reedsport, (503) 271-3611.

Camp Notes: Lagoon and Waxmyrtle are so similar and so close to each other that they are really more like two loops of the same campground. A large camping area for off road vehicles, called Driftwood II, is located within the primary dune area less than a mile west (just continue straight ahead on the access road, past Lagoon & Waxmyrtle). Also, a small 14 unit campground with limited facilities, Tyee, is located on the east side of U.S. 101 near milepost 197, just north of here.

Oregon 22

TAHKENITCH
Oregon Dunes National Recreation Area

Location: Central Oregon Coast north of Reedsport.

Access: From U.S. Highway 101 at milepost 203 +.5 (8 miles north of Reedsport, 13 miles south of Florence), turn west into the campground.

Facilities: 34 campsites; sites are small+ to medium-sized, with fair separation; most parking pads are paved, medium-length straight-ins, a few sites have pull-throughs; some pads may require a little additional leveling; small to medium-sized tent areas; there are a couple of walk-in sites suitable for small tents; fireplaces; firewood is available for gathering; water at faucets throughout; restrooms; paved driveway; adequate supplies and services are available in Reedsport.

Activities & Attractions: Tahkenitch Trail leads through dense forest to the open dunes area along the coast; fishing and boating on Tahkenitch Lake; Three-Mile Lake, a little less than 3 miles south, is a favorite hike-in fishing spot; like most lakes in the nra, Tahkenitch and Three-Mile are stocked with species that include trout, perch, and crappie; elevation 50'.

Natural Features: Located in a heavily forested area, but with some 'open' campsites; Tahkenitch Lake, one of the larger lakes on this section of the coast, is a short distance from here, on the east side of the highway; elevation 50'.

Season, Fees & Phone: Open all year; $9.00; 10 day limit; Oregon Dunes National Recreation Area Headquarters, Reedsport, (503) 271-3611.

Camp Notes: Tahkenitch is quite different from the other Oregon Dunes National Recreation Area campgrounds in this region. It really looks more like a state park campground. Another nra campground near here which might be worth considering is Carter Lake, 4.5 miles north, on the west side of the highway.

Oregon 23

WINDY COVE
Douglas County Park

Location: Central Oregon Coast south of Reedsport.

Access: From U.S. Highway 101 at milepost 215 +.8 at the south end of the small community of Winchester Bay (4 miles south of Reedsport, 23 miles north of Coos Bay), turn southwest onto Salmon Harbor Drive (Douglas County Road 251) and proceed 0.2 mile to the campground; (watch for signs indicating "Windy Cove Park" at the intersection of U.S. 101 and Salmon Harbor Drive).

Facilities: 97 campsites, including 4 with electrical hookups and 64 with full hookups, in 2 areas (A & B); sites are small to medium in size, with little or no separation; parking areas are paved in the hookup sections and oiled gravel in the tent section; no fire facilities; water at hookup sites or from several faucets; restrooms with showers; paved driveways; limited supplies in Winchester Bay; adequate supplies and services are available in Reedsport.

Activities & Attractions: Beach and dune access (most of the beach south of here is closed to vehicles); county fishing and crabbing dock; a unique county park, "Children's Fort", is across the road; cable TV.

Natural Features: Located harborside on an open flat, with sandy/grassy areas in and around the campsites; forested hillside to the east, behind the camping area; sea level.

Season, Fees & Phone: Open all year; $9.50 for a standard site, $11.50 for a full hookup site, $2.00 extra for a cable TV hookup; 10 day limit; park office (503) 271-5634.

Camp Notes: Windy Cove has a unique waterfront setting. Just watching the goings-on of a small harbor is an interesting 'activity' in itself. There's also camping for self-contained units in the landscaped parking lot ("The Slab") near the harbormaster's office, directly across the highway from Windy Cove.

UMPQUA LIGHTHOUSE
Umpqua Lighthouse State Park

Location: Southern Oregon Coast southwest of Reedsport.

Access: From U.S. Highway 101 at milepost 216 +.7 (0.7 mile south of Winchester Bay, 5 miles south of Reedsport, 22 miles north of Coos Bay), turn west for 0.15 mile up a hill to a fork; take the right fork and continue up the hill for another 0.35 mile, then turn left to the campground entrance.

Facilities: 63 campsites, including 22 with full hookups; (hiker-biker campsites are also available); most hookup units are near the campground entrance in a side-by-side 'parking lot' arrangement, and have long, level, paved, straight-in parking pads; the main part of the campground is located a short distance beyond the hookup area; most sites here are level, with medium to long, paved pads and good-sized, grassy tent areas; site spacing is fairly close throughout the campground; fire rings; firewood is usually for sale, or b-y-o; water at faucets throughout; restrooms with showers; waste water receptacles; limited supplies in Winchester Bay; adequate supplies and services are available in Reedsport.

Activities & Attractions: Umpqua Lighthouse and Visitor Center, just above the campground; trails to and around Lake Marie; small swimming beach on the lake; whale-watching station (platform) at the lighthouse; adjacent to Oregon Dunes National Recreation Area.

Natural Features: Located on moderately to densely forested, hilly terrain above a small gem of a lake-- Lake Marie; views of the Pacific Ocean are 'up-and-over' the hill from the campground; elevation 100'.

Season, Fees & Phone: April to October; please see Appendix for standard Oregon state park fees; 10 day limit; park office (503) 271-4118.

Camp Notes: You can walk up to the lighthouse from the camping areas. (If you prefer to drive, there is parking up there.) The 200,000-candlepower light directs its rotating beam as far as 19 miles seaward. Spending a night at the campground could be a very illuminating experience.

WILLIAM M. TUGMAN
William M. Tugman State Park

Location: Southern Oregon Coast south of Reedsport.

Access: From U.S. Highway 101 at milepost 221 +.4 (10 miles south of Reedsport, 11 miles north of Coos Bay), turn east/northeast and proceed 0.1 mile to the park entrance; turn right into the campground.

Facilities: 115 campsites, all with partial-hookups; (a hiker-biker camp is also available); sites are small to small+, level, with fair to fairly good separation; parking pads are paved, medium to long straight-ins; tent areas are medium to large and have a grass/sand surface; fireplaces; firewood is usually for sale, or b-y-o; water at each site; restrooms with showers; waste water receptacles throughout the campground; holding tank disposal station; paved driveways; limited supplies in Lakeside, 1 mile south; adequate supplies in Reedsport; complete supplies and services are available in the Coos Bay-North Bend area.

Activities & Attractions: Paved trails; playground; displays with information about local flora and fauna; swimming; fishing; boat launch and dock; large day use area with large shelter.

Natural Features: Located on a large flat; campsites are among moderately dense, medium-height conifers; evergreens have been planted between campsites; Eel Creek flows along the east side of the camp areas; Eel Lake is on the northeast side of the park; elevation 50'.

Season, Fees & Phone: April to October; please see Appendix for standard Oregon state park fees; park office (503) 759-3604.

Camp Notes: This is *really* a nice-looking place. The designers of the park have achieved a good balance between forest and open space. Typical of Oregon Coast parks, the campsites are rather closely spaced, but otherwise it's an excellent facility.

NORTH EEL
Oregon Dunes National Recreation Area

Location: Southern Oregon Coast north of Coos Bay.

Access: From U.S. Highway 101 at milepost 222 +.3 (10 miles north of Coos Bay, 11 miles south of Reedsport), turn west onto the campground access road and proceed 0.1 mile to the campground.

Facilities: 53 campsites in 2 loops; sites are small+ to medium-sized, with fair separation; parking pads are medium to long, paved/oiled gravel straight-ins or pull-throughs; fireplaces; some firewood is available for gathering; water at faucets throughout; restrooms; paved/oiled gravel driveways; limited supplies in Lakeside, 0.5 mile; adequate supplies in Reedsport; complete supplies and services are available in the Coos Bay-North Bend area.

Activities & Attractions: Several hiking trails, including one along Eel Creek and another to Umpqua Dunes; (no orv sand access from here).

Natural Features: Located in a moderately forested area along Eel Creek; some camp units are in the open, others are sheltered by trees; Umpqua Scenic Dunes section of the national recreation area lies to the west; elevation 50'.

Season, Fees & Phone: Open all year; $9.00; 10 day limit; Oregon Dunes National Recreation Area Headquarters, Reedsport, (503) 271-3611.

Camp Notes: This campground experiences somewhat less activity and provides more seclusion than Tugman State Park, 1 mile north. However, Tugman does have showers and other comforts, so take your pick. Two other nra campgrounds directly south of here, Middle Eel and South Eel, provide camping on weekends and reserved group camping only, respectively. A third local nra campground, Spinreel, 2 miles south, serves as a major orv area and tends to be dusty.

Oregon 27

BLUEBILL
Oregon Dunes National Recreation Area

Location: Southern Oregon Coast north of Coos Bay.

Access: From U.S. Highway 101 at a point 0.7 mile north of the great bridge which spans Coos Bay (4 miles north of midtown Coos Bay, 23 miles south of Reedsport), turn west/southwest onto a causeway that crosses the north end of the bay; proceed 1 mile, then bear northwest (right) just before the Weyerhauser plant and continue another 1.4 miles to the campground on the south (left) side of the road.

Facilities: 19 campsites; most sites are medium-sized, level, with nominal separation; most parking pads are medium-length straight-ins, several units have pull-throughs; large areas for tents in most sites; fireplaces; a minimal amount of firewood is available for gathering in the vicinity, b-y-o is recommended; water at several faucets; restrooms; complete supplies and services are available in the Coos Bay-North Bend area.

Activities & Attractions: Off road vehicle (orv) access to dunes; beach access 1 mile west; Wild Mare horse camp near here; hiking.

Natural Features: Located on the northwest corner of Bluebill Lake in a moderately forested lowland area; Bluebill Lake is small, shallow, and usually dry in summer; there are several other small coastal lakes and ponds in the vicinity; sea level.

Season, Fees & Phone: Open all year; $9.00; 10 day limit; Oregon Dunes National Recreation Area Headquarters, Reedsport, (503) 271-3611.

Camp Notes: This one is perhaps a little "iffy" (and possibly "whiffy"). The surroundings are quite nice and there is limited beach access. It's quite popular with orv enthusiasts and tends to be busy in summer, even in mid-week. You may catch an occasional whiff of some of the vapors from the forest products plant near here, however. This is somewhat balanced by the convenience of being close to the services of the largest metropolitan area along the Oregon Coast.

Oregon 28

BASTENDORFF BEACH
Coos County Park

Location: Southern Oregon Coast southwest of Coos Bay.

Access: From U.S. Highway 101 in midtown Coos Bay, travel west on Commercial Avenue and follow signs for "Sunset Bay" along a zigzag, winding, generally westerly and southwesterly route on Commercial Avenue, North 7th St., Central Avenue, Ocean Boulevard, Newmark Avenue, South Empire Boulevard, and Cape Arago Highway for 8.7 miles to the village of Charleston; continue southwesterly on Cape Arago Highway for another 1.7 miles; turn northerly (right) onto the paved park access road and proceed 0.3 mile to the campground. **Alternate Access:** From U.S. 101 in midtown North Bend, turn west onto Virginia Street and follow the signed route west/southwest for 9.5 miles to the campground turnoff. (The abbreviated directions above should be adequate under most conditions. An approach from the north, or a night arrival, might warrant taking the route from North Bend, since it is somewhat more straightforward than the way from Coos Bay.)

Facilities: 81 campsites, including 43 with partial hookups and 13 with full hookups, in 4 loops; (a group camp area is also available); sites are small+ to medium-sized, with fair to very good separation; parking pads are paved, mostly medium to long straight-ins; a bit of additional leveling may be needed in some hookup sites; small+ to medium+, grassy tent spots; fireplaces; b-y-o firewood; water at faucets throughout; central restrooms with showers, plus auxiliary vaults; waste water receptacles; holding tank disposal station; paved driveways; camper supplies in Charleston; complete supplies and services are available in the Coos Bay-North Bend metro area.

Activities & Attractions: Beachcombing; designated swimming area; dandy playground; horseshoe and basketball courts; day use area.

Natural Features: Located in a forested area a few yards from an ocean beach; most sites are well-sheltered by dense conifers and hardwoods; sea level.

Season, Fees & Phone: May to October; $10.00 for a standard site, $12.00 for a hookup site; 10 day limit; park office (503) 888-5353.

Camp Notes: Particularly if you have a longer camping outfit, this local park is certainly worth considering as a nice option to the nearby state park (Sunset Bay). Campsites at Bastendorff Beach are somewhat narrow, but they extend deep into the woods. In fact, taking into account the better privacy factor and its closeness to the beach, this park might have the edge over the state unit.

Oregon 29

Sunset Bay
Sunset Bay State Park

Location: Southern Oregon Coast southwest of Coos Bay.

Access: From U.S. Highway 101 in midtown Coos Bay, travel west on Commercial Avenue and follow signs for Sunset Bay along a zigzag, winding, generally westerly and southwesterly route on Commercial Avenue, North 7th St., Central Avenue, Ocean Boulevard, Newmark Avenue, South Empire Boulevard, and Cape Arago Highway for 8.7 miles to the village of Charleston; continue southwesterly on Cape Arago Highway for another 4 miles; turn northeast (left) into the campground. **Alternate Access:** From U.S. 101 in midtown North Bend, turn west onto Virginia Street and follow the signed route west/southwest for 11.5 miles to the campground. (The abbreviated directions above should be adequate under most conditions. An approach from the north, or a night arrival, might warrant taking the route from North Bend.)

Facilities: 137 campsites, including 29 with full hookups, in 4 loops; sites are small to small+, level, with nominal to fair separation; parking pads are paved, most are short to medium-length straight-ins; adequate space for medium to large tents; fire rings; firewood is usually for sale, or b-y-o; water at faucets throughout; restrooms with showers; paved driveways; camper supplies in Charleston, 3 miles northeast; complete supplies and services are available in Coos Bay-North Bend.

Activities & Attractions: Swimming beach; fishing; boating; boat launch; hiking trail; Cape Arago Lighthouse, just northwest of the park; day use areas, large shelter.

Natural Features: Located along and near Sunset Bay; sandstone bluffs shelter the small bay on the north and south; a sandy beach is on the east edge of the bay; the campground is a few hundred yards east of the bay; campsites receive light to medium shade/shelter from medium to tall conifers, hardwoods, and shrubs; a small creek flows through the campground; sea level.

Season, Fees & Phone: Open all year; please see Appendix for standard Oregon state park fees; 10 day limit; campsite reservations recommended for summer weekends and holidays, please see Appendix; park office (503) 888-4902 or (503) 888-3778.

Camp Notes: Sunset Bay, with its snug passage to the open ocean, isn't one of those grand, splashy places where the waves boom all day and night long. It's more like a small, quiet cove. The campground is quite well sheltered from wind.

BULLARDS BEACH
Bullards Beach State Park

Location: Southern Oregon Coast north of Bandon.

Access: From U.S. Highway 101 at milepost 259 +.3 (near the north end of the Coquille River bridge, 2 miles north of Bandon, 20 miles south of Coos Bay), turn west into the park entrance and proceed 0.1 mile; turn north into the campground.

Facilities: 192 campsites, including 100 with partial hookups and 92 with full hookups; (hiker-biker sites and an 8-site equestrian camp are also available); sites are generally small to medium-sized, level, with nominal to fairly good separation; parking pads are short + to long, paved straight-ins; large, grassy tent areas; fire rings; firewood is usually for sale, or b-y-o; water at each site; restrooms with showers; waste water receptacles; holding tank disposal station; paved driveways; adequate supplies and services are available in Bandon.

Activities & Attractions: Paved, level walkway (no bikes) leads 1.5 miles through beautifully landscaped parkland to the beach; other minor trails are in the park; abandoned Coquille River Lighthouse; nice playground; boat launch and dock on the river; salmon fishing, clamming and crabbing; amphitheater; large day use areas with shelters.

Natural Features: Located on a large flat along the Coquille River estuary, on the north bank of the river; mature conifers and smaller evergreens, shrubbery and mown grass are in and around the camping areas; long, mown-grass flats border portions of the river; 4 miles of ocean and riverfront beach are within the park; sea level.

Season, Fees & Phone: Open all year; please see Appendix for standard Oregon state park fees; 10 day limit; park office (503) 347-2209 or (503) 347-3501.

Camp Notes: What a showplace! The campground and surrounding parklands are elegant in their simplicity. While there aren't any 'big' attractions here, there are plenty of neat little things to do in this area.

CAPE BLANCO
Cape Blanco State Park

Location: Southern Oregon Coast north of Port Orford.

Access: From U.S. Highway 101 at milepost 296 +.5 (4.5 miles north of Port Orford, 23 miles south of Bandon), turn west onto Cape Blanco Road and proceed 4 miles to the day use area and boat launch; or bear left and continue for another 1.5 miles to the campground.

Facilities: 58 campsites with partial hookups; (hiker-biker sites and an equestrian camp are also available); sites are small + to medium + in size, generally level, with good to excellent separation; parking pads are paved, medium to long, straight-ins; some sites are designated as trailer units; medium to large, grassy tent areas; fire rings; firewood is usually for sale, or b-y-o; water at each site; restrooms with showers; waste water receptacles at each site; holding tank disposal station; paved driveways; limited + supplies and services are available in Port Orford.

Activities & Attractions: Absolutely superb views; a first-rate beach; boat launch for river access; reportedly very good fishing for salmon and steelhead on the river; very steep trail down to the beach from the small parking lot south of the campground; Cape Blanco Lighthouse; the park is near Port Orford, oldest townsite on the Oregon Coast.

Natural Features: Located on a high, windswept bluff overlooking the Pacific Ocean; some campsites are lightly sheltered, but many are very well sheltered by conifers and tall, dense shrubbery; long, wide, black sand beach below the campground; elevation 200'.

Season, Fees & Phone: April to October; please see Appendix for standard Oregon state park fees; 10 day limit; park office (503) 332-6774.

Camp Notes: Cape Blanco is the second-westernmost point, and this is the most westerly state park, in the contiguous 48 states. Many of the campsites are the most private of any coastal park. If you're looking for an easily accessible campground that maintains an atmosphere of remoteness and seclusion, this is it.

HUMBUG MOUNTAIN
Humbug Mountain State Park

Location: Southern Oregon Coast south of Port Orford.

Access: From U.S. Highway 101 at milepost 307 (6 miles south of Port Orford, 22 miles north of Gold Beach), turn east (a very sharp right turn if you're northbound) onto the campground access road and curve 0.2 mile westerly to the campground. (Note: the normally north-south U.S. 101 makes several curves around the mountain in this section; under certain traffic or weather conditions, the turnoff may not be highly visible until you've almost passed it.)

Facilities: 107 campsites, including 30 with full hookups, in 3 loops; (hiker-biker sites are also available); sites are small+ to medium-sized, with nominal to fair separation; parking pads are paved, and vary in length from short to medium+; adequate space for large tents in most sites; barbecue grills and fire rings in most sites; firewood is usually for sale, or b-y-o; water at faucets throughout; restrooms with showers; waste water disposal receptacles throughout; holding tank disposal station; paved driveways; limited+ supplies and services are available in Port Orford and Gold Beach.

Activities & Attractions: Humbug Mountain Trail leads 3 miles to the summit of the mountain; trail to the beach from the campground (0.2 mile); trail from the campground to a nice picnic area; footbridges across the streams.

Natural Features: Located at the foot of Humbug Mountain, a prominent, densely forested peak which rises 1756' from the ocean shore; the campground is on a semi-open, grassy flat down off the highway; campsites generally receive light to light-medium shade/shelter from conifers and hardwoods; sea level.

Season, Fees & Phone: April to October; please see Appendix for standard Oregon state park fees; 10 day limit; park office (503) 332-6774.

Camp Notes: If you approach the park from the north, it'll probably be obvious to you which of the local promontories is Humbug Mountain. It'll probably also be quite apparent why a lot of campers take the time and effort to hike up the mountain to savor the South Coast view from the summit.

HARRIS BEACH
Harris Beach State Park

Location: Southern Oregon Coast north of Brookings.

Access: From U.S. Highway 101 at milepost 355 +.7 (1 mile north of midtown Brookings), turn northwest onto the park access road and proceed 0.35 mile; turn north (right) into the campground entrance.

Facilities: 151 campsites, including 51 with partial hookups, and 34 with full hookups, in 4 loops; (hiker-biker sites are also available); sites are small to medium sized, with nominal to fairly good separation; level to sloped; parking pads are paved, short to medium-length straight-ins; some pads will require additional leveling; fireplaces; firewood is usually for sale, or b-y-o; water at faucets throughout; restrooms with showers; holding tank disposal station; paved driveways; adequate supplies and services are available in Brookings.

Activities & Attractions: Trail to the top of Harris Butte; swimming/wading; reportedly excellent beachcombing and fishing.

Natural Features: Located on a hillside a short distance east of an ocean beach; Harris Butte rises between the campground and the beach; vegetation in the campground varies from light to rather dense sections of tall hardwoods and conifers with a considerable amount of flowering bushes and underbrush; numerous rock spires and stack formations stand offshore; great ocean views; elevation 200'.

Season, Fees & Phone: Open all year; please see Appendix for standard Oregon state park fees; 10 day limit; campsite reservations recommended for anytime during the summer, please see Appendix; park office (503) 469-2021.

Camp Notes: If you get out of your bunk or sleeping bag early and find a vantage on a high point in the park, you can watch the commercial and sport fishing fleet congregate offshore. Starting with a few craft, the assemblage seems to double in size every few minutes until there are sometimes hundreds of boats bobbing in the briny blue sea.

LOEB
Loeb State Park

Location: Southwest corner of Oregon northeast of Brookings.

Access: From U.S. Highway 101 on the southeast corner of Brookings at the north end of the Chetco River Bridge, drive northeasterly on North Bank Road (Curry County Road 784, a winding, paved road) for 7.5 miles; turn southeast (right) into the park, proceed 0.1 mile, then turn right into the campground.

Facilities: 53 campsites with partial hookups; sites are mostly small to medium-sized, level, with fair to good separation; parking pads are paved, medium-length straight-ins; some good-sized areas for tents; fireplaces or fire rings; firewood is usually for sale, or b-y-o; water at sites; restrooms with showers; paved driveways; adequate supplies and services are available in Brookings.

Activities & Attractions: Fishing; rafting/drifting; carry-in boat launch area; swimming beach; trails in the vicinity lead up into the Kalmiopsis Wilderness a few miles east.

Natural Features: Located in the Coast Range on the north bank of the Chetco River; tall conifers and hardwoods, including old growth myrtlewoods, offer shelter and privacy for most campsites; nearby forested peaks rise to almost 3000' above the park; the typically deep blue-green Chetco River is quite wide at this point; elevation 100'.

Season, Fees & Phone: Open all year; please see Appendix for standard Oregon state park fees; phone c/o Harris Beach State Park (503) 469-2021.

Camp Notes: Loeb Park was dedicated to the preservation of the myrtlewoods located within its boundary. Myrtles are commercially prized for the intricate grain pattern in their wood, and grow only in certain areas of Southern Oregon and Northern California. Some people use the leathery, pungently aromatic leaves of the myrtle as a spice for camp soup or stew. (Sort of a backcountry bay leaf.)

Oregon

North Western

Please refer to the Oregon map in the Appendix

CHAMPOEG
Champoeg State Park

Location: Western Oregon southwest of Portland.

Access: From Interstate 5 Exit 278 for Aurora/Donald, (midway between Portland and Salem), travel west on Ehlen Road and Champoeg Road following the "Champoeg" signs for a total of 6 miles from the Interstate; turn north (right) into the park; continue for 0.2 mile (past the visitor center to a 3-way intersection; continue east (right) for 1 mile to the campground.

Facilities: 48 campsites with partial hookups; (an rv group camp is also available, by reservation only); sites are small+, level, with minimal to nominal separation; parking pads are paved, medium to long straight-ins; good tent areas on the lawns; separate group area for rv's; fireplaces or fire rings; firewood is usually for sale, or b-y-o; restrooms with showers; holding tank disposal station; paved driveways; adequate supplies and services are available in Aurora, 8 miles east.

Activities & Attractions: Visitor center; historical museum; replica of a pioneer's log cabin and a restored original settler's house; paved hikeway/bikeway; a hiking-only trail follows the river; rv group meeting hall in the campground; historical pageant; 2 large day use areas.

Natural Features: Located on prairie flatland on the east bank of the Willamette River; the camp area is landscaped with mown lawns, decorative bushes and shrubs, and tall oaks; one of the oldest groves of white oak trees in Oregon is a prominent feature of the park; elevation 100'.

Season, Fees & Phone: Open all year; please see Appendix for standard Oregon state park fees; 10 day limit; park office (503) 678-1251.

Camp Notes: A traditional or 'city park' atmosphere prevails here, even though the spacious, manicured grounds are surrounded by miles of fertile farmland. And when we say 'manicured' it's meant literally--

they don't just swing a scythe to cut the lawn and use a chain saw to prune the rose bushes. Champoeg is steeped in history--it is the site of Oregon's provisional government, established in 1843, which paved the way to statehood. If you're interested in Northwest history, you probably couldn't come to a better park than this. *Champoeg* (sham-poo-ee) is a French-Indian word which is thought to mean *Prairie of the Blue Flowers*.

Oregon 36

MILO MCIVER
Milo McIver State Park

Location: Western Oregon southeast of Portland.

Access: From the junction of Oregon State Highways 224 & 211 at the south end of the city of Estacada, turn west onto Highway 211 and proceed 0.9 mile; as Highway 211 bears southwest, continue west/northwest (right) up the steep hill on South Hayden Road for 1.2 miles; turn north/northwest (right) onto Springwater Road and travel another 1.2 miles; turn northeast (right) onto the park access road and proceed down the hill for 2.1 miles to the campground. (This is the most straightforward route to the park, but it's just one of at least a half-dozen ways of getting in here, depending upon exactly where in metropolitan Portland you start; if you're good at following trails marked with small signs, you might consider another of the signed routes along the district's hilly highways and byways to the park.)

Facilities: 44 campsites with partial hookups; (a group tent camping area is also available); sites are small+ to medium-sized, with good to excellent separation; parking pads are paved, short to medium-length straight-ins; some pads will require a touch of additional leveling; medium to large areas for tents; fireplaces; b-y-o firewood; water at sites; restrooms with showers; holding tank disposal station; paved driveways; adequate supplies and services are available in Estacada.

Activities & Attractions: Boating, rafting; boat launches; fishing (top stream for winter steelhead); hiking and equestrian trails; sports field; model airplane field; viewpoint; large day use areas.

Natural Features: Located on naturally terraced, hilly terrain along and above the south/west bank of the Clackamas River; campsites are very well shaded/sheltered by conifers and hardwoods; elevation 200'.

Season, Fees & Phone: Open all year; please see Appendix for standard Oregon state park fees; 10 day limit; park office (503) 630-7150.

Camp Notes: The campsites are really cozy little spots hugged by shrubs and tucked into their own densely forested cubicles. Views of the Cascades, including Mounts Hood, Adams and St. Helens, from the uppermost level of the park (before you start down to the campground level) are pretty impressive.

Oregon 37

SILVER FALLS
Silver Falls State Park

Location: Western Oregon southeast of Salem.

Access: From Oregon State Highway 214 at milepost 25 (9 miles east of the junction of Oregon State Highways 214 and 22 southeast of Salem, 16 miles south of Silverton), turn southeast into the main campground.

Facilities: 104 campsites, including 53 with partial hookups; (a youth group camp, a standard group camp, and a horse camp are also available--all by reservation); sites are small to medium-sized, with minimal to fairly good separation; parking pads are paved, short to medium-length straight-ins; many good tent spots are located on grassy areas or on a carpet of pine needles; fireplaces; water at faucets throughout; restrooms with solar showers; holding tank disposal station; paved driveways; adequate supplies and services are available in Silverton.

Activities & Attractions: Trail of Ten Falls passes the number of waterfalls in its name; 4 miles of paved bicycle trails; 3 mile jogging trail; 12 miles of equestrian trails; community building; swimming area; playground; basic horse-handling facilities; visitor center features nature talks and displays; several day use areas.

Natural Features: Located in the foothills of the Cascade Range along the banks of the North and South Forks of Silver Creek; vegetation consists of a moderately dense mixture of conifers and hardwoods with dense undercover, plus some meadows; elevation 600'.

Season, Fees & Phone: Open all year; please see Appendix for standard Oregon state park fees; 10 day limit; park office (503) 873-8681.

Camp Notes: The road to Silver Falls winds through hilly forest and fertile farmland. Once you arrive, you'll see that most of the waterfalls are no mere trickles like those found in some "falls" parks--they're the real McCoys.

Oregon 38

FISHERMEN'S BEND
Public Lands/BLM Recreation Area

Location: Western Oregon east of Salem.

Access: From Oregon State Highway 22 at milepost 28 +.5 (1.5 miles west of Mill City, 30 miles east of Salem), turn south onto a paved access road; drive south, then west for 0.4 mile to the camping area.

Facilities: 35 campsites, including some with electrical hookups; (several small group areas are also available); sites are medium-sized to spacious, level, and well separated; parking pads are paved; sites on the interior of the loop are straight-ins with nice tent spots; sites on the exterior of the loop are pull-throughs with electrical hookups; fireplaces; firewood is often for sale, or b-y-o; water at faucets throughout; restrooms with showers; holding tank disposal station; paved driveways; limited supplies in Mill City; complete supplies and services are available in Salem.

Activities & Attractions: Boating; paved boat ramp with large parking area; fishing for steelhead and trout; encircling the campground is a self-guided nature trail connected to a number of additional river access trails; several day use areas with picnic shelters, open grassy areas, ball fields and horseshoe pits.

Natural Features: Located at the west edge of the Cascade Range and on the eastern edge of the great Willamette Valley; campsites are all situated in densely wooded areas with a considerable amount of leafy vegetation, tall conifers, and hanging moss; the North Santiam River flows west past this point and into the Willamette River; elevation 800'.

Season, Fees & Phone: Open all year; $8.00 for a standard site, $10.00 for a partial-hookup site; 10 day limit; Bureau of Land Management Salem district office (503) 375-5646.

Camp Notes: Fishermen's Bend, built in 1963, is one of the nicest BLM campgrounds you'll find anywhere. A 'bend' in the North Santiam River here gives the campground its appropriate name.

Oregon 39

DETROIT LAKE
Detroit Lake State Park

Location: Western Oregon southeast of Salem.

Access: From Oregon State Highway 22 at milepost 48 (2 miles west/southwest of Detroit, 15 miles east of Mill City), turn south into the campground.

Facilities: 311 campsites, including 70 with partial hookups and 107 with full hookups, in 8 loops; sites are small to medium-sized, with minimal to nominal separation; parking pads are paved, tolerably level, short to long straight-ins; medium to large tent areas; fire rings; firewood is usually for sale, or b-y-o; water at faucets throughout; restrooms with showers; paved driveways; limited supplies are available in Detroit.

Activities & Attractions: Boating; boat launches and docks adjacent to the campground; fishing; fishing pier off the campground; designated swimming beach and ski beach nearby; ranger-naturalist programs on summer evenings; large day use area.

Natural Features: Located on the north/west shore of 3000-acre Detroit Lake in the North Santiam River Canyon; campsites are in or near a medium-dense forest of tall conifers and some hardwoods; the forested slopes of the Cascade Range rise all around the lake; elevation 1600'.

Season, Fees & Phone: April to October; please see Appendix for standard Oregon state park fees; 10 day limit; park office (503) 854-3406 or (509) 854-3346.

Camp Notes: Campsites at Detroit Lakes are all situated on a narrow strip of land between the lake and the highway. Sites along the lake tend to be a bit overused, and other sites are rather close to the highway. You may wish to request a preview before settling-in. If you're a boater, you might prefer the F or H Loop--both of them have docks a few yards from the campsites. Hundreds of thousands of rainbow trout and kokanee salmon are annually stocked in Detroit Lake, helping to make this one of the more popular campgrounds in the state.

HOOVER
Willamette National Forest

Location: Western Oregon southeast of Salem.

Access: From Oregon State Highway 22 at milepost 53 +.1 (3 miles east of Detroit, 2 miles west of Idanha), turn southwest onto Blowout Road (Forest Road 10); proceed west on Blowout Road for 0.9 mile to the campground.

Facilities: 37 campsites, including several multiple-occupancy sites; sites are fairly open and spacious, with some separation; parking pads are paved, most are straight-ins, but a few are pull-throughs spacious enough to accommodate larger rv's; some nice tent sites in open forest areas; fire rings; some firewood may be available for gathering in the vicinity; water at several faucets; restrooms; waste water receptacles; paved driveways; limited supplies and services are available in Detroit.

Activities & Attractions: Boating; large boat launch; fishing; handicapped-access fishing platform; ranger-naturalist programs may be scheduled on summer weekend evenings; tours at Big Cliffs and Detroit Dams; several nearby forest roads lead up into the surrounding mountain areas.

Natural Features: Located in a moderately forested area at the east tip of Detroit Lake on the west slope of the Cascades; the lake, with 32 miles of shoreline is a major reservoir on the North Santiam River; flanked by the steep walls of North Santiam Canyon; elevation 1600'.

Season, Fees & Phone: Open all year, with limited services October to April; $8.00 for a single unit, $16.00 for a multiple unit; 14 day limit; Detroit Ranger District, Mill City, (503) 854-3366.

Camp Notes: Hoover Campground has some terrific campspots, many with river/lake views. Sites are far enough from the highway to provide reasonable solitude. Boating access to Detroit Lake is through a narrow river channel, so Hoover is somewhat removed from the mainstream of boating traffic as well. For something a little farther off the highway, you may elect to continue for another three miles on FR 10 along the south shore of the lake down to South Shore Campground. It has 32 sites, hand pumps and vaults. A large island offshore of the South Shore has a promontory with the curious name of Piety Knob, which rises 500' above the lake surface.

RIVERSIDE
Willamette National Forest

Location: Western Oregon southeast of Salem.

Access: From Oregon State Highway 22 at milepost 64 +.3 (14 miles east of Detroit, 16 miles north of the junction of Highway 22 & U.S. Highway 20), turn southwest into the campground.

Facilities: 36 campsites; sites are average-sized, mostly level and quite well separated; parking pads are paved, with adequate space for medium-sized vehicles; some nice, private tent sites; fireplaces or fire rings; firewood is available for gathering in the vicinity; water at several faucets; vault facilities; paved driveways; limited supplies and services are available in Idanha, 9 miles northwest.

Activities & Attractions: Stream fishing; Detroit Lakes, 15 miles west, has boating, fishing and swimming; there are a number of nearby forest roads leading up into the surrounding mountains.

Natural Features: Located on the west slope of the Cascades along the rushing North Santiam River; sites are in a double row on the east bank of the river, which flows through a narrows at this point; dense campground vegetation is of tall conifers, with rhododendrons and ferns; high, forested peaks are visible to the west; Mount Jefferson Wilderness is to the east; elevation 2400'.

Season, Fees & Phone: Open all year, with limited services October to April; $7.00 for a single unit, $14.00 for a multiple unit; 16 day limit; Detroit Ranger District, Mill City, (503) 854-3366.

Camp Notes: This densely forested campground offers an atmosphere of privacy and seclusion. Many sites are right on the riverbank. Another small campground, Whispering Falls, is located near milepost 58, about 7 miles northwest of Riverside on Highway 22. It is much smaller (15 sites), has similar sites, restrooms instead of vaults, and is open April to September.

SUNNYSIDE
Linn County Park

Location: Western Oregon southeast of Albany.

Access: From U.S. Highway 20 near milepost 33 (6 miles east of Sweet Home, 7 miles west of Cascadia), turn north onto Quartzville Drive (a paved local road) and proceed 1.4 miles north and east; turn sharply south (right) onto a paved access road and go 0.4 mile, then bear left into the campground. (Note for this and the other camps on this route: Midtown Sweet Home isn't readily definable, since the c.b.d. stretches for several miles along the highway; for navigation purposes, we've plotted a midtown fix at approximately milepost 27 on U.S. 20.)

Facilities: 136 campsites, about half with partial hookups, in 2 sections; sites are small+ to medium-sized, level, with minimal separation; most parking pads are paved, medium to long, wide straight-ins; huge, grassy spaces for tents; fireplaces; b-y-o firewood; water at sites and at several additional faucets; restrooms with showers; holding tank disposal station; waste water receptacles; paved driveways; adequate+ supplies and services are available in Sweet Home.

Activities & Attractions: Boating; boat launch and dock; fishing; hiking trails; playground; volleyball, tennis, basketball and horseshoe courts; day use areas.

Natural Features: Located on a large flat on the west shore of Foster Lake (Reservoir), a flood control impoundment on the South and Middle Santiam Rivers; vegetation consists of acres of mown grass dotted with planted hardwoods and evergreens; bordered by the forested foothills of the west slope of the Cascade Range; elevation 700'.

Season, Fees & Phone: April to November; $11.00 for a standard site, $12.00 for a hookup site; 10 day limit; Linn County Parks Department (503) 967-3917.

Camp Notes: Even without seeing the signs, you can readily recognize this as a park that was originally developed by the Corps of Engineers. The large tracts of grass in and around the campground are a 'trademark' of most CoE parks throughout the West. The campsites are closely spaced 'horizontally', but they're also quite 'deep', (i.e., there's plenty of room behind each unit in the 'infield' or the 'outfield'). There's easy lake access--but it might take you a while to walk there from the far end of the campground! This is a good-sized place.

CASCADIA
Cascadia State Park

Location: Western Oregon southeast of Albany.

Access: From U.S Highway 20 at milepost 41 +.4 (14 miles east of midtown Sweet Home, a few yards west of the Dobbin Creek bridge), turn north onto the park access road, proceed 0.1 mile, bear to the right around the picnic area for another 0.1 mile to the campground.

Facilities: 26 campsites; (2 group camps are also available); sites are small to small+, with nominal to fair separation; parking pads are packed gravel, reasonably level, short to medium-length straight-ins; adequate space for small to medium+ tents in most sites (a few are larger); fireplaces; firewood is usually for sale, or b-y-o; water at several faucets; restrooms with showers; waste water receptacles; paved driveways; adequate+ supplies and services are available in Sweet Home.

Activities & Attractions: Fishing; 2-mile hiking trail to Soda Creek Falls; trails down to the river; soda water from a hand pump at Soda Springs; day use area with shelters.

Natural Features: Located on level or very gently sloping terrain near the north bank of the South Santiam River; campsites are well shaded/sheltered by tall conifers, dense hardwoods and brush; bordered by densely forested hills; elevation 800'.

Season, Fees & Phone: April to October; please see Appendix for standard Oregon state park fees; 10 day limit; phone c/o Armitage State Park (503) 686-7592.

Camp Notes: It's intriguing how the foliage in so many Oregon parks maintains its translucent brilliance even on rainy, overcast days. This nice place is no exception.

TROUT CREEK
Willamette National Forest

Location: Western Oregon southeast of Albany.

Access: From U.S. Highway 20 at milepost 48 +.7 (14 miles west of the summit of Tombstone Pass, 22 miles east of Sweet Home) turn south into the campground.

Facilities: 24 campsites; sites are small+ to medium-sized, basically level, with good to excellent separation; parking pads are packed gravel, mostly medium-length straight-ins, plus a few long pull-throughs; small tent areas; fire rings; firewood is available for gathering in the vicinity; water at a hand pump; vault facilities; waste water receptacles; hard-surfaced driveway; adequate+ supplies and services are available in Sweet Home.

Activities & Attractions: Fishing; picnic shelter.

Natural Features: Located on a flat along the South Santiam River; sites are well sheltered by dense conifers and hardwoods; elevation 1100'.

Season, Fees & Phone: May to October; $7.00 for a single site, $14.00 for double occupancy; 14 day limit; Sweet Home Ranger District (503) 367-5168.

Camp Notes: Unless you have claustrophobic tendencies, you'll really like it here. Ditto all the camps east of Trout Creek. Even then, you could gain some visual relief by gazing straight up through the holes in the forest to the sky. (Use discretion on drizzly days; a sudden, big drip from the trees may give you a free cold shower. We know.)

YUKWAH
Willamette National Forest

Location: Western Oregon southeast of Albany.

Access: From U.S. Highway 20 at milepost 49 (14 miles west of the summit of Tombstone Pass, 22 miles east of Sweet Home), turn south into the campground.

Facilities: 20 campsites; sites are small+ to medium+, level, with good to excellent separation; parking pads are gravel, medium to medium+ straight-ins, plus several long pull-throughs; small to medium-sized tent areas; fire rings; firewood is available for gathering in the vicinity (may be damp); water at hand pumps; vault facilities; waste water receptacles; narrow, gravel driveway (turnaround at east end); adequate+ supplies and services are available in Sweet Home.

Activities & Attractions: Trail; fishing.

Natural Features: Located on a small bench just above the South Santiam River; campground vegetation consists of dense conifers, hardwoods and undergrowth; bordered by densely forested hills and mountains; elevation 1200'.

Season, Fees & Phone: May to October; $7.00 for a single site, $14.00 for double occupancy; 14 day limit; Sweet Home Ranger District (503) 367-5168.

Camp Notes: When you consider the local mountainous terrain, Yukwah, as well the other camps along this stretch of '20' offers surprisingly level spots for tents or camping vehicles. Yukwah or one of the neighboring low-altitude camps is usually available for winter camping with no services and no fee.

FERNVIEW
Willamette National Forest

Location: Western Oregon southeast of Albany.

Access: From U.S. Highway 20 at milepost 51 +.3 (12 miles west of the summit of Tombstone Pass, 24 miles east of Sweet Home), turn south into the campground.

Facilities: 11 campsites; sites are small, with excellent separation; parking pads are gravel, short straight-ins; small tent areas; fire rings; firewood is available for gathering in the vicinity (may be damp); water at a hand pump; vault facilities; waste water receptacles; narrow, gravel driveway (turnaround at far east end); adequate+ supplies and services are available in Sweet Home.

Activities & Attractions: Trail from the east end of the campground; fishing.

Natural Features: Located on a flat in a dense forest of conifers, hardwoods, and dense undergrowth, including a lush carpet of ferns, on the west slope of the Cascade Range; elevation 1300'.

Season, Fees & Phone: May to October; $5.00 for a single site, $10.00 for double occupancy; 14 day limit; Sweet Home Ranger District (503) 367-5168.

Camp Notes: Like the other forest camps in this area, the access road is so tightly flanked by the forest that larger vehicles may get 'pinstripes' from overhanging or outstretched twigs and branches. You can hear the highway traffic from the campsites, but you certainly can't see it. Likewise, the stream which flows past far below the campground can be heard but not viewed. Once you're settled into a 'campnook', you, your tent, and your vehicle will be closely cuddled by the forest as well. If you like backpacking, but don't want to go through all the work and the sweat, this kind of spot might satisfy your craving for seclusion.

HOUSE ROCK
Willamette National Forest

Location: Western Oregon southeast of Albany.

Access: From U.S. Highway 20 at milepost 54 +.3 (9 miles west of the summit of Tombstone Pass, 27 miles east of Sweet Home), turn south (a hard left if you're westbound) onto a gravel access road and proceed 0.3 mile down into the campground. (Note: The access road is very narrow, signed as "not suitable for trailers or large rv's".)

Facilities: 17 campsites; sites are small to small+, acceptably level, with very good to excellent separation; parking pads are gravel, short straight-ins; small to medium-sized tent areas; fire rings; firewood is available for gathering in the vicinity (may be wet); water at hand pumps; vault facilities; waste water receptacles; narrow, gravel driveway; adequate+ supplies and services are available in Sweet Home.

Activities & Attractions: House Rock Loop Trail; footbridge across the stream; picnic area; possible fishing.

Natural Features: Located on hilly terrain in a canyon along 2 creeks in the Cascade Range; super dense canopy of conifers, hardwoods, moss and undergrowth covers and surrounds the campground; elevation 1700'.

Season, Fees & Phone: May to late October; $7.00 for a single site, $14.00 for double occupancy; 14 day limit; Sweet Home Ranger District (503) 367-5168.

Camp Notes: Most of the campsites are in their own little pockets of foliage. The spacing between them isn't much--but you can't see your neighbors. About half of the sites are streamside, the remainder are just above the streams. This looks like the kind of place where you wouldn't be at all surprised to catch a glimpse of a tiny guy with pointed ears dressed in a green suit, lugging a pot o' gold and a shovel.

LOST PRAIRIE
Willamette National Forest

Location: Western Oregon southeast of Albany.

Access: From U.S. Highway 20 at milepost 67 +.3 (14 miles west of the summit of Santiam Pass, 3.5 miles east of the summit of Tombstone Pass, 40 miles east of Sweet Home), turn south into the campground.

Facilities: 10 campsites, including several park 'n walk camp/picnic units; sites are small to medium-sized, level, with fair to good separation; parking pads are paved, short straight-ins or pull-offs; adequate space for medium to large tents on a surface of grass and conifer needles; fire rings; firewood is available for gathering in the area; water at hand pumps; vault facilities; waste water receptacles; paved driveway, parking area and footpaths; adequate+ supplies and services are available in Sweet Home.

Activities & Attractions: Possible fishing for small trout; several trailheads within 1 mile west of the campground.

Natural Features: Located on a streamside flat on the west slope of the Cascade Range; campground vegetation consists of large areas of tall grass and wildflowers, and medium-dense, tall conifers; Hackleman Creek flows past the campsites; bordered by densely forested hills and mountains; elevation 3300'.

Season, Fees & Phone: May to late November; $7.00 for a single site, $14.00 for double occupancy; 14 day limit; Sweet Home Ranger District (503) 367-5168.

Camp Notes: Lost Prairie's recorded history dates back to April 1859 when a group of settlers from the Willamette Valley camped on this grassy flat during a trailblazing trip to central Oregon. Some of the group's members thought they were lost. So the party's leader, one Andrew Wiley, climbed a tree on a nearby mountain to get a better look at the territory and became the first white man to glimpse Santiam Pass from this side of the Cascades. Nowadays, Lost Prairie serves as the easternmost roadside camp along this segment of highway. There's plenty of vegetation between the campground and the road. The park 'n walk sites look inviting.

Oregon 49

BIG LAKE
Willamette National Forest

Location: West-central Oregon northwest of Bend.

Access: From U.S. Highway 20 near milepost 80 (8.5 miles east of the junction of U.S. 20 with Oregon State Highway 126, 40 miles northwest of Bend), turn south onto Forest Road 2690 (paved); proceed 0.7 mile south to a fork in the road; take the left fork, and continue for 2 miles to the campground.

Facilities: 49 campsites; sites are average or better in size, with mostly good separation; north shore units may be a bit roomier; parking pads are gravel, and some pads are spacious enough for large vehicles; a few pads may require additional leveling; some very nice, grassy tent spots; fire rings; limited firewood is available for gathering in the vicinity, b-y-o is suggested; water at several faucets; restrooms; paved driveways; limited supplies and services are available in Sisters.

Activities & Attractions: Boating; sailing; boat launch; fishing; swimming area; the Pacific Crest Trail passes within 0.5 mile.

Natural Features: Located on the north and west shores of beautiful Big Lake in Hidden Valley on the upper west slope of the Cascades; all sites are in an open conifer forest, including some right on the shore of the lake; Mount Washington rises commandingly in full view from the south shore of the lake; Three Fingered Jack Peak can be seen to the north; Mount Washington Wilderness is located just a few miles from the southern edge of the lake; elevation 4600'.

Season, Fees & Phone: May to October; $8.00; 10 day limit; McKenzie Ranger District (503) 822-3381.

Camp Notes: Though only a few campsites are right along the lake, most units have views of the exceptionally picturesque lake and surrounding mountains. The sight of razor-backed Mount Washington rising from the south shore of Big Lake is incredibly impressive! Definitely recommended.

Oregon 50

FISH LAKE
Willamette National Forest

Location: Western Oregon northeast of Springfield.

Access: From Oregon State Highway 126 at milepost 1 +.5 (1.5 miles south of the junction of Highway 126 & U.S. Highway 20, 18 miles north of the junction of State Highways 126 & 242 near McKenzie Bridge), turn west into the campground.

Facilities: Approximately 8 campsites; sites are small+, level, with fair separation; parking pads are gravel/dirt, medium-length straight-ins or pull-offs; adequate space for tents; fire rings; firewood is available for gathering in the vicinity; water at a couple of faucets; vault facilities; gravel driveway; camper supplies at a resort at nearby Clear Lake.

Activities & Attractions: Fishing; possibility for hand-launched boating access.

Natural Features: Located on the east shore of evergreen-ringed Fish Lake in the Cascade Range; sites are lightly shaded/sheltered by tall conifers and some hardwoods; surrounded by lava fields; elevation 3300'.

Season, Fees & Phone: May to October; $6.00; 14 day limit; McKenzie Ranger District (503) 822-3381.

Camp Notes: Ordinarily, a tiny, rough spot like this would merit just a 'thumbnail' mention. But the views are so excellent and the highwayside access so convenient that it has been given a small measure of its own space so you'll take note of it, and maybe stop to take a look.

COLDWATER COVE
Willamette National Forest

Location: Western Oregon northeast of Springfield.

Access: From Oregon State Highway 126 at milepost 4 +.6 (4.6 miles south of the junction of Highway 126 & U.S. 20, 15 miles north of the junction of State Highways 126 & 242), turn east onto a paved access road; continue for 0.5 mile to the campground.

Facilities: 34 campsites; most sites are small to medium in size, and fairly well separated; parking pads are paved, most are smaller straight-ins, but there are a few pull-throughs long enough to accommodate medium-sized vehicles; many pads may require additional leveling; mostly small tent spots which may be a bit sloped; fire rings plus some barbecue grills; water at faucets and a hand pump; vault facilities; paved driveways; camper supplies at a nearby resort; gas and groceries are available in the community of McKenzie Bridge.

Activities & Attractions: Fishing; motorless boating; boat launch; a paved trail leads from the campground down to the lake; the McKenzie River Trail passes by the campground; picnic area on the west shore of Clear Lake.

Natural Features: Located on a hillside overlooking the south shore of beautiful, blue-green, 140-acre Clear Lake in the Cascade Range; the lake is the headwater of the McKenzie River; campground vegetation consists of fairly dense conifers and underbrush; deposits of volcanic rock surround the camp area; elevation 3000'.

Season, Fees & Phone: May to October; $8.00; 14 day limit; McKenzie Ranger Dist. (503) 822-3381.

Camp Notes: Although only a few of the best campsites overlook the lake, all the sites enjoy the tranquility of the forested setting at this picturesque lake. In the not uncommon event that Coldwater Cove is full when you roll in, an inexpensive night's stay might be had at Fish Lake Campground (see info above). Excellent mountain/lake views are also included in the Fish Lake package.

ICE CAP CREEK
Willamette National Forest

Location: Western Oregon northeast of Springfield.

Access: From Oregon State Highway 126 at milepost 5 +.5 (5.5 miles south of the junction of Highway 126 & U.S. 20, 14.5 miles north of the junction of State Highways 126 and 242), turn west onto a paved access road; continue for 0.2 mile west to the campground.

Facilities: 22 campsites; most sites are rather small, with fairly good to very good separation; parking pads are gravel, short to medium-length straight-ins; some additional leveling may be required; tent spots tend to be a bit small and some are rather sloped or bumpy; fire rings; firewood is available for gathering in the vicinity; water at faucets throughout; restrooms; paved driveways; gas and groceries are available in the community of McKenzie Bridge, 17 miles southwest.

Activities & Attractions: Stream fishing; fishing, motorless boating and boat launch on Carmen Reservoir, near the campground; adjacent picnic area; a short foot trail leads to viewpoints at Koosah Falls and Sahalie Falls; the McKenzie River Trail follows along the west bank of the river.

Natural Features: Located on a forested hillside east of the McKenzie River in the Cascade Range; tiny Carmen Reservoir is within view; Ice Cap Creek flows through a narrow deep gorge here, and into the McKenzie River; surrounded by dense forest, the campground itself is a bit more open, with tall timber and a pine needle forest floor; elevation 2900'.

Season, Fees & Phone: May to September; $6.00; 14 day limit; McKenzie R.D. (503) 822-3381.

Camp Notes: Since Ice Cap Creek Campground is situated away from the main highway, and no motors are allowed on Carmen Reservoir, the only real 'noise' here is the rush of the stream over the falls.

TRAIL BRIDGE
Willamette National Forest

Location: Western Oregon northeast of Springfield.

Access: From Oregon State Highway 126 at milepost 10 +.8 (11 miles south of the junction of Highway 126 & U.S. Highway 20, 9 miles north of the junction of State Highways 126 & 242), turn west onto Forest Road 730 (paved); drive 0.2 mile across a McKenzie River bridge, to a "T" intersection; turn south (left) and proceed 0.5 mile to the campground.

Facilities: 28 campsites; sites are located in one central area with minimal to nominal separation; ample space for tents; parking spaces are on a gravel driveway which encircles the units; fire rings; a limited amount of firewood is available for gathering in the vicinity; water at several faucets; vault facilities; gravel driveways; gas and groceries are available in the community of McKenzie Bridge.

Activities & Attractions: Boating; boat launch; fishing; McKenzie River Trail; a foot trail leads to nearby Smith River Reservoir.

Natural Features: Located along the west shore of Trail Bridge Reservoir, a deep-green 120-acre lake formed on the McKenzie River, in the Cascade Range; the campground is situated in dense forest which is quite clear of underbrush; elevation 2100'.

Season, Fees & Phone: April to November; $5.00-$6.00; 14 day limit; McKenzie Ranger District (503) 822-3381.

Camp Notes: This is a really different camp spot with uncommon facilities. Vehicle campers will find that their outdoor 'kitchen' probably won't be right out the rear door of the camper. (The name of the reservoir and campground are often spelled as a single word, Trailbridge.)

Oregon 54

OLLALIE
Willamette National Forest

Location: Western Oregon northeast of Springfield.

Access: From Oregon State Highway 126 at milepost 12 +.9 (13 miles south of the junction of Oregon State Highway 126 with U.S. 20, 7 miles north of the junction of Oregon State Highways 126 & 242 near McKenzie Bridge), turn west into the campground.

Facilities: 17 campsites in 2 tiers; site size varies from small sites along the river to fairly large sites in the upper tier; camp units have minimal to fair separation; parking pads are gravel, short straight-ins or long pull-throughs; some pads may require additional leveling; tent spots are mostly for smaller tents; fire rings; a limited amount of firewood is available for gathering in the vicinity; water at a hand pump; vault facilities; gravel driveways; gas and groceries are available in McKenzie Bridge, 9 miles southwest.

Activities & Attractions: Fishing on the McKenzie River; rafting; boating; a boat launch is located 0.3 mile south of this camping area; the 26-mile-long McKenzie River Trail passes by on the opposite bank of the river.

Natural Features: Located on a tree-dotted hillside overlooking the confluence of Ollalie Creek with the McKenzie River in the Cascade Range; Three Sisters Wilderness lies just to the south and the Mount Washington Wilderness Area is to the east; elevation 2000'.

Season, Fees & Phone: April to October; $6.00; 14 day limit; McKenzie Ranger District (503) 822-3381.

Camp Notes: The upper sites, a few yards from the highway, have somewhat limited views, but are relatively spacious. The lower sites are right on the grassy riverbank, and enjoy a somewhat quieter atmosphere.

Oregon 55

PARADISE
Willamette National Forest

Location: Western Oregon northeast of Springfield.

Access: From Oregon State Highway 126 at milepost 54 +.1 (4 miles east of the community of McKenzie Bridge, 2 miles west of the junction of Highways 126 & 242), turn north onto a paved access road, then immediately west (left); proceed west for 0.1 mile to the campground.

Facilities: 64 campsites; sites are medium-sized, level with good separation; 'premium' sites, along the river, are a bit smaller than sites along the highway; parking pads are paved, with some pull-throughs spacious enough to accommodate large vehicles; some nice, grassy tent sites, including some riverside areas; fire rings; limited firewood is available for gathering in the vicinity; water at faucets throughout; restrooms, plus supplementary vault facilities; paved driveways; gas and groceries are available in the small community of McKenzie Bridge.

Activities & Attractions: Fishing; rafting; boat launch located east of the camping area; a trail through the campground connects with the 26-mile-long McKenzie River Trail.

Natural Features: Located along the south bank of the McKenzie River on the west slope of the Cascades; units are all situated amid tall trees and hardy ferns over a lush green forest floor; Blue River Reservoir is a few miles west; Three Sisters Wilderness is to the south and east, the Mount Washington Wilderness Area is to the east; elevation 1600'.

Season, Fees & Phone: May to October; $8.00-$9.00; 14 day limit; McKenzie Ranger District (503) 822-3381.

Camp Notes: The dense forest here at Paradise creates a 'coastal rain forest' atmosphere. The campground trail passes through a virtual tunnel of thick vegetation.

Oregon 56

McKenzie Bridge
Willamette National Forest

Location: Western Oregon northeast of Springfield.

Access: From Oregon State Highway 126 at milepost 49 +.8 (1 mile west of the community of McKenzie Bridge, 9 miles east of Blue River), turn south onto a gravel access road and continue for 100 yards to the campground.

Facilities: 20 campsites in 2 loops; most sites are fairly large, level, with good separation; A Loop sites are a bit larger than B Loop sites; parking pads are gravel, many are short+ straight-ins but some are pull-throughs spacious enough to accommodate very large vehicles; some nice grassy tent sites; fire rings; firewood is available for gathering in the vicinity; water at hand pumps; vault facilities; gravel driveways; gas and groceries in McKenzie Bridge; nearest source of complete supplies and services is Springfield, 47 miles west.

Activities & Attractions: Boating; boat launch adjacent; fishing on the McKenzie River; day use area; variety of water recreation activities at Blue River Reservoir.

Natural Features: Located along the north bank of the McKenzie River in the Cascade Range; sites are situated amid tall conifers and moderate underbrush; Blue River Reservoir is a few miles west; elevation 1400'.

Season, Fees & Phone: May to October; $6.00; 14 day limit; McKenzie Ranger District (503) 822-3381.

Camp Notes: Some sites have river access within a few yards. McKenzie Bridge has a nice, sheltered/shady, forested atmosphere with lots of elbow room.

Oregon 57

Delta
Willamette National Forest

Location: Western Oregon northeast of Springfield.

Access: From Oregon State Highway 126 at milepost 45 +.4 (4.5 miles east of Blue River, 5.5 miles west of McKenzie Bridge), turn south onto Forest Road 19; drive 0.2 mile, across a trestle bridge; turn west (right) and continue (parallel to Highway 126) for 1 mile to the campground.

Facilities: 39 campsites; most sites are spacious, level, and well separated; parking pads are gravel, medium to long, straight-ins or pull-throughs; some large, level, grassy tent spots; fire rings at all sites; fire rings and barbecue grills at multiple sites; water at a hand pump; vault facilities; gravel driveways; limited supplies in Blue River.

Activities & Attractions: Stream fishing; an "Old Growth Timber Grove" nature trail starts from across a footbridge at the west end of the campground; Blue River Lake, a few miles north, offers most types of water recreation; Cougar Reservoir, to the south, is right on the west edge of the Three Sisters Wilderness.

Natural Features: Located in a narrow valley on the west slopes of the Cascades; most sites are in moderately dense forest; the main stream of the McKenzie River flows past the north edge of the campground, the South Fork of the McKenzie flows along the south boundary; an open grassy flat stretches along the riverbank; elevation 1200'.

Season, Fees & Phone: May to September; $7.00 for a single site, $14.00 for a multiple site; 14 day limit; Blue River Ranger District (503) 822-3317.

Camp Notes: Delta's position across the river from the highway makes it secluded enough to be quiet and peaceful. Though there are many recreation opportunities in the nearby area, Delta isn't often filled to capacity.

Oregon
South Western
Please refer to the Oregon map in the Appendix

Oregon 58

BLACK CANYON
Willamette National Forest

Location: Western Oregon southeast of Eugene.

Access: From Oregon State Highway 58 at milepost 27 +.3 (8 miles northwest of Oakridge, 33 miles southeast of Eugene), turn north into the campground.

Facilities: 75 campsites in 6 loops; sites are good-sized, with nominal to fair separation; parking pads are paved, some are spacious pull-through units located rather close to the highway; some very nice tent spots, several with gravel tent pads; fire rings; some gatherable firewood is available in the vicinity; water at several faucets; vault facilities; paved driveways; adequate supplies and services are available in Oakridge.

Activities & Attractions: Boating; rafting; paved boat ramp; stream fishing; nature programs may be scheduled on summer evenings; a trail leads through the campground to a gravel river beach; day use area.

Natural Features: Located in the Black Canyon of the Middle Fork of the Willamette River on the west slopes of the Cascades; sites are deeply sheltered/shaded by conifers and hardwoods; many sites are right along the south bank of the stream; a deep channel is just offbank of here, at a bend in the river; elevation 1000'.

Season, Fees & Phone: May to October; $6.00 for a standard single site, $9.00 for a 'premium' (riverside) site, $12.00 for a multiple site, $16.00 for a multiple riverside site; 14 day limit; Lowell Ranger District (503) 937-2129.

Camp Notes: Black Canyon is the last campground on the free-flowing river. A few miles downstream, a dam restricts the Middle Fork's flow by creating 12 mile-long, mile-wide Lookout Point Lake. The rain forest atmosphere at this campground suggests settings on the Oregon Coast. The so-called 'premium' sites along the river offer some really nice views. Another nearby campground is Shady Dell, located at milepost 29. It has 10 sites, a pump and vaults, and a fee, rather near the highway.

Oregon 59

BLUE POOL
Willamette National Forest

Location: Western Oregon southeast of Eugene.

Access: From Oregon State Highway 58 at milepost 44 +.7 (10 miles southeast of Oakridge, 41 miles northwest of the junction of Oregon State Highway 58 & U.S. 97), turn south into the campground.

Facilities: 24 campsites in 3 loops; most sites are small, with average to good separation; parking pads are paved, short to medium-length straight-ins; pads are fairly level, though the campground is built on a slight slope; several rather small, but private tent spots, including some walk-in sites, are located toward the west end of the campground; fire rings; limited firewood is available for gathering in the area, b-y-o is suggested; water at several faucets; vault facilities; paved driveways; adequate supplies and services are available in Oakridge.

Activities & Attractions: Nice 'poolside' picnic area; fishing; Salt Creek Falls, a 266-foot cascade, is located along the highway, 10 miles southeast.

Natural Features: Located along the bank of Salt Creek in a narrow valley in the Cascade Range; tall conifers, maples and a considerable amount of underbrush provide shelter and separation for the sites; elevation 2000'.

Season, Fees & Phone: May to September; $7.00 for a single unit, $14.00 for a double unit; 14 day limit; Oakridge Ranger District (503) 782-2291.

Camp Notes: The 'Blue Pool' is a deep, liquid sapphire on Salt Creek in the campground area. It provides a tranquil rest spot for campers and anyone else who needs a break while traveling Highway 58. This route is the *terrortory* of flatbeds, reefers, log trucks and other demonic diesels possessed by yellow-line fever that make sport of passing other vehicles on this narrow, two-lane, curvy road. Take care.

Oregon 60

SHADOW BAY
Willamette National Forest

Location: Western Oregon southeast of Eugene.

Access: From Oregon State Highway 58 at milepost 58 +.9 (26 miles east of Oakridge, 3 miles northwest of Willamette Pass, 25 miles west of the junction of Oregon State Highway 58 & U.S. 97), turn north onto Forest Road 5897 (paved); travel northeasterly for 6.5 miles; turn northwest (left) onto Forest Road 5896; continue for an additional 1.8 miles on a fairly steep access road down to the campground.

Facilities: 103 campsites, including a few walk-in sites, in 6 loops; sites are medium to large, with average to good separation; parking pads are gravel, most are straight-ins, several are long enough for large rv's; some beautiful tent spots; fireplaces; some firewood is available for gathering in the area; water at several faucets; restrooms; holding tank disposal station; paved driveways; adequate supplies and services are available in Oakridge.

Activities & Attractions: Limited boating (10 mph); boat launch; fishing; swimming; foot trails in the area include the Shoreline Trail and the Waldo Lake Trail; the Pacific Crest Trail passes nearby.

Natural Features: Located in the heart of the Cascade Range on the southeast shore of Waldo Lake; sites farthest from the lake shore are on a grassy hilltop, with some trees for shelter and visual separation; sites closer to the lake are on a forested slope; elevation 5500'.

Season, Fees & Phone: May to September; $8.00 for a single unit, $16.00 for a multiple unit; 14 day limit; Oakridge Ranger District (503) 782-2291.

Camp Notes: If the proper weather conditions exist, Waldo Lake becomes a mirror that reflects the images of surrounding mountain peaks. Shadow Bay has the easiest access of the camps along the lake shore, yet is filled to capacity only on weekends.

Oregon 61

NORTH WALDO & ISLET
Willamette National Forest

Location: Western Oregon southeast of Eugene.

Access: From Oregon State Highway 58 at milepost 58 +.9 (26 miles east of Oakridge, 3 miles northwest of Willamette Pass, 25 miles west of the junction of Oregon State Highway 58 with U.S. 97), head north/northeast on Forest Road 5897 (paved) for 12.7 miles to a "T" intersection; (note that the road takes a very sharp turn to the northwest/left at about the 12-mile point); take the north (right) fork of the "T" for 0.4 mile to North Waldo, or the south (left) fork for 1.2 miles to Islet.

Facilities: 58 campsites in North Waldo, 55 campsites in Islet; sites vary from small+ to large, with fair to good separation; parking pads are gravel, mostly short to medium-length straight-ins; most pads will require some additional leveling; medium to large tent areas (but many may be bumpy, rocky, stumpy or slopey); fireplaces or fire rings; firewood is available for gathering in the surrounding area; water at several faucets; restrooms; waste water receptacles; holding tank disposal station in Islet; paved driveways; adequate supplies and services are available in Oakridge.

Activities & Attractions: Limited boating (10 mph); boat launches; fishing; designated swimming areas; foot trails in the area include the Shoreline Trail and the Waldo Lake Trail; the Pacific Crest Trail passes nearby.

Natural Features: Located on forested slopes and hilltops above the northeast shore of Waldo Lake in the heart of the Cascade Range; campground vegetation consists of moderately dense to dense tall conifers and a small quantity of underbrush; elevation 5500'.

Season, Fees & Phone: May to September; $8.00 for a single unit, $16.00 for a multiple unit; 14 day limit; Oakridge Ranger District (503) 782-2291.

Camp Notes: There are a few subtle differences between these two camps; but they're basically just a pair of loops of the same campground--separated by a mile of dense forest. Of the trio of large lakes in this vicinity (also see Lakes Odell and Crescent), Waldo is the largest, and maybe the prettiest too. Worth the dozen-mile trip off the highway.

TRAPPER CREEK
Deschutes National Forest

Location: Western Oregon north of Crater Lake.

Access: From Oregon State Highway 58 at milepost 62 +.3 (0.4 mile southeast of Willamette Pass, 29 miles east of Oakridge, 22 miles west of the junction of Oregon State Highway 58 with U.S. 97), turn south onto Forest Road 5810 (paved) and follow it as it curves around the northwest tip of the lake for 2 miles; turn north (left) into the campground.

Facilities: 32 campsites in 2 loops; sites are medium to large, with fair to good separation; parking pads are gravel, acceptably level, mostly short to medium-length straight-ins, plus a few pull-throughs; medium to large, mostly level, areas for tents; fire rings; firewood is available for gathering in the area; water at several faucets; vault facilities; paved driveways; gas and groceries along Highway 58 in Crescent Lake; adequate supplies and services are available in Oakridge.

Activities & Attractions: Boating; boat launch; fishing; footbridge across the creek.

Natural Features: Located on a slightly sloping, streamside/lakeside flat; swift and clear Trapper Creek enters Odell Lake at this point; sites receive light to medium shelter/shade from tall conifers and some brush; bordered by the heavily timbered mountains of the Cascade Range; elevation 4800'.

Season, Fees & Phone: May to October; $8.00 for a single unit, $16.00 for a double unit; 14 day limit; Crescent Ranger District (503) 433-2234.

Camp Notes: Camper's choice (if you get here early): lakeside or streamside. But all sites are at least within a few minutes' stroll of either the lake or the stream. Chances are you'll agree that this is the best of the camps on scenic Odell Lake.

PRINCESS CREEK
Deschutes National Forest

Location: Western Oregon southeast of Eugene.

Access: From Oregon State Highway 58 at milepost 63 +.8 (2 miles east of Willamette Pass, 30 miles east of Oakridge, 21 miles west of the junction of Oregon State Highway 58 & U.S. 97), turn south into the campground.

Facilities: 46 campsites in 2 loops; sites are good-sized and fairly well separated; parking pads are gravel mostly level pull-throughs, many ample enough for large rv's; some very nice tent sites, especially in the east loop; fireplaces; some firewood is available for gathering in the area; water at several faucets; vault facilities; paved driveways; adequate supplies and services are available in Oakridge.

Activities & Attractions: Boating; boat launch and dock are located between the 2 loops; fishing; the Pacific Crest Trail passes by the lake's west shore; about 8 miles to the west just off the highway is 266-foot Salt Creek Falls.

Natural Features: Located in the heart of the Cascade Range on the north shore of Odell Lake; striking Diamond Peak pierces the skyline across the lake to the south; lakeside campsites are adequately sheltered/shaded, while units away from the shore are heavily forested; all sites have a lake view; Willamette Pass, at 5126', is just a short distance up the highway to the west; campground elevation 4800'.

Season, Fees & Phone: May to October; $8.00 for a single unit, $16.00 for a double unit; 14 day limit; Crescent Ranger District (503) 433-2234.

Camp Notes: Odell Lake is beautiful, and Princess Creek Campground is convenient, relatively spacious and generally well maintained. Though many of the sites are close to the highway, there is an abundance of forest cover to muffle the traffic tumult.

SUNSET COVE
Deschutes National Forest

Location: Southwest Oregon north of Crater Lake.

Access: From Oregon State Highway 58 at milepost 66 +.8 (19 miles west of the junction of Oregon State Highway 58 & U.S. 97, 32 miles east of Oakridge), turn south into the campground.

Facilities: 21 campsites; sites are mostly medium-sized, with fair to good separation; parking pads are gravel, mostly short to medium-length straight-ins, plus a few longer pull-offs; many pads may require additional leveling; some good spots for smaller tents; fireplaces; firewood is available for gathering in the area; water at several faucets; vault facilities; waste water receptacles; hard-surfaced driveway; adequate supplies and services are available in Oakridge.

Activities & Attractions: Boating; boat launch and dock; fishing; views through the trees of Odell Lake and Diamond Peak from most sites; the drive along Highway 58 and over Willamette Pass offers travelers some fine mountain scenery.

Natural Features: Located on a forested hillside along the north shore of Odell Lake in the Cascade Range; campsites are situated in a dense conifer forest with very little underbrush; very prominent Diamond Peak rises to almost 9000' across the lake to the south; campground elevation 4800'.

Season, Fees & Phone: May to October; $7.00 for a single unit, $14.00 for a double unit; 14 day limit; Crescent Ranger District (503) 433-2234.

Camp Notes: Odell Lake is a beautiful, sapphire-blue pool surrounded by emerald-green forested slopes. Add Diamond Peak and the gold of the sunset into the picture and you have a gem of a picture postcard to take back home. (Incidentally, some commercial sources spell the lake and its inlet stream as *O'Dell*, but all national forest references spell it *Odell*.)

Oregon 65

ODELL CREEK
Willamette National Forest

Location: West-central Oregon north of Crater Lake.

Access: From Oregon State Highway 58 at milepost 67 +.5 (34 miles southeast of Oakridge, 17 miles west of the junction of Oregon State Highway 58 & U.S. 97), turn south onto a gravel access road and proceed 0.4 mile; turn west (right) down into the campground.

Facilities: 19 campsites; sites are small to small+, with nominal to fairly good separation; parking pads are gravel, short to short+ straight-ins; some pads may require a little additional leveling; small tent areas; fire rings; firewood is available for gathering in the vicinity; water at a hand pump; vault facilities; narrow, paved driveway; gas and groceries along Highway 58 in Crescent Lake; adequate supplies and services are available in Oakridge.

Activities & Attractions: Fishing; boating; boat launch at nearby Sunset Cove Campground.

Natural Features: Located on a narrow flat along the southeast tip of Odell Lake in the Cascade Range; campsites are moderately shaded/sheltered by tall, thin pines and some undercover; nearly all sites are lakeside; Odell Creek exits the lake at this point; encircled by high, densely forested mountains; elevation 4800'.

Season, Fees & Phone: May to October; $6.00; 14 day limit; Crescent Ranger District (503) 433-2234.

Camp Notes: Odell's small, tight, simple facility is a bit snug for anything longer than a vehicle with a small trailer. (Trapper Creek Campground, at the opposite tip of the lake, has more maneuvering room for longer outfits.) An additional observation: Compared to other lakeside forest camps throughout the west, Odell Creek's location on an outlet creek is somewhat of a rarity. For some uncertain reason, a majority of forest camps of this type are along inlet streams.

Oregon 66

CRESCENT LAKE
Deschutes National Forest

Location: West-central Oregon north of Crater Lake.

Access: From Oregon State Highway 58 at milepost 69 +.5 in the small community of Crescent Lake (15 miles northwest of the junction of Oregon State Highway 58 & U.S. 97, 35 miles southeast of Oakridge), turn southwest onto Forest Road 60 (paved); proceed 2.7 miles (the road jogs southeast, then southwest again at about the 2 mile mark); turn south (left) into the campground.

Facilities: 46 campsites; most sites are medium-sized, with fair separation; most parking pads are gravel, medium-length straight-ins; several units have long pull-throughs; many pads will require some additional leveling; medium to large areas for tents, may be sloped; fireplaces; some firewood is available for gathering in the vicinity; water at faucets throughout; vault facilities; paved driveways; gas and camper supplies on Highway 58; nearest source of adequate supplies and services is Oakridge.

Activities & Attractions: Boating; paved boat launch; fishing; designated swimming area; foot trails in the area; nearby Whitefish Horse Camp is located at a trailhead to Summit Lake.

Natural Features: Located on a forested slope above a bay at the north tip of Crescent Lake, where Crescent Creek enter the lake; tall timber and grass are the predominant forms of campground vegetation; some sites are right along the bay and some are creekside; encircled by the high, forested mountains of the Cascade Range; elevation 4800'.

Season, Fees & Phone: May to October; $8.00 for a single unit, $16.00 for a double unit; 14 day limit.

Camp Notes: Most sites have at least limited views through the trees of glacially formed Crescent Lake. Because of its proximity to the highway and a marina, this campground tends to be very popular with weekend boaters. For a more secluded camp spot, you might want to check out Spring Campground, on the lake's south shore (see details below).

Oregon 67

SPRING
Deschutes National Forest

Location: West-central Oregon north of Crater Lake.

Access: From Oregon State Highway 58 at milepost 69 +.5 in the small community of Crescent Lake (15 miles northwest of the junction of Oregon State Highway 58 with U.S. 97, 35 miles southeast of Oakridge), turn southwest onto Forest Road 60 (paved); travel along the west shore of the lake, then around the southwest end of the lake for a total of 8 miles; turn north (left) onto the campground access road for a final 0.6 mile to the campground. (Note that the road jogs southeast, then southwest again at about the 2-mile mark, then passes Crescent Lake CG; the road is paved all the way to Spring.)

Facilities: 68 campsites; sites are medium to medium+ in size, with nominal to fair separation; parking pads are gravel, medium-length straight-ins, plus a few pull-throughs; a little additional leveling will probably be needed in most sites; adequate, possibly slightly sloped, space for medium to large tents; fireplaces; firewood is available for gathering; water at several faucets; vault facilities; waste water receptacles; hard-surfaced driveways; gas and groceries along Highway 58 in Crescent Lake; nearest source of adequate supplies and services is Oakridge.

Activities & Attractions: Designated swimming beach; boating; boat launch; fishing; day use area.

Natural Features: Located on a slope near the south shore of Crescent Lake; sites are lightly sheltered/shaded by tall, thin conifers and very little underbrush; surrounded by the densely forested mountains of the Cascade Range; elevation 4800'.

Season, Fees & Phone: May to October; $8.00 for a single unit, $16.00 for a double unit; 14 day limit; Crescent Ranger District (503) 433-2234.

Camp Notes: If you overlook the local area's vegetational shortcomings and concentrate on the distant views, you'll have an enjoyable stay. Nice lake.

Oregon 68

EAST DAVIS LAKE
Deschutes National Forest

Location: West-central Oregon southwest of Bend.

Access: From Oregon State Highway 58 at milepost 72 +.5 (3 miles southeast of Crescent Lake), take Klamath County Road 61 (Crescent Road, paved) east/northeast for 3.3 miles to a 3-way intersection; turn north (left) onto Forest Road 46 (paved) and travel 7.9 miles; turn west (left) onto a short paved road to a "T" intersection; turn southwest (left) onto FR 855 (gravel) and proceed 2 miles; turn north (right) for a final 0.3 mile to the campground.

Facilities: 32 campsites; sites are generally large, level, with fair to good separation; parking pads are gravel, mostly long pull-throughs; adequate space for medium to large tents; fireplaces; firewood is available for gathering; water at a hand pump; vault facilities; waste water basins; gravel driveways; nearest reliable sources of supplies (gas and groceries) are La Pine and Crescent, on U.S. 97.

Activities & Attractions: Hiking trail; fishing; boating.

Natural Features: Located on a flat on the edge of a meadow near the south shore of Davis Lake, on the east slope of the Cascade Range; a sizeable stream--Odell Creek--flows past the campground; sites are lightly sheltered/shaded by tall conifers and some second growth timber; several impressive, conical peaks rise in the distance, north of the lake; elevation 4400'.

Season, Fees & Phone: May to October; $6.00 for a single site, $12.00 for a double site; 14 day limit; Crescent Ranger District (503) 433-2234.

Camp Notes: This is another one of those "The campground isn't all that great, but, gosh, look at the *view* out there!" places. You can seek further seclusion at West Davis Lake Camp, on the opposite side of the inlet/bay from East Davis. West Davis can be reached from East Davis, or from FR 46 at a point 4 miles south of the East Davis turnoff, then northwest via FR 4660. Either way, it's a 5-mile drive on gravel. (But it's only *0.5* mile by foot trail from East Davis.)

Oregon 69

ROCK CREEK
Deschutes National Forest

Location: West-central Oregon southwest of Bend.

Access: From U.S. Highway 97 at Wickiup Junction (3 miles north of La Pine, 27 miles south of Bend) travel west on Deschutes County Road 43 (paved) for 11.5 miles; pick up CR 42 (paved) for another 9.2 miles westerly to its junction with County Road 46; turn north (right) onto CR 46 (paved) for 2.5 miles; turn east (right) onto a paved access road for 0.25 mile to the campground. **Alternate Access:** From Oregon State Highway 58 at milepost 72 +.5 (3 miles southeast of Crescent Lake), take Klamath County Road 61 (Crescent Road, paved) east/northeast for 3.3 miles to a 3-way intersection; turn north (left) onto Forest Road 46/County Road 46 (paved) and travel 18 miles to the campground turnoff.

Facilities: 32 campsites in 4 loops; sites are medium+ in size, with fair separation; parking pads are gravel, medium-length straight-ins, and some may require a little additional leveling; medium to large, basically level, spaces for tents; fire rings; firewood is available for gathering in the area; water at hand pumps; vault facilities; paved driveways; gas and groceries+ in La Pine.

Activities & Attractions: Fishing (bass and trout, special limits); boating; boat launch; day use area.

Natural Features: Located on a gently sloping flat near the west shore of Crane Prairie Reservoir; sites receive light to medium shelter/shade from tall pines and light ground vegetation; bordered by the forested hills and mountains of the Cascade Range; elevation 4500'.

Season, Fees & Phone: May to October; $8.00 for a single site, $16.00 for a double site; 14 day limit; Bend Ranger District (503) 388-5664.

Camp Notes: Rock Creek is a little closer to the lake than its sister Camp, Quinn River (see separate info). The Alternate Access (above) from Highway 58 will also work for Quinn River. It is also useful, with a slight adjustment, for Gull Point and Crane Prairie Campgrounds (see separate information and maps).

Oregon 70

QUINN RIVER
Deschutes National Forest

Location: West-central Oregon southwest of Bend.

Access: From U.S. Highway 97 in the whistle stop of Wickiup Junction (3 miles north of La Pine, 27 miles south of Bend) travel westerly on Deschutes County Road 43 (paved) for 11.5 miles; pick up County Road 42 (paved) for another 9.2 miles westerly to its junction with County Road 46; turn north (right) onto CR 46 and proceed 4 miles; turn east (right) into the campground.

Facilities: 41 campsites in 2 loops; sites are medium to large, essentially level, with nominal to fairly good separation; parking pads are sandy gravel, medium to medium+ straight-ins or pull-throughs; large tent areas; fire rings; firewood is available for gathering in the surrounding area; water at a hand pump; vault facilities; waste water basins; gravel driveways; gas and groceries+ in La Pine.

Activities & Attractions: Osprey Point Observation Trail, a half-mile south of the campground; fishing (bass and trout, special limits); boating; boat launch.

Natural Features: Located on a gently sloping, forested flat, a short distance from a large bay on the west shore of Crane Prairie Reservoir, an impoundment on the Deschutes and Cultus Rivers; sites are moderately sheltered/shaded by tall pines and light ground vegetation; a good-sized stream flows past the campground; bordered by the forested hills and mountains of the Cascade Range; elevation 4500'.

Season, Fees & Phone: May to October; $8.00; 14 day limit; Bend Ranger District (503) 388-5664.

Camp Notes: The lodgepole pine forest in this region has been decimated by an infestation of mountain pine beetles, so the scenic merit of the area is something you'll have to judge for yourself. The old forest is being logged-off, and new, more-resistant trees are being planted. The trees in the campground so far seem to have withstood the beetle barrage a bit better than those in the surrounding area.

Oregon 71

CRANE PRAIRIE
Deschutes National Forest

Location: West-central Oregon southwest of Bend.

Access: From U.S. Highway 97 at Wickiup Junction (3 miles north of La Pine, 27 miles south of Bend), travel westerly on Deschutes County Road 43 (paved) for 11.5 miles; pick up Deschutes County Road 42 (paved) and continue west for another 5.6 miles; turn north (right, 1 mile past the Twin Lakes turnoff) onto Forest Road 4270 (paved) and proceed 4 final miles to the campground.

Facilities: 147 campsites, including 6 park 'n walk tent sites, in 4 loops; sites are small to medium-sized, with nominal to fair separation; parking pads are gravel, medium to long straight-ins or pull-throughs; ample space for tents; fireplaces; firewood is available for gathering in the vicinity; water at several faucets; vault facilities; paved driveways; gas and camper supplies at a local resort; gas and groceries+ in La Pine.

Activities & Attractions: Boating; boat launches and docks; fishing for bass and rainbow trout; day use area.

Natural Features: Located along a bay on the northeast corner of Crane Prairie Reservoir, an impoundment on the Deschutes and Cultus Rivers; campsites receive light-medium to medium shade/shelter from tall pines and light ground cover; tent sites offer a little more seclusion than standard sites; bordered by the forested hills and mountains of the lower east slopes of the Cascade Range; elevation 4500'.

Season, Fees & Phone: May to October; $9.00; 14 day limit; Bend Ranger District (503) 388-5664.

Camp Notes: Crane Prairie and the other campgrounds in this section are the largest and best-equipped camps on the three major bodies of water (Crane Prairie and Wickiup Reservoirs and Davis Lake) in the Deschutes River Region. The information presented here provides you with an introduction to the area. There are a half-dozen other camps on lesser lakes off of back roads in the area. A conversation with local campground hosts or the rangers who regularly make their rounds should provide you with details and directions to the other campgrounds if you need them.

Oregon 72

GULL POINT
Deschutes National Forest

Location: West-central Oregon southwest of Bend.

Access: From U.S. Highway 97 at Wickiup Junction (3 miles north of La Pine, 27 miles south of Bend), travel westerly on Deschutes County Road 43 (paved) for 11.5 miles; pick up Deschutes County Road 42 (paved) and continue west for another 4.6 miles; turn southwest (left) onto Twin Lakes Road (paved) and proceed southwest, south, then southeast for 2.7 miles to the campground.

Facilities: 81 campsites in 2 loops; sites are medium to large, reasonably level, with nominal to fair separation; parking pads are gravel, medium to long pull-throughs, plus some straight-ins; large tent spots; fireplaces; some firewood is available for gathering in the surrounding area; water at several faucets; vault facilities; disposal station; paved driveways; gas and groceries+ in La Pine.

Activities & Attractions: Limited boating; boat launch; fishing.

Natural Features: Located on a bayside flat adjacent to a meadow on the northwest corner of Wickiup Reservoir, an impoundment on the Deschutes River; sites are lightly to moderately sheltered/shaded by tall conifers and some brush; bordered by forested hills; elevation 4200'.

Season, Fees & Phone: May to October; $9.00; 14 day limit; Bend Ranger District (503) 388-5664.

Camp Notes: Why is Gull Point sometimes jammed when some other camps in the Cascade Lakes region (like those on Davis Lake and Crane Prairie Reservoir) still have room to spare? OK, maybe 'cause it's a few minutes closer to U.S. 97; and you may be able to grab a shower at the local resort. Speaking of which, near the resort there's another public camp--South Twin Lake--with several dozen sites in 2 sections flanking the access road. You'll pass it on the way in to Gull Point. Same fee and facilities as

Gull Point. They really pack 'em in on some weekends there, too. There are also a pair of good-sized, roughcut, but pleasant and piney, free campgrounds in the neighborhood.

Oregon 73

BAKER BAY
Lane County Park

Location: Western Oregon southeast of Eugene.

Access: From Interstate 5 Exit 174 for Dorena Lake and Cottage Grove, (20 miles south of Eugene), head east on Row River Road for 4.1 miles; continue ahead (southeast) on Government Road (past the turnoff to the dam and Schwartz Park, then along the south side of the lake) for another 2.9 miles; turn north (left) onto a paved park access road and proceed 0.1 mile, then turn east (right) for a final 0.2 mile to the campground.

Facilities: 52 campsites; sites are smallish, with minimal to fair separation; parking pads are gravel, short+ to medium+ straight-ins, plus some pull-throughs/pull-offs; most pads will require some additional leveling; generally small, sloped areas for tents; fire rings; some firewood may be available for gathering in the surrounding area, b-y-o to be sure; water at several faucets; restrooms with showers, plus auxiliary vaults; holding tank disposal station; gravel driveways; gas and groceries along Row River Road; adequate supplies and services are available in Cottage Grove, 9 miles west.

Activities & Attractions: Swimming beach; boating; boat launch; fishing; day use area.

Natural Features: Located on the south shore of Dorena Lake, a 5-mile-long, 1900-acre impoundment on the Middle Fork of the Willamette River; low-level vegetation consists mainly of tall bushes and a few ferns; super tall conifers form a high 'canopy' over the campground; bordered by forested hills; elevation 900'.

Season, Fees & Phone: April to late-October; $10.00; 14 day limit; Lane County Parks Department, Eugene, (503) 341-6940.

Camp Notes: There are a number of nice campsites along the lake shore; most sites, however, are 20 or more feet up on the slope. The day use area on the opposite side of the bay from the camp looks like a good place to spend some time. Easy access is provided via a footbridge that spans the gap between the campground and day use area.

Oregon 74

PINE MEADOWS
Cottage Grove Lake/Corps of Engineers Park

Location: Western Oregon south of Eugene.

Access: From Interstate 5 Exit 170 for Cottage Grove Lake/London Road (in the city of Cottage Grove, 20 miles south of Eugene), proceed to the south-east side of the freeway, then pick up London Road; follow London Road south for 3.7 miles; turn southeast (left) onto Cottage Grove Reservoir Road and proceed 2.1 miles (past the dam, across the outlet stream, then along the east shore of the lake); turn west (right) into the campground.

Facilities: 93 campsites in 2 loops; sites are small to medium-sized, with minimal to fairly good separation; parking pads are paved, medium-length straight-ins or medium to medium+ pull-throughs; a little additional leveling might be required in some sites; ample space for large tents on a grass/pine needle surface; fire rings; b-y-o firewood; water at several faucets; restrooms with showers; holding tank disposal station; paved driveways; adequate supplies and services are available in Cottage Grove.

Activities & Attractions: Small, sandy swimming beach; boating; boat launch; fishing; playground; scheduled nature walks and programs on weekend afternoons and evenings.

Natural Features: Located on a gently rolling and sloping flat on the northeast shore of Cottage Grove Lake; the lake is a 3-mile-long, 1100-acre flood-control reservoir on the Coast Fork of the Willamette River; sites receive light to moderately dense shade/shelter from very tall conifers; bordered by forested hills; elevation 800'.

Season, Fees & Phone: Late May to early September; $11.00; 14 day limit; Corps of Engineers Cottage Grove Project Office (503) 942-5631.

Camp Notes: Nice environment, good-looking camp. (If you've previously camped here and were disappointed, you may be interested in knowing that the Corps and the Oregon SP have recently been making a concerted effort to maintain a more tranquil atmosphere at Pine Meadows.)

PASS CREEK
Douglas County Park

Location: Western Oregon south of Eugene.

Access: From Interstate 5 Exit 163 for Curtin (7 miles south of Cottage Grove, 38 miles north of Roseburg), go west from the exit for 0.1 mile, then swing north (right) onto a park access road and proceed 0.2 mile to the campground.

Facilities: 35 campsites, including 30 with full hookups; sites are small to medium-sized, level, with minimal to nominal separation; parking pads are paved, short to long straight-ins; ample space for tents on a grassy surface; fireplaces; b-y-o firewood; water at hookup sites and at central faucets; restrooms with showers; paved driveways; gas and cafes at the freeway exit; adequate supplies and services are available in Cottage Grove.

Activities & Attractions: Freewayside convenience; playgrounds; small community building; day use area.

Natural Features: Located on a wooded flat in a narrow, green valley; most sites receive light to medium shade/shelter from tall conifers and an assortment of hardwoods, shrubs, flowers and other plants on mown lawns; low hills, densely forested with conifers and hardwoods, flank the valley; elevation 500'.

Season, Fees & Phone: Open all year; $9.00 for a standard site, $11.00 for a full hookup site; 14 day limit; park office (503) 942-3281.

Camp Notes: Included within the nice landscaping arrangement here is small duck pond (lagoon) for a bit of added interest. With freewayside convenience, however, comes the flip side of the location: The campground is only a few yards from the multi-lane maelstrom on the other side of the wall of trees that borders the east edge of the park. (The railroad tracks along the west edge of the park offer their own, latent intimidation.) But with all the greenery around here, you might not notice these items once you get settled-in.

HORSESHOE BEND
Umpqua National Forest

Location: Southwest Oregon east of Roseburg.

Access: From Oregon State Highway 138 near milepost 48 (30 miles east of Glide, 28 miles west/northwest of Diamond Lake), turn south onto Forest Road 4750 (paved), then almost immediately swing right and continue for 0.3 mile to the campground.

Facilities: 24 campsites, including 2 double units, in 2 loops and a string; (a group camp in a third loop is also available, by reservation); sites are small+ to medium-sized, with fair separation; parking pads are paved, short to medium-length straight-ins; adequate space for tents; firelaces; firewood is available for gathering in the vicinity; water at several faucets; restrooms; paved driveways; gas and groceries at a small store 4 miles east; nearest source of complete supplies is Roseburg, 48 miles west.

Activities & Attractions: Fly fishing for trout; river floating; launch area; hiking trails.

Natural Features: Located on the inside of a sharp bend on the North Umpqua River; sites are on a shelf above the north bank of the river and receive light to medium shade/shelter from old-growth firs and pines; bordered by the forested mountains of the west slope of the Cascade Range; elevation 1300'.

Season, Fees & Phone: May to October; $7.00 for a single site, $9.00 for a double site; 14 day limit; North Umpqua Ranger District Glide, (503) 496-3532.

Camp Notes: There's just enough space for the access road and the campground between the 'pincers' formed by the river channel, which nearly loops-back onto itself here. There are four other, considerably smaller forest camps along or very near the highway between Glide and Horseshoe Bend. From west to east they are: Bogus Creek, on the north side of the road near mp 37 (19 miles from Glide); Canton Creek , on a side road, 0.3 mile north of the highway near mp 41; Island, on the south side of the road near mp 43; and Apple Creek also snuggly along the south edge of the road in the vicinity if mp 45. Bogus Creek and Canton Creek have drinking water, restrooms and fees; the others have vaults, no water and no fees. Of the bunch, the best-equipped overall is Bogus Creek. However, Apple Creek and Island are usually available for limited 'off season' use when the more posh camps are closed.

EAGLE ROCK
Umpqua National Forest

Location: Southwest Oregon east of Roseburg.

Access: From Oregon State Highway 138 at a point 35 miles east of Glide and 23 miles west/northwest of Diamond Lake, turn north into the campground.

Facilities: 25 campsites, including 2 double units, in 2 loops connected by a string; sites are small+ to medium-sized, with fair to good separation; parking pads are paved, short to medium+ straight-ins; medium to large areas for tents; firelaces; firewood is available for gathering in the vicinity; water at hand pumps; vault facilities; waste water receptacles; paved driveways; gas and groceries at a small store 3 miles west; nearest source of complete supplies is Roseburg, 53 miles west.

Activities & Attractions: Fly fishing; river floating/kayaking.

Natural Features: Located along the south bank of the North Umpqua River in the Cascade Range; sites are moderately sheltered/shaded by tall conifers and some undercover; bordered by forested mountains; elevation 1700'.

Season, Fees & Phone: May to October; $5.00 for a single site, $7.00 for a double site; 14 day limit; North Umpqua Ranger District, Glide, (503) 496-3532.

Camp Notes: Eagle Rock's namsesake and another large rock formation, Rattlesnake Rock, loom over the campground. The majority of the sites are nearly streamside. Roughly similar accomodations, minus the drinking water and fee, can be had at Boulder Flat Campground, a mile east of Eagle Rock, also on the north side of the highway.

DIAMOND LAKE
Umpqua National Forest

Location: Southwest Oregon north of Crater Lake.

Access: From the junction of Oregon State Highways 138 & 230 (3 miles south of the community of Diamond Lake, 80 miles northeast of Medford), drive northwest on Highway 230 for 0.3 mile; turn north (right) onto Forest Road 4795 (paved); continue for 2.3 miles along the East Shore Road to the campground. **Alternate Access:** From Oregon State Highway 138 in the small community of Diamond Lake, proceed west on a paved connecting road for 0.2 mile to a "T"; turn south (left) onto East Shore Road and follow this paved road for 1.2 miles to the campground turnoff. (Note: East Shore Road closely parallels Highway 138 for about 4 miles, but the roads aren't in view of each other; the junctions are a bit tricky, so watch for directional signs.)

Facilities: 240 campsites in a multitude of loops on 3 tiers; sites are rather small and closely spaced; most parking pads are paved straight-ins; additional leveling may be necessary; a few good-sized tent sites, but many are small; fire rings; some firewood is available for gathering on nearby forest lands; water at several faucets; restrooms; waste water receptacles; holding tank disposal station; paved driveways; camper supplies at nearby small stores and resorts.

Activities & Attractions: Boating; boat launches; fishing; swimming; foot and equestrian trails in the area, including access to the Pacific Crest Scenic Trail; information center located near the entrance; evening programs may be scheduled during the summer in the campground amphitheater.

Natural Features: Located on sloping terrain on the middle-east east shore of Diamond Lake in the southern Cascades; campground vegetation consists primarily of tall conifers, moderate underbrush, and a pine needle-and-grass forest floor; the 3000-acre lake is completely surrounded by heavily forested mountains; elevation 5200'.

Season, Fees & Phone: May to October; $8.00 for a single unit, $11.00 for a double unit, $3.00 extra for a lakeside unit; 14 day limit; Diamond Lake Ranger District (503) 498-2531.

Camp Notes: As remote as it is, Diamond Lake is still a very popular recreation area. An important attraction here is the fantastic scenery. The campsites are strung out for almost a mile along the campground driveway. All sites have views, across the lake, of Mount Bailey. Sunsets on the lake can be phenomenal!

BROKEN ARROW
Umpqua National Forest

Location: Southwest Oregon north of Crater Lake.

Access: From the junction of Oregon State Highways 138 & 230 (3 miles south of Diamond Lake, 80 miles northeast of Medford), drive northwest on Highway 230 for 0.3 mile; turn north (right) onto Forest Road 4795 (paved); proceed 0.7 mile; turn west (left) onto South Shore Road; continue for 0.5 mile, then turn south (left) into the campground.

Facilities: 148 campsites in 11 loops; sites are medium to large, with minimal to good separation; parking pads are paved, and some are long enough for large vehicles; many units have large, level tent spots; fire rings and/or barbecue grills; firewood is often for sale, some firewood is available for gathering in the area; water at several faucets; restrooms; holding tank disposal station; paved driveways; camper supplies at a small store about 1 mile north.

Activities & Attractions: Boating; boat ramp nearby; fishing; picnic area; nearby foot and equestrian trails, including access to the Pacific Crest Scenic Trail; information center in Diamond Lake, 3 miles north.

Natural Features: Located in the southern Cascades on a lightly forested hillside near the south shore of Diamond Lake; the lake is visible through the trees from some sites; campground vegetation consists mostly of grass, conifers, and very little underbrush; elevation 5200'.

Season, Fees & Phone: May to September; $7.00 for a single unit, $9.00 for a double unit; 14 day limit; Diamond Lake Ranger District (503) 498-2531.

Camp Notes: A striking attraction in the Diamond Lake area is the fantastic scenery! Striking Mount Thielsen, just to the east, reaches to nearly 9200'. It's visible from many points around the lake, and from the approaching highways.

STANTON
Douglas County Park

Location: Southwest Oregon south of Roseburg.

Access: From Interstate 5 Exit 99 on the north edge of Canyonville (23 miles south of Roseburg), proceed to the east side of the freeway, then take a frontage road north for 0.4 mile to the park entrance and the campground.

Facilities: 43 campsites with full hookups, plus several standard sites; sites are small to medium-sized, level, with nominal to fairly good separation; parking pads are paved, mostly medium to long straight-ins; adequate space for large tents; assorted fire facilities; b-y-o firewood; water at faucets throughout; restrooms with showers; paved driveways; adequate supplies and services are available in Canyonville.

Activities & Attractions: Trail along the river; playground; boating; day use area.

Natural Features: Located in a canyon on flats at 2 levels along the bank of the South Umpqua River; sites are generally well sheltered/shaded by tall conifers and hardwoods on a surface of mown grass; bordered by densely forested hills and mountains; elevation 1700'.

Season, Fees & Phone: Open all year; $9.00 for a standard site, $11.00 for a full hookup site; 14 day limit; park office (503) 839-4483.

Camp Notes: Canyonville's name befits the location: The closely bordering, forested hills come right straight down to the canyon floor. This is the larger of a pair of Douglas County Parks along I-5. The other freewayside stop is Pass Creek Park, in the little burg of Curtin, at least an hour's drive north of here. (See separate information.) There aren't more than a half-dozen public campgrounds within 15-minutes' drive of I-5 in Oregon, so both of these attractive camps are very welcome.

SCHROEDER
Josephine County Park

Location: Southwest Oregon west of Grants Pass.

Access: From U.S. Highway 199 at milepost 3 (3 miles west of Grants Pass, 40 miles northeast of the Oregon-California border), turn north onto Willow Lane; drive north for 1.2 miles to the park entrance, on the east side of the road.

Facilities: Approximately 30 campsites, including some with full hookups; most sites are small to small+, with minimal to nominal separation; parking pads are paved and fairly level; some really nice, grassy tent spots; fireplaces and/or barbecue grills; b-y-o firewood; water at several faucets; restrooms with showers; paved driveways; complete supplies and services are available in Grants Pass.

Activities & Attractions: Rafting on the Wild and Scenic Rogue River; adjacent day use area has lush lawns, formal gardens, a fountain, picnic area, children's playground, and swimming beach.

Natural Features: Located in a grassy park on the south bank of the Rogue River; sites at the north end of the campground are separated by tall hardwoods and shrubbery; other sites are out on an open, grassy lawn; the park is surrounded by rolling, forested hills; elevation 900'.

Season, Fees & Phone: Open all year; $9.00 for a standard site, $11.00 for a hookup site; 14 day limit; Josephine County Parks Office, Grants Pass, (503) 474-5285.

Camp Notes: This campground, with its lawns and gardens, looks almost like a deluxe private rv park. Its strategic location--on the outskirts of the sizeable community of Grants Pass--also accounts for its undeniable popularity.

Oregon 82

LAKE SELMAC
Josephine County Park

Location: Southwest Oregon southwest of Grants Pass.

Access: From U.S. Highway 199 at milepost 20 +.8 in the community of Selma (22 miles north of the Oregon-California border, 20 miles southwest of Grants Pass), turn east onto a paved access road (should be signed for Selmac Lake); drive 2 miles to the park entrance; Loops A, B & C are around the south end of the lake (right) and loops D & E are around the north side of the lake (left).

Facilities: Approximately 80 campsites, some with partial hookups; Loops A & B have average-sized, mostly level sites with fair separation; Loops C, D & E have smaller sites, with minimal separation; all parking pads are gravel; pads in Loops A & B are mostly straight-ins, long enough for medium to large vehicles; maneuvering room is tight in Loops C, D, and E, and pads may need additional leveling; water at several faucets; fireplaces; b-y-o firewood is recommended; restrooms with showers in Loops A & B, vaults in Loops C, D & E; paved driveways; gas and camper supplies are available locally along the highway; complete supplies and services are available in Grants Pass.

Activities & Attractions: Fishing; swimming beach; boat ramp and dock; open, grassy day use area with playground, barbecue grills, covered tables and a bridge over a creek.

Natural Features: Located in an open forest surrounding Lake Selmac, in the southern Oregon mountains; elevation 1300'.

Season, Fees & Phone: April to October; $9.00; 14 day limit; Josephine County Parks Office, Grants Pass, (503) 474-5285.

Camp Notes: The camping facilities here vary considerably--"comfortable" camping a short distance from the lake, or "roughing it" camping in a tight spot where you can pitch a small tent and throw a line in from your picnic table.

Oregon 83

VALLEY OF THE ROGUE
Valley of the Rogue State Park

Location: Southwest Oregon east of Grants Pass.

Access: From Interstate 5 Exit 45B (10 miles east of Grants Pass, 15 miles northwest of Medford, turn south into the park, then turn right into the campground. (Note: If you're southbound, the exit leads directly to the park; if you're northbound, from the exit you'll need to take the viaduct to the south side of the Interstate, then west for 0.2 mile on a frontage road to the park; note also that I-5 lies in an east-west direction in this area.)

Facilities: 174 campsites, including 55 with partial hookups and 97 with full hookups, in 6 loops; (small group camping areas are also available); sites are small+ to medium+ in size, essentially level, with minimal to fair separation; parking pads are paved, short to medium+ straight-ins or medium to long pull-throughs; ample space for large tents in most sites; fireplaces or fire rings; firewood is usually for sale, or b-y-o; restrooms with showers; water at faucets throughout; holding tank disposal station; paved driveways; limited supplies and services are available in Rogue River and Gold Hill.

Activities & Attractions: Boating; boat launch; limited fishing; playground; amphitheater for evening programs in summer; day use area with shelter.

Natural Features: Located on a large, gently rolling flat above the Rogue River; park vegetation consists of several-dozen acres of mown grass well shaded/sheltered by hardwoods and conifers; closely bordered by forested mountains; elevation 1000'.

Season, Fees & Phone: Open all year; please see Appendix for standard Oregon state park fees; 10 day limit; park office (503) 582-1118.

Camp Notes: Nearly three miles of high riverbank are available for strolling or fishing. Veteran campers and park people who know the river agree that, while there are some trout still lurking in the Rogue, a lot of them in this stretch "have been run off by the jet boats"--referring to the jet-propelled excursion boats that regularly run the river. An excellent freewayside stop--notwithstanding the passing eighteen-wheelers and jet boats.

Oregon 84

EMIGRANT LAKE
Jackson County Park

Location: Southwest Oregon east of Ashland.

Access: From Oregon State Highway 66 at milepost 4 +.7 (3.5 miles east of Interstate 5 Exit 14 in Ashland, 11 miles west of Green Springs Mountain Summit, 56 miles west of Klamath Falls) turn northeast onto a paved access road and proceed 0.5 mile to the park entrance station; continue ahead, then curve north (left) for an additional 0.75 mile to the campground, on the west (left).

Facilities: 42 campsites; sites are small to medium-sized, with nominal separation; parking pads are paved, medium to long, mostly straight-ins, plus a few long pull-throughs; most pads will require a little to a lot of additional leveling; small to medium-sized, generally sloped, tent spots; fireplaces; b-y-o firewood; water at several faucets; restrooms with showers; holding tank disposal station; paved driveways; adequate+ supplies and services are available in Ashland.

Activities & Attractions: Sandy swimming beach and waterslide; hiking trail; boating; boat launch; fishing; central shelters; athletic field; day use facilities.

Natural Features: Located on a hillside in the foothills of the Cascade Range above Emigrant Lake; sites receive light to medium shelter/shade from medium to large oaks on a grassy surface; bordered by grass-and-tree covered hills and mountains; elevation 2400'.

Season, Fees & Phone: April to October; $11.00 for up to 2 adults, $2.00 for each additional adult (16 or older), $1.00 per pet; 14 day limit; Jackson County Parks Department, Medford, (503) 776-7001.

Camp Notes: A few of the sites "on top" have dandy, lake-and-mountain views. (But bring along a winch just in case the site selection is limited when you arrive--you may need a little extra power to angle up into one of the more sloped sites.) The local vegetation suggests a warmer and drier micro-climate than is found elsewhere in Western Oregon.

Oregon 85

HYATT LAKE
Public Lands/Bureau of Land Management

Location: Southwest Oregon east of Ashland.

Access: From Oregon State Highway 66 at milepost 17 +.5 (16.5 miles east of Interstate 5 Exit 14 in Ashland, 1.8 miles east of Green Springs Mountain Summit, 45 miles west of Klamath Falls) turn north onto a paved access road and proceed 3 miles to a major fork/intersection; bear slightly northeast (right) for another 0.1 mile; continue ahead to the main campground or east (right) to the tent camping area.

Facilities: 35 campsites, including 7 park n' walk tent sites, in 3 loops; sites are small+ to medium+, with fair to very good separation; parking pads are paved, short to medium-length straight-ins or medium+ pull-throughs; some pads will require a little additional leveling; medium to large areas for tents; fireplaces; firewood is available for gathering in the area; water at faucets throughout; restrooms with showers; holding tank disposal station; paved driveways; camper supplies on the highway; adequate+ supplies and services are available in Ashland.

Activities & Attractions: Limited boating (10 mph); boat launch; fishing; hiking trail along the lake shore; campfire circle; access to Pacific Crest Trail nearby; day use area.

Natural Features: Located on a forested, gentle slope along and near the south shore of Hyatt Lake; campground vegetation consists of moderately dense, tall conifers, a considerable quantity of underbrush and a lush carpet of grass; surrounded by forested mountains of the Cascade Range; elevation 4500'.

Season, Fees & Phone: Available all year, subject to weather conditions, with limited services October to May; $9.00 for a standard site, $7.00 for a tent site; 14 day limit; BLM Hyatt Lake park office (503) 482-2031 or BLM Medford District Office (503) 770-2200.

Camp Notes: This is one of the highest, greenest BLM camps you'll find anywhere. *Generally* speaking, it's also a very quiet spot (partly due to the 10 mph limit on the lake.) The view across the lake to a solitary, conical peak, is terrific.

Oregon 86

THREEHORN
Umpqua National Forest

Location: Southwest Oregon northeast of Medford.

Access: From Oregon State Highway 227 at milepost 39 +.1 (25 miles north of the junction of State Highways 227 & 62 near Shady Cove, 6 miles south of the hamlet of Drew, 37 miles southeast of Canyonville), turn east, go 100 yards to a fork, then bear left and continue for 0.1 mile to the campground.

Facilities: 5 campsites; sites are small+, slightly sloped, with nominal separation; parking pads are gravel, short to medium-length straight-ins; medium to large areas for tents; fireplaces; firewood is available for gathering; water at a hand pump; (may be unreliable, so b-y-o drinking water is recommended); vault facilities; pack-it-in/pack-it-out trash system; gravel driveway; groceries in Tiller, 11 miles north; nearest limited to adequate supplies are in Canyonville and Shady Cove.

Activities & Attractions: Highwayside convenience; small picnic area.

Natural Features: Located in a glen in the western foothills of the Cascade Range; sites are lightly shaded by tall timber, some shrubbery and scrub oak; elevation 2600'.

Season, Fees & Phone: Open all year; no fee; 14 day limit; Tiller Ranger District (503) 825-3201.

Camp Notes: This little hideaway could provide you with a simple but pleasant, free 'n easy, cool camp along a scenic 'backway'. The campground takes its name from Threehorn Mountain, a local promontory that rises a couple of miles southwest of here.

Oregon 87

ROGUE ELK
Jackson County Park

Location: Southwest Oregon northeast of Medford.

Access: From Oregon State Highway 62 at milepost 25 +.8 (6 miles northeast of Shady Cove, 26 miles northeast of Medford), turn south into the campground.

Facilities: Approximately 37 campsites, some with partial hookups; sites are small, level, with minimal separation; parking pads are paved, mostly short straight-ins; medium to large areas for tents; fire rings; b-y-o firewood; water at central faucets; restrooms with showers; paved driveways; limited to adequate supplies and services are available in Shady Cove.

Activities & Attractions: Boating/floating; boat ramp; fishing for Chinook salmon, trout, steelhead (seasonally); day use area.

Natural Features: Located on the north bank of the Rogue River at the river's confluences with Elk Creek; sites receive light to light-medium shade from large hardwoods on a grassy surface; bordered by the forested foothills of the Cascade Range; elevation 1500'.

Season, Fees & Phone: April to October; $11.00 for a standard site, $12.00 for a hookup site; 14 day limit; Jackson County Parks Department, Medford, (503) 776-7001.

Camp Notes: During the prime recreation season, the Rogue flows clear and deep and swift past here. This good-sized park is a very popular place with 'river rats' (or 'river runners', if you prefer a more formal appellation), but it could serve as a quick and easy overnight stop for anyone looking for riverfront property. The campsites stretch along the riverbank for about a half-mile. Highway traffic in midsummer moves by at a fast, tightly packed clip, so you'll only have one shot at turning onto the park driveway.

Depending upon your direction of travel, if you miss the turnoff you'll be in Crater Lake or Medford before a reasonable swingaround opportunity presents itself.

Oregon 88

JOSEPH P. STEWART
Joseph P. Stewart State Park

Location: Southwest Oregon northeast of Medford.

Access: From Oregon State Highway 62 at milepost 34 +.2 (14 miles northeast of Shady Cove, 9 miles southwest of Prospect), turn northwest onto the campground access road and proceed 0.3 mile to the entrance station; continue ahead for 0.1 mile to the campground. (Note that the campground access road is 0.9 mile *east* of the main park entrance.)

Facilities: 201 campsites, including 151 with partial hookups, in 4 loops; (a reservable group camp is also available); sites are medium to large, typically level or nearly so, with nominal to fair separation; parking pads are paved, medium to very long straight-ins; plenty of space for tents; fire rings and barbecue grills; firewood is usually for sale, or b-y-o; water at faucets throughout; restrooms with showers; holding tank disposal station; paved driveways; limited to adequate supplies and services are available in Shady Cove.

Activities & Attractions: Boating; boat launch; fishing for stocked trout and bass (reportedly very good); swimming beach with bathhouse; playground; 3 miles of paved hiking trails; 5 miles of paved bicycle trails; athletic field; CoE hiking trail circumnavigates the lake; day use areas.

Natural Features: Located on very gently sloping terrain near the south-east shore of 3400-acre Lost Creek Lake (Reservoir), an impoundment on the Rogue River; vegetation in the campground consists of dozens of acres of mown lawns well-dotted with small to medium-sized hardwoods and conifers; surrounded by densely forested mountains; elevation 1900'.

Season, Fees & Phone: April to October; please see Appendix for standard Oregon state park fees; 10 day limit; park office (503) 560-3334.

Camp Notes: You could fit an entire 201-site national park campground in just one of Stewart's four camp loops. Packing a tarp or something to supplement the camp's light natural shade might be a good idea in case you get one of the less-sheltered sites. Great views in all directions across acres and acres and acres of grass.

Oregon 89

UNION CREEK
Rogue River National Forest

Location: Southwest Oregon west of Crater Lake.

Access: From Oregon State Highway 62 at milepost 56 +.1 (1 mile south of the junction of State Highways 62 & 230, 15 miles west of the Annie Springs entrance to Crater Lake National Park, 11 miles north of Prospect), turn west into the campground.

Facilities: 99 campsites in 5 loops; sites are large, with good to very good separation; parking pads are gravel, fairly level, straight-ins; many pads can accommodate large vehicle combinations; some nice, secluded tent spots; fireplaces; firewood is available for gathering in the area; water at several faucets; vault facilities; waste water receptacles; paved driveways; camper supplies at a resort 0.5 mile north on Highway 62.

Activities & Attractions: Rogue River Gorge viewpoint, 0.5 mile north, overlooks the river where it rushes through a narrow gorge; trailhead for the Upper Rogue River Trail is located a few miles south; foot trails follow Union Creek along both banks; picnic area with shelters; Crater Lake National Park is 15 miles east; nature programs may be scheduled for summer evenings.

Natural Features: Located on a heavily timbered flat along both sides of Union Creek, where Union Creek flows into the Rogue River; campground vegetation consists mainly of tall conifers, fairly dense underbrush and a conifer-needle forest floor; elevation 1000'.

Season, Fees & Phone: May to September; $6.00; 14 day limit; Prospect Ranger District (503) 560-3623.

Camp Notes: The campsites at Union Creek are spacious and private--and some are creekside. The campground is neatly divided into two sections by this clear, mountain stream spanned by a picturesque wooden bridge.

FAREWELL BEND
Rogue River National Forest

Location: Southwest Oregon west of Crater Lake.

Access: From Oregon State Highway 62 at milepost 56 +.9 (0.2 mile south of the junction of State Highways 62 & 230, 14 miles west of the Annie Springs entrance to Crater Lake National Park, 12 miles north of Prospect), turn west into the campground.

Facilities: 61 campsites in 3 loops; sites are large, most are level, and well separated; parking pads are paved straight-ins, some long enough to accommodate large vehicles; adequate space for tents; fire rings and barbecue grills; firewood is available for gathering in the area; water at several faucets; restrooms; waste water receptacles; paved driveways; camper supplies at a resort 0.5 mile south on Highway 62; nearest source of complete supplies and services is Medford.

Activities & Attractions: Large, grassy, central area with children's playground (most of the play equipment was constructed from natural materials); Rogue River Gorge viewpoint, 0.5 miles south, overlooks the historic river where it rushes through a narrow gorge; Crater Lake National Park is 15 miles northeast; trailhead for the Upper Rogue River Trail is located a few miles south.

Natural Features: Located in the southern Cascades on the southeast bank of the Rogue River; most of the sites are well sheltered and separated by tall hardwoods, conifers and considerable underbrush; about half the sites are streamside; elevation 1000'.

Season, Fees & Phone: May to September; $8.00; 14 day limit; Prospect Ranger District (503) 560-3623.

Camp Notes: Though a few sites may be rather close to the highway, the forest serves as an effective partition between most campsites and the traffic. The closeness of the legendary Rogue River creates a distinctive spirit at Farewell Bend.

MAZAMA
Crater Lake National Park

Location: Southwest Oregon south of Crater Lake.

Access: From Oregon State Highway 62 at the Annie Springs entrance station for Crater Lake National Park (14 miles east of the junction of State Highways 62 & 230, 57 miles northwest of Klamath Falls, 71 miles northeast of Medford), drive north for 100 yards, then turn east (right) into the campground.

Facilities: 198 campsites in 7 loops; sites are medium-sized, level, and fairly well separated; parking pads are paved, many are medium+ pull-throughs; some very nice, spacious tent areas; fireplaces; b-y-o firewood; water at several faucets; restrooms; (showers may be available at a private lodge nearby); holding tank disposal station; paved driveways; gas, camper supplies, laundromat and showers at a nearby store; nearest sources of complete supplies and services are Klamath Falls and Medford.

Activities & Attractions: Annie Creek Nature Trail descends 1.7 miles to Annie Creek; Pacific Crest Trail passes near the campground and extends the length of the park; visitor center at Rim Village; Rim Drive completely circles the lake; lake cruises; fishing permitted on the lake and streams of the park; campground nature programs scheduled for summer evenings.

Natural Features: Located on a lightly to moderately forested flat; sites are in among tall trees, or on open grassy areas; Crater Lake itself is located 4 miles north; peaks of the Cascades encircle this lake, which has formed in a volcanic caldera; Annie Creek flows through a chasm several hundred feet below the campground level; elevation 6000'.

Season, Fees & Phone: June to October; $12.00; 14 day limit; operated by concessionaire; park headquarters (503) 594-2211.

Camp Notes: Crater Lake, the second deepest lake in the western hemisphere, is a magnificent sight--from the Rim Drive or from the surface of the lake itself. However, Mazama Campground is nowhere close to the lake. Many of Mazama's campsites are very near the edge of the Annie Creek chasm, though. If all you can handle is an economy-class ticket, the park also has a primitive campground, Lost Creek, near the southeast rim of the lake. It's accessible from about the 'five o'clock' position on the circular Rim Drive (north being 12 o'clock), then 3 miles southeast. Lost Creek has 12 small sites, piped water and vaults, at a budget price.

COLLIER
Collier State Park

Location: Southwest Oregon north of Klamath Falls.

Access: From U.S. Highway 97 at milepost 243 +.8 (5 miles north of Chiloquin, 30 miles north of Klamath Falls, 107 miles south of Bend) at the north end of the Spring Creek bridge, turn east onto a paved access road and proceed east and south for 0.4 mile to the campground.

Facilities: 68 campsites, including 50 with full hookups; sites are small to medium-sized, level, with nominal separation; parking pads are paved, medium to long straight-ins or pull-throughs; roomy, level spaces for tents; fireplaces; firewood is usually for sale, or b-y-o; water at hookups and at several faucets; restrooms with showers; holding tank disposal station; paved driveways; gas and groceries are available in Chiloquin, 5 miles south.

Activities & Attractions: Collier Memorial Logging Museum--an outdoor display of logging machinery and a Pioneer Village of authentic, relocated log cabins filled with artifacts from a bygone era; hiking trails along the river; excellent trout fishing on Spring Creek and the Williamson River; playground; evening programs in summer.

Natural Features: Located in an open forest in a large valley between the southern Cascades and the Fremont Mountains; Spring Creek enters the Williamson River within the park; vegetation consists of light to medium-dense conifers, light underbrush, sparse grass, and some sage; elevation 4200'.

Season, Fees & Phone: April to October; please see Appendix for standard Oregon state park fees; 10 day limit; park office (503) 783-2471.

Camp Notes: Collier is in a lovely setting along deep, clear, rushing streams. It's popular with campers, fishermen and mosquitoes. (An ongoing mosquito control program helps to take the bite out of the bugs.) If you would like a much simpler place to pitch your tent or park your pickup, Jackson F. Kimball State Park, on State Highway 232, 3 miles north of Fort Klamath and 4 miles south of Sun Pass, is within a half-hour's drive from Collier. (Some maps don't depict the road as Highway 232, but whatever they call it, it's there.) Kimball has a half-dozen campsites, vaults, but no drinking water, in an informal, roadside setting at the headwaters of the Wood River.

SPRING CREEK
Winema National Forest

Location: Southwest Oregon north of Klamath Falls.

Access: From U.S. Highway 97, 100 yards south of milepost 241 (8 miles north of Chiloquin, 33 miles north of Klamath Falls, 104 miles south of Bend), turn west onto Forest Road 9732 (gravel); drive west and south on a steep and winding road for 3 miles to the campground entrance; continue for 0.6 mile to the campsites.

Facilities: 26 campsites; sites are large and well spaced; parking pads are gravel, mostly level, and generally spacious enough for large vehicles; large, level spots for tents; fireplaces; plenty of firewood is available for gathering; no drinking water in the campground; vault facilities; piped water and restrooms are available in the nearby day use area; waste water receptacles; gravel driveways; gas and groceries in Chiloquin; complete supplies and services are available in Klamath Falls.

Activities & Attractions: Fishing on Spring Creek; foot trail from the campsites down to the creek and a picnic area.

Natural Features: Located on a forested flat near Spring Creek, where the stream is wide, deep and slow-moving; vegetation is moderately dense, with very tall conifers, underbrush and tall grass; timbered hills and mountains surround the campground; elevation 4200'.

Season, Fees & Phone: May to October; no fee (subject to change); 14 day limit; Chiloquin Ranger District (503) 783-2221.

Camp Notes: Spring Creek Campground is not usually busy--probably due, in part, to its rough access. Maneuvering the access road might be a little difficult for some towing vehicles. This secluded retreat has lots of elbow room at a good price. Mosquitoes seem to be less of a problem here than at other camps in the area. On the way in or out, or while you're camping, save a few minutes or more to savor the view at Oux-Kanee Overlook. (*Oux-Kanee* is the traditional name of the Klamath Indians and means "People of the Marsh".) This viewpoint along the campground access road provides a fantastic vista of the Klamath Basin. Another local forest camp, Williamson River, might also be to your liking. It's a little less secluded, but the access road is easier to handle. From the same turnoff point as Collier SP (above), travel 1.5 miles northeast on a gravel forest road to the small, simple camp along the west bank of the Williamson River. It has a hand pump, vaults and a nominal fee.

Oregon 94

WHISKEY SPRINGS
Rogue River National Forest

Location: Southwest Oregon east of Medford.

Access: From Oregon State Highway 140 at milepost 28 + .6 (40 miles east of Medford, 40 miles west of Klamath Falls), turn north onto Jackson County Road 30/37 (may be signed as the turnoff for "Willow Lake"); drive 9 miles north on a curvy paved road; turn east (right) at milepost 25 + .3 onto a surfaced access road and proceed 0.4 mile to the campground.

Facilities: 36 campsites; campsites are large, level and well spaced; parking pads are gravel, some are double-wide straight-ins, some are pull-throughs spacious enough to accommodate very large rv's; some large, level tent areas; fireplaces; firewood is available for gathering in the area; water at faucets throughout; vault facilities; gravel driveways; camper supplies at a small store on Willow Lake, 4 miles west; complete supplies and services are available in Medford and Klamath Falls.

Activities & Attractions: Nature trail; footbridge across the small creek; day use area has picnic sites, barbecue grills, and horseshoe pits; forest roads lead up into the Cascades toward the Sky Lakes Wilderness Area; Willow Lake, 4 miles west, is popular for boating, fishing, swimming and other water sports.

Natural Features: Located on a moderately forested flat in the southern Cascades, just west of the Sky Lakes Wilderness Area; fairly clear of underbrush; the soil and gravel are an unusual reddish color; a small stream flows through the campground; elevation 3200'.

Season, Fees & Phone: May to September; $6.00; 14 day limit; Butte Falls Ranger District (503) 865-3581.

Camp Notes: The sites at Whiskey Springs are easily accessible, secluded, and roomy. It's unlikely that this nice campground is often filled to capacity because the major local water feature, Willow Lake, is several miles from here.

Oregon 95

WILLOW LAKE
Jackson County Park

Location: Southwest Oregon east of Medford.

Access: From Oregon State Highway 140 at milepost 28 + .6 (40 miles east of Medford, 40 miles west of Klamath Falls), turn north onto Jackson County Road 30/37 (may be signed for "Willow Lake"); drive 10.7 miles north on a curvy paved road; at milepost 23 + .5, turn sharply left onto Willow Lake Road (Forest Road 3020); proceed southwest for 1.5 (paved) miles to the park entrance and the campground.

Facilities: 71 campsites, including some with hookups; sites are average-sized and generally well separated; parking pads are gravel, and many pull-throughs are long enough for large vehicles; some pads may require additional leveling; about 30 sites have nice, large tent areas in an open forest setting; fireplaces; some firewood is available for gathering in the vicinity; water at several faucets; restrooms with showers; supplementary vault facilities; holding tank disposal station; gravel driveways; camper supplies and laundry facilities are available in the park.

Activities & Attractions: Boating; boat launch and dock; rental boats; fishing; sailing; swimming beach; day use area.

Natural Features: Located on the forested west shore of Willow Lake; vegetation in the camping area consists of tall, thin conifers and moderate underbrush; timbered peaks of the southern Cascades, including 9500' Mount McLaughlin, surround the lake; elevation 3000'.

Season, Fees & Phone: May to September; $11.00 for a standard site, $12.00 for a partial-hookup site, $13.00 for a full-hookup site; $2.00 extra for each adult beyond 2 per site; 14 day limit; Jackson County Parks Department, Medford, (503) 776-7001.

Camp Notes: The drive to this fairly secluded lake is enjoyable in its own right. Mount McLaughlin's stately presence adds a touch of near-surrealism to the local landscape. The lake is also known as Willow Creek Reservoir.

Oregon 96

DOE POINT
Rogue River National Forest

Location: Southwest Oregon between Klamath Falls and Medford.

Access: From Oregon State Highway 140 at milepost 30 +.4 (38 miles west of Klamath Falls, 42 miles east of Medford), turn south, then immediately west onto a paved access road which parallels the highway; drive west for 0.2 mile to the campground.

Facilities: 25 campsites in 2 loops; sites are medium to large and fairly well-separated; some pads are very long, and many are double-wide in order to accommodate a vehicle and trailer side-by-side; a few pads may require additional leveling; most sites have adequately level tent spots; fireplaces; some firewood is available for gathering in the vicinity; water at several faucets; restrooms; paved driveways; limited supplies about 1 mile east on Highway 140; complete supplies and services are available in Medford and Klamath Falls.

Activities & Attractions: Nature trail along the lake; fishing; picnic area; boat ramp and dock at Fish Lake Campground, 0.7 mile east; great views across the lake.

Natural Features: Located on the forested north shore of Fish Lake in the southern Cascades; a number of sites are right along the lake, which is encircled by timbered slopes; vegetation in the campground consists primarily of tall conifers and a considerable amount of underbrush, providing good separation between sites; elevation 4700'.

Season, Fees & Phone: May to September; $8.00; 14 day limit; Butte Falls R.D. (503) 865-3581.

Camp Notes: This campground is located in a mountain setting with hard-to-top scenery and generally excellent fishing near at hand. Extensive lava fields partly surround the general lake area.

Oregon 97

FISH LAKE
Rogue River National Forest

Location: Southwest Oregon between Klamath Falls and Medford.

Access: From Oregon State Highway 140 at milepost 30 +.4 (38 miles west of Klamath Falls, 42 miles east of Medford), turn south and immediately east onto a paved access road which parallels the highway; drive east for 0.5 mile to the campground.

Facilities: 17 campsites; sites are mostly average-sized with nominal separation; parking pads are gravel, typically long, and some are double-wide; most sites are level enough for tents; fireplaces; some firewood is available for gathering in the vicinity; water at several faucets; restrooms; waste water receptacles; paved driveways; limited supplies are available less than 1 mile east, on Highway 140; complete supplies and services are available in Medford and Klamath Falls.

Activities & Attractions: Fishing; boating; paved and lighted boat launch and dock; picnic area, with kitchen shelters; a foot trail leads around the east end of the lake and connects with the Pacific Crest Trail; visitor information center nearby at Lake of the Woods.

Natural Features: Located on a timbered hillside on the north shore of Fish Lake in the southern Cascades; the campground area has an open forest atmosphere with tall pines and very little underbrush; views of the lake through the trees from many sites; elevation 4700'.

Season, Fees & Phone: May to September; $8.00; 14 day limit; Butte Falls R.D. (503) 865-3581.

Camp Notes: Fish Lake has earned its title. Fishing here is reportedly in the very good-to-excellent category. An annual stocking program, an abundance of food and nearly ideal environmental conditions are cited as reasons for the good fish production.

Oregon 98

ASPEN POINT
Winema National Forest

Location: Southwest Oregon northwest of Klamath Falls.

Access: From Oregon State Highway 140 at milepost 36 +.3 (32 miles west of Klamath Falls, 48 miles east of Medford), turn south onto Forest Road 3704 (paved); drive southerly for 0.6 mile, then turn west (right) into the campground.

Facilities: 60 campsites in 2 loops; sites are fairly large with good separation for the most part; parking pads are gravel, mostly level straight-ins, plus several pull-throughs spacious enough to accommodate very large vehicles; adequate space for tents; fireplaces; some firewood is available for gathering in the area; water at faucets throughout; restrooms; disposal station; paved driveways; camper supplies at a nearby resort; complete supplies and services are available in Klamath Falls.

Activities & Attractions: Fishing; boating; boat launch and dock; swimming beach; picnic area; Billie Creek Nature Trail is one of several foot trails in the area; Lake of the Woods Visitor Center nearby.

Natural Features: Located in an open forest setting along the northeast shore of Lake of the Woods in the southern Cascades; campground vegetation consists mostly of tall conifers and very little underbrush; Mountain Lakes Wilderness lies to the east, and Sky Lakes Wilderness is to the north; elevation 5000'.

Season, Fees & Phone: May to September; $8.00; 14 day limit; Klamath Ranger District (503) 883-6824.

Camp Notes: Aspen Point has been a popular campground since the 1920's. There are huge stone fireplaces and picnic tables here which were built in the 1930's.

Oregon 99

SUNSET
Winema National Forest

Location: Southwest Oregon northwest of Klamath Falls.

Access: From Oregon State Highway 140 at milepost 36 +.3 (32 miles west of Klamath Falls, 48 miles northeast of Medford), turn south onto Forest Road 3704 (paved); drive 1.3 miles south and east to a "T"; turn south (right) onto Dead Indian Road, go 0.9 mile, then turn west (right) into the campground.

Facilities: 66 campsites in 3 loops; sites are good-sized and fairly well-separated; parking pads are paved, mostly level, straight-ins, and some are roomy enough to accommodate very large vehicles; a number of sites have large, level, gravel tent pads; fireplaces; firewood is available for gathering in the vicinity; water at faucets throughout; restrooms; holding tank disposal station, 2 miles north near Aspen Point Campground; paved driveways; camper supplies at a nearby resort; complete supplies and services are available in Klamath Falls.

Activities & Attractions: Boat launch and dock; fishing; swimming; Sunset Trail leads 1 mile along the shore to Rainbow Bay Picnic Area; Lake of the Woods Visitor Center is located on Highway 140.

Natural Features: Located on the forested east shore of Lake of the Woods in the southern Cascades; campground vegetation consists of fairly dense conifers with considerable underbrush; Mountain Lakes Wilderness lies to the east and Sky Lakes Wilderness is to the north; elevation 5000'.

Season, Fees & Phone: May to September; $8.00; 14 day limit; Klamath Ranger District (503) 883-6824.

Camp Notes: Mount McLaughlin, rising to 9500', is visible across the lake to the north. This national forest is named for the Modoc Indian woman Winema (Wih-*nee*-mah) who served as a liaison between the Modocs and pioneer settlers in Southern Oregon and Northern California during the Modoc War of 1872.

Oregon
Columbia Gorge & North Central
Please refer to the Oregon map in the Appendix

Oregon 100

AINSWORTH
Ainsworth State Park

Location: Northern Oregon border east of Portland.

Access: From Interstate 84 Exit 35 (9 miles west of Cascade Locks, 18 miles east of Troutdale), turn south, then west, onto the Columbia River Scenic Highway, U.S. 30; proceed west 0.5 mile to the campground entrance, on the south (left) side of the highway.

Facilities: 45 campsites with full hookups in 2 loops; sites are generally medium-sized, with fair to good separation; parking pads are paved, and many are pull-throughs long enough for very large rv's; some additional leveling may be required; adequate space for a small to medium sized tent in most sites; fireplaces; b-y-o firewood; water at sites; restrooms with showers; paved driveways; limited supplies in Cascade Locks; adequate supplies and services are available in Troutdale and Hood River.

Activities & Attractions: A 4-mile section of the Columbia Gorge Trail links Ainsworth to John Yeon State Park, east of here; Horsetail Falls (176' high) is a half-mile west of the campground on the Scenic Highway.

Natural Features: Located on a forested slope a short distance from the south bank of the Columbia River, in the Columbia Gorge (although there is no river access from the park); campground vegetation consists of mown grass, medium-height conifers, and tall hardwoods; elevation 100'.

Season, Fees & Phone: April to October; please see Appendix for standard Oregon state park fees; phone c/o Rooster Rock State Park (503) 695-2261.

Camp Notes: John Yeon State Park, mentioned above, is a small natural area on the south slopes of the Gorge. Trails lead up the densely forested slopes to Elowah Falls (0.8 mile) and Upper McCord Creek Falls (1.1 miles). Beacon Rock, a celebrated Columbia River landmark mentioned as far back in recorded history as the Lewis and Clark Journals, can be viewed from Yeon's trailhead and parking lot.

Oregon 101

EAGLE CREEK
Mount Hood National Forest

Location: Northern Oregon border west of Hood River.

Access: From Interstate 84 eastbound, take Exit 41 (3 miles west of Cascade Locks, 24 miles east of Troutdale); proceed east 0.2 mile on the off-ramp to the fish hatchery; turn south (right) into the recreation area entrance, then east (left) on a fairly steep, paved road for 0.4 mile to the campground. (Note: Exit 41 is an eastbound exit only; if westbound, take Exit 44 at Cascade Locks and proceed 3 miles west on a frontage road to the recreation area.)

Facilities: 19 campsites; most sites are medium-sized and moderately well separated; parking pads are paved, fairly level, medium-length straight-ins; adequate space for medium-sized tents in most sites; fireplaces, plus a few barbecue grills; a small quantity of firewood is available for gathering in the vicinity, b-y-o is suggested; water at several faucets; restrooms; paved driveway; limited supplies and services are available in Cascade Locks.

Activities & Attractions: Shady Glen Interpretive Trail leads off from an associated day use area; suspension bridge over the creek; Eagle Creek Trailhead, 0.5 mile south.

Natural Features: Located on a densely forested hill overlooking the Columbia River; campground vegetation consists of alder, maple, Douglas fir, and ferns; Eagle Creek enters the Columbia River below the campground, a short distance to the north; elevation 200'.

Season, Fees & Phone: Late-May to October; $6.00; 7 day limit; Columbia Gorge Ranger District (503) 695-2276.

Camp Notes: Eagle Creek is an historic campground of the first order of magnitude. Set your WayBack™ Time Machine to the year *1915* and you'll see Eagle Creek Campground being built. It is considered to be the *first national forest public campground* constructed in the United States. Want another 'first'? The restrooms here were the first with flusheroos installed in a Forest Service campground. Neat, huh? The pathways and trails in the area are popular with joggers. (And, considering the 11+ percent grade on some of the trails, they're quite invigorating as well.) A number of the campsites have very impressive views of the Columbia Gorge.

Oregon 102

WYETH
Mount Hood National Forest

Location: Northern Oregon border west of Hood River.

Access: From Interstate 84 Exit 51 (13 miles west of Hood River, 6 miles east of Cascade Locks), turn south off the Interstate, then head immediately west (right) onto Herman Creek Road (paved); continue west for 0.1 mile to the campground entrance on the south (left) side of the road.

Facilities: 14 campsites; (6 small group sites are also available; most units are spacious, with fair separation; parking pads are paved, long, wide, level straight-ins; generally good areas for tents, but a few spots might be slightly off-level; fire rings; some firewood is available for gathering in the area; water at faucets throughout; restrooms; paved driveways; limited supplies at Cascade Locks; adequate supplies and services are available in Hood River.

Activities & Attractions: Trailhead parking at the south end of the campground; museum and visitor center in Cascade Locks.

Natural Features: Great views of the Columbia River Gorge from the campground area; tall pine and spruce forest, along with big leafy hardwoods; very little low-level vegetation other than ferns; set against the south face of the gorge; elevation 150'.

Season, Fees & Phone: Mid-May to October; $6.00; 7 day limit; Columbia Gorge Ranger District (503) 695-2276.

Camp Notes: An extensive landscaping project accomplished by various government and volunteer groups has turned Wyeth into one of the most attractive campgrounds in this part of the country. The rockwork alone is worth a king's ransom. Definitely worth the stop--even if it's just to take a look. Taking a good look just about everywhere in this region is mandatory. Wyeth and the other camps in this vicinity are within the Columbia River Gorge National Scenic Area. This unique, quarter-million-acre scenic entity was established by Act of Congress in 1986 and transcends national, state, local and private boundaries. It is the first creation of its kind in the United States.

Oregon 103

VIENTO
Viento State Park

Location: Northern Oregon border west of Hood River.

Access: From Interstate 84 Exit 56 for Viento Park (8 miles west of Hood River, 39 miles east of Troutdale), proceed to the north side of the freeway, then 0.1 mile east on a park access road to the main campground; a second camp loop for standard/tent camping is located on the south side of the freeway, 0.3 mile east of the exit.

Facilities: 75 campsites, including 58 with partial hookups; sites are small to medium-sized, with nominal to fair separation; parking pads are paved, short to medium length straight-ins, and are fairly well leveled; adequate space for medium to large tents; fireplaces or fire rings; firewood is usually for sale, or b-y-o; water at faucets in most sites; restrooms with showers; paved driveways; adequate supplies and services are available in Hood River.

Activities & Attractions: Hiking trails in this park and in several other small, undeveloped state parks in the vicinity; picnic area; limited river access.

Natural Features: Located on a hillside above the south bank of the Columbia River; the heavily forested south walls of the Columbia Gorge rise steeply, directly behind the park; grassy campsites are quite well shaded/sheltered by tall conifers, hardwoods, and shrubbery; elevation 100'.

Season, Fees & Phone: April to October; please see Appendix for standard Oregon state park fees; 10 day limit; park office (503) 374-8811.

Camp Notes: Viento is more of a 'sitting' campground rather than a 'doing' camp--and that's just fine. However, the park is situated between the Interstate and a very active railroad line, so one or the other could be a bit of a bother at times. But the grounds are grassy and inviting and provide a verdant stop for Interstate travelers. Views of the Columbia River and the Columbia Gorge along this stretch are fabulous!

Oregon 104

MEMALOOSE
Memaloose State Park

Location: Northern Oregon border east of Hood River.

Access: From Interstate 84, (westbound) at milepost 73 (9 miles east of Hood River, 12 miles west of The Dalles), take the exit for "Rest Area, Memaloose Park"; continue west through the rest area parking lot to the park entrance and the campground. **Alternate Access:** From I-84, eastbound, take Exit 76, backtrack on I-84 westbound to the "Rest Area" exit at milepost 73, then continue as above.

Facilities: 110 campsites, including 43 with full hookups; most sites are average-sized, with fair separation; parking pads are paved, reasonably level, and some are large enough for very large rv's;

adequate space for medium to large tents; fireplaces; b-y-o firewood is recommended; water at faucets throughout; restrooms with showers; holding tank disposal station; adequate supplies in Hood River; complete supplies and services are available in The Dalles.

Activities & Attractions: Large, grassy area for general recreation.

Natural Features: Located on a mown, grassy flat above the south bank of the Columbia River; assorted conifers, hardwoods, and bushes dot the park area; elevation 100'.

Season, Fees & Phone: April to October; please see Appendix for standard Oregon state park fees; 10 day limit; phone c/o Rooster Rock State Park (503) 695-2261.

Camp Notes: The park's name was derived from an island in the Columbia River which was used as a burial ground by Indians. The nearby town of Hood River bills itself as the 'Windsurfing Capitol of the World'.

Oregon 105

DESCHUTES RIVER
Deschutes River State Recreation Area

Location: North-central Oregon east of The Dalles.

Access: From Interstate 84 (eastbound) Exit 97, (12 miles east of The Dalles, 7 miles west of the junction of U. S. 97 with I-84), turn east onto Oregon State Highway 206; continue for 3.2 miles (Highway 206 parallels I-84), and over the Deschutes River Bridge; turn south (right) into the park. From I-84 (westbound) Exit 104 (at the junction of I-84 with U.S 97), turn west onto State Highway 206; continue 4.5 miles, then turn south (left) into the park.

Facilities: 34 campsites; sites are small, with nominal separation; parking pads are paved, fairly level, short+ straight-ins; gently sloping grassy areas for tents; fireplaces; b-y-o firewood is recommended; water at several faucets; restrooms; paved driveways; gas and groceries in Celilo Village, 5 miles west; complete supplies and services are available in The Dalles.

Activities & Attractions: Fishing and floating on the Deschutes River; Oregon Trail point of interest; The Dalles Dam Visitor Center is 15 miles west.

Natural Features: Located along the east bank of the Deschutes River; the campground is situated in a grove of tall hardwoods and a few evergreens; the Deschutes enters the Columbia River just downstream of this point; the park is bordered by fairly steep and rocky canyon walls and rolling, grassy hillsides; elevation 150'.

Season, Fees & Phone: April to October; please see Appendix for standard Oregon state park fees; 10 day limit; park office (503) 739-2322.

Camp Notes: Actually, there are more complete camping facilities in a Washington state park (Maryhill) just across the river; or cheaper accommodations in a CoE Park (LePage, described below). But Deschutes River SRA does provide a strong motivator for sportsmen--the park's namesake. Fishing and floating/boating are usually good on the Deschutes.

Oregon 106

LePAGE
Lake Umatilla/Corps of Engineers Park

Location: Northern Oregon border east of The Dalles.

Access: From Interstate 84 Exit 114 for Le Page Park/John Day River Recreation Area, (5 miles east of Rufus, 29 miles east of The Dalles, 24 miles west of Arlington), at the south side of the freeway proceed south on a paved access road for 0.3 mile (past the day use area) to the campground.

Facilities: Approximately 12 campsites in a string and a loop; sites are small, level, with nominal to fair separation; parking pads are gravel, short+ pull-offs; enough space for a small tent; water in the nearby day use area; vault facilities; (restrooms with freshwater rinse showers in the day use area); complete supplies and services are available in The Dalles.

Activities & Attractions: Designated swimming area; boating; boat launch; fishing; large day use area with several small picnic shelters.

Natural Features: Located near the mouth of a canyon along the bank of the John Day River at its confluence with the Columbia River; this segment of the Columbia has been dammed to form Lake

Umatilla; sites are lightly shaded by large hardwoods; about half of the sites are riverside; bordered by dry, rocky hills and bluffs; elevation 200'.

Season, Fees & Phone: Open all year; no fee; 14 day limit; Corps of Engineers John Day Project Office, The Dalles, (503) 296-1181.

Camp Notes: Great little freewayside stop (especially for a freebie). The terrific day use area has watered/mown lawns dotted with hardwoods. Golf course grooming there. From near here are commanding views down through the Columbia Gorge and of Mount Hood rising prominently (on a clear day) in the distance.

Oregon 107

TOLL BRIDGE
Hood River County Park

Location: Northern Oregon south of Hood River.

Access: From Oregon State Highway 35 at milepost 84 (12 miles south of Hood River, 29 miles northeast of the junction of Highway 35 & U.S. 26), proceed 0.4 mile west and south on a paved, 2-lane access road; turn west (right) into the campground; (look for a "Tollbridge Park Junction" sign on Highway 35).

Facilities: 38 campsites, including 20 with full hookups and 18 for tents, in 2 loops; sites are small+ to medium-sized, level, with nominal to fair separation; parking pads are paved or oiled gravel; many pads are long enough to accommodate large rv's; fireplaces; b-y-o firewood is recommended; water at faucets throughout; restrooms with showers; paved driveways; limited supplies in the community of Mt. Hood, 2 miles north; adequate supplies and services are available in Hood River.

Activities & Attractions: Fishing; hiking trails in the area; adjacent day use area has barbecue grills, kitchen shelter, children's play area, ball diamond and a large lawn.

Natural Features: Located on a flat along the East Fork of the Hood River in the forested Hood River Valley; the East Fork rushes by the campground, just a few yards to the west of many sites; the campground has some grassy areas, and some conifers and hardwoods for shelter and separation; timbered ridges border the valley on the east and west; majestic Mount Hood rises a few miles to the west; elevation 1900'.

Season, Fees & Phone: April to November $9.00 for a standard site, $12.00 for a full hookup site; Hood River County Parks Department, Hood River, (503) 386-6323.

Camp Notes: Toll Bridge is situated right along a lovely river and surrounded by the tall peaks of the Cascades. It's located just far enough off the main highway to provide easy access, yet retain its tranquility.

Oregon 108

SHERWOOD
Mount Hood National Forest

Location: Northern Oregon south of Hood River.

Access: From Oregon State Highway 35 at milepost 72 +.1 (24 miles south of Hood River, 17 miles northeast of the junction of Highway 35 & U.S. 26), turn west into the campground.

Facilities: 18 campsites; sites are small+ to medium-sized, reasonably level, with fair separation; parking pads are gravel, short to medium-length straight-ins; adequate space for smaller tents; fireplaces; firewood is available for gathering in the area; water at faucets and a hand pump; vault facilities; paved driveways; limited supplies in the community of Mount Hood, 10 miles north; adequate supplies and services are available in Hood River.

Activities & Attractions: Stream fishing; foot bridge over the river; several foot trails lead off from the campground, including trails to Tamanawas Falls and toward the Mount Hood Wilderness; adjacent picnic area.

Natural Features: Located in a very forested atmosphere, typical of the Hood River Valley, in the Cascade Mountains; some sites are located right along the East Fork of the Hood River, which flows past toward the Columbia River, 30 miles north; timbered ridges to the east and west; Mount Hood and the Mount Hood Wilderness Area are located a few miles west; elevation 3000'.

Season, Fees & Phone: April to October; $7.00; 14 day limit; Hood River Ranger District (503) 666-0701.

Camp Notes: The fine scenery and overall environment of the Hood River Valley are manifested here in the tranquility of Sherwood's forest. Whoever christened this campground may have done so in order to upstage the individual who named the area described below.

Oregon 109

ROBINHOOD
Mount Hood National Forest

Location: Northern Oregon south of Hood River.

Access: From Oregon State Highway 35 at milepost 68 +.1 (28 miles south of Hood River, 13 miles northeast of the junction of Highway 35 & U.S. 26), turn west into the campground.

Facilities: 24 campsites; sites are small+ to medium-sized, essentially level, with fair separation; parking pads are gravel, short to medium-length, mostly straight-ins; a number of sites have good, level spaces for tents; fireplaces; firewood is available for gathering in the area; water at several faucets; vault facilities; oiled gravel driveways; limited supplies in the community of Mt. Hood, 14 miles north; adequate supplies and services are available in Hood River.

Activities & Attractions: Fishing; foot bridge over the river; several foot trails lead off from the campground, including one to Horsethief Meadow.

Natural Features: Located along the East Fork of the Hood River; smaller creeks flow into the East Fork here as it rushes by the campsites; moderately dense vegetation in the campground consists of conifers, hardwoods, and a considerable amount of underbrush; high, timbered ridges flank the Hood River Valley; the extinct volcano, Mount Hood, rises a few miles west; elevation 3500'.

Season, Fees & Phone: April to October; $7.00; 14 day limit; Hood River Ranger District (503) 666-0701.

Camp Notes: Robinhood's forested atmosphere is typical of this section of the Cascade Mountains. While some sites are rather close to the highway, some riverside sites are nicely tucked away in the forest. The campground, spelled as one word rather than as the "Robin Hood" we might expect, was named for Robinhood Creek, which passes by a half-mile west of the campground, on the other side of Horsethief Meadow.

Oregon 110

TOLLGATE
Mount Hood National Forest

Location: Western Oregon southeast of Portland.

Access: From U.S. Highway 26 at milepost 44 +.9 (0.4 mile east of Rhododendron, 10 miles west of Government Camp), turn south onto a paved access road and continue for 0.1 mile to the campground. (The driveway through the camping area is rather narrow, and may prove a bit tight for maneuvering larger vehicles.)

Facilities: 15 campsites; sites are fairly good-sized and well separated; parking pads are gravel, double-wide straight-ins or long pull-throughs; some pads may require additional leveling; some very nice tent spots; fireplaces; firewood is available for gathering in the area; water at faucets throughout; vault facilities; paved driveways; gas and groceries in Zigzag, 2 miles west.

Activities & Attractions: Stream fishing; an extensive day use area has a picnic shelter; a number of forest roads in the area provide access to the nearby mountains; Mount Hood Wilderness is accessible by foot trail from near Rhododendron.

Natural Features: Located along Camp Creek which flows into Zigzag River on the west slope of the Cascade Range; campsites are in a fairly dense forest, surrounded by tall conifers, bushes, ferns and moss-covered rocks; a few units are creekside; elevation 1700'.

Season, Fees & Phone: May to September; $6.00-$8.00; 14 day limit; Zigzag Ranger District (503) 666-0704.

Camp Notes: Tollgate is located near the site of an historic tollgate on the Barlow Trail. There are a number of large stone fireplaces and rock retaining walls along parking pads and pathways in the campground. A rail fence borders some really pleasant creekside sites.

CAMP CREEK
Mount Hood National Forest

Location: Western Oregon southeast of Portland.

Access: From U.S. Highway 26 at milepost 47 + .1 (2.5 miles east of Rhododendron, 8 miles west of Government Camp), turn south onto a paved access road and continue for 0.2 mile to the campground.

Facilities: 24 campsites, including 6 double units, in 2 loops; sites are fairly large and well spaced; parking pads are gravel, double-wide straight-ins or long pull-throughs; many pads may require additional leveling; some nicely forested tent spots; fireplaces; firewood is available for gathering in the area; water at hand pumps; vault facilities; waste water receptacles; gravel driveways (somewhat narrow for maneuvering larger vehicles); gas and groceries in Zigzag, 4 miles west.

Activities & Attractions: A foot trail follows along the creek and a wooden footbridge crosses the stream; a number of forest roads in the area provide mountain access; Mount Hood Wilderness is located just to the north of Zigzag River.

Natural Features: Located on the west slope of the Cascades on a forested hillside along Camp Creek, which flows into Zigzag River; camp area vegetation is not as dense here as at nearby Tollgate; conifers, ferns and leafy bushes are interspersed with open grassy areas; a number of sites are located right on the creek bank; elevation 2100'.

Season, Fees & Phone: May to September; $7.00-$9.00 for a single site, $12.00 for double site; 14 day limit; Zigzag Ranger District (503) 666-0704.

Camp Notes: Camp Creek is a refreshing stream which attracts fishermen, hikers and picnickers. There are a number of large, old, stone fireplaces and rock retaining walls along the parking pads and pathways in this campground. These were built by CCC crews in the 1930's. The community of Government Camp takes its name from that bygone era.

STILL CREEK
Mount Hood National Forest

Location: Western Oregon southeast of Portland.

Access: From U.S. Highway 26 at milepost 55 + .5 (0.5 mile south of Government Camp, 60 miles north of Madras), turn west onto a steep, paved access road and continue for 0.5 mile down to the campground.

Facilities: 27 campsites; sites are medium+ to large, with fair separation; parking pads are paved, level, mostly long straight-ins; some very nice tent spots; fireplaces; firewood is available for gathering in the area; water at faucets throughout; vault facilities; waste water receptacles; paved driveways; camper supplies in Government Camp.

Activities & Attractions: Fishing on Still Creek and Zigzag River; Trillium Lake, 2 miles south via a forest road, offers motorless boating, fishing, swimming and a sizable day use facility.

Natural Features: Located in the heart of the northern Cascades in a narrow valley along Still Creek, a rivulet which flows into the Zigzag River; the surrounding territory is very densely forested, but the camp area itself is fairly open, with tall conifers and only a little underbrush; Mount Hood, of volcanic origin, rises to over 11,000' just a few miles north; elevation 3300'.

Season, Fees & Phone: May to September; $6.00; 14 day limit; Zigzag Ranger District (503) 666-0704.

Camp Notes: All the sites at Still Creek are in good locations, but a few top-notch sites are located right along the creek. The overall atmosphere here is quiet and casual.

TRILLIUM LAKE
Mount Hood National Forest

Location: Western Oregon between Portland and Madras.

Access: From U.S. Highway 26 at milepost 56 + .8 (1.8 miles south of Government Camp, 59 miles north of Madras), turn southwest onto a steep access road and proceed 1.5 miles down to the campground.

Facilities: 49 campsites, including 5 double units; most sites are small to medium-sized and fairly well separated; parking pads are paved, medium to long straight-ins; a few pads may require a little additional leveling; many nice, secluded tent spots; fireplaces; firewood is available for gathering in the vicinity; water at faucets throughout; vault facilities; waste water receptacles; paved driveways; camper supplies in Government Camp.

Activities & Attractions: Motorless boating; fishing; swimming; a sizable day use facility is adjacent to the camping area; a number of forest roads nearby provide access to the surrounding mountains.

Natural Features: Located on the east shore of Trillium Lake in the Cascade Range; a dense conifer forest provides privacy and shelter for the sites; the small mountain lake (roughly 100 acres) is completely surrounded by forested slopes; Mount Hood, the loftiest peak in Oregon, is visible across the lake as it rises to over 11,000' just a few miles north; elevation 3200'.

Season, Fees & Phone: May to September; $8.00-$10.00 for a single site, $12.00 for a double site; 14 day limit; Zigzag Ranger District (503) 666-0704.

Camp Notes: Trillium Lake is a mountain gem! Really superscenic sights in this basin! A few campsites are located close enough to the lake to provide lake views through the trees. The campground and adjacent day use facility are typically bustling with activity.

FROG LAKE
Mount Hood National Forest

Location: West-central Oregon between Portland and Madras.

Access: From U.S. Highway 26 at milepost 62 (7 miles south of Government Camp, 53 miles north of Madras), turn east onto a paved access road and proceed 0.5 mile; turn left into the campground.

Facilities: 33 campsites; sites are mostly average-sized with nominal separation between interior sites, and fairly good separation between sites around the perimeter; parking pads are gravel, level, and mostly medium-length straight-ins; some nice, level tent spots; fireplaces; firewood is available for gathering in the area; water at hand pumps; vault facilities; paved driveways; camper supplies in Government Camp; nearest source of adequate supplies and services is Madras.

Activities & Attractions: Motorless boating; fishing; large day use facility adjacent to the camping area; a foot trail leads toward the Pacific Crest Scenic Trail.

Natural Features: Located near the shore of Frog Lake high in the Cascade Range; the center of the camp area is fairly open, with only some tall trees, grass and a little underbrush; sites around the exterior are situated in dense forest; waters of Frog Lake feed into Frog Creek, which flows eastward to the Deschutes River; Mount Hood rises to over 11,000' just a few miles north; elevation 3900'.

Season, Fees & Phone: May to September; $9.00; 14 day limit; Bear Springs Ranger District, Maupin, (503) 328-6211.

Camp Notes: Frog Lake is situated just about as high in the Cascades as you can get along this highway. It's off a slight 'dip' in the highway, roughly midway along the one mile between 3952' Wapinitia Pass to the north-west and 4042' Blue Box Pass to the south-east. Its drainage pattern places it on the east slope of the Cascades. A few of the sites are located close enough to Frog Lake to provide a lake view through the trees.

CLEAR LAKE
Mount Hood National Forest

Location: West-central Oregon between Madras and Portland.

Access: From U.S. Highway 26 at milepost 64 +.5 (1 mile south-east of Blue Box Pass summit, 10 miles south of Government Camp, 50 miles northwest of Madras), turn west onto a winding, paved access road and continue for 1.1 miles down to the campground.

Facilities: 26 campsites; sites are medium to large, with mostly average separation; parking pads are gravel straight-ins or pull-throughs; some are spacious enough to accommodate fairly large rv's; pads may require some additional leveling; tent spaces tend to be sloped, the most level sites are on the hilltop; fireplaces; firewood is available for gathering in the area; water at a hand pump; vault facilities; paved driveways; camper supplies in Government Camp; adequate supplies and services are available in Madras.

Activities & Attractions: Windsurfing; boating; boat launch.

Natural Features: Located on a slope above the northeast shore of Clear Lake in the Cascade Range; campground vegetation consists of a few large trees, grass and many small scrub pines; surrounded by forested hills and ridges; elevation 3600'.

Season, Fees & Phone: May to September; $8.00; may be operated by concessionaire; Bear Springs Ranger District, Maupin, (503) 328-6211.

Camp Notes: Clear Lake Campground provides good facilities. But in August, or other low water times, Clear Lake's surface may be speckled with tree stumps that poke their way up through the shallow waters. If you can look between the tree stumps, you'll enjoy a stay here.

Oregon
West Central
Please refer to the Oregon map in the Appendix

Oregon 116

BLUE BAY & SOUTH SHORE
Deschutes National Forest

Location: West-central Oregon northwest of Bend.

Access: From U.S. Highway 20/Oregon State Highway 126 at milepost 87 +.3 (10 miles northwest of Sisters, 6 miles east of Santiam Pass), turn southwest onto a paved lake access road and proceed 0.9 mile to Blue Bay; or continue for an additional 0.15 mile to South Shore; turn northwest (right) into the campgrounds.

Facilities: 25 campsites in Blue Bay, 39 campsites in South Shore; sites are generally medium to large, with fair to good separation; parking pads are gravel, mostly medium-length straight-ins, plus a number of long pull-throughs or pull-offs; majority of pads will require additional leveling; adequate space for medium to large tents, but generally a little sloped; fireplaces; some firewood may be available for gathering in the surrounding area, b-y-o to be sure; water at several faucets; vault facilities; waste water receptacles; paved driveways; camper supplies at a nearby store; nearest source of limited supplies and services is Sisters.

Activities & Attractions: Lake Shore Trail; boating; boat launch and dock; fishing; fish cleaning station.

Natural Features: Located on a sloping shelf a few feet above the south shore of Suttle Lake; sites are moderately sheltered/shaded by tall conifers and some hardwoods; bordered by the heavily timbered, low hills and mountains of the Cascade Range; elevation 3400'.

Season, Fees & Phone: May to October; $8.00; 14 day limit; Sisters Ranger District (503) 549-2111.

Camp Notes: Only a few subtle differences distinguish these two camps from each other. Blue Bay may have a bit of an edge in site separation. South Shore, however, is the slightly more level campground of the two. Lake access is also a little better at South Shore. Both campgrounds have quite a few nice lakefront sites.

Oregon 117

LINK CREEK
Deschutes National Forest

Location: West-central Oregon northwest of Bend.

Access: From U.S. Highway 20/Oregon State Highway 126 at milepost 87 +.3 (10 miles northwest of Sisters, 6 miles east of Santiam Pass), turn southwest onto a paved lake access road and proceed 2.2 miles along the south shore of the lake and around to the southwest end; turn northeast (right) into the campground.

Facilities: 33 campsites in a complex of loops; sites are medium-sized to quite large, with fair to good separation; parking pads are gravel, medium-length straight-ins or long pull-throughs; majority of the pads will require additional leveling; tent spaces vary from small to large, and many are sloped; fireplaces; some firewood may be available for gathering in the surrounding area, b-y-o just in case; water at several faucets; vault facilities; paved driveways; camper supplies at a nearby store; nearest source of limited supplies and services is Sisters.

Activities & Attractions: Lake Shore Trail; boating; boat launch; fishing.

Natural Features: Located on rolling. sloping terrain at the southwest tip of Suttle Lake on the east slope of the Cascade Range; campground vegetation consists of some tall grass and moderate underbrush capped by medium to moderately dense, tall conifers; bordered by low hills and mountains; elevation 3400'.

Season, Fees & Phone: May to October; $8.00; 14 day limit; Sisters Ranger District (503) 549-2111.

Camp Notes: Suttle Lake was hewn by glaciers about 10,000 years ago and is situated in an elongated basin. Consequently, there aren't any really distant views available here except out toward the hills on the far shores of this medium-sized lake. However, there's a good highwayside viewpoint of spectacular Mount Washington, on U.S. 20 just three miles west of the lake road turnoff.

Oregon 118

CAMP SHERMAN & ALLINGHAM
Deschutes National Forest

Location: West-central Oregon northwest of Bend.

Access: From U.S. Highway 20/Oregon State Highway 126 at milepost 90 +.9 (10 miles northwest of Sisters, 10 miles east of Santiam Pass), turn north onto Jefferson County Road 14 (paved) and proceed 2.7 miles to a fork; take the right fork onto Forest Road 14 and travel another 3.4 miles; turn west (left) and drop down to a paved road at river-level; turn north (right) again for 0.1 mile to Camp Sherman, or continue for another half-mile to Allingham; turn west (left) into the campgrounds.

Facilities: 15 campsites in Camp Sherman, 6 campsites in Allingham; sites are medium to large, level, with nominal to fair separation; parking pads are gravel/earth, medium to long straight-ins or pull-throughs; medium to large tent areas; fireplaces; firewood is available for gathering in the area; water at faucets; vault facilities; paved driveways; limited supplies and services are available in Sisters.

Activities & Attractions: Head of the Metolius Interpretive Center nearby; fly fishing; central kitchen shelter in Camp Sherman.

Natural Features: Located on a flat in a canyon on the east bank of the Metolius River in the Cascade Range; sites are sheltered/shaded by light to medium-dense conifers over a surface of tall grass and brush; elevation. 3300'.

Season, Fees & Phone: May to October; $8.00; 14 day limit; Sisters Ranger District (503) 549-2111.

Camp Notes: Although the Metolius isn't one of the West's best-known rivers, it nonetheless is a fine stream. Unlike most Western rivers, it's headwaters aren't merely mountain trickles which gradually gather water from other streams on their passage to the sea. Instead, icy waters from gigantic springs gush forth from the mountains a mile upstream of these campgrounds. Thus the Metolius is no infant stream as it passes by your campsite, but is born nearly full-grown.

Oregon 119

SMILING RIVER
Deschutes National Forest

Location: West-central Oregon northwest of Bend.

Access: From U.S. Highway 20 & Oregon State Highway 126 at milepost 90 +.9 (10 miles northwest of Sisters, 10 miles east of Santiam Pass), turn north onto Jefferson County Road 14 (paved) and proceed 2.7 miles to a fork; take the right fork onto Forest Road 14 and travel another 3.4 miles; turn west (left) and drop down to a paved road at river-level; head north (right) again and continue northward (parallel to the river and the "high" road) for 1.2 miles; turn west (left) into the campground.

Facilities: 37 campsites; sites are medium to large, level or nearly so, with nominal to good separation; parking pads are gravel/earth, medium-length straight-ins, plus some long pull-throughs; medium to large tent spots; fireplaces; firewood is available for gathering in the general area; water at several faucets; vault facilities; paved driveway; nearest source of supplies and services (limited) is Sisters.

Activities & Attractions: Fly fishing; interpretive center nearby.

Natural Features: Located on a streamside flat along the east bank of the Metolius River on the east slope of the Cascade Range; sites are generally well-sheltered/ shaded by tall conifers on a surface of tall grass; bordered by forested hills; elevation 3300'.

Season, Fees & Phone: May to October; $8.00; 14 day limit; Sisters Ranger District (503) 549-2111.

Camp Notes: Smiling River has the highest number of riverside sites of all the campgrounds in this area. That, plus other unexplained reasons, make it the most favored camp as well. (Maybe the campground host serves complimentary flapjack breakfasts. Ed.) Tell you what, though. If you take a tumble into the frosty waters of the Smiling River with a smile on your face, you'll be wearing that silly, frozen grin for at least a week. Guaranteed!

Oregon 120

PINE REST & GORGE
Deschutes National Forest

Location: West-central Oregon northwest of Bend.

Access: From U.S. Highway 20/Oregon State Highway 126 at milepost 90 +.9 (10 miles northwest of Sisters, 10 miles east of Santiam Pass), turn north onto Jefferson County Road 14 (paved) and proceed 2.7 miles to a fork; take the right fork onto Forest Road 14 and travel another 3.4 miles; turn west (left) and drop down to a paved road at river-level; head north (right) again and proceed parallel to the river and the "high" road for 1.7 miles to Pine Rest or 1.9 miles to Gorge, both on the west (left).

Facilities: 18 campsites in Gorge, 8 sites in Pine Rest; sites are medium to large, level, with fair to fairly good separation; parking pads are gravel/earth, medium to long pull-throughs or pull-offs in Gorge, straight-ins in Pine Rest; adequate space for medium to large tents; fireplaces; firewood is available for gathering in the area; water at several faucets; vault facilities; paved driveways; nearest source of supplies and services (limited) is Sisters.

Activities & Attractions: Hiking trail; fly fishing; kitchen shelter in Pine Rest.

Natural Features: Located on a flat in a forested canyon on the east bank of the Metolius River on the east slope of the Cascade Range; sites receive light to medium shelter/shade from tall conifers; elevation 3300'.

Season, Fees & Phone: May to October; $8.00; 14 day limit; Sisters Ranger District (503) 549-2111.

Camp Notes: Gorge is the last (northernmost) of the campgrounds on this stretch of the Metolius River Road. If your primary reason for coming up here is to get away from it all (or from everybody), these popular camps might not do. For that, you can try heading up the river road for another half-dozen miles to a second group of small camps. They're up near the point where the Metolius forms the natural boundary between the national forest and the Warm Springs Indian Reservation.

Oregon 121

INDIAN FORD
Deschutes National Forest

Location: West-central Oregon northwest of Bend.

Access: From U.S. Highway 20/Oregon State Highway 126 at milepost 94 +.95 (6 miles northwest of Sisters, many miles east of nowhere else), turn north onto a paved road for 0.05 mile, then turn east (right) into the campground.

Facilities: 25 campsites in 2 loops; sites are medium+ to very large, basically level, with fair to good separation; parking pads are earthen, long straight-ins or pull-throughs; plenty of space for tents; fireplaces, plus some barbecue grills; some firewood is available for gathering in the surrounding area; water at a hand pump; vault facilities; waste water receptacles; gravel driveways; limited supplies and services are available in Sisters.

Activities & Attractions: Possibly fishing for small trout.

Natural Features: Located on a forested flat along Indian Ford Creek in the foothills of the Cascade Range; campground vegetation consists of some tall grass and brush and light to medium-dense, tall conifers; bordered by well-forested hills and low mountains; elevation 3200'.

Season, Fees & Phone: May to October; $7.00; 14 day limit; Sisters Ranger District (503) 549-2111.

Camp Notes: For a camp with restrooms, several water hydrants, a few electrical hookups, and about the same price as Indian Ford, the city park in Sisters might be worth a look. It's on the east edge of town, off the south side of the main drag. The 20 or so small, level campsites stretch several hundred yards back from the highway, so you might find a spot that's a little quieter than those at Indian Ford. (You'll not find many campgrounds along this highway that have sites *larger* than Indian Ford's, though.) The local community was named for the majestic triplets in the Cascade Range known as the Three Sisters. The great gray ladies may be viewed from near town.

TUMALO
Tumalo State Park

Location: Central Oregon northwest of Bend.

Access: From U.S. Highway 20 at milepost 14 +.8 in the hamlet of Tumalo (7 miles northwest of Bend, 16 miles southeast of Sisters), turn southerly (i.e., an easy right if eastbound) onto a paved local road and proceed 1.1 miles; just past the Deschutes River bridge, turn east (left) into the campground. (Note: if westbound from Bend on U.S. 20, you could opt to take the slightly more scenic route by following the signs from milepost 16 +.7, east of the park; but taking the narrow, winding, steep route probably won't save any time over the more direct route given above.)

Facilities: 88 campsites, including 20 with full hookups, in 3 loops; (two small group camps and hiker-biker sites are also available); sites are small, with minimal separation; parking pads are paved, short to medium-length straight-ins, and most will require a little additional leveling; small to medium-sized, level to slightly off-level, spaces for tents; fireplaces; firewood is usually for sale, or b-y-o; water at faucets throughout; restrooms with solar showers; waste water receptacles; paved driveways; complete supplies and services are available in Bend.

Activities & Attractions: River trail; designated swimming hole and grassy beach; fishing (rainbow and brown trout, best in spring and late summer); amphitheater; day use area.

Natural Features: Located on a slope along the Deschutes River (day use area) and on a hill/knoll above the river (campground); picnic and camp sites are lightly shaded by hardwoods, junipers and pines; surrounded by rolling/hilly semi-arid plains; the eastern foothills of the Cascade Range lie a dozen or so miles to the west; elevation 3200'.

Season, Fees & Phone: April to October; please see Appendix for standard Oregon state park fees; 10 day limit; park office (503) 388-6055 or (503) 382-3586.

Camp Notes: The Deschutes is a fine stream, and it's particularly appealing as it passes through the small canyon in which this park is located. The swimmin' hole is on a deep, slow-moving segment of the river. The campground is extremely popular, so get here before noon and hope for the best. Although the main things to do in the park itself are fishing, swimming and camping, you can be occupied by a multitude of other attractions in and around Bend. Although this is indeed a nice little park with nice little campsites, it might best serve you as a base of ops for exploring what some literature calls the "volcanic wonderland" of this region. South of Bend is the 50,000-acre Newberry National Volcanic Monument, with a visitor center and trails around the rims of volcanic craters. In the same vicinity are Lava River Caves, where you can walk through a mile-long lava tube.

LA PINE
La Pine State Recreation Area

Location: West-central Oregon southwest of Bend.

Access: From U.S. Highway 97 at milepost 160 +.5 (7 miles north of La Pine, 23 miles south of Bend), head west on State Rec Road (paved) for 3.9 miles, then curve northerly and westerly for another 1.2 miles to the campground entrance station; continue for a final 0.5 mile to the camp loops.

Facilities: 145 campsites, including 50 with partial hookups and 95 with full hookups, in 7 loops; sites are small+ to medium+, with nominal to good separation; parking pads are paved, medium to long straight-ins or long pull-throughs; some pads will require a touch of additional leveling; medium to large, tolerably level tent areas; fireplaces; some firewood may be provided, b-y-o to be sure; water at faucets throughout; restrooms with showers; holding tank disposal station; paved driveways; gas and groceries in La Pine; complete supplies and services are available in Bend.

Activities & Attractions: Fishing (the Deschutes is one of the West's great trout streams; limited boating/floating; designated swimming area; amphitheater.

Natural Features: Located on a slightly rolling bluff above the west bank of the Deschutes River; sites are lightly shaded/sheltered by tall pines; the largest pine tree (191' high) in Oregon is in the park; bordered by low, pine-and-brush-covered slopes and low hills; the Cascade Range rises in the distant west; elevation 4200'.

Season, Fees & Phone: April to October; please see Appendix for standard Oregon state park fees; 10 day limit; park office (503) 536-2428.

Camp Notes: The wide, deep, clear Deschutes is the major attraction in the recreation area. It's a bit more river than is typically found in a leeside environment such as this. (By the way, if you've grown particularly fond of a mosquito you met here, keep him/her inside your tent or camper while the fog truck rolls through.)

CROOKED RIVER
The Cove Palisades State Park

Location: Central Oregon north of Bend.

Access: From U.S. Highway 97/Oregon State Highway 26 at Avenue D in midtown Madras, proceed west and south on Avenue D for 2 blocks, then southwest on Culver Highway (through the town of Metolius) for 7.5 miles to a point between the communities of Metolius and Culver; turn west onto Gem Lane, cross the railroad tracks, and follow this paved road west for 1 mile, then south for 0.8 mile to a turnoff signed for the park; turn west (right) onto the paved park access road and continue for 1.5 miles; turn south (left) into Crooked River Campground. (Total distance from Madras to Crooked River is 10 miles.)

Facilities: 91 campsites with partial hookups; sites are small to small+, generally level, with minimal separation; parking pads are paved, short to medium-length straight-ins; some grassy spots for tents; fire rings; firewood is usually for sale, or b-y-o; water at sites; restrooms with showers; holding tank disposal station; paved driveways; minimal supplies at a general store, 1 mile east; adequate supplies and services are available in Madras.

Activities & Attractions: Boating; boat launches and docks; fishing (reportedly very good for trout, steelhead, salmon); water skiing; swimming beaches; the drive along the canyon's east rim provides spectacular views of the area.

Natural Features: Located on the east rim above a deep basaltic canyon above Lake Billy Chinook, a reservoir located at the confluence of 3 rivers--Crooked, Deschutes and Metolius; campground vegetation consists of mown lawns and planted hardwoods which provide limited shade; bordered by a sage plain; elevation 2600'.

Season, Fees & Phone: Open all year, with limited services October to April; please see Appendix for standard Oregon state park fees; 10 day limit; campsite reservations recommended for summer weekends, please see Appendix; park office (503) 546-3412.

Camp Notes: If you've ever been to the great canyon lakes of the Desert Southwest, such as Lakes Mead or Powell, you'll have a good idea of what this place looks like. Crooked River Campground's high-level breeziness may make it a better midsummer choice than its sister camp, Deschutes River, which is far below the canyon rim.

DESCHUTES RIVER
The Cove Palisades State Park

Location: Central Oregon north of Bend.

Access: From U.S. Highway 97/Oregon State Highway 26 at Avenue D in midtown Madras, proceed west and south on Avenue D for 2 blocks, then southwest on Culver Highway (through the town of Metolius) for 7.5 miles to a point between the communities of Metolius and Culver; turn west onto Gem Lane, cross the railroad tracks, and follow this paved road west for 1 mile, then south for 0.8 mile to a turnoff signed for the park; turn west (right) onto the paved park access road; continue (you'll pass Crooked River Campground on the left) down a steep, winding road and across the Crooked River bridge for an additional 6.5 miles to Deschutes River Campground. (Total distance from Madras--15 miles.) Whew!

Facilities: 181 campsites, including 87 with full hookups; (a group camp is also available); sites are small to small+, with minimal to fair separation; parking pads are paved, mostly short to medium-length straight-ins, plus about a dozen pull-throughs; some pads may require a little additional leveling; medium to large tent spots; fire rings or fireplaces; firewood is usually for sale, or b-y-o; water at faucets throughout; restrooms with showers; paved driveways; gas and camper supplies in the park; adequate supplies and services are available in Madras.

Activities & Attractions: Boating; boat launches and docks; fishing (reportedly very good for trout, steelhead, salmon); water skiing; designated swimming beaches; hiking trails; amphitheater for scheduled programs in summer; river access from several points.

Natural Features: Located deep in a dry, rocky canyon on the Deschutes River Arm of Lake Billy Chinook; campsites are lightly to moderately shaded by hardwoods and junipers; the 'fork' at the confluence of the Deschutes and Crooked Rivers is split by an enormous, rocky landmass called "The Island"; surrounded by sage slopes and sheer-walled escarpments as viewed from the lake shore; elevation 1900'.

Season, Fees & Phone: Open all year, with limited services October to April; please see Appendix for standard Oregon state park fees; 10 day limit; campsite reservations recommended for summer weekends, please see Appendix; park office (503) 546-3412.

Camp Notes: A number of these sites are distinctively different: they're built into rocky walls with huge boulders for separation. Other sites have grass and trees for cool comfort. The drive along the canyon rim and down to the campground at lake level provides spectacular views of the area.

Oregon 126

SMITH ROCK
Smith Rock State Park

Location: Central Oregon north of Bend.

Access: From U.S. Highway 97 in midtown Terrebonne (6 miles north of Redmond), turn east onto B Avenue (Smith Rock Way) and proceed 0.6 mile; turn north (left) onto NE 1st Street and go 0.4 mile, then curve east (right) onto NE Wilcox Avenue and continue for another 1.5 miles; turn north (left) onto NE 25th Street for a final 0.6 mile to the park.

Facilities: Bivouac/primitive camping in a small, walk-in camp; drinking water, restrooms and parking lot along the main park road.

Activities & Attractions: 7 miles of hiking and equestrian trails follow the river and switchback up the canyon walls to the ridge tops; rock climbing ("clean" climbing equipment preferred, experienced/trained climbers only, please).

Natural Features: Located above the banks of the Crooked River; campsite vegetation consists mainly of junipers, pines, sage and sparse grass; imposing rock spires and jagged ridges dominate the terrain; elevation 3000'.

Season, Fees & Phone: Open all year, subject to weather conditions; principal season is April to October; please see Appendix for standard Oregon state park fees; 10 day limit; phone c/o The Cove Palisades State Park (503) 546-3412.

Camp Notes: According to local legend, the Rock was named back in the middle 1800's for a U.S. Army soldier named Smith who fell to his demise while climbing its heights. Nowadays, Smith Rock is now a nationally recognized rock climbing site. But just because the park has a reputation for its climbs doesn't mean there aren't a lot of good things to see and do for someone other than Spiderman. The local scenery is unlike any other that you'll come across in Oregon.

Oregon 127

PRINEVILLE RESERVOIR
Prineville Reservoir State Park

Location: Central Oregon east of Bend.

Access: From U.S. Highway 26 at milepost 19 + .8 on the east edge of Prineville (0.85 mile east of the county courthouse), turn south onto Combs Flat Road (paved) and proceed southeast for 1.3 miles; bear south (right) onto Juniper Canyon Road (paved) and travel 14 miles south then southeast to the park and a "T" intersection; turn left for 0.1 mile to the campground entrance.

Facilities: 70 campsites, including 22 with full hookups, in 3 loops; sites are small, with nominal to fair separation; parking pads are paved, short to medium-length straight-ins; pads are respectably level (considering the slope), but a little additional leveling may still be required in some sites; medium to large, acceptably level spaces for tents; fire rings; firewood is usually for sale, or b-y-o; water at several faucets; restrooms with showers; paved driveways; adequate+ supplies and services are available in Prineville.

Activities & Attractions: Boating; boat launch, docks; swimming area; fishing for trout, bass, catfish; amphitheater; day use area with shelter.

Natural Features: Located on a steep hillside above the middle-north shore of Prineville Reservoir, a major impoundment on the Crooked River; vegetation consists of sections of lawns dotted with tall junipers and hardwoods which provide light to light-medium shade/shelter for most campsites; the reservoir is surrounded by rocky hills and mountains covered by sage and crunchgrass and specked with junipers; elevation 3200'.

Season, Fees & Phone: April to October; please see Appendix for standard Oregon state park fees; 10 day limit; campsite reservations highly recommended for July and August weekends, please see Appendix; park office (503) 447-4363.

Camp Notes: Nearly all campsites have a lake view. Since the sites are high on a hillside, they actually provide campers with better views than those afforded to day trippers. One needs no profound deduction to determine why so many visitors from the (often cloudy and rainy) Willamette Valley take an annual trip or two to Prineville to enjoy the sunshine and crisp, dry air of this high desert park. However, because the reservoir's water is used for irrigation, the water level is subject to deep drawdown by mid or late summer.

OCHOCO LAKE
Ochoco Lake State Park

Location: Central Oregon east of Bend.

Access: From U.S. Highway 26 at milepost 26 +.2 (7 miles east of Prineville, 43 miles west of Mitchell), turn south into the park entrance and continue ahead for a few yards to the campground.

Facilities: 22 campsites; (hiker-biker sites are also available); sites are small to small+ in size, with minimal to fair separation; parking pads are paved, mostly short to medium-length straight-ins; some pads may require additional leveling; fireplaces or fire rings; firewood is usually for sale, or b-y-o; water at several faucets; restrooms; waste water receptacles; paved driveways; adequate+ supplies and services are available in Prineville.

Activities & Attractions: Boating; boat launch; windsurfing; fishing; Painted Hills Unit of John Day Fossil Beds National Monument, with its domed hills striped with color, is located northwest of Mitchell.

Natural Features: Located on a lightly forested hill above the north shore of Ochoco Lake (Reservoir), an impoundment on Ochoco Creek; short to medium-height junipers are the predominant trees in the park; bordered by rugged, dry-looking hills and low mountains dotted with junipers; the moderately forested Ochoco Mountains, north and east of the lake, rise to almost 7000'; park elevation 3100'.

Season, Fees & Phone: April to October; please see Appendix for standard Oregon state park fees; 10 day limit; phone c/o Prineville Reservoir State Park (503) 447-4363.

Camp Notes: Ochoco Lake's surroundings may be slightly less-parched than some of the other locales in these parts. But the area nonetheless retains the overall atmosphere of the windswept, rocky, high desert which many vacationers seek in summer.

OCHOCO DIVIDE
Ochoco National Forest

Location: Central Oregon between Prineville and John Day.

Access: From U.S. Highway 26 just west of milepost 50 (16 miles west of Mitchell, 34 miles east of Prineville), turn south into the campground.

Facilities: 28 campsites; sites are medium to large, with minimal separation; parking pads are gravel, some are short straight-ins and others are pull-throughs large enough to accommodate medium-sized rv's; some pads may require additional leveling; many nice, grassy tent spots; steps are cut into the slope at many sites to provide easier access to tables and fireplaces; limited firewood is available for gathering in the vicinity; water at central faucets; vault facilities; waste water receptacles; paved driveways; limited supplies and services are available in Mitchell.

Activities & Attractions: Commanding vistas from atop Ochoco Divide--especially to the east; a jeep trail leads off from the east end of the campground; the drive along Highway 26, east of here, passes some interesting geological formations; 2 sections of the John Day Fossil Beds National Monument are located near Mitchell and, further east, near Dayville.

Natural Features: Located in the Ochoco Mountains just west of Ochoco Divide (Ochoco Summit); campsites are on a grassy, pine-dotted, gentle slope; a rivulet near the divide flows westward down to Ochoco Lake and ultimately to the Deschutes River; elevation 4600'.

Season, Fees & Phone: May to September; $5.00; 14 day limit; Big Summit Ranger District (Prineville), (503) 447-9645.

Camp Notes: Ochoco Divide Campground has an 'airy' quality as a result of its mountainside position in a high, dry, open forest. The campsites are not very far from the highway, but the traffic on U.S. 26 is generally light anyway. Good price, too. (*Spelling* the name of this campground, the pass, the lake, the mountains and the national forest is a lot easier than explaining how to *pronounce* it. Try *Oh*-ch-*koh*, with moderate, even accents on the first and last syllables if you'd like to sound just like a local-in-the-know. The meaning of the word? "Willow". It was also the name of a local group of Snake Indians.)

Oregon 130

SHELTON
Shelton State Wayside

Location: Central Oregon north of Mitchell.

Access: From Oregon State Highway 19 at milepost 69 +.7 (1.4 miles south of the summit of Butte Creek Pass, 11 miles south of Fossil, 9 miles north of the junction of State Highways 19 & 207 near Service Creek), turn west onto a gravel access road and proceed 0.1 mile into the park; turn north (right) to a small group of campsites, or south to the main string of campsites.

Facilities: Approximately 40 campsites; sites are small+ to large, slightly sloped, with nominal to fairly good separation; parking surfaces are grass, of various lengths, pull-offs or straight-ins; plenty of space for tents; fire rings or fireplaces; firewood may be available for gathering in the surrounding area, b-y-o just in case; water at several faucets; vault facilities; gravel driveways; camper supplies are available in Service Creek.

Activities & Attractions: Nature trail (at the north end of the park); footbridges across the stream bed.

Natural Features: Located in a shallow canyon/draw along a mile-long stretch of a brushy stream bed; campsites receive light shade/shelter from tall conifers on a grassy surface; closely flanked by forested mountains; elevation 3600'.

Season, Fees & Phone: Open all year, subject to weather conditions, with limited services October to April; please see Appendix for standard Oregon state park fees; 10 day limit; phone c/o Clyde Holliday State Park (503) 575-2773.

Camp Notes: Shelton's camp facilities are some of the most roughcut of any in an Oregon state park unit. The wayside apparently mostly serves summer weekend campers looking for a cool spot to pitch a tent and hang a water jug in otherwise hot and dry Central Oregon. It also looks like a place that's used as a hunters' camp during the fall. Most of the land in this region is privately owned, so the best you can do is sit back and enjoy the scenery as it passes your windshield. Although this highway crosses forested mountains, other main roads follow portions of the great John Day River through semi-arid, irrigated country. The lower John Day River (west and north of Shelton) is classified as a Scenic Waterway. River access is quite limited, though.

Oregon
Northeast
Please refer to the Oregon map in the Appendix

Oregon 131

UKIAH-DALE FOREST
Ukiah-Dale Forest State Wayside

Location: Northeast Oregon southwest of La Grande.

Access: From U.S. Highway 395 at milepost 51 (1.4 miles south of the junction of U.S. 395 & State Highway 244 near Ukiah, 14 miles north of Dale), turn east into the campground.

Facilities: 25 campsites; sites are small, with minimal to fair separation; parking pads are paved, essentially level, short to medium-length straight-ins; adequate space for large tents; fire rings; some firewood is available for gathering in the surrounding area; water at several faucets; restrooms; paved driveways; limited supplies and services are available in Ukiah.

Activities & Attractions: Trout fishing.

Natural Features: Located in a narrow canyon on a slightly rolling flat along the west bank of Camas Creek in the Blue Mountains; campsites are very lightly to moderately shaded/sheltered by tall conifers on a surface of mown grass; bordered by forested hills and mountains; elevation 3200'.

Season, Fees & Phone: April to October; please see Appendix for standard Oregon state park fees; 10 day limit; phone c/o Emigrant Springs State Park (503) 983-2277.

Camp Notes: Camas Creek is a classic mountain stream. It's wide, clear and deep, with a lively but not overwhelming current. Most campsites have a stream view.

Oregon 132

LANE CREEK & BEAR WALLOW
Umatilla National Forest

Location: Northeast Oregon southwest of La Grande.

Access: From Oregon State Highway 244 at milepost 11, (10 miles northeast of Ukiah, 37 miles southwest of Interstate 84 Exit 252 at Hilgard Junction), turn north into Lane Creek Campground; or at milepost 11 +.8 (0.8 mile northeast of Lane Creek), turn north into Bear Wallow Campground.

Facilities: 5 campsites in each campground; sites are small to medium-sized, level, with fair separation; parking pads are gravel, short to medium-length straight-ins; medium-sized areas for tents; fire rings; a very limited amount of firewood is available for gathering in the area, b-y-o to be sure; no drinking water; vault facilities; gravel driveways; gas and groceries+ in Ukiah; adequate supplies and services are available in La Grande.

Activities & Attractions: Fishing.

Natural Features: Located on streamside flats along the banks of Camas Creek at its confluences with Lane Creek and Bear Wallow Creek in the Blue Mountains; sites receive light to light-medium shade/shelter from short to tall conifers and brush; bordered by low hills covered with sections of timber and grass; elevation 3900'.

Season, Fees & Phone: May to November; no fee; 14 day limit; North Fork John Day Ranger District, Ukiah, (503) 427-3231.

Camp Notes: Bear Wallow is slightly farther off the highway than Lane Creek, so it may be the camp of choice. The scenery along Highway 244 between the Interstate and Ukiah may not be spectacular, but it is certainly quite pleasant. Traffic is generally light.

Oregon 133

FRAZIER
Umatilla National Forest

Location: Northeast Oregon southwest of La Grande.

Access: From Oregon State Highway 244 at milepost 18 +.2, (17 miles northeast of Ukiah, 30 miles southwest of Interstate 84 Exit 252 at Hilgard Junction), turn south onto Forest Road 5226 (gravel) and proceed 0.7 mile; turn northeast (left) onto the gravel campground access road and proceed 0.1 mile to the campground.

Facilities: 31 campsites; sites are small to medium-sized, level, with fair to fairly good separation; parking pads are gravel, short to medium-length straight-ins; medium-sized areas for tents; fire rings; some firewood is available for gathering in the area; no drinking water; vault facilities; gravel driveways; gas and groceries+ in Ukiah; adequate supplies and services are available in La Grande.

Activities & Attractions: Fishing; hunting.

Natural Features: Located on a flat along the banks of Frazier Creek, a tributary of Camas Creek in the Blue Mountains; sites are moderately shaded/sheltered by medium to tall conifers and some undercover; bordered by partially forested low hills; elevation 4300'.

Season, Fees & Phone: May to November; no fee; 14 day limit; North Fork John Day Ranger District, Ukiah, (503) 427-3231.

Camp Notes: This region is widely respected as a good hunting ground for elk and mule deer. Consequently, during the fall big game season, Frazier is heavily used as a hunting camp.

Oregon 134

CLYDE HOLLIDAY
Clyde Holliday State Park

Location: Central Oregon west of John Day.

Access: From U.S. Highway 26 at milepost 155 +.2 (1.3 miles east of Mt. Vernon, 7 miles west of John Day), turn south into the park and the campground.

Facilities: 30 campsites with partial hookups; (several hiker-biker sites are also available); sites are medium+ in size, level, with nominal separation; parking pads are paved, and most are spacious enough for large rv's; some very nice, large tent spots on the lawns; fireplaces; firewood is usually for sale, or b-y-o; water at sites; restrooms with showers; holding tank disposal station; paved driveways; adequate supplies and services are available in John Day.

Activities & Attractions: Fishing; day use area.

Natural Features: Located on a flat in the semi-arid John Day Valley near the banks of the John Day River; the park has manicured lawns, and a variety of large hardwoods and a few conifers which provide limited to light shade for campsites; lightly timbered ridges border the valley; the Strawberry Range, with peaks rising to 9000', lies to the southeast; elevation 3200'.

Season, Fees & Phone: April to October; please see Appendix for standard Oregon state park fees; 10 day limit; park office (503) 575-2773.

Camp Notes: The Clyde Holliday oasis is one of the best all-around highwayside stops in dry East-Central Oregon. Some striking geological features can be seen in and around the John Day Valley.

Oregon 135

DEPOT
Grant County Park

Location: East-central Oregon southwest of Baker in Prairie City.

Access: From U.S. Highway 26 (Front Street) at milepost 175 in midtown Prairie City (15 miles northeast of John Day, 65 miles southwest of Baker), turn south onto Main Street; continue south for 0.4 mile, then turn east (left) into the park.

Facilities: 23 campsites, some with hookups; sites are small+ to medium sized, fairly level, with minimal separation; parking pads are paved and should accommodate medium-sized vehicles; a nice, level lawn area is designated for tents; fireplaces; b-y-o firewood; water at many sites and at a central faucet; restrooms with showers; holding tank disposal station; paved driveways; limited supplies and services are available in Prairie City.

Activities & Attractions: The park has an open, grassy area for recreation; picnic shelter and gezebo; the Depot Museum is located in a renovated railroad depot building which was moved to this location; access to the Strawberry Mountain Wilderness, south of Prairie City.

Natural Features: Located in the John Day River Valley, north of the John Day River; campsites are quite open, on lawns, with a few tall hardwoods for limited shelter/shade; views of the Strawberry Mountains to the south; elevation 3500'.

Season, Fees & Phone: May to September; $6.00 for a tent site, $9.00 for a partial-hookup site, $3.00 for a hike-bike site; $2.00 for disposal station use; Prairie City Hall (503) 820-3605.

Camp Notes: Depot Park's pleasant, green surroundings stand in marked contrast to the region's semi-arid terrain. A good stop for central Oregon travelers.

Oregon 136

DIXIE
Malheur National Forest

Location: Eastern Oregon southwest of Baker.

Access: From U.S. Highway 26 at milepost 184 +.9 (9.5 miles east of Prairie City, 23 miles west of Unity), turn northwest onto a gravel forest road and continue for 0.3 mile to the campground.

Facilities: 11 campsites; sites are medium to medium+, with good to excellent separation; parking pads are gravel, some large enough to accommodate medium-sized vehicles; additional leveling may be necessary in many sites; some nice, secluded tent sites; fireplaces; firewood is usually abundant; water at a hand pump; vault facilities; waste water receptacle; pack-it-in/pack-it-out trash removal system; gravel driveways; limited supplies and services are available in Prairie City.

Activities & Attractions: Hiking; huckleberry picking in spring and early summer; day use area adjacent to the campground has picnic facilities and a picturesque wooden foot bridge over the small stream.

Natural Features: Located on a forested hillside near the southern end of the Blue Mountains; a small creek flows through the campground and adjacent picnic area; vegetation in the camp area consists of light-medium dense tall timber and a little underbrush; Dixie Summit, just west of here on Highway 26, is at 5280'; campground elevation 5000'.

Season, Fees & Phone: April to November; no fee; 14 day limit; Prairie City Ranger District (503) 820-3311.

Camp Notes: This mile-high campground will seldom be full to its limited capacity because it's a bit off the beaten path, and has no major water feature to attract crowds. It's just a pleasant, simple, secluded forest camp, and would be a cool stop in the warmth of the Eastern Oregon summer. Hopefully, it will remain a bargain.

Oregon 137

UNITY LAKE
Unity Lake State Park

Location: Eastern Oregon southwest of Baker.

Access: From U.S. Highway 26 at milepost 210 +.3 (2 miles west of Unity, 19 miles east of the intersection of U.S. 26 with Oregon State Highway 7), turn northeast onto Oregon State Highway 245; proceed east and north for 2.2 miles; turn left onto a paved access road and continue for 0.4 mile to the park and the campground.

Facilities: 21 campsites, including 10 with partial hookups; (hiker-biker sites are also available); sites are small+ to medium-sized, level, with minimal separation; parking pads are paved or gravel and some are long enough for large vehicles; fireplaces; b-y-o firewood; restrooms with solar showers; water at hookups and at several faucets; holding tank disposal station; paved driveways; limited supplies and services are available in Unity.

Activities & Attractions: Boating; boat launch; fishing; nearby mountains, lakes and streams are accessible by forest roads; day use area.

Natural Features: Located on a sage flat on a breezy bluff slightly above man-made Unity Lake; park area is landscaped with watered and mown lawns, and planted hardwoods which provide very light to light shade for campsites; bordered by dry hills and mountains, plus a few trees and some natural grass and sage around the lake; the Blue Mountains rise in the north and west; elevation 3800'.

Season, Fees & Phone: April to October; please see Appendix for standard Oregon state park fees; 10 day limit; phone c/o Clyde Holliday State Park (503) 575-2773.

Camp Notes: This is a pleasant place to enjoy eastern Oregon if you prefer a hills-and-prairie environment over a forested mountain setting. There's enough local geological relief, plus some distant mountain views, to add a touch of embellishment to the semi-arid scene.

Oregon 138

EMIGRANT SPRINGS
Emigrant Springs State Park

Location: Northeast Oregon southeast of Pendleton.

Access: From Interstate 84 Exit 234 eastbound (24 miles southeast of Pendleton), travel east along the frontage road on the south side of I-84 for 0.6 mile; turn south (right) into the park; turn easterly (left) into the campground. **Alternate Access:** From I-84 Exit 234 westbound (28 miles west of La Grande), cross over the Interstate to the south frontage road, then proceed west 0.5 mile, then turn right into the park.

Facilities: 51 campsites, including 18 with full hookups; sites are small+ to medium-sized, essentially level, with nominal to fair separation; parking pads are paved, mostly short to medium-length straight-ins, plus some pads long enough for large vehicles; many excellent spots for tents; fire rings; firewood is usually for sale, or b-y-o; water at faucets throughout; restrooms with showers; paved driveways; gas and groceries at Meacham, 1 mile east; adequate+ supplies and services are available in Pendleton and La Grande.

Activities & Attractions: Nature trail; Conestoga wagon and oxen display near the park entrance; the historic spring for which the park is named is located just west of the park; large community building with very large, outdoor, stone fireplace (available to groups by reservation); playground; amphitheater; day use area with shelters.

Natural Features: Located on a flat and on a gentle slope in the Blue Mountains; campsites are moderately shaded/sheltered by tall conifers and some low-level vegetation; sections of the campground are trimmed by a pole fence; located 7 miles east of Blue Mountain Summit; generally quite mild temps during the summer; elevation 4000'.

Season, Fees & Phone: April to October; please see Appendix for standard Oregon state park fees; 10 day limit; park office (503) 983-2277.

Camp Notes: Emigrant Springs was the site of a scheduled pit stop on the Old Oregon Trail. Near here, travelers camped for a few days and filled their water casks from the spring. The place remains an excellent stop for Interstate travelers, particularly those who've spent a day or two crossing the barrens of Southern Idaho and Eastern Oregon.

Oregon 139

HILGARD JUNCTION
Hilgard Junction State Park

Location: Northeast Oregon west of La Grande.

Access: From Interstate 84 Exit 252 at Hilgard Junction (9 miles west of La Grande, 43 miles east of Pendleton), turn south onto Oregon State Highway 244, and proceed 0.1 mile to the campground entrance on the east (left) side of the highway.

Facilities: 18 campsites; most sites are small to medium-sized, level, with minimal separation; parking pads are paved, short to medium-length straight-ins; excellent tent spots; fire rings; a limited amount of firewood available for gathering in the vicinity, b-y-o is suggested; water at several faucets; restrooms; holding tank disposal station; paved driveways; fairly complete supplies and services are available in La Grande.

Activities & Attractions: Fishing; day use area.

Natural Features: Located in a canyon along the north-west bank of the Grande Ronde River; campsites are lightly shaded/sheltered by rows of tall hardwoods and a few conifers; bordered by grassy, tree-dotted hills; elevation 3100'.

Season, Fees & Phone: Open all year, with limited services October to April; please see Appendix for standard Oregon state park fees; 10 day limit; phone c/o Emigrant Springs State Park (503) 983-2277.

Camp Notes: This is a nice camp spot except for one minor drawback: it's only about a hundred feet off the Interstate. And by "a hundred feet off" we mean a hundred feet south and a hundred feet *below* I-84. Look at the bright side: at this angle, and with the help of the trees, you mostly *hear* the big rigs whizzing by, you don't really *see* much of them.

Oregon 140

WOODWARD
Umatilla National Forest

Location: Northeast Oregon east of Pendleton.

Access: From Oregon State Highway 204 near milepost 19 +.7 (18 miles east of Weston, 19 miles north/northwest of Elgin, turn south into the campground.

Facilities: 18 campsites; sites are small to medium-sized, with nominal to fair separation; parking pads are gravel, short to medium-length straight-ins; a few pads may require a little additional leveling; adequate space for tents; fireplaces; firewood is available for gathering in the vicinity; water at several faucets; vault facilities; holding tank disposal station at Tollgate Visitor Center, 0.5 mile east; paved driveway; gas and camper supplies 1 mile west; gas and groceries in Weston; limited+ supplies and services are available in Elgin.

Activities & Attractions: Short hiking trail; day use area with large picnic shelter, built by the CCC in the 1930's.

Natural Features: Located on a hillside above the west shore of Langdon Lake in the Blue Mountains; sites receive moderately dense shade/shelter from tall conifers and huckleberry undercover; elevation 5000'.

Season, Fees & Phone: Mid-June to mid-September; $5.00; 14 day limit; Walla Walla Ranger District (509) 522-6290.

Camp Notes: Langdon Lake is privately owned, but the pleasant scenic views are available to everyone. There's another roadside camp along this highway, named Woodland, five miles southeast of Woodward, on the east side of the highway near milepost 24. Woodland has seven sites in a forested setting, vaults, no drinking water and no fee. The namesake of this national forest is the Umatilla River, which rises a few miles southwest of Woodward Campground. *Umatilla* means "Waters Rippling Over Sand".

Oregon 141

TARGET MEADOWS
Umatilla National Forest

Location: Northeast Oregon east of Pendleton.

Access: From Oregon State Highway 204 near milepost 20 +.3 (18 miles east of Weston, 19 miles north/northwest of Elgin, turn north-east onto Forest Road 64 (gravel) and proceed 0.5 mile (past the Tollgate Visitor Center); turn northwest (left) onto Forest Road 6401 and go 2 miles, then turn northerly (right) onto Spur 050 for a to the campground.

Facilities: 20 campsites; sites are small+ to medium-sized, with fair to fairly good separation; parking pads are gravel, short to short+ straight-ins; small to medium-sized areas for tents; fireplaces; firewood is available for gathering in the vicinity; water at faucets; vault facilities; holding tank disposal station at Tollgate Visitor Center; gravel driveway; gas and camper supplies 1 mile west of the highway turnoff; gas and groceries in Weston; limited+ supplies and services are available in Elgin.

Activities & Attractions: Historical significance; Burnt Cabin Trailhead; excellent huckleberry picking; wildlife observation.

Natural Features: Located in a forested area on gently rolling terrain along the west edge of 400-acre Target Meadows in the Blue Mountains; sites are well shaded/sheltered by tall conifers and a plenitude of huckleberry bushes; elevation 4800'.

Season, Fees & Phone: Mid-June to mid-September; $4.00; 14 day limit; Walla Walla Ranger District (509) 522-6290.

Camp Notes: Horse soldiers from the U.S. Cavalry detachment at Fort Walla Walla regularly used the large open meadow for marksmanship practice during the late 1800's, thus its name. Wildlife grazing in the marshy meadow can often be observed from the campground area. If you don't mind a lot of gravel travel (instead of just the couple of miles to get to Target Meadows), a large, popular campground awaits at Jubilee Lake. Use the same basic instructions for getting to Target Meadows, but instead of turning off Forest Road 64, just keep heading northeasterly on FR 64 for 12 more miles to the lake. Jubilee Lake's campground has 50 forested campsites that can handle tents and medium to long rv's, piped water and restrooms, for several dollars more than camping here or at nearby Woodward Campground. Local activities include fishing for stocked rainbow trout, boating (hand propelled or electric motors), boat ramp and dock, and a 2.8 mile National Recreation Trail that circumnavigates the lake.

Oregon 142

MINAM
Minam State Recreation Area

Location: Northeast corner of Oregon north of La Grande.

Access: From Oregon State Highway 82 at milepost 33 +.6 (0.1 mile west of the hamlet of Minam, 14 miles northeast of Elgin, 34 miles north of La Grande), turn north at the west end of the Wallowa River bridge; follow a narrow gravel road which parallels the river for 1.6 miles to the campground.

Facilities: 12 campsites; sites are small to medium-sized, level, with minimal separation; parking pads are gravel, mostly short to medium-length straight-ins; very good tent-pitching possibilities; fireplaces; firewood is available for gathering in the area; water at a faucet; vault facilities; paved loop driveway; camper supplies in Minam; adequate+ supplies and services are available in La Grande.

Activities & Attractions: Plenty of river access points between the highway and the campground and beyond; many deep pools in the river, which reportedly provide good fishing.

Natural Features: Located on a small, grassy flat in a narrow canyon on the Wallowa River, (downstream of the confluence of the Wallowa and Minam Rivers at Minam); some shelter/shade is provided by tall conifers around the perimeter of the camp area; bordered by grassy, tree-dotted hills; elevation 2500'.

Season, Fees & Phone: April to October; please see Appendix for standard Oregon state park fees; 10 day limit; phone c/o Wallowa Lake State Park (503) 432-8855 or (503) 432-4185.

Camp Notes: This is a nice little campground which is surprisingly quite popular. It's a good sportsman's access, and is one of the few public camping areas in these parts.

Oregon 143

WALLOWA LAKE
Wallowa Lake State Park

Location: Northeast corner of Oregon south of Enterprise.

Access: From midtown Enterprise, travel south on Oregon State Highway 82, through the small community of Joseph, then along the east shore of Wallowa Lake to the park (a total of 12 miles from Enterprise); turn west (right) into campground.

Facilities: 210 campsites, including 120 with full hookups, in 5 loops; sites are small+ to medium-sized, most are level, with minimal to fair separation; parking pads are paved, mostly short to medium-length straight-ins, plus about 3 dozen long pull-throughs; excellent spots for tents; fireplaces; firewood is usually for sale, or b-y-o; water at faucets throughout; restrooms with showers; holding tank disposal station; paved driveways; gas and groceries in Joseph; adequate supplies and services are available in Enterprise.

Activities & Attractions: Boating; boat launch; marina; fishing; swimming area; nature trail; hiking trails, including trails into the 200,000-acre Eagle Cap Wilderness; amphitheater for scheduled programs in summer; playground; 2 day use areas.

Natural Features: Located at the south end of 283-foot-deep Wallowa Lake along the Wallowa River in the Wallowa Mountains; campground vegetation consists of light to medium-dense, tall conifers, some bushes and other low-level plants, and large grassy areas; glacial moraines tower 1200 feet above the lake surface; elevation 4600'.

Season, Fees & Phone: April to October; please see Appendix for standard Oregon state park fees; 10 day limit; campsite reservations suggested for summer weekends and holidays, please see Appendix; park office (503) 432-8855 or (503) 432-4185.

Camp Notes: Although it is in a relatively isolated region, Wallowa Lake is *very* popular. Certainly the area offers scenic pleasures of the first order. (Local promoters compare the Wallowa Mountain region to the Alps as "The Switzerland of America". Other regions in the West are labeled "The American Alps", "The Western Alps", and "Little Switzerland". Does anyone believe that our Western mountains can stand tall on their own merits, and that just maybe it is the supercilious *Swiss* who should be comparing *their* fine scenery to *our* outstanding geography? Ed.)

Oregon 144

CATHERINE CREEK
Catherine Creek State Park

Location: Northeast Oregon southeast of La Grande.

Access: From Oregon State Highway 203 at milepost 8 +.1 (8.1 miles southeast of Union, 29.5 miles northeast of Interstate 84 Exit 298), turn west into the campground.

Facilities: Approximately 15 campsites; sites are small+, level, with nominal separation; parking surfaces are grass, with ample space for medium to long vehicle combinations; large tent areas; fire rings; firewood is usually for sale, and some firewood may be available for gathering in the vicinity; water at several faucets; restrooms; gravel driveway; limited supplies and services are available in Union.

Activities & Attractions: Fishing; day use area.

Natural Features: Located in a canyon on a large, grassy flat along the east bank of Catherine Creek; campsites are streamside or nearly so, and receive light to medium shade/shelter from very tall conifers and hardwoods; bordered by forested hills; elevation 3100'.

Season, Fees & Phone: Open all year, with limited services October to April; please see Appendix for standard Oregon state park fees; 10 day limit; park office (503) 963-0430.

Camp Notes: Catherine Creek is the kind of place that, once you've camped here, you'll not tell anyone else about it. The pleasant simplicity of this little park is what "makes" it. The classic, arched wooden footbridge across the wide, clear, swift stream adds a certain country "charm" (if that's the proper phrase). And it's far enough from civilization that it should only be populated on summer weekends. (So please, don't spread the word around.)

FAREWELL BEND
Farewell Bend State Park

Location: Eastern Oregon northwest of Ontario.

Access: From Interstate 84 Exit 353 (22 miles northwest of Ontario, 50 miles southeast of Baker), drive north on Huntington Road, parallel to I-84, for 1.0 mile; turn east (right) into the park entrance, then swing left into the primitive campground, just beyond the entrance; or continue northeast and east for another 0.2 mile to the hookup camp loop.

Facilities: 96 campsites, including 53 with partial hookups; (2 small group camping areas are also available); sites are small to small+, level, with minimal to fair separation; parking pads are short to medium-length straight-ins; pads are paved in the hookup loop, gravel in the primitive zone; adequate space for large tents in most sites; fireplaces or fire rings; firewood is usually for sale, or b-y-o; water at faucets throughout; restrooms with showers; holding tank disposal station; paved driveways in the hookup loop, gravel driveways in the primitive loop; gas and groceries near the freeway; complete supplies and services are available in Ontario.

Activities & Attractions: Boating; excellent, large, boat launch and docks; fishing (said to be very good for bass and catfish); swimming beach; Oregon Trail interpretive exhibits; large day use areas.

Natural Features: Located on a bluff at a wide, sweeping bend on the Snake River; the primitive camp loop receives light to medium shade/shelter from large hardwoods; the hookup camp loop is shaded/sheltered by large hardwoods and shrubs; the desert plains are crowned by virtually treeless hills and high mountains which border the river; typically breezy; elevation 2100'.

Season, Fees & Phone: Open all year, with limited services October to April; please see Appendix for standard Oregon state park fees; 10 day limit; park office (503) 869-2365.

Camp Notes: Oregon Trail pioneers bound for the promised land of cool, green Western Oregon bid farewell to the Snake River and its stern surroundings here and headed cross-country toward the Columbia River and thence to the Willamette Valley. Below this point, the Snake would be nothing but trouble anyway as it carved its way through Hells Canyon. Farewell Bend is now the greenest campground along Interstate 84 between Oregon's Blue Mountains and a state park down in Utah. (The campground in Three Island SP in Idaho, several miles off I-84, might be worth considering, depending upon current local conditions. See info for same.)

Oregon
Southeast
Please refer to the Oregon map in the Appendix

GOOSE LAKE
Goose Lake State Park

Location: South-central Oregon on the Oregon-California border.

Access: From U.S. Highway 395 in the hamlet of New Pine Creek (15 miles south of Lakeview, 43 miles north of Alturas, California), turn west onto State Line Road; proceed 1.2 miles, then turn north (right) into the campground.

Facilities: 48 campsites with partial hookups; sites are narrow and long, level, with minimal to nominal separation; parking pads are paved, medium-length straight-ins; excellent, large, grassy tent spots; fireplaces; firewood is usually for sale, or b-y-o; water at sites; restrooms with showers; paved driveway; gas and groceries in New Pine Creek; adequate supplies and services are available in Lakeview and Alturas.

Activities & Attractions: Fishing for warm-water species (bullhead, perch, etc.); boating; small, simple, boat launch area; also good to excellent fishing in the local mountains.

Natural Features: Located on the northeast shore of Goose Lake; picnic sites are on a grassy flat along the lake shore and are lightly shaded by large hardwoods; campground vegetation consists of watered and mown grass and hardwoods which provide limited to light shade for most campsites; the lake is in a large, high desert valley surrounded by low, rounded, mountains covered by grass, sage, and some trees; elevation 4700'.

Season, Fees & Phone: April to October; please see Appendix for standard Oregon state park fees; 10 day limit; park office (503) 947-3111.

Camp Notes: This is a nice campground that's near a primary highway, and yet in many respects it's really somewhat off the beaten path, too. Goose Lake could be described as an enormous, blue puddle that straddles the Oregon-California border. Although it has been sounded to 24 feet, it's average depth is only 8 feet. Advice from the locals: If you plan to fish, bring a boat.

CHERRY CREEK
Lake Owyhee State Park

Location: Eastern Oregon southwest of Ontario.

Access: From Oregon State Highway 201 at milepost 10 +20 yards (2 miles south of the hamlet of Owyhee, 1.8 miles north of Adrian), turn west onto Overstreet Road and proceed 5.3 miles; (the first 3 miles are straight west, then the road curves south and goes down a hill, then west again); at a "T" intersection, turn south (left) onto Owyhee Dam Road and travel 7.4 miles to the dam; continue past the dam for another 3.3 miles to the campground, on the northwest (right) side of the road. (Note: From the tiny burg of Owyhee, you can also head west on Owyhee Avenue, which becomes Owyhee Dam Road, but the primary access given above is a bit quicker; both roads from Highway 201 are depicted on the Oregon highway map.)

Facilities: 40 campsites, including 10 with electrical hookups; sites are small, with nil to nominal separation; parking pads are paved, short to medium-length straight-ins; a little additional leveling probably will be needed in some sites; medium to large areas for tents; barbecue grills; b-y-o firewood; water at several faucets; restrooms with showers; holding tank disposal station; paved driveways; gas and camper supplies at a nearby resort; gas and groceries in Owyhee; limited supplies and services are available in Adrian.

Activities & Attractions: Boating; boat launches; good fishing for bass, crappie, cats, and trout.

Natural Features: Located above the east shore of Lake Owyhee, a 53-mile-long reservoir on the Owyhee River; campsites are on a small point and receive very light to medium shade from hardwoods; (the tent sites at the bottom of the slope near the tip of the point have the best grass and shade); bordered by the lofty, rugged, rocky Owyhee Mountains; near-arid climate; elevation 2800'.

Season, Fees & Phone: Open all year; please see Appendix for standard Oregon state park fees; phone c/o Farewell Bend State Park (503) 869-2365.

Camp Notes: Allow a couple of hours driving time to the lake (including some scenic stops) from the Interstate. Even though all roads are paved, your speedo will be reading only in the 30's and 40's during much of the drive. Indeed, half the fun of a trip to Lake Owyhee is the scenic drive along the road that follows the Owyhee River. When you finally reach the lake, you'll wonder how *all* that liquid has been stored from so small of a stream. Soon you realize that you're seeing only a fraction of the total square mileage of this immense body of water. This region resembles the Desert Southwest much more than it the does the cool, evergreen Pacific Northwest.

If Lake Owyhee *still* isn't far enough from home and you *still* can hear the drone of freeway traffic between your sun-reddened ears.....there's *still* one more campground in Oregon you can try. It's in Succor Creek State Recreation Area. To get there, first find your way to milepost 19 +.9 on Oregon State Highway 201 (8 miles south of Adrian, 7 miles west of Homedale, ID). Head south on Succor Creek Road (gravel) for 15 miles. Succor Creek has about 20 primitive campsites, drinking water and vaults, in a colorful, rocky, narrow, deep, desert canyon.

169

One final item: *Owyhee* is said to be the original, Old American name for *Hawaii*. We'll leave that one to your imagination, at least for now .....

Idaho

Public Campgrounds

The Idaho map is located in the Appendix.

Idaho 1

INDIAN CREEK
Priest Lake State Park

Location: Idaho Panhandle north of Priest River.

Access: From the junction of U.S. Highway 2 and Idaho State Highway 57 in the city of Priest River, drive north on Highway 57 for 22 miles to the Coolin Fork (Dickensheet Junction); turn east (right) at the fork and proceed 6.1 miles to Coolin; travel north on East Shore Road (paved) for 4 miles to Cavanaugh Bay (road turns to good gravel here); continue for another 7 miles; turn west (left) into the park and the campground.

Facilities: 92 campsites; sites are small to small+, level, with minimal to nominal separation; parking pads are gravel, short to medium-length straight-ins; some excellent tent-pitching areas; fireplaces; b-y-o firewood is recommended; water at several faucets; restrooms with showers; holding tank disposal station; gravel driveways; camper supplies at a store at the park entrance; limited to adequate supplies and services are available in Priest River.

Activities & Attractions: Boating; boat launch and docks; fishing; swimming; large, sandy beach; cross-country skiing and snowmobiling on literally hundreds of miles of marked and groomed trails in the region; large day use area.

Natural Features: Located on a large, moderately forested flat along Indian Creek Bay on the middle-east shore of Priest Lake; vegetation in the campground consists of sparse grass and assorted tall conifers and hardwoods; the lake stretches 19 miles north to south between densely forested mountains; elevation 2400'.

Season, Fees & Phone: Open all year, with limited services in winter; please see Appendix for standard Idaho state park fees and campsite reservation information; park office (208) 443-2200.

Camp Notes: Indian Creek is the largest and most popular of the park's trio of campgrounds. Two smaller units, Dickensheet and Lionhead, might also be of interest to you. You'll pass the Dickensheet camp on the way into Coolin. The area has primitive camping facilities, no drinking water, vaults, plus a launch zone for canoers and rafters planning to float the Priest River downstream of the lake. Lionhead is a dozen gravel miles north of Indian Creek at the north tip of Priest Lake. In addition to primitive campsites, it has drinking water, vaults, a nice sandy beach and a boat launch.

Idaho 2

LUBY BAY
Idaho Panhandle National Forests

Location: Idaho Panhandle north of Priest River.

Access: From the junction of U.S. Highway 2 & Idaho State Highway 57 in the city of Priest River, travel north on Highway 57 for 28 miles to a junction in Van's Corner (at "Frizzy O'Leary's"); (about 5 miles before arriving at this point, you'll pass Dickensheet Junction mentioned in the access for Indian Creek Campground, above); turn northeast (right) onto a paved local road and proceed 1.4 miles to a "T" intersection; turn north (left) onto a gravel access road for a final 0.5 mile to the campground.

Facilities: 52 campsites, including 24 smaller sites close to the lake in the east (lower) loop, and 28 larger sites on a hillside on the west (upper) side of the access road; parking pads are gravel, mostly straight-ins, and some may require additional leveling; sites in the upper loop may be better for larger rv's; adequate space for medium to large tents, though some tent sites are rather sloped; fire rings; firewood is available for gathering in the area; water at several faucets; restrooms; holding tank disposal station; paved driveways; minimal supplies at a store 2 miles south on Highway 57; adequate supplies and services are available in Priest River.

Activities & Attractions: Boating; boat launch; fishing for trout and kokanee salmon; hiking trails to Upper Priest Lake and Roosevelt Grove of Ancient Cedars; Hanna Flats Nature Trail; nature programs may be scheduled for weekends.

Natural Features: Located in a wide valley between two mountain crests on the west shore of 25,000-acre Priest Lake; campground vegetation consists of tall conifers, limited underbrush and a thick carpet of pine needles; the lake is bordered by densely forested mountains; elevation 2500'.

Season, Fees & Phone: May to mid-September; $8.00 in the upper (west) loop, $7.00 in the lower (east) loop; 10 day limit; Priest Lake Ranger District (208) 443-2512.

Camp Notes: It's worth the long trip off the main highways to see the scenes at Priest Lake. But get here early on midsummer weekends. If you plan to fish, bring a boat, plenty of deep-water trolling gear, and a big ice chest.

Idaho 3

PRIEST RIVER
Pend Oreille River/Corps of Engineers Park

Location: Idaho Panhandle east of Priest River.

Access: From U.S. Highway 2 at milepost 7 +.1 (on the east edge of the city of Priest River, just east of the Priest River Bridge), turn south into the park entrance, then turn right into the campground.

Facilities: 19 campsites; sites are medium to large, basically level, with typically good separation; parking pads are gravel, many are pull-throughs large enough to accommodate good-sized rv's; some good tent-pitching areas; fireplaces; b-y-o firewood; water at several faucets; restrooms with showers; paved driveways; limited to adequate supplies and services are available in Priest River, 1 mile west.

Activities & Attractions: Fishing; boating; adjacent Priest River City Park has extensive day use facilities including lawns, ball diamond, children's play area, sandy beach with floating docks; annual Huckleberry Festival held in Priest River in August; public tours of Albeni Falls Dam, which spans the Pend Oreille River west of town.

Natural Features: Located in a fairly dense stand of timber at the confluence of the Priest River and the Pend Oreille River; sites are well sheltered/shaded by tall conifers and a considerable quantity of underbrush; adjacent to the campground is an expansive recreational park on the grassy northeast bank of the river; the Cabinet Mountains lie to the south and the Selkirks to the north; elevation 2100'.

Season, Fees & Phone: May to September; $8.00; 14 day limit; Corps of Engineers Albeni Falls Dam Project Office, Priest River, (208) 437-3133.

Camp Notes: This very nice campground is just far enough from the highway to be quiet, and close enough to the town of Priest River to be convenient. The setting is beautiful--at the meeting of two rivers, and framed by distant, densely forested mountains. The adjacent city park is a bonus if you have kids or like to lawn-stroll. Another CoE campground in the Priest River area is Albeni Cove, located on the south bank of the Pend Oreille River between the city and Albeni Falls Dam. Take the bridge from near downtown across to the south side of the river, than turn west onto a paved road for 3 miles to the campground. Albeni Cove has 13 campsites, including 3 for tent camping only, drinking water, showerless restrooms, a swim beach and a boat launch. It's just onshore of Strong's Island, which sits prominently in midriver.

Idaho 4

RILEY CREEK
Pend Oreille River/Corps of Engineers Park

Location: Idaho Panhandle southwest of Sandpoint.

Access: From U.S. Highway 2 at milepost 14 +.5 in midtown Laclede, (7 miles east of Priest River, 14 miles southwest of Sandpoint), turn south onto a local access road and proceed south, then west for 1.1 miles to the campground.

Facilities: 68 campsites in 2 loops; sites are average or better in size, level, with fairly good separation; parking pads are gravel, medium to long straight-ins; some very nice tenting opportunities in among the tall cedars; fire rings; b-y-o firewood is recommended; water at faucets throughout; restrooms with showers; holding tank disposal station; paved driveways; gas and groceries in Laclede; limited to adequate supplies and services are available in Priest River.

Activities & Attractions: Boating; boat launch and docks; fishing; hiking (foot trails through the park); 2-mile, packed gravel bicycle trail; large day use area includes extensive lawns, playground, and sandy swimming beach; Albeni Falls Dam, located west of Priest River, is open for tours during the summer.

Natural Features: Located on a forested flat along the north bank of the Pend Oreille River, between Albeni Falls Dam and Lake Pend Oreille; tall cedars and very little underbrush provide separation and shelter in the campground; a large, open, grassy area separates the campground from the river; forested slopes flank the river as it winds its way through the Idaho Panhandle; elevation 2100'.

Season, Fees & Phone: May to September; $9.00; 14 day limit; campsite reservations accepted ($5.00 res. fee), call the park entrance station (208) 263-1502; off-season information phone Corps of Engineers Albeni Falls Dam Project Office, Priest River, (208) 437-3133.

Camp Notes: Though most campsites are a short distance from the river's edge, there are some sites with views through the trees of the river and the forested hills beyond. Some of the sites are quite 'deep'. This is a *very nice* facility that's very well-maintained.

Idaho 5

COPPER CREEK
Idaho Panhandle National Forests

Location: Northern tip of Idaho near the U.S.-Canada border.

Access: From U.S. Highway 95 at a point 1 mile south of Eastport and 27 miles north of Bonners Ferry, turn east onto Forest Road 2517 (gravel); drive easterly for 0.9 mile to the campground.

Facilities: 16 campsites; sites are medium-sized, with fair separation; parking pads are gravel and some are large enough to accommodate larger rv's; some good tent spots in the open forest; fireplaces; firewood is available for gathering; water at several faucets; vault facilities; pack-it-in/pack-it-out trash system; gravel driveway; gas and groceries in Eastport.

Activities & Attractions: Copper Falls is a major attraction; the Falls are accessible by continuing on Forest Road 2517 for 1.5 miles beyond the campground and then taking a 0.3 mile foot trail to the falls; another foot trail leads over Copper Ridge past 6196' Copper Mountain and on up to Copper Lake; fishing on the Moyie River.

Natural Features: Located on a forested flat along the Moyie River; peaks rise to 6000' in the Purcell Mountains just to the southwest; campground elevation 2500'.

Season, Fees & Phone: Mid-May to October; $5.00; 14 day limit; Bonners Ferry Ranger District (208) 267-5561.

Camp Notes: The surrounding lush forest is a pleasant setting for this campground. Many of the sites are right on the riverbank.

Idaho 6

ROBINSON LAKE
Idaho Panhandle National Forests

Location: Northern tip of Idaho near the U.S.-Canada border.

Access: From U.S. Highway 95 at a point 6 miles south-west of Eastport, 22 miles north of Bonners Ferry, turn north onto a gravel access road and drive 0.5 mile on this winding, narrow road to the campground.

Facilities: 10 campsites; sites are small to medium-sized, with fair to good separation; parking pads are gravel, large enough to accommodate small to medium-sized vehicles; a few nice tent spots in among the trees; fire rings; firewood is available for gathering in the vicinity; water at several faucets; vault facilities; pack-it-in/pack-it-out trash system; gravel driveway; gas and groceries in Eastport.

Activities & Attractions: Motorless boating; launch area and dock; fishing; several foot trails in the immediate vicinity, including a level and very easy 1 mile loop trail around the lake.

Natural Features: Located on the densely forested shore of 60-acre Robinson Lake; the Purcell Mountains rise in the south; elevation 2300'.

Season, Fees & Phone: May to October; $5.00; 14 day limit; Bonners Ferry R.D. (208) 267-5561.

Camp Notes: Robinson Lake is a beautiful pond surrounded by a lush green forest. It's a pleasant setting for this campground which is generally quite quiet and peaceful.

Idaho 7

SMITH LAKE
Idaho Panhandle National Forests

Location: Northern tip of Idaho north of Bonners Ferry.

Access: From U.S. Highway 95 at a point 2 miles north of the junction of U.S. Highways 2 & 95, 4 miles north of Bonners Ferry turn east onto Forest Road 1005 (gravel) and proceed east, north and northeast for 2 miles on a narrow, winding road that leads up to the lake and the campground.

Facilities: 7 campsites, plus limited overflow camping; sites are small+, with fair separation; parking pads are gravel, short to medium-length straight-ins, and may require some additional levelling; some nice tent-pitching opportunities; fireplaces; firewood is available for gathering in the vicinity; water at hand pumps; vault facilities; pack-it-in/pack-it-out trash system; gravel driveway; adequate supplies and services are available in Bonners Ferry.

Activities & Attractions: Limited boating; boat launch and dock; trout fishing; several foot trails in the immediate vicinity, including one which leads part way around the lake shore; nearby Dawson Lake, 1 mile east, is accessible by foot trail from here; huckleberry picking is popular in season.

Natural Features: Located on moderately sloping terrain above 40-acre Smith Lake; some sites are in open areas and some are heavily forested; peaks rise to 6000' just to the northeast in the densely forested Purcell Mountains; campground elevation 3000'.

Season, Fees & Phone: Mid-May to October; no fee (contributions welcome); 14 day limit; Bonners Ferry Ranger District (208) 267-5561.

Camp Notes: Smith Lake is a pleasant setting for this campground as well as for a number of summer homes. The lake is stocked with rainbow trout each year.

Idaho 8

SPRINGY POINT
Lake Pend Oreille/Corps of Engineers Park

Location: Idaho Panhandle south of Sandpoint.

Access: From U.S. Highway 95 at milepost 471 +.7 (3 miles south of Sandpoint, 40 miles north of Coeur d' Alene), turn west onto Lake Drive (just south of the bridge over Lake Pend Oreille); proceed 3.1 miles on a narrow, rough and twisty paved road; turn north (right) into the campground.

Facilities: 39 campsites in 2 loops; sites are small to average in size, with nominal to fairly good separation; parking pads are gravel, short to medium-length, straight-ins or pull-throughs; many pads will require some additional leveling; limited tent-pitching possibilities, mostly for smaller tents; assorted fire facilities; b-y-o firewood is recommended; water at several faucets; restrooms with showers; holding tank disposal station; paved or gravel driveways; complete supplies and services are available in Sandpoint.

Activities & Attractions: Boating; paved boat launch and floating dock; fishing; swimming; sandy beach; day use area for picnicking.

Natural Features: Located on a forested slope above the south shore of beautiful Lake Pend Oreille; tall cedars and hardwoods provide shelter, plus an abundance of ferns for ground cover; glimpses of the lake through the trees from some sites; great views, from the lake shore, of tall, timbered mountains across the lake to the north; elevation 2100'.

Season, Fees & Phone: May to October; $9.00; 14 day limit; Corps of Engineers Albeni Falls Dam Project Office, Priest River, (208) 437-3133.

Camp Notes: Sites at Springy Point are rather close together with limited room for maneuvering large vehicles along the narrow driveway. All sites are within a short walk of the lake. It appears to be a very popular campground, perhaps because the city of Sandpoint is so near.

Idaho 9

SAMOWEN
Idaho Panhandle National Forests

Location: Idaho Panhandle east of Sandpoint.

Access: From Idaho State Highway 200 at milepost 48 +.1 (18 miles east of Sandpoint, 7 miles west of Clark Fork), turn south onto Samowen Road; proceed south 0.9 mile, then turn west (right), and continue for 0.1 mile to the campground.

Facilities: 56 campsites in 3 loops; sites are small to average in size, with nominal to fairly good separation; parking pads are gravel, straight-ins or pull-throughs; sites closer to the lake are more level, but are typically smaller; some sites farther from the lake have larger parking pads which may require additional leveling; a few designated tent sites along the lake shore; fireplaces or fire rings; some firewood is available for gathering, b-y-o to be sure; restrooms; freshwater-rinse showers in the bathhouse; holding tank disposal station; paved driveways; minimal supplies in East Hope, 2 miles west; complete supplies and services are available in Sandpoint, 18 miles west.

Activities & Attractions: Fishing; boating; gravel boat ramp; swimming (rocky beach); day use area with picnic shelters and barbecue grills; an historically significant fur trade center, Kullyspell House, is nearby.

Natural Features: Located on the northeast shore of 43-mile-long Lake Pend Oreille; fairly dense campground vegetation consists of tall conifers, a thick forest carpet, but very little underbrush; surrounded by emerald hills and distant mountains; elevation 2100'.

Season, Fees & Phone: May to October; $8.00; 14 day limit; Sandpoint Ranger District (208) 263-5111.

Camp Notes: Samowen Campground is justifiably popular, so arrival should be early on summer weekends. Lake Pend Oreille (Pond-oh-*ray*) holds world records for kamloops trout, dolly varden trout and kokanee salmon. *Pend Oreille* is a French word for "earring". Perhaps the lake does resemble a brilliant sapphire encircled by emeralds. (As seen from the space shuttle. Ed.)

Idaho 10

ROUND LAKE
Round Lake State Park

Location: Idaho Panhandle southwest of Sandpoint.

Access: From U. S. Highway 95 at milepost 465 +.5 (1.5 miles north of Westmond, 9 miles southwest of Sandpoint), turn west onto Dufort Road (paved) and proceed 1.9 miles; turn south into the park and go 0.1 mile to the campground.

Facilities: 53 campsites in 2 loops; sites are small to small+, with nominal to fair separation; parking pads are gravel, short to medium-length straight-ins; about half of the pads will require additional leveling; medium to large tent spots; fireplaces; some firewood is available for gathering in the surrounding area, b-y-o is suggested; water at several faucets; restrooms with showers, plus supplemental vault facilities; holding tank disposal station; paved driveways; gas and groceries+ in Westmond; complete supplies and services are available in Sandpoint.

Activities & Attractions: Swimming beach, flanked by piers; 2-mile hiking trail around the lake; fishing; limited boating (no gas motors); boat launch; small visitor center; amphitheater for summer evening programs; cross-country skiing, ice fishing, ice skating, and other quiet winter sports.

Natural Features: Located around the shore of 58-acre Round Lake; picnic and camp areas are well-shaded by tall conifers and a moderate amount of underbrush; Cocolalla Creek flows into and out of the lake; bordered by heavily timbered hills; elevation 2100'.

Season, Fees & Phone: Open all year, with limited services in winter; please see Appendix for standard Idaho state park fees; 14 day limit; park office (208) 263-3489.

Camp Notes: Maximum depth of the small, glacially formed lake is only 37 feet. In midsummer the shallow water warms to a very tolerable temp, and swimming becomes the number one pastime here. Nice little place.

Idaho 11

GARFIELD BAY
Idaho Panhandle National Forests

Location: Northern Idaho southeast of Sandpoint.

Access: From U.S. Highway 95 at a point 6 miles south of Sandpoint and 38 miles north of Coeur d' Alene, turn east onto Sagle Road; proceed east for 7.5 miles on this paved, but winding, county road to a fork; take the right fork for another 1.5 miles to Garfield Bay; continue for 0.4 mile (beyond the boat ramp and day use area), on a narrow, steep, twisty, paved, access road up to the campground.

Facilities: 27 campsites in 2 loops; sites are medium-sized, with good separation; parking pads are medium-length, some are long enough to accommodate large rv's; some pads may require additional leveling; many sites have very good tent-pitching areas; fireplaces; some firewood is available for gathering in the area; water at several faucets; vault facilities (restrooms in the nearby day use area); paved driveways; camper supplies at a marina; adequate to complete supplies and services are available in Sandpoint.

Activities & Attractions: Boating; sailing; windsurfing; boat launch; fishing; day use area below the campground has picnicking facilities; a number of small lakes in the area are accessible by county roads.

Natural Features: Located on a hill 200 feet above Garfield Bay on Lake Pend Oreille, the largest lake in Idaho; campground vegetation consists of lush ferns, underbrush and tall timber; the lake is surrounded by densely forested mountains; elevation 2300'.

Season, Fees & Phone: May to September; $6.00; 14 day limit; Sandpoint Ranger District (208) 263-5111.

Camp Notes: Since the campground is slightly removed from Garfield Bay's center of activity, it usually maintains a quiet atmosphere. Access to very beautiful Lake Pend Oreille is only a short walk or drive from the campsites.

Idaho 12

WHITETAIL
Farragut State Park

Location: Idaho Panhandle north of Coeur d'Alene.

Access: From the junction of U.S. Highway 95 & Idaho State Highway 54 in the small community of Athol (19 miles north of Coeur d'Alene, 25 miles south of Sandpoint), travel east on Highway 54 for 4.3 miles; as the highway curves northeasterly, bear east (right) off the highway to the park entrance station/visitor center; just beyond the entrance station, swing right onto South Road, and travel northeasterly (parallel to the main highway) for 2.4 miles; turn south (right) to Whitetail Campground.

Facilities: 97 campsites; (several nearby group camps are also available, by reservation); sites are small to medium-sized, with nominal to fairly good separation; parking pads are gravel/earth, short to medium-length straight-ins; most pads will require additional leveling; medium to large tent areas; fireplaces; b-y-o firewood; water at central faucets; restrooms with showers; holding tank disposal station; paved driveways; gas and groceries+ in Athol.

Activities & Attractions: Large day use area with sports courts nearby; swimming beach; boating; boat launch and docks; fishing; visitor center/museum; amphitheater; interpretive programs; nature trail; hiking and equestrian trails; bicycle routes; model airplane flying field; shooting ranges; cross-country skiing; snowmobiling.

Natural Features: Located above the southwest shore of Lake Pend Oreille; the campground is situated on moderately sloping terrain some distance above the lake shore; campsites receive light to medium shade/shelter from tall conifers and moderate underbrush; the forested Coeur d'Alene Mountains are visible to the east across the lake; elevation 2500'.

Season, Fees & Phone: Open all year, with limited services in winter; please see Appendix for standard Idaho state park fees and campsite reservation information; 10 day limit; park office (208) 683-2425.

Camp Notes: Early in World War II, this property was chosen as the site for the new Farragut Naval Training Station. In only 15 months, Farragut graduated 293,000 sailors. In its time, the facility was the second-largest naval training center in the world. After the war, the base was mothballed and eventually became today's 4700-acre state park.

Idaho 13

SNOWBERRY
Farragut State Park

Location: Idaho Panhandle north of Coeur d'Alene.

Access: From the junction of U.S. Highway 95 & Idaho State Highway 54 in the small community of Athol (19 miles north of Coeur d'Alene, 25 miles south of Sandpoint), travel east on Highway 54 for 4.3 miles; as the highway curves northeasterly, bear east (right) off the highway to the park entrance station/visitor center; just beyond the entrance station, swing right onto South Road, and travel northeasterly (parallel to the main highway) for 2.4 miles; turn northwest (left) into Snowberry Campground.

Facilities: 45 campsites with partial hookups; sites are medium-sized, with fair to fairly good separation; parking pads are paved/gravel, medium-length straight-ins or long pull-throughs; many pads will require a little additional leveling; medium to large tent areas; fireplaces; b-y-o firewood; water at central faucets; restrooms with showers; holding tank disposal station; paved driveways; (several reservable group camps are also available); gas and groceries+ in Athol.

Activities & Attractions: Large play areas nearby; swimming beach; boating; boat launch and docks; fishing; visitor center/museum; amphitheater; interpretive programs; nature, hiking and equestrian trails; bicycle routes; model airplane flying field; shooting ranges; cross-country skiing; snowmobiling.

Natural Features: Located on a gentle, forested slope above Idlewild Bay and the southwest shore of Lake Pend Oreille; campsites receive light to medium shade/shelter from tall conifers and some undercover; the Coeur d'Alene Mountains rise sharply from the east shore of the lake across from the campground; elevation 2500'.

Season, Fees & Phone: Open all year, with limited services in winter; please see Appendix for standard Idaho state park fees and campsite reservation information; 10 day limit; park office (208) 683-2425.

Camp Notes: Lake Pend Oreille is one of the most beautiful of the larger lakes in the Northern Rockies. It is the largest lake in Idaho and has 100 miles of shoreline and a maximum depth of 1150 feet. That's one heckuva puddle.

Idaho 14

BUMBLEBEE
Idaho Panhandle National Forests

Location: Northern Idaho east of Coeur d'Alene.

Access: From Interstate 90 Exit 43 at Kingston (30 miles east of Coeur d' Alene, 8 miles west of Kellogg), proceed through Kingston east/north on the Coeur d'Alene River-Prichard Road for 4.7 miles; turn northwest (left) onto Forest Road 209 (paved); drive 3 miles and turn east (right) onto Forest Road 796 (paved) for 0.2 mile to the campground.

Facilities: 25 campsites in 2 loops; sites are medium to large, level, with fair to very good separation; parking pads are gravel, and some are pull-throughs spacious enough to accommodate very large rv's; good tent-pitching opportunities beneath tall conifers; fire rings; firewood is available for gathering; water at hand pumps; vault facilities; gravel driveways; gas and groceries in Kingston; complete supplies and services are available in Coeur d'Alene.

Activities & Attractions: Fishing; hiking.

Natural Features: Located in a fairly open forest surrounded by large, grassy Bumblebee Meadow near the confluence of Bumblebee Creek and the North Fork of the Coeur d'Alene River; campground vegetation consists of tall conifers and light underbrush; Bumblebee Peak rises to 4746' just a few miles to the north; elevation 2200'.

Season, Fees & Phone: May to mid-September; $7.00; 14 day limit; Fernan Ranger District, Coeur d' Alene, (208) 765-7381.

Camp Notes: This quiet, secluded spot is reached by driving along the gently curving Coeur d'Alene River Road that passes through a very pleasant pastoral landscape. The drive itself is worth the trip, but, in addition, Bumblebee Campground offers relatively spacious sites in a peaceful setting.

Idaho 15

KIT PRICE
Idaho Panhandle National Forests

Location: Northern Idaho east of Coeur d'Alene.

Access: From Interstate 90 Exit 43 at Kingston (30 miles east of Coeur d' Alene, 8 miles west of Kellogg), travel through Kingston east/north on the Coeur d'Alene River-Prichard Road for 21 miles to the Prichard Fork; take the left fork onto Forest Road 208 (paved); proceed northerly for 10 miles to milepost 10; turn east (right) into the campground. **Alternate Access:** From I-90 at Wallace, access is available over the serpentine Dobson Pass Road to Forest Road 208 near Prichard.

Facilities: 52 campsites in 3 loops; most sites are medium-sized, level and well-spaced; parking pads are paved, many are pull-throughs or double-wide straight-ins spacious enough to accommodate even the largest rv's; most tent spots are large and level; water at faucets throughout; vault facilities; holding tank disposal station at the Shoshone Work Center near milepost 6; fire rings and/or barbecue grills at each site; firewood is available for gathering in the area; paved driveways; camper supplies in Prichard; complete supplies and services are available in Coeur d'Alene.

Activities & Attractions: Fishing; river floating.

Natural Features: Located along the bank of the Coeur d'Alene River, which meanders through a narrow, forested valley in this area; most campsites are surrounded by tall timber and moderate underbrush; some sites are right along the river's edge; peaks of the Shoshone Range rise to over 6000' to the east; campground elevation 2600'.

Season, Fees & Phone: May to September; $7.00; 14 day limit; Wallace Ranger District (208) 752-1221.

Camp Notes: Kit Price is typically inhabited by fishermen who stay a few days or more. The drive along the Coeur d'Alene River is eminently pleasant; the drive through Dobson Pass to or from Wallace is an adventure!

Idaho 16

DEVIL'S ELBOW
Idaho Panhandle National Forests

Location: Northern Idaho east of Coeur d'Alene.

Access: From Interstate 90 Exit 43 at Kingston (30 miles east of Coeur d' Alene, 8 miles west of Kellogg), proceed through Kingston east/north on the Coeur d'Alene River-Prichard Road for 21 miles to the Prichard Fork; take the left fork onto Forest Road 208 (paved); travel northerly for 13 miles to milepost 13; turn east (right) into the campground. **Alternate Access:** From I-90 at Wallace, access is available over the snakey, steep, sometimes narrow, Dobson Pass Road to Forest Road 208 near Prichard.

Facilities: 19 campsites; sites are medium-sized, generally level and well spaced, with average or better visual separation; most parking pads are paved, and some are pull-throughs or double-wide straight-ins spacious enough for very large rv's; large, level tent spaces; fire rings; firewood is available for gathering in the area; water at a hand pump; vault facilities; holding tank disposal station at the Shoshone Work Center near milepost 6; paved driveways; camper supplies in Prichard; complete supplies and services are available in Coeur d'Alene.

Activities & Attractions: Fishing; limited river floating; hiking trails.

Natural Features: Located in an open forest on the west bank of the Coeur d'Alene River; most sites are situated around a small grassy meadow; tall conifers, moderate underbrush and flowering beargrass provide shelter and privacy for most sites; some units have views of the river, which flows by within a few yards of some of the sites; peaks of the Shoshone Range rise to over 6000' just to the east; campground elevation 2700'.

Season, Fees & Phone: June to September; $7.00; 14 day limit; Wallace Ranger District (208) 752-1221.

Camp Notes: This typically quiet, somewhat secluded spot has some very sheltered sites and some open ones. This entire stretch along the Coeur d'Alene River almost seems like part of a different world. Rafting and canoeing have become favorite river sports. In a typical year, it's possible to float the upper Coeur d'Alene from late spring to early July. The segment below Kit Price Campground can be floated for a couple of weeks beyond that mark, although some low-water spots may be encountered.

Idaho 17

BIG HANK
Idaho Panhandle National Forests

Location: Northern Idaho east of Coeur d'Alene.

Access: From Interstate 90 Exit 43 at Kingston (30 miles east of Coeur d' Alene, 8 miles west of Kellogg), go through Kingston and head east/north on the Coeur d'Alene River-Prichard Road for 21 miles to the Prichard Fork; take the left fork onto Forest Road 208 (paved); proceed northerly for 18.8 miles to milepost 18 +.8; turn west (left) into the campground. **Alternate Access:** From I-90 at Wallace, access is available over the snakey, steep (but paved) Dobson Pass Road to Forest Road 208 at Prichard.

Facilities: 30 campsites; sites are medium-sized, level, nicely spaced, with considerable privacy; parking pads are paved, level, and large enough, double-wide in some sites, to accommodate large rv's; some very roomy tent spaces are located in grassy areas beneath tall trees; fire rings and barbecue grills; firewood is available for gathering in the area; water at hand pumps; vault facilities; holding tank disposal station at the Shoshone Work Center near milepost 6; paved driveways; camper supplies in Prichard; complete supplies and services are available in Coeur d'Alene.

Activities & Attractions: Fishing; river floating (early in the season); hiking trails in the campground area.

Natural Features: Located on the bank of the typically crystal clear Coeur d'Alene River in a fairly dense forest setting; campground vegetation consists of tall conifers and considerable underbrush; though the river flows within a few yards of many sites, there are no real riverside sites with open river views; often showery in summer; elevation 2900'.

Season, Fees & Phone: May to September; $7.00; 14 day limit; Wallace Ranger District (208) 752-1221.

Camp Notes: Though Big Hank Campground is located quite a distance from the main highway (I-90), it's worth the trip. How many campgrounds in regions as nice as this are 40 miles from the nearest numbered highway, yet are reachable via a paved route all the way to the parking pad?

Idaho 18

BEAUTY CREEK
Idaho Panhandle National Forests

Location: Northern Idaho east of Coeur d'Alene.

Access: From Interstate 90 Exit 22 (9 miles east of Coeur d'Alene, 29 miles west of Kellogg), proceed south on Idaho State Highway 97 for 2.3 miles; turn east (left) onto a paved access road; continue east for 0.3 mile to the campground.

Facilities: 12 campsites; most sites are small to medium in size, level with minimal separation; parking pads are paved, fairly level, short to medium in length; level, grassy tent spots; fireplaces; b-y-o firewood is recommended; water at a hand pump; vault facilities; narrow driveway; complete supplies and services are available in Coeur d'Alene.

Activities & Attractions: Boating; boat launch and dock at Mineral Ridge on the shore of Lake Coeur d'Alene; fishing; Caribou Ridge interpretive trail; a nearby BLM Mineral Ridge hiking trail leads almost 5 miles up to a Mount Coeur d'Alene viewpoint.

Natural Features: Located in a long, narrow canyon at the southeast end of Beauty Bay on Lake Coeur d'Alene; sites are stretched out in a grassy meadow along Beauty Creek; peaks of the Coeur d'Alene Mountains rise to over 6000' just to the east; sites are separated mostly by tall grass and some brush; elevation 2200'.

Season, Fees & Phone: May to September; $7.00; 14 day limit; Fernan Ranger District, Coeur d'Alene, (208) 765-7381..

Camp Notes: Beauty Creek Campground is located in a pleasant open canyon very near one of the most beautiful lakes in Idaho. Beauty Creek meanders past the sites on its way to Lake Coeur d'Alene. Beauty Bay is actually just a cove on the south shore of much larger Wolf Lodge Bay, on the main east 'arm' of the lake. A couple of sites are quite a distance to the east past the main camp area--so don't give up looking for them. *Coeur d'Alene* was the name given to the local Indians by French-Canadian trappers and traders. The phrase is freely translated as "heart like a sharp pick". It refers to the Indians' shrewd trading practices.

Idaho 19

HAWLEY'S LANDING
Heyburn State Park

Location: Idaho Panhandle south of Coeur d'Alene.

Access: From Idaho State Highway 5 at milepost 6 +.4 (6 miles east of Plummer, 13 miles west of Saint Maries), turn north onto a paved access road for a few yards, then swing east (right) into the campground.

Facilities: 52 campsites, including 42 with partial hookups, and 5 park n' walk sites, in 2 loops; sites are small+ to medium-sized, with nominal to fair separation; parking pads are gravel, mostly medium-length straight-ins, plus a number of long pull-throughs; many pads will require some additional leveling; enough space for a medium-sized tent on gravel tent pads in hookup sites; large tent spots in the tent loop; fireplaces; b-y-o firewood is suggested; water at hookup sites and at central faucets; restrooms; waste water receptacles; gravel driveways; limited supplies and services are available in Plummer.

Activities & Attractions: Boating; trail to the park's boat dock below the campground; fishing; 5 hiking trails in the vicinity; public boat launch, dock, and swimming beach at the park's nearby Chatcolet area; designated swimming area and sandy beach at the park's Rocky Point area.

Natural Features: Located on a hill/bluff above Chatcolet Lake; campsites are generally well-sheltered/shaded by tall conifers; the St. Joe Mountains rise to above 5000' and are visible across the lake to the east; elevation 2100'.

Season, Fees & Phone: Open all year, with limited services April to October; please see Appendix for standard Idaho state park fees; 14 day limit; park office (208) 686-1308.

Camp Notes: A few of the campground's hookup sites have views of the lake, but the tents-only loop really is better in that respect. They're on a nice-sized flat near the edge of the tree line. Heyburn lays claim to being the first state park in the Pacific Northwest.

Idaho 20

BENEWAH
Heyburn State Park

Location: Idaho Panhandle south of Coeur d'Alene.

Access: From Idaho State Highway 5 at milepost 11 +.7 (at the east end of the Benewah Creek bridge, 12 miles east of Plummer, 7 miles west of Saint Maries), turn north onto a paved access road and proceed 1.3 miles (past the private resort) to the campground.

Facilities: 39 campsites including 15 with full hookups, in 3 loops; sites are very small to small+, with minimal to fairly good separation; parking pads are gravel/earth, short to medium-length straight-ins, plus a few medium-length pull-throughs; a few good tent spots, but most are small to medium-sized; fireplaces; a limited quantity of firewood is available for gathering in the vicinity, b-y-o is suggested; water at hookups and at central faucets; restrooms with showers; camper supplies at the resort store; adequate supplies and services are available in St. Maries.

Activities & Attractions: Boating; boat launch, docks; fishing.

Natural Features: Located on a hill above the east shore of Benewah Lake; most sites are lightly to moderately shaded/sheltered by tall conifers and brush; a few sites have commanding views of Benewah Lake; quantities of wild rice grow nearby in a marsh at the south end of Benewah Lake; the St. Joe Mountains form the eastern backdrop for the lake; elevation 2200'.

Season, Fees & Phone: April to October; please see Appendix for standard Idaho state park fees; 14 day limit; park office (208) 686-1308.

Camp Notes: Don't let the "very small" in the objective description of the campsites turn you off. There are a number of tiny but cozy sites that overlook the lake--but anything larger than a pickup or a van need not apply for admission to those spots. The many miles of navigable waterways in this region are all part of what could be called the "Greater Coeur d'Alene Lake System", since they share common waters with giant Coeur d'Alene Lake north of here.

Idaho 21

EMERALD CREEK
Idaho Panhandle National Forests

Location: Northern Idaho south of Coeur d'Alene.

Access: From Idaho State Highway 3 at a point 4 miles south of Fernwood, 31 miles south of St. Maries and 6 miles north of Clarkia (just south of the Benewah/Shoshone County Line) turn southwest at the "Emerald Creek Recreation Area" sign onto Forest Road 447 (gravel); proceed southwest for 3.3 miles; at the fork in the road, take the left fork and continue for 1.4 miles farther on a narrow dirt road to the campground.

Facilities: 18 campsites; sites are reasonably roomy, with good separation; parking pads are gravel, level, medium to long straight-ins; medium to large areas for tents; barbecue grills; firewood is available for gathering in the area; water at hand pumps; vault facilities; gravel driveways; gas and groceries in Clarkia; adequate supplies and services are available in St. Maries.

Activities & Attractions: Garnet digging is the primary activity in the area; (an administration building is located at the "dig" to provided information to diggers and visitors); fee for using the 'dig'; (days and hours vary, additional info is available from the ranger station in Clarkia; fishing.

Natural Features: Located in a grove of trees surrounded by a grassy meadow; Emerald Creek flows past the campground and into the St. Maries River to the east; the campground is within 3 miles of the Emerald Creek Garnet Area; elevation 2900'.

Season, Fees & Phone: May to October; $6.00; 14 day limit; St. Maries Ranger District (208) 245-2531.

Camp Notes: This secluded campground offers an inviting place to enjoy nature, whether or not you include a side trip to one of the two places in the world where star garnets can be found. On a side road east of the city of St. Maries are several other national forests campgrounds which you might consider if you have the time to do some local exploring. All of them are streamside camps located along the St. Joe River Road. Water and vaults are provided at most of the campgrounds. The St. Joe River Road is paved for half of its 120-mile course between St. Maries and Interstate 90 near St. Regis, Montana. The unpaved sections are usually well-maintained during midsummer, but check about road conditions and log truck traffic with a knowledgeable source before heading out. It's an adventure through beautifully wild country.

Idaho 22

HELLS GATE
Hells Gate State Park

Location: Western Idaho on the south edge of Lewiston.

Access: From U.S. Highway 12 at the west edge of Lewiston (just east of the Snake River Bridge), proceed south on Snake Avenue for 3.5 miles (along the east bank of the Snake River); turn west (right) into the park, then swing south and go 1.2 miles (past the day use areas) to the campground.

Facilities: 93 campsites, including 64 with partial hookups; sites are small+ to medium-sized, with nominal to fair separation; parking pads are paved, medium to long straight-ins or pull-throughs; many pads will require a bit of additional leveling; very good to excellent tent-pitching possibilities; barbecue grills; b-y-o firewood; water at faucets throughout; restrooms with showers; disposal station; paved driveways; complete supplies and services are available in Lewiston.

Activities & Attractions: Boating; boat launch; fishing; swimming beach; playground; sports field; volleyball court; several miles of hiking, jogging and biking trails; evening campfire programs in summer; visitor center; day use area with shelters.

Natural Features: Located on the east bank of the Snake River; campsites are lightly to moderately shaded/sheltered by large hardwoods and a few conifers on a surface of watered and mown grass; high, dry, grassy, nearly treeless bluffs border the river; typically breezy; elevation 700'.

Season, Fees & Phone: March to November; please see Appendix for standard Idaho state park fees and campsite reservation information; 14 day limit; park office (208) 743-2363.

Camp Notes: As the name implies, this is the gateway to North America's deepest canyon--5500' deep Hells Canyon--and Hells Canyon National Recreation Area. Mostly because this riverside strip (about a mile-and-a-quarter long and 300 yards wide) is at one of the lowest elevations in the state, the early spring/late fall weather is milder here than in most other campgrounds in Idaho. The groomed lawns and mild climate make this a good, three-season camp.

Idaho 23

LAPWAII & NEZ PERCE
Winchester Lake State Park

Location: Western Idaho south of Lewiston.

Access: From U.S. Highway 95 at a point 40 miles south of Lewiston and 33 miles north of Grangeville, travel west/north on Business Route 95A into Winchester; turn west onto Joseph Avenue; proceed southwest for 0.3 mile, then turn southeast (left) to the park entrance station, then proceed another 0.2 mile to the campgrounds.

Facilities: 60 campsites, including 28 sites in the Lapwaii Camp and 32 sites in the Nez Perce Camp; parking pads are gravel, short to medium-length, mostly straight-ins; additional leveling may be required in many sites; some good areas for tent-pitching; fireplaces; b-y-o firewood is recommended; water at several faucets; vault facilities; holding tank disposal station; paved driveways; gas and groceries in Winchester.

Activities & Attractions: Fishing (including ice fishing) for stocked rainbow trout; motorless boating; boat launch; nature trails; evening campfire programs in summer; ice skating, sledding and cross-country skiing; day use areas.

Natural Features: Located on the west shore of 103-acre Winchester Lake, on a forested high plateau at the foot of the Craig Mountains; campground vegetation consists of medium-dense, tall conifers and some underbrush, bordered by some open grassy sections along the lake shore; some sites in the Nez Perce camp unit have lake views; elevation 3900'.

Season, Fees & Phone: Open all year, with limited services in winter; please see Appendix for standard Idaho state park fees; 14 day limit; park office (208) 924-7563.

Camp Notes: Winchester Lake lies in one of the country's more intense climatic zones. Summers are usually short, with very warm days and cool nights. Winters tend to be long, cold and snowy.

Idaho 24

FREEMAN CREEK
Dworshak State Park

Location: Western Idaho northeast of Lewiston.

Access: From U.S. Highway 12 on the south edge of Orofino (39 miles east of Lewiston), drive north through midtown Orofino and follow a well-signed route for 24 miles (paved, then gravel then a final 2 miles of curvy, steep downgrade) to the campground.

Facilities: 102 campsites, including 46 with partial hookups, in 3 loops and a separate tent camping area; (3 small group camps are also available, reservations accepted); sites are small+, with nominal to fairly good separation; parking pads are gravel, mostly short to medium-length straight-ins; medium to large areas for tents; fireplaces; firewood is available for gathering in the surrounding area; water at hookups and at several faucets; restrooms with showers, plus supplementary vault facilities; holding tank disposal station; adequate supplies and services are available in Orofino.

Activities & Attractions: Boating; boat launch; fishing for rainbows and kokanee; swimming beach; playground; day use area.

Natural Features: Located on hilly terrain on the southwest shore of 54-mile long Dworshak Reservoir, an impoundment on the North Fork of the Clearwater River; vegetation consists of stands of tall conifers and large, grassy areas; bordered by forested mountains; elevation 1500'.

Season, Fees & Phone: April to October; please see Appendix for standard Idaho state park fees; 14 day limit; park office (208) 476-5994.

Camp Notes: Just about anywhere you go in Idaho you're "getting away from it all", but this place is *really* out in the woods. Campsites are located in four areas (including a nice, lakeside, tent-camping section) so the number of close neighbors you'll have is relatively small.

Idaho 25

WILD GOOSE
Clearwater National Forest

Location: Northern Idaho east of Lewiston.

Access: From U.S Highway 12 at milepost 95 +.2 (21 miles northeast of Kooskia, 79 miles southwest of Lolo Pass), turn south into the campground.

Facilities: 6 campsites; sites are medium-sized, reasonably level, with fair separation; parking pads are gravel, short to medium-length straight-ins; adequate space for tents; fire rings; some firewood is available for gathering in the area; water at central faucets; vault facilities; gravel driveway; limited to adequate supplies and services are available in Kooskia.

Activities & Attractions: Rafting, floating; fishing.

Natural Features: Located on a flat in a canyon along the north bank of the Clearwater River; the Lochsa and Selway Rivers join 2 miles east of the campground to form the Middle Fork of the Clearwater River; sites receive medium shade/shelter from conifers and hardwoods; a few sites are riverside; flanked by densely forested slopes; elevation 1500'.

Season, Fees & Phone: April to November; $6.00; (no fee if drinking water is not available); 14 day limit; Lochsa Ranger District (208) 926-4275.

Camp Notes: Wild Goose is the westernmost campground along this highway, and it is the only campground along the Clearwater River. Also, it is usually one of the first camps (along with Wilderness Gateway) to be available in spring and the last to close in fall. (Because of the definite possibility of freezing temps in early spring and late summer, the drinking water system is turned on only from about Memorial Day to Labor Day.) Please note that supplies and services on this section of U.S. 12 are quite scarce. It might be a good idea to fill up with gas and groceries in Lewiston, Idaho, or Missoula, Montana prior to venturing out onto what is one of the most wildly beautiful passages in this region.

Idaho 26

APGAR
Clearwater National Forest

Location: Northern Idaho east of Lewiston.

Access: From U.S Highway 12 at milepost 104 +.4 (30 miles northeast of Kooskia, 70 miles southwest of Lolo Pass), turn south into the campground.

Facilities: 7 campsites; sites are fairly large, level, and well separated; parking pads are gravel, medium-length straight-ins; adequate space for medium to large tents in most sites; fire rings; firewood is available for gathering in the area; water at faucets; vault facilities; gravel driveway; limited to adequate supplies and services are available in Kooskia.

Activities & Attractions: Lochsa Historic Ranger Station and Visitor Center, 17 miles northeast, has displays and self-guided tours; fishing and rafting on several rivers in the area; mini-amphitheater (a large fire ring encircled by several benches).

Natural Features: Located on a small flat along the north bank of the Lochsa River, a few miles northeast of the Lochsa's confluence with the Selway River; the Middle Fork of the Clearwater River is formed at that merger; sites are moderately sheltered/shaded and have a river view; a few camp spots are streamside; the river flows through a fairly densely forested narrow valley in this section; several small sandy beaches along the river are within a half-dozen miles east and west of here; elevation 1200'.

Season, Fees & Phone: May to October; $6.00; 14 day limit; Lochsa Ranger District (208) 926-4275.

Camp Notes: Even though Apgar (also called Apgar Creek) is somewhat small, it is, nevertheless, one of the nicer campgrounds along this route. There are some really beautiful views of the river from most of the sites. It tends to be a bit less populated than Wild Goose Campground (above). The Lochsa River is part of the Middle Fork Clearwater Wild and Scenic River System, and is one of the premier white-water rafting and kayaking streams in the West. The river is usually floatable from May to August. It has yet to be 'discovered' by the masses.

Idaho 27

WILDERNESS GATEWAY
Clearwater National Forest

Location: Northern Idaho east of Lewiston.

Access: From U.S. Highway 12 at milepost 122 +.8 (48 miles northeast of Kooskia, 52 miles southwest of Lolo Pass), turn south, cross the Lochsa River bridge, and follow a paved access road 0.2 mile to the campground.

Facilities: 89 campsites in 4 loops; sites are generally large and private; parking pads are paved, level, short to medium in length; many pads are double-wide; sites have some possibilities for pitching small to medium-sized tents, but are probably better suited for smaller camping vehicles; several handicapped access units; fire rings; firewood is available for gathering nearby; water at faucets throughout; restrooms, plus auxiliary vault facilities; holding tank disposal station; paved driveways; nearest reliable source of limited to adequate supplies is in Kooskia.

Activities & Attractions: Lochsa Historic Ranger Station, 1 mile west, has displays and self-guided tours; amphitheater and children's play area in the campground; river trail; the campground serves as a major staging area for wilderness trips.

Natural Features: Located on a large flat along the Lochsa River, in a moderately wide spot in a valley bordered by the timbered ridges of the Bitterroot Range; conifers mixed with an abundance of small hardwoods and large ferns shelter the camp area; elevation 2100'.

Season, Fees & Phone: Mid-May to early September, plus pre- and post- season availability with limited services; $6.00; 14 day limit; Lochsa Ranger District (208) 926-4275.

Camp Notes: This is probably one of the best campgrounds on this highway, and yet it is usually not crowded. While camping at Wilderness Gateway, you probably would enjoy spending some time roaming around the Lochsa Historic Ranger Station. The simply furnished log buildings were built around 1930 and housed upwards of 200 national forest workers. Local materials were used throughout the eight-building complex, since any "store-bought" supplies had to be brought in by pack train from Lolo,

Montana. The completion of the highway in 1952 ended an era, but it opened up a myriad of opportunities for recreation and exploration to the rest of us.

Idaho 28

JERRY JOHNSON
Clearwater National Forest

Location: Northern Idaho east of Lewiston near Lolo Pass.

Access: From U.S. Highway 12 at milepost 150 +.3 (24 miles southwest of Lolo Pass, 76 miles northeast of Kooskia), turn north into the campground.

Facilities: 15 campsites; sites are medium to large, with fair separation; parking pads are paved; adequate space for tents in most sites; fireplaces; plenty of firewood is available for gathering; water at hand pumps; vault facilities; paved driveway; nearest reliable source of limited to adequate supplies is in Kooskia, Idaho or Lolo, Montana, 60 miles northeast; nearest sources of complete supplies and services are Lewiston, Idaho, 150 miles west, or Missoula, Montana, 70 miles east.

Activities & Attractions: Fishing (catch and release) on the Lochsa River, (a foot trail leads from the campground across the highway and down a steep bank to the water's edge); 4-wheel-drive trail leads north from the campground into the nearby primitive areas.

Natural Features: Located on a fairly level portion of a hillside above the Lochsa River on the west slope of the Bitterroot Range; campground has moderate forestation without much underbrush; relatively low timbered ridges flank the campground north and south; elevation 3000'.

Season, Fees & Phone: May to mid-September; $6.00; 14 day limit; Powell Ranger District (208) 942-3113.

Camp Notes: This spot is perhaps not as fully equipped as some of the other campgrounds along Highway 12, but it also tends to be less crowded. It may also be slightly more comfortable than some of the other camping areas near here, since it is positioned somewhat above the cold and dampness of the river level.

Idaho 29

WENDOVER
Clearwater National Forest

Location: Northern Idaho east of Lewiston near Lolo Pass.

Access: From U.S. Highway 12 at milepost 158 +.2 (16 miles southwest of Lolo Pass, 84 miles northeast of Kooskia), turn south into the campground.

Facilities: 28 campsites in two loops; sites are medium-sized, level, with fair to fairly good separation; parking pads are paved, medium to medium+ straight-ins; most sites are quite suitable for tents: fireplaces, plus some barbecue grills; firewood is available for gathering in the area; water at a hand pump; vault facilities; paved driveways; nearest reliable sources of supplies are Lolo, Montana, 52 miles east, or Kooskia, Idaho, 84 miles west.

Activities & Attractions: Fishing on the river and adjacent side streams; numerous primitive roads and foot trails in the region.

Natural Features: Located on the north bank of the Lochsa (Lock-saw) River, part of the National Wild and Scenic River System; the campsites receive medium shade/shelter from tall conifers and some bushes; a small creek trickles down through the campground between the loops; large gravel and sand beach areas along the river just to the west of the campground; closely flanked by the forested mountains of the Bitterroot Range; elevation 3300'.

Season, Fees & Phone: May to mid-September; $6.00; 14 day limit; Powell Ranger District (208) 942-3113.

Camp Notes: Wendover is nearly a twin of Whitehouse Campground, 0.3 mile east. Wendover, however, has fewer sites with a river view. It also has a slightly more "open" environment.

Idaho 30

WHITEHOUSE
Clearwater National Forest

Location: Northern Idaho east of Lewiston near Lolo Pass.

Access: From U.S. Highway 12 at milepost 158 +.5 (16 miles west of Lolo Pass, 85 miles northeast of Kooskia), turn south off the highway into the campground. (Note that the driveway entrance may be difficult to see until you're almost past it.)

Facilities: 14 campsites; campsites are large, level and reasonably well-spaced; parking pads are paved, medium to long enough for larger vehicles; nice, level tent spaces; fireplaces; firewood is available for gathering in the area; water at a hand pump; vault facilities; wide, paved driveway, with a narrow turnaround at the east end; camper supplies at a resort, 3 miles west; limited to adequate supplies are available in Kooskia, Idaho, 85 miles west, and Lolo, Montana, 51 miles east.

Activities & Attractions: Fairly good fishing on the Lochsa River; many 4 wheel drive and foot trails in the area.

Natural Features: Located on the north bank of the Lochsa River, part of the National Wild and Scenic River System; quite a few camp spots have river frontage, and most at least have a river view; mostly tall pine combined with tall grass and hardwoods within the campground; campsites are moderately sheltered/shaded; dense conifer forest throughout this region; elevation 3300'.

Season, Fees & Phone: May to September; $6.00; 14 day limit; Powell Ranger District (208) 942-3113.

Camp Notes: The size of this campground is quite large in proportion to the relatively small number of sites. Very few vehicles travel this winding highway through the Bitterroots between dusk and dawn; so a good night's sleep in this roadside spot, while not guaranteed, is a reasonable expectation.

Idaho 31

POWELL
Clearwater National Forest

Location: Northern Idaho east of Lewiston near Lolo Pass.

Access: From U.S Highway 12 at milepost 161 +.8 (12 miles southwest of Lolo Pass, 87 miles northeast of Kooskia), turn south off the highway onto a paved road which leads 0.2 mile to the campground.

Facilities: 39 campsites in 3 loops; sites are medium-sized, with dense vegetation providing very good separation between most sites; parking pads are paved or gravel, wide, level, with plenty of space for larger vehicles; adequate room for tents; fireplaces; firewood is available for gathering in the area; water at several faucets; restrooms, plus auxiliary vaults; paved driveways; ranger station just east of the campground; camper supplies at a nearby lodge; nearest reliable sources of limited to adequate supplies and services are Kooskia, Idaho 87 miles west, and Lolo, Montana, 49 miles east.

Activities & Attractions: Good views of the Lochsa River and the mountains of the nearby Idaho wilderness; fishing; national forest visitor center at the summit of Lolo Pass (staffed by volunteers, open during midsummer).

Natural Features: Located on the densely forested north bank of the Lochsa River, part of the National Wild and Scenic River System; the river can be heard but not actually viewed from the campsites, except from a half dozen spots in the A Loop; large, open, grassy recreation area in the center of the B Loop; bordered by the high densely timbered peaks of the Bitterroot Range north and south; elevation 3400'.

Season, Fees & Phone: May to October; $6.00; 14 day limit; Powell Ranger District (208) 942-3113.

Camp Notes: Lolo Pass was traveled by Lewis and Clark's Corps of Discovery on both the trip West in September 1805, and upon their return eastward in June 1806. Their journals note that the way was extremely rugged on the Indian trails along the densely forested riverbank, and game for food was scarce. Even though this highway became a 'through' route in 1952, supplies and services are still hard to come by on the 130-mile stretch of U.S. 12 between Kooskia, Idaho, and Lolo, Montana.

Idaho 32

TWIN CREEK
Salmon National Forest

Location: North-eastern Idaho north of Salmon near the Montana border.

Access: From U.S. Highway 93 at milepost 342 +.4 (8.6 miles south of Lost Trail Pass and the Idaho-Montana border, 5 miles north of Gibbonsville), turn west; proceed 0.3 mile on a gravel road up to the campground.

Facilities: 44 campsites in 2 loops; sites are quite spacious, with generally good separation; parking pads are gravel, most are medium to long straight-ins; many pads may require additional leveling; some nice large tent spots, perhaps a bit sloped; fire rings and/or barbecue grills; firewood is available for gathering; water at several faucets; vault facilities; gravel driveways; gas and groceries in Gibbonsville; adequate supplies and services are available in Salmon, 38 miles south.

Activities & Attractions: Fishing on the North Fork of the Salmon River and at Allan Lake (accessible by a 10-mile-long foot trail); hiking; river rafting at North Fork, 16 miles south on Highway 93; superscenic (though twisty) drive along Highway 93 between Lost Trail Pass and Salmon.

Natural Features: Located along a forested, sloping gulch high in the Bitterroot Range; most campsites are surrounded by dense, tall timber with hanging moss, plus hardwoods and smaller conifers; a few sites are in more open forest; Twin Creek, a clear mountain stream, tumbles past the sites, through a wide ravine, and into the North Fork of the Salmon River; often showery in the afternoon; elevation 5100'.

Season, Fees & Phone: May to mid-September; $5.00; 14 day limit; North Fork Ranger District (208) 865-2383.

Camp Notes: The forest here provides a really nice, sheltered setting for a campground. The Lewis & Clark Expedition camped in this vicinity on September 2, 1805.

Idaho
South West
Please refer to the Idaho map in the Appendix

Idaho 33

COLD SPRINGS
Payette National Forest

Location: Western Idaho northeast of Weiser.

Access: From Idaho State Highway 55 at milepost 152 +.5 (9 miles southwest of New Meadows, 15 miles north of Council), turn west onto Lost Creek Road (gravel, with steep sections) and proceed 4 miles to the campground.

Facilities: 31 campsites; sites are small+ to medium-sized, with fair separation; parking pads are gravel, some are long enough for medium to large rv's; fairly level spots for tents in among the trees; fire rings or barbecue grills; firewood is available for gathering in the vicinity; water at several faucets; vault facilities; pack-it-in/pack-it-out trash system; holding tank disposal station gravel driveway; gas and camper supplies at the highway turnoff; adequate supplies and services are available in New Meadows.

Activities & Attractions: Hiking; good berry picking in season; boating, boat launch, fishing, swimming area on Lost Valley Reservoir.

Natural Features: Located on a forested, gentle slope bordered by forested hills and mountains; Lost Valley Reservoir is 1 mile northwest; elevation 4800'.

Season, Fees & Phone: June to October; $5.00; 14 day limit; New Meadows Ranger District (208) 347-2141.

Camp Notes: Lost Valley Reservoir is an attractive mountain lake surrounded by forested slopes. It's large enough to accommodate most water activities. Another, roughly similar campground, though only about half the size of Cold Springs, Slaughter Gulch, is two miles northwest of Cold Springs.

Idaho 34

EVERGREEN
Payette National Forest

Location: Western Idaho northeast of Weiser.

Access: From U.S. Highway 95 at milepost 149 (13 miles north of Council, 11 miles south of New Meadows), turn east, cross a bridge over the Weiser River, and into the campground.

Facilities: 12 campsites in 3 loops; sites are small+ to medium-sized, with good separation; parking pads are gravel, most are short to medium-length straight-ins; many pads may require additional leveling; a few designated tent sites are on cleared, level terrain; fireplaces and some barbecue grills; firewood is available for gathering in the area; water at several faucets; vault facilities; gravel driveways; camper supplies, 3 miles north; limited to adequate supplies are available in Council and New Meadows.

Activities & Attractions: Fishing; hiking; berry-picking in season; boating on nearby Lost Valley Reservoir, about 8 miles northwest; adjacent day use area has large tables and a campfire circle.

Natural Features: Located on a slope in a densely forested canyon along the Weiser River; the river flows swiftly by the campground, and a number of sites are right above the river's edge; tall timber and brush separate the sites nicely; to the east are the West Mountains, where peaks rise to 8000'; campground elevation 3800'.

Season, Fees & Phone: May to October; $5.00; 14 day limit; Council Ranger District (208) 253-4215.

Camp Notes: Nice streamside location. The Weiser River, with the *i* following the *e*, looks like it should be pronounced like *Wize*-r, with a long *i*; but it's regionally pronounced *Weez*-r, (*ala* sneezer).

Idaho 35

MANN CREEK RESERVOIR
Mann Creek/Bureau of Reclamation Area

Location: Western Idaho northeast of Weiser.

Access: From U.S. Highway 95 at milepost 95 +.2 (13 miles north of Weiser, 19 miles south of Cambridge), turn west onto Mann Creek Road; drive west (paved for 1 mile), north and west again, past the dam; continue northerly along the east shore of the reservoir; turn west (left) onto a gravel access road and proceed 0.1 mile to the campground. (The campground is at the far end of the reservoir in a grove of trees, a total of 3 miles from U.S. 95.)

Facilities: 10 campsites; sites are small+, level, with nominal separation; parking pads are gravel, medium-length straight-ins or pull-offs; 5 sites are park 'n walk units, with sheltered tables; fire rings; a limited amount of firewood is available for gathering in the area, so b-y-o is suggested; water at a hand pump; vault facilities; gravel driveway; camper supplies at a small store on Highway 95, south of Mann Creek Road; limited supplies in Midvale, 10 miles north; adequate supplies are available in Weiser.

Activities & Attractions: Boating; boat ramp 1 mile south of the campground; fishing; picnic area with restrooms at the dam; foot trail leads along the creek.

Natural Features: Located at the far north end of Mann Creek Reservoir, where Mann Creek rushes past the campground and flows into the lake; 5 sites are on a lawn near a stand of hardwoods; 5 less-sheltered sites are bordered by boulders and bunchgrass; the Hitt Mountains rise to about 7000' just north of here; campground elevation 2800'.

Season, Fees & Phone: Open all year, subject to weather and road conditions; no fee (subject to change); 14 day limit; BuRec Boise District Office (208) 334-1937 or (208) 334-1128.

Camp Notes: The campground is really a pleasant surprise for this part of the country. There is a nice view of the lake through the trees from several of the sites. A rest area on U.S. 95, near milepost 101 a few miles north of here, overlooks a terrific panorama of this region.

Idaho 36

PONDEROSA
Ponderosa State Park

Location: Western Idaho north of Boise.

Access: From Idaho State Highway 55 at milepost 144 in midtown McCall, follow the well-marked route northeast through town on a paved local road for 1.6 miles to the park entrance and the campground, just beyond.

Facilities: 170 campsites, including 108 with partial hookups, in 3 loops; sites are small to medium-sized, reasonably level, with fair to fairly good separation; parking pads are paved or oiled gravel and many are long enough to accommodate large rv's; good to excellent tent-pitching spots; fireplaces; b-y-o firewood is suggested; water at hookups and at central faucets; restrooms with showers; disposal station; paved driveways; adequate supplies and services are available in McCall.

Activities & Attractions: Boating; sailing; boat launches and docks; fishing; swimming area; nature trails; visitor center with interpretive displays; summer evening campfire programs; playground; ice skating, sledding and cross-country skiing; old mining towns in the surrounding area.

Natural Features: Located on a peninsula on the east side of Payette Lake, a glacial lake fed by the Payette River; vegetation consists of moderately dense stands of very tall conifers, plus an assortment of marshes and sage flats; surrounded by forested mountains; elevation 5000'.

Season, Fees & Phone: Open all year, with limited services in winter; please see Appendix for standard Idaho state park fees and campsite reservation information; 10 day limit; park office (208) 634-2164.

Camp Notes: Ponderosa is located on the shores of a beautiful mountain lake in a high mountain valley. The lake becomes one of those picture-perfect places on sunny days when small sailboats and colorful windsurfers are plying its waters. The park has excellent camping and other recreational opportunities. It does indeed get very cold and snowy during the winter here, but the local area is becoming a relatively popular place for winter campers who are ready for the weather.

Idaho 37

RAINBOW POINT
Cascade Reservoir/Boise National Forest

Location: Western Idaho north of Boise.

Access: From Idaho State Highway 55 at milepost 131+.3 in midtown Donnelly (25 miles south of New Meadows, 16 miles north of Cascade), turn west onto the Cascade Reservoir Loop Road (watch for a "Rainbow Point Campgrounds" sign); drive west across the Payette River on this winding paved access road for 4 miles to a "T" intersection (at Tamarack Falls); turn south (left) onto West Mountain Road and proceed 0.8 mile on gravel and turn east (left) into the campground.

Facilities: 13 campsites; sites are medium to medium+, mostly level, with good to excellent separation; parking pads are oiled gravel, a few may require additional leveling; some sites have pull-through pads spacious enough to accommodate large rv's; several very good tent spots in fairly dense vegetation; fireplaces; some firewood is available for gathering in the area; water at several faucets; vault facilities; gravel driveway; camper supplies+ in Donnelly; adequate supplies and services are available in Cascade.

Activities & Attractions: Fishing (reportedly some of the best fishing in Idaho); boating; boat launch.

Natural Features: Located on the densely forested northwest shore of Cascade Reservoir in Long Valley; the reservoir was formed by a dam on the North Fork of the Payette River; the West Mountains, with peaks loftier than 7000', rise just to the west; campground elevation 4800'.

Season, Fees & Phone: June to October; $7.00; 14 day limit; Cascade Ranger District (208) 382-4271.

Camp Notes: Views east across Cascade Reservoir and Long Valley are quite impressive. Campsites at both Rainbow Point and Amanita (below) are more sheltered than those at the Bureau of Reclamation campgrounds farther south on the west shore.

Idaho 38

AMANITA
Cascade Reservoir/Boise National Forest

Location: Western Idaho north of Boise.

Access: From Idaho State Highway 55 at milepost 131+.3 in midtown Donnelly, (25 miles south of New Meadows, 16 miles north of Cascade), turn west onto the Cascade Reservoir Loop Road; drive west across the Payette River on this winding paved access road for 4 miles to a "T" intersection (at Tamarack Falls); turn south (left) onto West Mountain Road; proceed 0.9 mile on gravel, then turn east (left) into the campground.

Facilities: 10 campsites; sites are medium-sized, with fair to good separation; parking pads are oiled gravel, mostly level, a few sites have long pull-through pads; several good-sized tent spots; fireplaces; some firewood is available for gathering in the area; water at several faucets; vault facilities; gravel driveway; camper supplies+ in Donnelly; adequate supplies and services are available in Cascade.

Activities & Attractions: Fishing; boating; boat launch nearby; Long Valley Museum in Donnelly.

Natural Features: Located in Long Valley on the forested northwest shore of Cascade Reservoir, an impoundment on the North Fork of the Payette River; the West Mountains lie to the west; elevation 4800'.

Season, Fees & Phone: June to October; $7.00; 14 day limit; Cascade Ranger District (208) 382-4271.

Camp Notes: Though campsites at Amanita are definitely forested, the forest is not quite so dense here as 'next door' to the north at Rainbow Point Campground. A number of these sites are lakeside, offering superscenic views across Cascade Reservoir and Long Valley. If you prefer somewhat less rustic camping, you might want to check out the campgrounds farther south on West Mountain Road.

HUCKLEBERRY & WEST MOUNTAIN
Cascade Reservoir/Bureau of Reclamation Areas

Location: Western Idaho north of Boise.

Access: From Idaho State Highway 55 at milepost 131+.3 in midtown Donnelly, (25 miles south of New Meadows, 16 miles north of Cascade), turn west onto the Cascade Reservoir Loop Road (watch for a "Rainbow Point Campgrounds" sign); drive west across the Payette River on this winding paved access road for 4 miles to a "T" intersection (at Tamarack Falls); turn south (left) onto West Mountain Road; proceed south on gravel for 1.5 miles, then turn east (left) into Huckleberry; or continue for 1.5 miles further south and turn east into West Mountain.

Facilities: 33 campsites in Huckleberry and 36 campsites in West Mountain; sites are medium to large, level, with nominal separation; parking pads are paved and spacious enough to accommodate large rv's; lawns are perfect for tents; barbecue grills; firewood is occasionally for sale, some may be available for gathering locally; water at several faucets; vault facilities; holding tank disposal station nearby; paved driveways; camper supplies in Donnelly; adequate supplies and services are available in Cascade.

Activities & Attractions: Fishing (reportedly excellent) on Cascade Reservoir; boating.

Natural Features: Located in Long Valley in an open meadow on the west shore of Cascade Reservoir, which was formed by damming the North Fork of the Payette River; vegetation in the campgrounds consists of mown grass with a few large trees; the West Mountains, with peaks above 7000', rise within view to the west; campground elevation 4800'.

Season, Fees & Phone: May to September; $7.00; 14 day limit; BuRec Cascade Field Station (208) 382-4258.

Camp Notes: It's a bit of a surprise to find so many nice campgrounds on this lake. There are terrific views of the lake to the east and of the forested ridges to the west from Huckleberry and West Mountain. (These two units were originally called West Mountain North and West Mountain South; continuous confusion brought about the name changes.)

BUTTERCUP
Cascade Reservoir/Bureau of Reclamation Area

Location: Western Idaho north of Boise.

Access: From Idaho State Highway 55 at milepost 131+.3 in midtown Donnelly, (25 miles south of New Meadows, 16 miles north of Cascade), turn west onto the Cascade Reservoir Loop Road; drive west on this winding paved access road for 4 miles to a "T" intersection (at Tamarack Falls); turn south (left) onto West Mountain Road; proceed south for 2.5 miles on gravel; turn east (left) into the campground.

Facilities: 27 campsites; sites are medium to large, level, with nominal separation; parking pads are paved, mostly long straight-ins; excellent tent-pitching possibilities; barbecue grills; firewood is often available for sale, and some may be available for gathering in the area; water at several faucets; vault facilities; holding tank disposal station 0.4 mile south on West Mountain Road; paved driveways; camper supplies+ in Donnelly; adequate supplies and services are available in Cascade.

Activities & Attractions: Boating; boat launch at Rainbow Point; fishing.

Natural Features: Located in Long Valley on the grassy lake shore of a small peninsula which extends from this point eastward into Cascade Reservoir; campground vegetation consists of gently rolling grassy slopes dotted with conifers; elevation 4800'.

Season, Fees & Phone: May to September; $7.00; 14 day limit; BuRec Cascade Field Station (208) 382-4258.

Camp Notes: Buttercup is relatively new as campgrounds go--it first opened in 1986. Great lake views from here, perhaps a little better here than at other points on the west shore.

POISON CREEK
Cascade Reservoir/Bureau of Reclamation Area

Location: Western Idaho north of Boise.

Access: From Idaho State Highway 55 at milepost 131+.3 in midtown Donnelly (25 miles south of New Meadows, 16 miles north of Cascade), turn west onto the Cascade Reservoir Loop Road (watch for a sign "Rainbow Point Campgrounds"); drive west across the Payette River on this winding paved access road for 4 miles to a "T" intersection (at Tamarack Falls); turn south (left) onto West Mountain Road (gravel); proceed 3.7 miles, then turn east (left) into the campground.

Facilities: 36 campsites, including 17 park 'n walk tent sites; sites are medium to medium+, level, with nominal separation; parking pads are gravel, mostly long straight-ins; ample space for tents; barbecue grills; b-y-o firewood is recommended; water at several faucets; vault facilities; holding tank disposal station 0.6 miles north; gravel driveways; camper supplies+ in Donnelly; adequate supplies and services are available in Cascade.

Activities & Attractions: Boating; boat docks at this campground and boat ramps at the northern end of the lake; fishing; open grassy area for recreational activities.

Natural Features: Located in Long Valley on the west shore of Cascade Reservoir; campground vegetation consists of grass and a few more trees than at the campgrounds just to the north; some sites are lakeside and a number of other sites are situated in a stand of trees a few yards west of the lake; the West Mountains are visible to the west; elevation 4800'.

Season, Fees & Phone: June to October; $7.00; 14 day limit; BuRec Cascade Field Station (208) 382-4258.

Camp Notes: Poison Creek's name belies its attractiveness. It's one of the nicest of the half-dozen campgrounds along this shore. This and other west shore campgrounds are also somewhat accessible from the south at the town of Cascade. The drive is highly scenic, but a 15-mile section of West Mountain Road may be very rough, depending upon weather conditions.

Idaho 42

CROWN POINT
Cascade Reservoir/Bureau of Reclamation Area

Location: Western Idaho north of Boise.

Access: From Idaho State Highway 55 at a point 1 mile north of Cascade and 15 miles south of Donnelly (on the north side of the Payette River bridge near the dam), turn west onto a gravel access road (may eventually be paved) and proceed 0.5 mile to the campground.

Facilities: 148 campsites, including several tents-only units; sites are medium to large, with nominal separation; parking pads are paved, medium to long, reasonably level, straight-ins or pull-throughs; ample space for tents; barbecue grills; b-y-o firewood; water at several faucets; restrooms; paved driveways; adequate supplies and services are available in Cascade.

Activities & Attractions: Boating; boat launch nearby in the Van Wyck area; fishing for bass and crappie, plus some stocked trout.

Natural Features: Located on the gently sloping southeast shore of Cascade Reservoir, formed by the adjacent BuRec dam across the North Fork of the Payette River in Long Valley; sites receive light to medium shade/shelter from conifers; the forested West Mountains rise from the west shore of the lake, the North Fork Range and the Salmon River Mountains are to the east; all sites have lake views; elev. 4800'.

Season, Fees & Phone: May to September; $7.00; 14 day limit; BuRec Cascade Field Station (208) 382-4258; or BuRec Boise District Public Affairs Office (208) 334-1937.

Camp Notes: Crown Point is the largest, best-equipped and most popular campground on Cascade Reservoir. If you arrive after dark, you'll be able to see the lights of campers' lanterns and fires from a long way off. Hope for, but don't expect to find, a campsite available that late in the evening, though. There are, however, several other, smaller, BuRec campgrounds along the east and south shores of the lake along the highway. They include Sugarloaf, just onshore of an island, with 42 sites, water and vaults midway between Cascade and Donnelly; Van Wyck, inside the city limits of Cascade, with 22 sites, water and restrooms; and Blue Heron, a 12-site camp with water and vaults that was split-off from a large day use area just south of town. For more seclusion, take the road around the south shore of the lake for 9.5 miles (the first 7.2 miles are paved) to French Creek, a 21-site Boise National Forest Campground on the southwest shore of Cascade Reservoir.

Idaho 43

SWINGING BRIDGE
Boise National Forest

Location: Western Idaho north of Boise.

Access: From Idaho State Highway 55 near milepost 86 (2 miles north of the Boise/Valley County Line, 7 miles north of Banks, 30 miles south of Cascade), turn west at either of 2 entrances (south or north end) of the campground.

Facilities: 11 campsites; sites are medium to large with nominal to fairly good separation; parking pads are paved, short to medium-length straight-ins; some additional leveling may be necessary (although pads and tent areas are well leveled, considering the steep slope); fire rings and barbecue grills; some firewood is available for gathering in the vicinity; water at a hand pump; vault facilities; paved driveways (maneuvering may be a little difficult for large vehicles); camper supplies in Banks, 8 miles south; nearest source of complete supplies and services is Boise, 40 miles south.

Activities & Attractions: Fishing on the North Fork; foot trails in the camp area have steps built into the side of the slope.

Natural Features: Located on a densely forested hillside across the highway from the North Fork of the Payette River; campground vegetation consists of a fairly dense stand of very tall conifers with some underbrush; a rivulet runs through the campground on its way to the North Fork; the river flows through a deep, narrow canyon here between the West Mountains to the west and the Salmon River Mountains to the east; elevation 3700'.

Season, Fees & Phone: May to October; $5.00; 14 day limit; Emmett Ranger District (208) 365-4382.

Camp Notes: Remnants of a hand-cable suspension bridge span the river near the campground. Three other small campgrounds near here also serve Highway 55 travelers. From a half mile to three miles north are (from south to north): Canyon (also called Canyon Creek), Cold Springs and Big Eddy Campgrounds, all on the west side of the highway. Camp size varies from 3 to 7 sites, and facilities are quite similar to those in Swinging Bridge. A fee is charged in Canyon and Cold Springs. This section of Highway 55 is designated as part of the Payette River Scenic Route.

Idaho 44

BANKS
Boise National Forest

Location: Western Idaho north of Boise.

Access: From Idaho State Highway 55 at milepost 77 +.9 (1 mile south of Banks, 14 miles north of Horseshoe Bend), turn east into the upper section, or pull off the highway on the west for access to the lower section.

Facilities: 10 campsites; 4 sites in the lower section are walk-ins, built on a rocky shelf along the river, where parking is very limited and only smaller tents could easily fit into the small spaces; the upper section has short to medium-length straight-in parking pads, and is better than the lower section for larger tents; fire rings or barbecue grills; a limited amount of firewood is available for gathering in the area; water at several faucets; vault facilities; paved driveway in the upper section; camper supplies 2 miles south or 1 mile north on Highway 55; complete supplies and services are available in Boise, 37 miles south.

Activities & Attractions: River rafting; fishing; large, sandy river bar (subject to change); terrific scenery; a drive east from milepost 78 +.9 toward Lowman is a real experience!

Natural Features: Located on the east bank of the Payette River, in a steep-walled and rugged canyon situated between the West Mountains and Boise Ridge; sites in the lower section are right along the river; sites in the upper section are on a hill overlooking the river; campground vegetation consists of tall grass and a few trees clinging to a rocky slope in the lower section, open conifer forest in the upper section; elevation 2700'.

Season, Fees & Phone: May to October; $5.00; 14 day limit; Emmett Ranger District (208) 365-4382.

Camp Notes: The fact that enough room was found for campsites of any size along this stretch is amazing, considering the steep, rocky walls of the canyon. The campground is a mile downstream from the confluence of the sizeable North Fork of the Payette River with the river's main stream. The principal Payette enters this canyon from the east at that point.

Idaho 45

HOT SPRINGS
Boise National Forest

Location: Western Idaho northeast of Boise.

Access: From Idaho State Highway 55 at milepost 79 (0.1 mile north of Banks, 37 miles south of Cascade), turn east onto the Banks-Lowman Road (paved); travel easterly for 13.7 miles; turn north (left) into the campground.

Facilities: 10 campsites, including some multi-family and group units; sites are medium to large, with minimal to average separation; parking pads are gravel, level, short straight-ins or long pull-throughs; large tents will easily be accommodated in most of the sites; barbecue grills; a limited amount of firewood is available for gathering in the vicinity; water at hand pumps; vault facilities; gravel driveways; camper supplies in Garden Valley, 3 miles west; nearest source of complete supplies and services is Boise, 50 miles south.

Activities & Attractions: The hot springs are the main attraction here; fishing; hiking; river-floating; large day use area adjacent to the campground.

Natural Features: Located in an open forest area in a valley along the South Fork of the Payette River; some sites are fairly private because of the surrounding tall conifers; other sites are in more open grassy areas; a tall, forested ridge borders the campground on the north and the South Fork borders the campground across the highway to the south; the hot springs are accessible from the campground via a trail down to the river; the Salmon River Mountains lie just to the north and the Boise Mountains are to the south; elevation 3200'.

Season, Fees & Phone: April to October; $6.00; 14 day limit; Emmett Ranger District (208) 365-4382.

Camp Notes: This camp is located just a few miles from the heart of the river-running country near Banks. The road from Banks to Hot Springs Campground follows along a narrow, tree-dotted valley and then a wide, fertile valley. A long section of the road from Lowman to Hot Springs Campground is narrow, steep and winding, but it offers some spectacular views of this wild area.

Idaho 46

PINE FLATS
Boise National Forest

Location: Western Idaho northeast of Boise.

Access: From Idaho State Highway 21 in midtown Lowman, (70 miles northeast of Boise, 58 miles west of Stanley), turn west onto the Lowman-Banks Road; proceed west for 5 miles; turn south (left) onto a steep gravel access road leading 0.3 mile down into the camping area.

Facilities: 29 campsites; sites are medium to large, with average to very good separation; parking pads are gravel; some pads are long enough to accommodate larger rv's, but many may require additional leveling; (sites are quite well leveled for parking and tents, considering the slope); many large tent areas; fireplaces and/or barbecue grills; firewood is available for gathering in the area; water at hand pumps; vault facilities; dirt/gravel driveways (maneuvering larger vehicles is likely to be a challenge); camper supplies in Lowman; nearest source of complete supplies and services is Boise.

Activities & Attractions: River running; fishing; hiking; the drive west toward Banks is along a narrow, steep, twisty road which passes through some fantastic mountain scenery.

Natural Features: Located on a forested shelf 75' above the South Fork of the Payette River, which flows between two crests of mountain peaks through a very narrow canyon with steep, rocky walls; sites are stretched out along the shelf and many have views of the river below; campground vegetation consists of moderately dense stands of conifers, grass and some underbrush; elevation 4400'.

Season, Fees & Phone: June to September; $6.00; 14 day limit; Lowman Ranger District (208) 259-3361.

Camp Notes: Access to the wild South Fork of the Payette River here is not easy, but it is possible. The forested setting is inviting. The campground's location off the main highway provides it with a certain measure of seclusion.

Idaho 47

MOUNTAIN VIEW
Boise National Forest

Location: Western Idaho northeast of Boise.

Access: From Idaho State Highway 21 at milepost 73 +.2 (0.5 mile east of Lowman, 58 miles west of Stanley), turn south into the campground.

Facilities: 14 campsites; sites are medium to large, level, with mostly average separation; parking pads are paved and level; some pads are large enough to accommodate large rv's; some level areas for good-sized tents; fire rings and some barbecue grills; firewood is available for gathering in the area; water at a hand pump; vault facilities; paved driveways; ranger station adjacent to the campground; camper supplies in Lowman; nearest source of complete supplies and services is Boise, 75 miles south.

Activities & Attractions: River running; the river is easily accessible at this point; fishing; hiking; a number of forest roads and trails lead off into the mountain areas from near here.

Natural Features: Located on a forested flat that extends east and west slightly above the South Fork of the Payette River; a number of sites are riverside, with views of the tree-lined canyon; Deadwood Ridge is to the north and the Boise Mountains lie to the south; the campground has moderately dense stands of tall conifers, moderate underbrush, and tall grass; elevation 3900'.

Season, Fees & Phone: May to September; $6.00; 14 day limit; Lowman Ranger District (208) 259-3361.

Camp Notes: Mountain View Campground is situated in a very attractive river valley setting. A number of really fine sites are right along the river. This facility is one of the nicest campgrounds along the South Fork of the Payette River.

Idaho 48

KIRKHAM HOT SPRINGS
Boise National Forest

Location: Western Idaho northeast of Boise.

Access: From Idaho State Highway 21 at milepost 77 (4 miles east of Lowman, 54 miles west of Stanley), turn south, drive across a bridge over the South Fork of the Payette River and turn west (right) into the campground.

Facilities: 17 campsites in 2 loops; sites are medium-sized, mostly level, with minimal to good separation; parking pads are paved, and some are long enough to accommodate large rv's; medium to large areas for tents; barbecue grills; some firewood is available for gathering in the area; no drinking water; pack-it-in/pack-it-out system of trash removal; vault facilities; paved driveways; camper supplies in Lowman; nearest source of complete supplies and services is Boise, 80 miles southwest.

Activities & Attractions: The main attraction is the hot springs, accessible via a foot trail from the west end of the campground; hiking; fishing.

Natural Features: Located on a flat that extends east to west along the South Fork of the Payette River; the forested loop has medium-sized trees, moderate underbrush and tall grass for a forest floor; the more open loop has very few trees and tall grass; the ridge to the north across the river and highway is heavily forested; Kirkham Hot Springs are a series of rivulets bubbling out of the talus of a rock wall; elevation 4000'.

Season, Fees & Phone: May to September; no fee (subject to change); 14 day limit; Lowman Ranger District (208) 259-3361.

Camp Notes: The sites at Kirkham Hot Springs Campground are more open than at the other camps along this stretch. The South Fork of the Payette River passes through some very scenic canyon areas in this section. The drive along Highway 21, in both directions, offers outstanding mountain scenery.

Idaho 49

HELENDE
Boise National Forest

Location: Western Idaho northeast of Boise.

Access: From Idaho State Highway 21 at milepost 81 +.5 (8 miles east of Lowman, 50 miles west of Stanley), turn south onto a paved access road for about 100 yards to the campground.

Facilities: 10 campsites; sites are medium to large, with average or better separation; parking pads are paved; some pads are small, others will hold medium-sized rv's; most sites have level grassy areas that will readily accommodate large tents; fire rings and/or barbecue grills; firewood is available for gathering in the area; water at a hand pump; vault facilities; paved driveways; camper supplies in Lowman; nearest complete supplies and services are in Boise, 85 miles southwest.

Activities & Attractions: River running; fishing; Kirkham Hot Springs is 4 miles west on Highway 21; several forest roads and foot trails lead off into the mountains from near this point; the sprawling Sawtooth Wilderness and Sawtooth National Recreation Area are east of here.

Natural Features: Located on a grassy flat above the South Fork of the Payette River; campground vegetation consists of a moderately dense conifer forest over an extensive grass and brush floor; the Boise Mountains lie to the south and the Sawtooth Mountains are to the east; elevation 4100'.

Season, Fees & Phone: May to September; $6.00; 14 day limit; Lowman Ranger District (208) 259-3361.

Camp Notes: Though the campsites are not actually on the riverbank, the atmosphere created by the nearby river is apparent. The campground is shielded from the highway by a substantial stand of trees.

Idaho 50

TEN MILE
Boise National Forest

Location: Western Idaho northeast of Boise.

Access: From Idaho State Highway 21 at milepost 47 +.8 (9 miles north of Idaho City, 25 miles south of Lowman), turn right or left into the campground; (campsites are located on both sides of the highway.)

Facilities: 14 campsites; sites are average-sized and fairly well separated; parking pads are gravel, short to medium-length, and many may require a little additional leveling; the forest floor is rather rocky, so tent-pitching may require extra preparation; fire rings; firewood is available for gathering in the area; water at a hand pump; vault facilities; gravel driveways; limited supplies and services are available in Idaho City.

Activities & Attractions: Fishing; hiking in the vicinity; Idaho City has an information center and an historic mining town exhibit; the drive along Highway 21 is steep and curvy, but does offer some nice scenery.

Natural Features: Located in a very narrow, steep-walled canyon, where Ten Mile Creek flows into Mores Creek which flows south into the Boise River; tall trees and some creekside brush separate most sites nicely; a number of campsites are right along the swiftly flowing creek; elevation 5000'.

Season, Fees & Phone: June to September; $5.00; 14 day limit; Idaho City Ranger District (208) 392-6681.

Camp Notes: Because the campground is built in a very narrow valley (this territory is almost strictly vertical), many of the sites are rather close to the highway by necessity. Ten Mile is probably the best of four campgrounds along this stretch. Others are: Bad Bear at milepost 48, Hayfork at milepost 48 +.9, and Grayback Gulch, south of here at milepost 36 +.6. All have similar facilities and a typical mountain-forest environment. This segment of Highway 21 is a lot more serpentine than it looks on most maps.

Idaho 51

BULL TROUT LAKE
Boise National Forest

Location: Western Idaho northeast of Boise.

Access: From Idaho State Highway 21 at milepost 107 +.5 (1 mile north of Banner Summit, 34 miles northeast of Lowman, 24 miles west of Stanley), turn southwest onto Forest Road 100 (gravel, watch for a small sign); drive 2 miles on a graded gravel road to the campground.

Facilities: 17 campsites; sites are medium-sized, with nominal to fair separation; parking pads are gravelled, short straight-ins; medium to large areas for tents; fire rings; a limited amount of firewood is available for gathering; no drinking water; vault facilities; gravel driveway; limited+ supplies and services are available in Stanley.

Activities & Attractions: Trout fishing, hiking and photography are the main attractions; foot trails lead into the Sawtooth Wilderness Area from this vicinity; in nearby Sawtooth Recreation area are visitor centers and organized activities.

Natural Features: Located in an open forest high in the Sawtooth Mountains; sites are lightly shaded/sheltered by tall conifers; Banner Pass tops out at 7056' on the highway south of the campground turnoff; elevation 6800'.

Season, Fees & Phone: Mid-June to September; no fee (subject to change); 14 day limit; Lowman Ranger District (208) 259-3361.

Camp Notes: The campground is accessible only during a few short months because of its high altitude and consequent snowpack. The scenery in the area is magnificent. Eight miles northeast of the turnoff to Bull Trout Lake is a very nice small camp called Thatcher Creek in Challis National Forest. It's right off the south-west side of Highway 21. It has 5 sites, a hand pump and vault facilities. Views from Thatcher Creek are terrific.

Idaho 52

STANLEY LAKE
Sawtooth National Recreation Area

Location: Central Idaho west of Stanley.

Access: From Idaho State Highway 21 at milepost 125 +.9 (5 miles west of Stanley, 9 miles east of the western boundary of the Sawtooth National Recreation Area), turn southwest onto a good, wide gravel access road and proceed 3 miles to the camping areas.

Facilities: 33 campsites in 4 loops; sites vary considerably in size, levelness and separation; parking pads are gravel, medium to long, mostly straight-ins, plus a few pull-throughs; some good tent spots, though many are sloped; fireplaces; firewood is usually available for gathering in the area; water at hand pumps; vault facilities; gravel driveways; limited+ supplies in Stanley; adequate supplies and services are available in Ketchum, 65 miles southeast.

Activities & Attractions: Super scenery; boating; boat launch; designated swimming beach; hiking trails, including Alpine Lake and Summit Trails which lead off into the Sawtooth Wilderness Area.

Natural Features: Located on the northwest shore of Stanley Lake; campground vegetation is predominantly a light to moderate conifer forest with light underbrush; Stanley Lake is 1 mile long, 0.5 mile wide and 100' deep; the dramatic relief of the Sawtooth Range, including 9860' McGown Peak, is visible across the lake just a few miles to the south; elevation 6400'.

Season, Fees & Phone: June to October; $7.00; 10 day limit; Sawtooth NRA Headquarters, Ketchum, (208) 726-7672.

Camp Notes: Quite a varied selection of sites: Inlet Loop A has 6 lakeside sites, Inlet Loop B has 6 creekside sites, Stanley Lake Loop has 15 sites on a sloping bluff overlooking the lake, and Lakeview has 6 mostly level sites with very good lake views. Stanley Lake offers some magnificent scenery--the lake's waters wash right up against the sheer, jagged, rock-faced Sawtooth Range.

Idaho 53

MOUNTAIN VIEW & CHINOOK BAY
Sawtooth National Recreation Area

Location: Central Idaho south of Stanley.

Access: From Idaho State Highway 75 at milepost 185 (4.4 miles southeast of Stanley, 57 miles north of Ketchum), turn southwest onto the Redfish Lake Recreation Area Road (paved); proceed 0.1 mile southwest to Chinook Bay Campground and 0.3 mile to Mountain View Campground; turn right into either of the two camping areas.

Facilities: 13 campsites in Chinook Bay and 7 campsites in Mountain View; sites are small+, with some separation; parking pads are gravel, level, and most would accommodate medium-sized rv's; fireplaces; firewood is usually available for gathering in the area; water at several faucets; vault facilities; gravel driveways; camper supplies at a lodge on Redfish Lake, 4 miles west; limited+ supplies in Stanley; adequate supplies and services are available in Ketchum.

Activities & Attractions: Hiking, fishing; float boating; nearby Redfish Lake Rock Shelter holds archaeological artifacts dating back nearly 11,000 years; visitor center at Redfish Lake.

Natural Features: Located in an open forest on the shore of Little Redfish Lake, a small, clear mountain lake nestled at the foot of the dramatically jagged peaks of the Sawtooth Range; the Salmon River flows along next to Highway 75 within a mile of this camping area; campground vegetation consists of tall conifers, a grassy forest floor and very little underbrush; elevation 6500'.

Season, Fees & Phone: May to September; $8.00; 10 day limit; Sawtooth NRA Headquarters, Ketchum, (208) 726-7672.

Camp Notes: The scenery is magnificent as viewed from the shore of this beautiful mountain lake surrounded by towering forested peaks. On summer weekdays, there is somewhat less traffic and congestion here than at campgrounds nearer to the much more popular Redfish Lake.

POINT
Sawtooth National Recreation Area

Location: Central Idaho south of Stanley.

Access: From Idaho State Highway 75 at milepost 185 (4.4 miles southeast of Stanley, 57 miles north of Ketchum), turn southwest onto the Redfish Lake Recreation Area Road (paved); proceed 1.8 miles to a fork; take the right fork and continue for 1 mile around the north side of the lake, past the visitor center and lodge, to the campground.

Facilities: 17 campsites in 3 loops; sites are rather small but fairly well-spaced; parking aprons are gravel and fairly small; tent-camping only is permitted; fireplaces; firewood may be available for gathering in the general vicinity; water at several faucets; restrooms; gravel driveways; camper supplies and laundry at the lodge; limited + supplies and services in Stanley.

Activities & Attractions: Hiking trails lead into the Sawtooth Wilderness Area; fishing; boating; marina; swimming (probably the most popular swimming beach on the lake); visitor center.

Natural Features: Located on a flat point of land extending south into Redfish Lake; 2 loops are close to the beach and a third is above them on a short bluff; shelter and separation are provided at some sites by medium-sized trees and a little underbrush; the lake is located at the base of the towering Sawtooth Mountains; elevation 6500'.

Season, Fees & Phone: June to September; $8.00; 6 day limit; Sawtooth NRA Headquarters, Ketchum, (208) 726-7672.

Camp Notes: This is a favorite spot for water sports enthusiasts. Adjacent to Point Campground is a large and popular day use area with picnicking and swimming facilities. If you're interested in regional flora and fauna, the visitor center can provide you with a number of pamphlets related to birding, wildflower identification, and animal life. Fantastic vistas through the trees of Redfish Lake and the surrounding mountains!

REDFISH OUTLET
Sawtooth National Recreation Area

Location: Central Idaho south of Stanley.

Access: From Idaho State Highway 75 at milepost 185 (4.4 miles southeast of Stanley, 57 miles north of Ketchum), turn southwest onto the Redfish Lake Recreation Area Road (paved); proceed 2 miles (past the right-hand turnoff to the lodge and visitor center) on a curving, paved road; turn northwest (right) at the campground entrance and proceed down into the campground.

Facilities: 46 campsites; sites are mostly small to medium-sized with nominal to fair separation; parking pads are gravel, mostly short to medium-length straight-ins, plus a few longer pull-throughs; tent spots tend to be rather small; barbecue grills; firewood is usually available for gathering in the area; water at faucets throughout; vault facilities; holding tank disposal station near the lodge; paved driveways; camper supplies at the lodge; limited + supplies in Stanley.

Activities & Attractions: Hiking (Marshall Lake and Baron Creek Trailheads nearby); fishing; boating (ramps nearby at Sandy Beach); visitor center on Redfish Lake's north shore.

Natural Features: Located on a forested flat close to the northeast shore of Redfish Lake, a beautiful mountain lake nestled at the foot of some dramatically rugged peaks of the Sawtooth Range; tall timber and very little underbrush provide some privacy between sites; elevation 6500'.

Season, Fees & Phone: May to September; $8.00; 10 day limit; Sawtooth NRA Headquarters, Ketchum, (208) 726-7672.

Camp Notes: There is a commanding view from near here of this superscenic mountain lake and the rock face of the Sawtooth Mountains which encompass it. Neighboring Point Campground cannot accommodate trailers, so Outlet Campground is often occupied to capacity early in the day during the peak of the season.

GLACIER VIEW
Sawtooth National Recreation Area

Location: Central Idaho south of Stanley.

Access: From Idaho State Highway 75 at milepost 185 (4.4 miles southeast of Stanley, 57 miles north of Ketchum), turn southwest onto the Redfish Lake Recreation Area access road (paved); proceed 2 miles (past the right-hand turnoff to the lodge and visitor center) on a curving paved road; turn southwest (left) and proceed up into the campground.

Facilities: 17 campsites; sites are medium to medium+ in size, with nominal to good separation; parking pads are paved, mostly level, and many pads are long enough to accommodate very large rv's; most sites have large, level tent-pitching areas; fireplaces; firewood is usually available for gathering in the area; water at faucets throughout; vault facilities; holding tank disposal station near the lodge; paved driveways; camper supplies at the lodge; limited+ supplies in Stanley.

Activities & Attractions: Hiking (Marshall Lake and Baron Creek Trailheads are located nearby); fishing; boating (boat ramp and beach nearby at Sandy Beach); visitor center on Redfish Lake's north shore.

Natural Features: Located on a forested hilltop across the main roadway from beautiful Redfish Lake (and Outlet Campground) at the base of the Sawtooth Range; campground vegetation consists of light to moderately dense stands of conifers, grass and light underbrush; striking views of steep, rocky slopes; elevation 6500'.

Season, Fees & Phone: May to September; $8.00; 6 day limit; Sawtooth NRA Headquarters, Ketchum, (208) 726-7672.

Camp Notes: Glacier-clad mountains can be glimpsed through the trees from some really nice sites in this relatively tranquil forest setting. Glacier View Campground is a bit more spacious and often less congested than some of the more popular campgrounds nearer to the lake shore. A suggestion for camping anywhere in the Sawtooth: Bring plenty of warm clothing, even for a First-of-August campout. Expect occasional snow during May and June. Memorial Day Weekend may summon-up frost and flurries, but at least you'll have a good choice of campsites.

MOUNT HEYBURN
Sawtooth National Recreation Area

Location: Central Idaho south of Stanley.

Access: From Idaho State Highway 75 at milepost 185 (4.4 miles southeast of Stanley, 57 miles north of Ketchum), turn southwest onto the Redfish Lake Recreation Area Road (paved); proceed 3.5 miles (past the right-hand turnoff to the lodge and visitor center) on a curving paved road; turn southwest (left) into the campground.

Facilities: 42 campsites; sites are medium to large, level, with nominal to good separation; some parking pads are paved, most are straight-ins, plus a few long pull-throughs for very large rv's; most sites have good, large, level tent-pitching spots; fireplaces; firewood is usually available for gathering in the vicinity; water at faucets throughout; vault facilities; holding tank disposal station near the lodge; fairly wide, paved driveways; camper supplies and laundry at the lodge; limited+ supplies in Stanley.

Activities & Attractions: Hiking (trailhead to the Sawtooth Wilderness Area); boating; boat launch and beach at nearby Sandy Beach; fishing.

Natural Features: Located on a forested hill above Redfish Lake; campground vegetation consists of moderately dense stands of tall conifers with light underbrush; the jagged peaks of the Sawtooth Range rise from the opposite lake shore; elevation 6500'.

Season, Fees & Phone: June to September; $8.00; 10 day limit; Sawtooth NRA Headquarters, Ketchum, (208) 726-7672.

Camp Notes: Some of Mount Heyburn's sites offer lake views through the trees. You'll find additional, similar sites and facilities at Sockeye Campground, just south of Mount Heyburn.

SMOKEY BEAR
Sawtooth National Recreation Area

Location: Central Idaho northwest of Ketchum.

Access: From Idaho State Highway 75 at a point 10 miles south of Stanley and 51 miles north of Ketchum, turn west at a sign for "Alturas Lake"; travel west and south (past Perkins Lake on the right) for 3.5 miles; turn southeast (left) into the campground.

Facilities: 12 campsites in 2 loops; sites are medium to large, with moderate to good separation; parking pads are gravel, mostly level, medium-length straight-ins or pull-throughs; some good tent-pitching opportunities; fireplaces; firewood is available for gathering in the area; water at several faucets; vault facilities; gravel driveways with a turnaround loop at the east end of the campground; limited+ supplies in Stanley; adequate supplies and services are available in Ketchum.

Activities & Attractions: Boating; boat launch and dock at the east end of the campground; beach access; hiking; a nearby ghost town, Sawtooth City, is accessible by forest road.

Natural Features: Located on an open sage flat along the north shore of Alturas Lake, in the broad Salmon River Valley; campground vegetation includes grass and some thin pines between sites; peaks of the Sawtooth Range rise sharply from the lake's west shore to above 10,000'; elevation 7000'.

Season, Fees & Phone: June to September; $7.00; 10 day limit; Sawtooth NRA Headquarters, Ketchum, (208) 726-7672.

Camp Notes: Smokey Bear Campground is the easternmost campground on Alturas Lake. The superscenic lake and surrounding mountains are visible from virtually all sites. The ultra-wide vistas of the Sawtooth Range and Salmon River Valley are really spectacular from Galena Summit Overlook, on Highway 75 near the turnoff to Alturas Lake.

ALTURAS INLET
Sawtooth National Recreation Area

Location: Central Idaho northwest of Ketchum.

Access: From Idaho State Highway 75 at a point 10 miles south of Stanley and 51 miles north of Ketchum, turn west at a sign for "Alturas Lake"; proceed west and south (past Perkins Lake on the right) for 5 miles; turn southeast (left) into the campground.

Facilities: 29 level sites; sites are medium to large, with mostly good to excellent separation; parking pads are gravel, level and most are straight-ins large enough for medium-sized rv's; many good tent-pitching opportunities; fireplaces; firewood is available for gathering in the area; water at several faucets; vault facilities; gravel driveways; limited supplies in Stanley; adequate supplies and services are available in Ketchum.

Activities & Attractions: Boating; sailing, water-skiing, fishing, (boat ramp at Smokey Bear Campground, 2 miles east); hiking; an old ghost town, Sawtooth City, is accessible by forest road from near here; the drive along Highway 75, the Sawtooth Scenic Drive, follows the Salmon River Valley past a point very near the headwaters of the legendary 420-mile-long Salmon River.

Natural Features: Located on a forested flat along the west shore of Alturas Lake, where Alturas Lake Creek flows into the lake; this lovely mountain lake is 2 miles long, 0.5 mile wide and 300' deep; campground vegetation consists of tall pines, tall grass and very little underbrush; elevation 7000'.

Season, Fees & Phone: June to September; $7.00; 10 day limit; Sawtooth NRA Headquarters, Ketchum, (208) 726-7672.

Camp Notes: Alturas Inlet Campground is located in a pocket at the west end of the lake and up against the Sawtooth Mountain Range. Alturas Lake is a liquid sapphire surrounded by emerald-mantled mountain slopes. Very nice indeed.

EASLEY
Sawtooth National Recreation Area

Location: Central Idaho northwest of Ketchum.

Access: From Idaho State Highway 75 at a point 14 miles north of Ketchum and 47 miles south of Stanley, turn southwest onto a gravel access road; proceed 0.2 mile and turn northwest (right) into the campground.

Facilities: 17 campsites in 2 loops; (an adjacent group camping area is also available, by reservation); sites are medium-sized, with average to good separation; parking pads are gravel, level, and mostly short straight-ins, though some are quite wide; some good, level, grassy tent-pitching spaces; fireplaces; a limited quantity of firewood is available for gathering in the area; water at faucets; vault facilities; gravel driveway with a turnaround loop at the end; camper supplies at Easley Hot Springs, 0.1 mile southwest; adequate supplies and services are available in Ketchum.

Activities & Attractions: Great scenery on the drive along the Sawtooth Scenic Route (Highway 75) north from here toward Stanley; stream fishing; hiking trails in the nearby mountains.

Natural Features: Located in a broad, sweeping mountain meadow near the headwaters of the Big Wood River; campground vegetation consists of some tall grass and a few medium-sized trees; a few sites are within a few yards of the Big Wood River; the Boulder Mountains rise to the east; foothills of the Sawtooth Range are immediately to the west; elevation 6600'.

Season, Fees & Phone: June to September; $5.00; 10 day limit; Sawtooth NRA Headquarters, Ketchum, (208) 726-7672.

Camp Notes: The super scenery in this valley overshadows the unexceptional facilities at the campground itself. The official 'stats' for the three-quarter-million-acre Sawtooth NRA boast four mountain ranges, headwaters of five major rivers, and about 1,000 lakes. According to official sources, a grand total of 24,920 persons can be accommodated when the developed recreational facilities are maxxed-out. But would you really enjoy a visit here with a gang of that size?

Idaho 61

WOOD RIVER
Sawtooth National Recreation Area

Location: Central Idaho northwest of Ketchum.

Access: From Idaho State Highway 75 at a point 10 miles northwest of Ketchum and 51 miles south of Stanley, turn south (this stretch of the highway actually lies in an east/west direction) into the campground.

Facilities: 32 campsites in 3 loops; sites are medium to large, with mostly good separation; most parking pads are paved, level, medium-length straight-ins, plus a few longer pull-throughs; some good tent-pitching opportunities; fireplaces; firewood is available for gathering in the vicinity; water at faucets throughout; restrooms, supplemented by vault facilities; paved driveways; adequate supplies and services are available in Ketchum.

Activities & Attractions: Great scenery in the Big Wood River Valley and along the Sawtooth Scenic Route (Highway 75) especially northward toward Galena Summit Overlook and Stanley; amphitheater for campfire programs; self-guided nature trail from near the day use area; nearby on Highway 75, a jeep trail leads up to Boulder Basin, a 'high-in-the-sky' deserted mining camp; stream fishing; hiking.

Natural Features: Located on a forested flat along the Big Wood River; campground vegetation consists of moderately dense stands of conifers, grass and considerable underbrush; the Boulder Mountains rise to the east; foothills of the Sawtooth Range are immediately to the west; elevation 6300'.

Season, Fees & Phone: June to September; $7.00; 10 day limit; Sawtooth NRA Headquarters, Ketchum, (208) 726-7672.

Camp Notes: The rushing Big Wood River provides an ambient quality which helps to create what might be called a 'cordial' atmosphere at this very inviting campground. Some sites are forested, some are in the open, and some are streamside. All sites are really nice!

Idaho 62

NORTH FORK
Sawtooth National Recreation Area

Location: Central Idaho north of Ketchum.

Access: From Idaho State Highway 75 at a point 8 miles north of Ketchum and 53 miles south of Stanley, turn west into the campground; (there are 2 entrances fairly close together).

Facilities: 26 campsites in 2 loops; sites are average or better in size, with fairly good separation; most parking pads are gravel, level, and some are pull-throughs long enough to accommodate medium-sized rv's; some good tent-pitching possibilities; fireplaces; firewood is available for gathering in the vicinity; water at several faucets; vault facilities; gravel driveways; adequate supplies and services are available in Ketchum.

Activities & Attractions: The Sawtooth Scenic Route follows Highway 75 along the Big Wood River in this section and offers fantastic scenery, especially when you reach Galena Summit Overlook, north of here; stream fishing; hiking in the nearby mountains; the Sawtooth National Recreation Area Headquarters is located directly across the highway.

Natural Features: Located where the North Fork enters the main stream of the Big Wood River; campsites are within a fairly dense conifer forest with considerable underbrush; several riverside sites; an open meadow bordered by an aspen grove is located across the highway to the east; the Boulder Mountains rise to the east and the foothills of the Sawtooth Range are immediately to the west; elevation 5900'.

Season, Fees & Phone: June to September; $6.00; 10 day limit; Sawtooth NRA Headquarters, Ketchum, (208) 726-7672.

Camp Notes: This campground may be a step down from nearby Wood River Campground (see separate listing) as far as 'best' in this region north of Ketchum and ski-famous Sun Valley. It's slightly handier to town, though. Galena Summit, at 8700', mentioned in the Attractions section, divides the watersheds of the Salmon River and the Big Wood River. (The Big Wood River is also commonly called just Wood River.)

Idaho 63

SALMON RIVER
Sawtooth National Recreation Area

Location: Central Idaho east of Stanley.

Access: From Idaho State Highway 75 at milepost 193 +.7 (4 miles east of Stanley, 51 miles southwest of Challis), turn right or left into the campground; (campsites are both north and south of the highway).

Facilities: 32 campsites in 4 loops (2 on each side of the highway); sites are medium to large, with generally good separation; parking pads are gravel, most are medium to long straight-ins, and well-leveled, considering the slight slope of the hillside; good tent spots; fireplaces; ample firewood is available for gathering in the area; water at hand pumps; vault facilities; gravel driveways; limited+ supplies in Stanley; nearest sources of adequate supplies and services are Ketchum, 65 miles south, and Salmon, 110 miles northeast.

Activities & Attractions: River rafting; fishing; the superscenic drive along Highway 75 to the west offers fantastic views of the Sawtooth Range, as the Salmon River Canyon opens into a wider valley; Stanley Museum is 4 miles west.

Natural Features: Located on the gently sloping north bank of the Salmon River, where the river is fairly wide, shallow and slow-moving; two groves of trees above the highway and two groves below the highway provide shelter and separation for all but a few sites; a number of sites are right at the river's edge; a timbered ridge flanks the river on the south; the river's north boundary is a sage and grass covered hillside; tall mountain peaks beyond the canyon walls; elevation 6100'.

Season, Fees & Phone: Mid-June to September; $6.00; 10 day limit; Sawtooth NRA Headquarters, Ketchum, (208) 726-7672.

Camp Notes: This campground is the westernmost, and also the largest, of a half-dozen campgrounds located in the beautiful Salmon River Canyon in this section of the Sawtooth NRA. Opening dates are fairly late in spring not only because of snow cover, but because there's a lot more camper demand for the lake camps west of here.

Idaho 64

RIVERSIDE
Sawtooth National Recreation Area

Location: Central Idaho east of Stanley.

Access: From Idaho State Highway 75 at milepost 195 +.5 (5.1 miles east of Stanley, 50 miles southwest of Challis), turn right or left into the campground. (Campsites are both north and south of the highway.)

Facilities: 18 campsites in 2 loops; sites are small to medium-sized, with nominal to fair separation; parking pads are gravel, most are short to medium-length straight-ins; additional leveling may be required; fireplaces; firewood is available for gathering in the area; water at hand pumps; vault facilities; gravel driveways; limited+ supplies and services are available in Stanley.

Activities & Attractions: River rafting; fishing; hiking; Casino Creek Trail leads up into the White Cloud Peaks and to a number of mountain lakes; the Redfish Lake area, an exceptionally scenic (and popular) part of Sawtooth NRA, is 11 miles southwest.

Natural Features: Located along the forested bank of the Wild and Scenic Salmon River; most sites are nicely sheltered; some about half of the campsites are between the highway and the river, are a bit close together and also close to the highway; remaining sites, on a hillside across the highway from the river, are more roomy; White Cloud Peaks tower to greater than 11,000' to the south, and the Salmon River Mountains lie to the north; campground elevation 6100'.

Season, Fees & Phone: Mid-June to September; $6.00; 10 day limit; Sawtooth NRA Headquarters, Ketchum, (208) 726-7672.

Camp Notes: Though this campground is built on a slope and rather close to the highway, river access is excellent here, and the setting is beautiful. Riverside Campground is located just east of some of the most spectacular scenery in Idaho.

MORMON BEND
Sawtooth National Recreation Area

Location: Central Idaho east of Stanley.

Access: From Idaho State Highway 75 at mileposts 195 +.9 and 196 +.1 (there are 2 entrances, 5.5 miles east of Stanley, 50 miles southwest of Challis), turn south into the campground.

Facilities: 17 campsites; sites are medium-sized, mostly level, with average or better separation; parking pads are gravel, some are spacious enough to accommodate large rv's; good tent-pitching opportunities; fireplaces; firewood is available for gathering in the area; water at hand pumps; vault facilities; gravel driveways; limited+ supplies and services are available in Stanley.

Activities & Attractions: River rafting; fishing; hiking; Casino Creek Trail leads up into the White Cloud Peaks and to a number of mountain lakes; Sunbeam Hot Springs is 5 miles east; the Redfish Lake area, also part of Sawtooth NRA, is 12 miles southwest.

Natural Features: Located on a grassy riverbank in the timbered Salmon River Canyon; campsites at the eastern end, in a section dotted with clusters of trees, are more open; sites at the western end are more forested, but closer to the highway; a number of sites are riverside; the Salmon is a designated Wild and Scenic River along this segment; White Cloud Peaks rise to over 11,000' south of here, and the Salmon River Mountains are to the north; campground elevation 6000'.

Season, Fees & Phone: Mid-June to September; $6.00; 10 day limit; Sawtooth NRA Headquarters, Ketchum, (208) 726-7672.

Camp Notes: If you're planning to camp anywhere in Sawtooth NRA around Independence Day, Labor Day, or July 24th, you may want to consider adjusting your travel plans to either: (a) arrive early in order to grab a campsite. or (b) avoid the area until the smoke clears after the holidays. "OK", you say, "the reasons for the recommendations are obvious for Independence Day and Labor Day. But July 24th?" That's the day Mormons from throughout Idaho, Utah and neighboring states come here to celebrate the arrival of Brigham Young and the early Mormons at Salt Lake in 1847. It's a BIG time for friendly get-togethers and family reunions, and all the camps play to capacity crowds. As one Sawtooth employee told us: "I'm a Mormon, and I was 12 years old before I realized July 24th wasn't a national holiday".

BASIN CREEK
Sawtooth National Recreation Area

Location: Central Idaho east of Stanley.

Access: From Idaho State Highway 75 at milepost 197 +.5 (8 miles east of Stanley, 47 miles southwest of Challis), turn north into the campground.

Facilities: 15 campsites; sites are good-sized, level, with minimal separation for the most part; parking pads are gravel, mostly medium to long straight-ins; good tent-pitching opportunities; fireplaces; firewood is available for gathering in the vicinity; water at a hand pump; vault facilities; gravel driveways; camper supplies at Sunbeam, 4 miles east; limited+ supplies and services are available in Stanley.

Activities & Attractions: River rafting on the Wild and Scenic Salmon River; fishing; Basin Creek Road (gravel) leads off into the Salmon River Mountains and to a number of hiking trailheads; Yankee Fork Road leads north from Highway 75 (at Sunbeam) to the Custer Museum and historically significant mine diggings.

Natural Features: Located on an open grassy flat along Basin Creek where it flows into the Salmon River; the Salmon River Canyon, in this stretch, has steep timbered ridges above the south bank and steep rocky ridges rising from the north bank; campground vegetation consists of grass dotted with a few small conifers and some creekside brush; elevation 5900'.

Season, Fees & Phone: Mid-June to September; $6.00; 10 day limit; Sawtooth NRA Headquarters, Ketchum, (208) 726-7672.

Camp Notes: Of the several good campgrounds along this stretch of the river, this one is the most sunny (or least sheltered). If maneuvering a large vehicle is a consideration, this delta-like location would be ideal.

Idaho 67

O'BRIEN
Sawtooth National Recreation Area

Location: Central Idaho east of Stanley.

Access: From Idaho State Highway 75 at milepost 204 +.5 (15 miles east of Stanley, 40 miles southwest of Challis), turn south onto a gravel access road which leads down a short but steep hill and east across a wooden bridge over the Salmon River; Upper O'Brien Campground is located directly on the east side of the bridge; Lower O'Brien Campground is 0.2 mile farther east along the south bank of the river.

Facilities: 8 campsites in Upper O'Brien and 12 campsites in Lower O'Brien; sites are small+, with nominal to fair separation; parking pads are gravel, most are straight-ins, a few are pull-throughs; some pads may require a little additional leveling; good tent-pitching opportunities beneath tall trees; fireplaces or fire rings; firewood is available for gathering in the area; water at hand pumps; vault facilities; gravel driveways; camper supplies in Sunbeam, 3 miles west; limited+ supplies and services are available in Stanley.

Activities & Attractions: Fishing; river floating; hiking trail leads south along Warm Springs Creek into the White Cloud Peaks; Sunbeam Hot Springs, 3 miles east; Yankee Fork Road leads north from Highway 75 (at Sunbeam) to the Custer Museum, and a backcountry rich in mining history.

Natural Features: Located in the steep-walled, narrow Salmon River Canyon, with towering, forested peaks to the north and south; all units are situated on a slight slope along the riverbank in an open forest of tall timber, light underbrush and a carpet of pine needles; elevation 5800'.

Season, Fees & Phone: June to September; $6.00; 10 day limit; Sawtooth NRA Headquarters, Ketchum, (208) 726-7672.

Camp Notes: Lower O'Brien Campground has sites closer to the river, while Upper O'Brien's sites are on a short shelf above the stream. This is right on the eastern edge of some superscenic country!

Idaho 68

HOLMAN CREEK
Sawtooth National Recreation Area

Location: Central Idaho east of Stanley.

Access: From Idaho State Highway 75 at milepost 214 +.8 (25 miles east of Stanley, 30 miles southwest of Challis), turn south onto a gravel access road; campsites start about 75 yards south of the highway.

Facilities: 13 campsites; sites are small+, well-spaced, with little visual separation; parking pads are gravel, level, short to medium-length straight-ins; tent-pitching areas are good-sized and fairly level; fireplaces; a small amount of firewood is available in the immediate area, so gathering on national forest lands prior to arrival is suggested; water at a hand pump; vault facilities; gravel driveways; camper supplies and services in Clayton, 8 miles east; limited supplies in Stanley and Challis; nearest sources of adequate supplies are Salmon, 90 miles east, or Ketchum, 80 miles south.

Activities & Attractions: Fishing; river floating; access to the Salmon River, across the highway, is a little easier here than farther to the east; hiking; the heart of the Sawtooth National Recreation Area is 30 miles west.

Natural Features: Located just inside the northeast boundary of Challis National Forest and Sawtooth National Recreation Area; sites are in a single row at the base of a timbered slope; conifers dot the hillside which borders the sites on the south; sparse grass and sagebrush cover the flat between the campground and the river; Holman Creek flows into the Salmon River here, where the valley is narrower and more heavily forested than farther east; forested White Cloud Peaks are to the south; peaks of the Salmon River Range rise to the north; elevation 5600'.

Season, Fees & Phone: Open all year, subject to weather conditions, with limited services in winter; $5.00; 10 day limit; Sawtooth NRA Headquarters, Ketchum, (208) 726-7672.

Camp Notes: This campground is perhaps a happy compromise: more forested than the BLM campgrounds to the east, yet lower in altitude (and therefore less snowbound) than campgrounds to the west. Holman Creek is the easternmost campground in Sawtooth NRA. In addition to all of the foregoing developed campgrounds (beginning with Stanley Lake), the recreation area also maintains a number of 'undeveloped' camp areas with the most basic facilities (vaults), no drinking water, and a 16 day camping limit. A stop at the ranger stations in Stanley or Lowman, or the Sawtooth NRA visitor centers north of Ketchum or at Redfish Lake, will provide you with information about these other camping opportunities.

Idaho 69

EAST FORK
Public Lands/BLM Recreation Area

Location: Central Idaho southwest of Challis.

Access: From Idaho State Highway 75 at milepost 227 (17 miles southwest of the junction of Highway 75 & U.S. Highway 93 near Challis, 38 miles northeast of Stanley), turn northwest into the campground.

Facilities: 10 campsites; sites are rather small, level, with minimal separation; parking pads are gravel pull-throughs or pull-offs, large enough to accommodate medium-sized vehicles; tent spots are small and grassy; small sun shelters for some table areas; fireplaces; a very limited amount of firewood is available in the area, so b-y-o is recommended; water at faucets; vault facilities; gravel driveway; minimal supplies in Clayton, 4 miles west; limited supplies and services are available in Challis, 20 miles northeast.

Activities & Attractions: Fishing; river floating; a foot trail leads from the campsites down to the river's edge; access from the west, along either Highway 75 or Highway 21, is through the Sawtooth National Recreation Area, with the spectacular scenery of the rugged Sawtooth Range.

Natural Features: Located in the Salmon River Valley on a somewhat barren bluff overlooking the Salmon River, where the East Fork of the Salmon enters the Salmon; some brush and small trees are along the river, but vegetation in the campground itself consists of sparse grass with a few trees planted for future shelter; a steep canyon wall frames the opposite riverbank; typically breezy; the Salmon River Range rises to almost 10,000' to the north; campground elevation 5400'.

Season, Fees & Phone: Open all year, with limited services and no fee in winter; $5.00; 14 day limit; Bureau of Land Management Salmon District (208) 756-5400.

Camp Notes: The facilities at this campground are some of the best in this stretch of Highway 75. The campsites and the surrounding barren terrain are, however, quite exposed to the effects of the prevailing winds and the summer sun.

Idaho 70

BAYHORSE
Public Lands/BLM Recreation Area

Location: Central Idaho southwest of Challis.

Access: From Idaho State Highway 75 at milepost 237 (7 miles southwest of the junction of Highway 75 & U.S. Highway 93 near Challis, 48 miles northeast of Stanley), turn northwest into the campground.

Facilities: 12 campsites in 3 loops; sites are medium-sized, well-spaced, but with virtually no visual separation; parking pads are gravel, level, short to medium-length straight-ins; tent sites are level, grassy and quite sizeable; barbecue grills and/or fire rings; a very limited amount of firewood is available for gathering in the vicinity, so b-y-o is recommended; water at a hand pump; vault facilities; gravel driveways; limited supplies in Challis, 10 miles north, or Stanley, 48 miles west; nearest source of adequate supplies and services is Salmon, 70 miles northeast.

Activities & Attractions: Fishing; good river access; a small wooden footbridge spans an irrigation canal which flows between the campsites and the river; nearby Bayhorse Creek Road follows the creek for 7 miles to the Bayhorse and Little Bayhorse Lakes, at almost 8600'; hiking.

Natural Features: Located on a grassy, sage flat along the Salmon River, just below the level of the highway; campground vegetation consists of sparse grass, with some brush and trees along the river; the

Salmon River Mountains rise to almost 10,000' just to the west, and the White Cloud Peaks tower to over 11,000' to the southwest; campground elevation 5300'.

Season, Fees & Phone: Open all year, with limited services and no fee in winter; $5.00; 14 day limit; Bureau of Land Management Salmon District (208) 756-5400.

Camp Notes: Bayhorse is located in a fairly dry river valley flanked by high, dry hills and distant timbered mountains. Shelter is very limited, and, though the river is close at hand, there's a thirsty look about the locale. You may want to stock up with supplies before coming through this stretch of highway.

Idaho 71

SPRING GULCH
Public Lands/BLM Recreation Area

Location: Central Idaho southwest of Challis.

Access: From U.S. Highway 93 at milepost 256 +.7 (10 miles northeast of Challis, 50 miles south of Salmon), turn northwest into the campground; (the campground entrance is just 100 yards west of a Salmon River bridge.)

Facilities: 12 campsites in 2 loops; sites are medium-sized, level, with minimal to fair separation; most units have gravel, pull-off parking aprons which could accommodate larger vehicles; small to medium-sized, grassy tent areas; barbecue grills or fire rings; a limited amount of firewood is available for gathering in the vicinity; water at a hand pump (unreliable, so b-y-o); vault facilities; gravel/dirt driveway; limited supplies in Challis; adequate supplies and services are available in Salmon.

Natural Features: Located on a short bluff above the Salmon River; campground vegetation consists of patches of tall grass, some eye-level brush and a few tall cottonwoods; the river valley is flanked by dry, semi-barren mountains on either side; forested peaks of the Salmon River Mountains, rising to almost 10,000', are visible to the west; campground elevation 5100'.

Activities & Attractions: Limited access to the river; river floating; 'carry-in' boat launch area; good stream fishing here and on nearby Morgan Creek.

Season, Fees & Phone: Open all year, with limited services in winter; no fee; 14 day limit; Bureau of Land Management Salmon District (208) 756-5400.

Camp Notes: In addition to Spring Gulch, there are two other small BLM recreation sites in the vicinity: Cottonwood (5 miles east), and Morgan Creek (5 miles west and 4 miles north off Highway 93 on Morgan Creek Road). Of the trio, Spring Gulch has the most complete services and is the most easily accessible.

Idaho
South East
Please refer to the Idaho map in the Appendix

Idaho 72

MACKAY RESERVOIR
Public Lands/BLM Recreation Area

Location: Central Idaho northwest of Arco.

Access: From U. S. Highway 93 at milepost 113 +.6 (4.8 miles north of the town of Mackay, 46 miles south of Challis), turn west into the campground.

Facilities: 58 campsites in 2 loops; sites are small to medium-sized, with minimal to fair separation; Loop A has gravel, short to medium-length straight-in parking pads; Loop B has gravel pull-offs or long, level, parallel pull-throughs; some large tent sites in Loop A, but they may be a bit slopey; barbecue grills, plus some fireplaces; a few sites have sun/wind shelters; water at faucets throughout; vault facilities; holding tank disposal station; gravel driveways; limited supplies are available in Mackay, Challis and Arco.

Activities & Attractions: Boating; fishing; 4-wheel-drive trails lead from near here up into Challis National Forest.

Natural Features: Located on the east/northeast shore of Mackay Reservoir in the Big Lost River Valley; Loop A is on a sage slope overlooking the lake, Loop B is closer to the shore; the area surrounding the reservoir is semi-arid, with a few poplars planted in the campground area; the reservoir was formed by damming the Big Lost River; sage and grass-covered hills surround the lake; dry rocky peaks of the Lost River Range soar to well-above 12,600' to the east; the White Knob Mountains rise to nearly 11,300' in the southwest; campground elevation 5900'.

Season, Fees & Phone: May to October; $5.00; 14 day limit; Salmon BLM office (208) 756-5400.

Camp Notes: Considering the semi-arid conditions and the fairly constant breeze/wind/gale that persists here, this is a fine campground. The lake is large enough to offer good water recreation opportunities in an otherwise lakeless part of Idaho. This region is a study in contrasts: the semi-arid valley with its 1500-acre reservoir and abundance of small, seasonal streams, all topped by Idaho's highest point, 12,655' Borah Peak about a dozen miles north in the Lost River Range.

Idaho 73

LAVA FLOW
Craters of the Moon National Monument

Location: Central Idaho west of Arco.

Access: From U.S. Highways 20/26 at milepost 229 +.4 (18 miles southwest of Arco, 24 miles northeast of Carey), turn south into the Craters of the Moon National Monument and proceed 0.3 mile to the entrance station; continue for 0.1 mile beyond the entrance, then turn right into the campground.

Facilities: 52 campsites; (a group camp area is also available, by reservation only); sites are small to medium-sized, with minimal to fair separation; parking surfaces are cindered straight-ins or pull-offs, many are long enough to accommodate medium to large rv's; some additional leveling may be necessary; nice, medium to large, cleared tent areas; barbecue grills (charcoal fires only); water at faucets throughout; restrooms; paved driveways; limited supplies and services are available in Arco.

Activities & Attractions: 7-mile loop drive with side spurs; foot trails lead to fascinating features including the Craters of the Moon Wilderness Area; ranger-guided hikes in season; geological and historical exhibits at the visitor center; naturalist programs on summer evenings; x-c skiing on the loop road (best January-March).

Natural Features: Located on a rocky hill with many sites in among a number of knolls and dips and rock pockets; campground vegetation consists mostly of large and small brush; Craters of the Moon is so-named because of the moonscape terrain that encompasses an 83-square-mile volcanic area with lava flows, cinder cones and other unusual geological features; elevation 5900'.

Season, Fees & Phone: Open all year, with limited services and no fee October to May; $9.00; 14 day limit; park headquarters (208) 527-3257.

Camp Notes: Craters of the Moon has been called "the strangest 83 square miles on the North American Continent". Best time to visit is mid-June. Daytime high temperatures are still fairly moderate at that time, and the brilliant wildflowers blooming among the black lava rocks produce dazzling springtime displays. The volcanic features in this park are truly fascinating. The campground terrain is unique, and it's not uncommon for campers (particularly younger ones) to vividly imagine that they've been transported to somewhere else in the galaxy.

Idaho 74

BRUNEAU DUNES
Bruneau Dunes State Park

Location: Southwest Idaho south of Mountain Home.

Access: From Idaho State Highway 78 at milepost 84 +.3 (2 miles east of the junction of Idaho State Highways 51 & 78 south of Mountain Home, 14 miles west of the hamlet of Hammett), turn south onto a paved access road; proceed 1 mile to the park entrance; continue for 1.7 miles to the campground.

Facilities: 48 campsites, including 32 with partial hook-ups; sites are average-sized with minimal separation; parking pads are gravel, fairly level, medium to long straight-ins; excellent tent-pitching opportunities; many sites have sun/wind shelters; water at faucets throughout; restrooms with solar-heated showers; fireplaces; b-y-o firewood; paved driveways; adequate+ supplies and services are available in Mountain Home, 17 miles north.

Activities & Attractions: Sand dune exploration, limited to foot traffic; 5 miles of hiking and nature trails lead through marshes, desert prairie and sand dunes; equestrian trail; visitor center with interpretive displays; fishing for bass and bluegills; motorless boating on Bruneau Lake; boat launch; day use area.

Natural Features: Located on tree-dotted, mown grass surrounded by treeless sage hills and plains; small Bruneau Lake is within the park; typically breezy; temperatures can reach 110° F in summer to well below zero in winter; less than 10 inches of rainfall per year; elevation 2500'.

Season, Fees & Phone: Open all year; please see Appendix for standard Idaho state park fees; 14 day limit; park office (208) 366-7919.

Camp Notes: Bruneau Dunes is situated in a distinctively different environment. The terrain surrounding the park is barren, but the campground is rather inviting. The largest single sand dune in North America rises to nearly 500' above the level of this campground.

Idaho 75

THREE ISLAND
Three Island State Park

Location: Southwest Idaho southeast of Mountain Home.

Access: From Interstate 84 Exit 120 (eastbound) or Exit 121 (westbound) for Glenns Ferry, drive 1 mile on Business Route 84 into midtown Glenns Ferry; turn south onto Commercial Street and proceed to a "T" intersection; turn west (right) onto a paved local road and continue west to the park entrance; the campground is 0.1 mile beyond the entrance; (the well-signed route totals 2.6 miles from I-84 to the park.)

Facilities: 50 campsites, many with partial hookups; sites are medium-sized, level, with minimal separation; parking pads are paved straight-ins, typically spacious enough to accommodate large rv's; good tent-pitching opportunities on mown lawns; fireplaces; b-y-o firewood; restrooms with showers; holding tank disposal station; paved driveways; limited supplies and services are available in Glenns Ferry.

Activities & Attractions: Interpretive center has displays and historical information; Conestoga wagon display; the park maintains a small herd of buffalo and longhorn cattle; designated swimming beach; day use area with shelter.

Natural Features: Located on a bluff above the north bank of the Snake River; in summer, the mown lawns, dotted with a few tall hardwoods, stand in sharp contrast to the surrounding sage plains; elevation 2500'.

Season, Fees & Phone: Open all year, with limited services in winter; please see Appendix for standard Idaho state park fees; 14 day limit; park office (208) 366-2394.

Camp Notes: Three Island Crossing is a site where many Oregon Trail travelers crossed the Snake River to the Snake's north bank in order to follow a more advantageous route West. The campground is, at times, bothered by disagreeable odors, if the wind is from the wrong direction. Many campers (and midsummer insects) are not noticeably distressed.

Idaho 76

DEVIL'S GARDEN
Massacre Rocks State Park

Location: Southeast Idaho southwest of Pocatello.

Access: From Interstate 86 Exit 28, signed for "Massacre Rocks State Park", (43 miles east of Burley, 12 miles west of American Falls), proceed east on the north frontage road for 0.8 mile; turn left into the park; the campground is just beyond the visitor center.

Facilities: 52 campsites with partial hookups; (a group camp is also available); sites are small to medium-sized, with minimal separation; parking pads are gravel, and vary from short straight-ins to long pull-throughs; additional leveling may be required; tent-pitching could be a challenge; framed and leveled, gravel table pads; fireplaces; b-y-o firewood; restrooms with showers; gravel driveways; holding tank disposal station; adequate supplies and services are available in American Falls.

Activities & Attractions: Boat launch; visitor center provides exhibits and information; campfire programs during the summer season; "Meadows" self-guided nature trail leads down to the river.

Natural Features: Located on a hill overlooking the Snake River; the terrain is quite rocky, with some tall grass and short junipers; the most impressive attraction is "Devil's Garden", a unique geological formation with jagged lava rocks jutting up from the arid plains; elevation 4400'.

Season, Fees & Phone: Open all year, with limited services in winter; please see Appendix for standard Idaho state park fees; 14 day limit; park office (208) 548-2672

Camp Notes: The unusual terrain and arid conditions of the park stand in contrast to the impressive Snake River. From some campsites atop the hill the views are outstanding--across the plains and across the river to a prominent rock escarpment. This area was called "Gate of Death" or "Devil's Gate" by travelers on the old Oregon Trail because of fears of being bushwhacked by the Shoshone, who could easily be hidden among the rock formations. (If you're a bit squeamish about camping in places named for grisly events, you might take some solace in knowing that, according to historical reports, the "massacre" in "Massacre Rocks" never really happened.)

Idaho 77

TWIN SPRINGS
Curlew National Grassland

Location: Southern Idaho southwest of Pocatello.

Access: From Idaho State Highway 37 at milepost 32 +.5 (36 miles south of Interstate 86 Exit 36, 10 miles north of Holbrook), turn west onto a gravel access road and continue 0.1 mile to the campground.

Facilities: 5 campsites; sites are good-sized, fairly level with average separation; parking aprons are gravel, and sizable enough for large vehicles; small to medium-sized tents could be pitched among the tall sage and boulders; several sun/wind shelters; fire rings; b-y-o firewood is recommended; water at a hand pump; vault facilities; pack-it-in/pack-it-out trash removal system; gravel driveway; minimal supplies in Rockland, 23 miles north; limited to adequate supplies and services are available in Malad City, 32 miles east.

Activities & Attractions: Historic significance.

Natural Features: Located in a dry valley between 2 barren ridges; the treeless setting has only sparse grass and some massive sagebrush for vegetation; a tiny rivulet trickles through an otherwise harsh habitat; the barren Blue Spring Hills rise to the east; elevation 4700'.

Season, Fees & Phone: Open all year; no fee; 14 day limit; Malad Ranger District (208) 766-4743.

Camp Notes: Twin Springs was a very important water stop for gold rush travelers about 1849. Hudspeth's Trail is still visible on the ridge above the camp to the west. Though the campground itself is certainly not one of the best, it does have the necessary requirements, and it is the one and only public camp for many miles.

Idaho 78

HENRY'S LAKE
Henry's Lake State Park

Location: Eastern Idaho west of Yellowstone National Park.

Access: From U.S. Highway 20 at milepost 401 (16 miles west of West Yellowstone, Montana, 41 miles north of Ashton), turn west onto a paved, 2-lane road; proceed 2 miles, then turn north (right) into the campground.

Facilities: 32 campsites; sites are small+, with minimal separation; parking pads are paved, fairly well leveled, medium to long straight-ins; grassy areas will accommodate tents nicely; fireplaces; firewood is usually for sale, or b-y-o; water at several faucets; restrooms with showers; holding tank disposal station; paved driveways; gas and groceries at Mack's Inn, 9 miles south.

Activities & Attractions: Boating; boat launch; generally good fishing for trout and whitefish; short nature trail starts at the east end of the campground; trail around the lake.

Natural Features: Located on a grassy slope above the south shore of Henry's Lake, a natural lake enlarged by a dam on Henry's Fork of the Snake River; bordered by an immense sage flat; the lake lies in a great basin with mountains in all directions; elevation 6500'.

Season, Fees & Phone: May to late-September; please see Appendix for standard Idaho state park fees; 14 day limit; park office (208) 558-7523.

Camp Notes: Spectacular sunsets are common here. Just slightly short of spectacular is the fishing in this fairly shallow (12-foot average depth) lake and it's associated river. A rainbow-cutthroat hybrid is said to be the favorite fish. Insects can occasionally be bothersome, but are usually kept at bay by a good breeze during daylight hours.

BIG SPRINGS
Targhee National Forest

Location: Eastern Idaho west of Yellowstone National Park.

Access: From U.S. Highway 20 at milepost 392 +.6 at the south edge of the settlement of Mack's Inn, (25 miles southwest of West Yellowstone, Montana, 32 miles north of Ashton), turn southeast onto Big Springs Road (paved); proceed southeast then northeast for 4.7 miles, then turn east (right) into the campground.

Facilities: 17 campsites; sites are average to large, level, with mostly fair separation; parking pads are paved or gravel, medium to long straight-ins or pull-offs; large, level tent spots; assorted fire facilities; firewood is usually available for gathering in the area; water at several faucets; vault facilities; paved driveways; gas and camper supplies in Mack's Inn; adequate supplies and services are available in West Yellowstone and Ashton.

Activities & Attractions: Big Springs; historically significant John Sack's Cabin is adjacent to the Springs; interpretive trail; Big Springs Water Trail and boat ramp, 1 mile southwest.

Natural Features: Located on a lightly forested flat near Big Springs, a principal source for Henry's Fork of the Snake River; tall grass and a few scattered pines provide some shelter and separation for the sites; the peaks of the Rocky Mountains and Continental Divide rise within a few miles to the east; elevation 6400'.

Season, Fees & Phone: May to September; $7.00; 14 day limit; Island Park Ranger District (208) 558-7301.

Camp Notes: Though the campground setting itself is rather nondescript, the nearby phenomenon, and the campground's proximity to Yellowstone Park, are factors making a stay here worth considering. Big Springs has a constant temperature of 52° F, and 120 million gallons of water flow through here daily, thus making the river an ideal spawning ground for trout. The fish and their fry feast on swarms of mosquitoes.

FLAT ROCK
Targhee National Forest

Location: Eastern Idaho northeast of Idaho Falls.

Access: From U.S. Highway 20 at mileposts 392 and 392 +.5 (2 entrances) on the south edge of Mack's Inn, (25 miles southwest of West Yellowstone, Montana, 32 miles north of Ashton), turn west into the campground.

Facilities: 34 campsites in 2 loops; sites are mostly medium to large; sites in Loop B are more level and have a little better separation than those in Loop A; parking pads are gravel, many are large enough to accommodate medium-sized vehicles; some leveled, framed, gravel tent pads; water at several faucets; restrooms, plus supplemental vault facilities; holding tank disposal station nearby; fireplaces and barbecue grills; firewood is available for gathering in the area; gravel driveways; gas and camper supplies are available in Mack's Inn; adequate supplies and services are available in Ashton and West Yellowstone.

Activities & Attractions: Fishing and canoeing on Henry's Fork; hiking to nearby Coffeepot Rapids; boating, boat launch and fishing on nearby Island Park Reservoir; Yellowstone National Park is 30 miles northeast.

Natural Features: Located on Henry's Fork of the Snake River a few miles downstream from Big Springs, the river's headwaters; sites in Loop A are located very near the highway on a fairly open hillside in a terraced arrangement; sites in Loop B are located on a forested flat where sites are more level and have better shelter provided by tall conifers and considerable underbrush; tall peaks of the Rocky Mountains rise to the north and east; elevation 6400'.

Season, Fees & Phone: May to September; $9.00; 14 day limit; Island Park Ranger District (208) 558-7301.

Camp Notes: Flat Rock Campground seems to be a fairly well-designed facility, except, perhaps, for the sites closest to the busy Yellowstone Highway. It's a nice place--good fishin' around here, too.

COFFEE POT
Targhee National Forest

Location: Eastern Idaho northeast of Idaho Falls.

Access: From U.S. Highway 20 at milepost 392+.3 (0.2 mile south of Mack's Inn, 25 miles southwest of West Yellowstone, Montana, 32 miles north of Ashton), turn west onto a gravel forest road; proceed west and south for 1 mile to a fork in the road; bear right and continue for 0.5 mile west, then turn right into the campground.

Facilities: 14 campsites; sites are mostly medium-sized, fairly level, with minimal to average separation; parking pads are gravel, mostly level, and some are long enough to accommodate medium-sized vehicles; some nice grassy spots for tents in among the new growth of conifers; fireplaces; firewood is available for gathering in the vicinity; water at several faucets; vault facilities; gravel driveways with large turnaround loops at both ends; gas and camper supplies in Mack's Inn; adequate supplies and services are available in Ashton, and West Yellowstone, Montana.

Activities & Attractions: Fishing; hiking trail leads from the south end of the campground to Coffee Pot Rapids; Harriman State Park, 15 miles south; boating and fishing on nearby Island Park Reservoir.

Natural Features: Located on the grassy east riverbank of Henry's Fork of the Snake River; campsites are lightly to moderately shaded/sheltered by conifers and some brush; high mountain peaks rise to the north and east; elevation 6300'.

Season, Fees & Phone: May to September; $9.00; 14 day limit; Island Park R. D. (208) 558-7301.

Camp Notes: Coffee Pot Campground (also known as Upper Coffee Pot), is situated on a quiet stretch of Henry's Fork that's wide, crystal-clear, and lazily meanders through an open forest. Trout fishing on Henry's Fork is considered by many anglers to be World Class.

McCrea Bridge
Targhee National Forest

Location: Eastern Idaho west of Yellowstone National Park.

Access: From U.S. Highway 20 at milepost 389 +.2 (29 miles north of Ashton, 29 miles southwest of West Yellowstone, Montana), turn west onto Fremont County Road A2 (paved); travel 2.1 miles west, then turn south (left) into the campground.

Facilities: 24 campsites in 2 loops; sites are average to large, with minimal to nominal separation; parking pads are gravel, mostly medium-length, straight-ins or pull-throughs; many pads may require additional leveling; some large, grassy tent spots; barbecue grills; some firewood is available for gathering in the vicinity; water at several faucets; vault facilities; gravel driveways; gas and groceries+ in Mack's Inn and Island Park, 3 miles north and south, respectively; adequate supplies and services are available in Ashton and West Yellowstone.

Activities & Attractions: Fishing; boating; 2 boat launches are nearby; Yellowstone National Park is less than an hour's drive east.

Natural Features: Located on the grassy east bank of Henry's Fork of the Snake River at the inlet to Island Park Reservoir; rolling, grassy hillsides with a few thin pines are around the perimeter of the campground; views of distant forested ridges and mountains from several sites; river views from most sites; elevation 6200'.

Season, Fees & Phone: May to October; $7.00; 14 day limit; Island Park Ranger Dist. (208) 558-7301.

Camp Notes: Since it's right along the river, McCrea Bridge Campground is very popular with Island Park recreationers. Actually, in this area the river merges with the lake to form a long, thin arm (or perhaps more properly, a finger). The narrow inlet is respectably navigable by most boats along the four winding miles southwesterly to the main body of the lake.

BUTTERMILK
Targhee National Forest

Location: Eastern Idaho west of Yellowstone National Park.

Access: From U. S. Highway 20 at milepost 389 +.2 (29 miles north of Ashton, 29 miles southwest of West Yellowstone, Montana), turn west onto Fremont County Road A2 (paved); proceed west 1.8 miles, then turn south (left) onto Forest Road 126; continue south and east for 2.6 miles (still paved); turn south (right) onto Meadow Drive; continue for a final 0.2 mile south to the campground. (Note: Forest Road 126 is an elongated loop which connects to County Road A2 at a point 0.8 mile from the main highway in addition to the point 1.8 miles from the highway listed above; the access from 1.8 miles off the highway is the preferred, i.e., paved route.)

Facilities: 60 campsites in 4 loops; most sites are medium to large with good separation; most parking pads are reasonably level pull-throughs, spacious enough to accommodate larger rv's; many large, grassy tent spots; fire rings, plus a few barbecue grills; some firewood is available for gathering in the vicinity; water at several faucets; vault facilities; gravel driveways; gas and groceries+ in the Mack's Inn/Island Park area; adequate supplies and services are available in Ashton and West Yellowstone.

Activities & Attractions: Boating; boat launch and docks are nearby; fishing.

Natural Features: Located near the shore at the northeast tip of Island Park Reservoir, created by Island Park Dam across Henry's Fork of the Snake River; light to moderately dense pines shelter most of the campground, with just a few sites out in the open; most sites are on a grassy flat, a few are on a hillside; distant timbered ridges are visible east and north; elevation 6200'.

Season, Fees & Phone: May to October; $7.00; 14 day limit; may be operated by concessionaire; Island Park Ranger District (208) 558-7301.

Camp Notes: Island Park is a popular recreation area, but there is usually space for one more camper in Buttermilk Campground.

Idaho 84

BUFFALO
Targhee National Forest

Location: Eastern Idaho northeast of Idaho Falls.

Access: From U.S. Highway 20 at milepost 387 +.4 (1 mile north of Island Park, 27 miles north of Ashton, 30 miles southwest of West Yellowstone, Montana), turn east into the campground.

Facilities: 127 campsites in 7 loops; sites are medium to medium+, level, with minimal to good separation; parking pads are gravel or paved, and some are long enough to accommodate the largest rv's; some good, large, level tent-pitching areas; fireplaces and/or barbecue grills; firewood is available for gathering in the vicinity, or is often for sale; water at faucets throughout; restrooms, plus supplemental vault facilities; holding tank disposal station; gravel or paved driveways; gas and camper supplies+ in Island Park; adequate supplies and services are available in Ashton.

Activities & Attractions: Fishing on the Buffalo River; boating and fishing on nearby Island Park Reservoir; Yellowstone National Park is less than an hour's drive northeast.

Natural Features: Located on a fairly open forested flat along the north bank of the wide and slow-moving Buffalo River, about 2 miles upstream of the Buffalo's confluence with Henry's Fork of the Snake River; campground vegetation consists of tall grass and some new-growth timber in some loops, and more dense forest in other loops; Island Park Reservoir, formed on Henry's Fork, is a mile west; the Rockies rise to the north and east; elevation 6300'.

Season, Fees & Phone: May to October; $9.00; 14 day limit; may be operated by concessionaire; Island Park Ranger District (208) 558-7301.

Camp Notes: This is a BIG campground. Oddly enough, irrespective of its proximity to Yellowstone and the Island Park area, it doesn't swell to capacity very often. Occasionally, the river and its attendant campground are spelled in the traditional manner, Buffaloe, with an archaic *e* at the end.

Idaho 85

BOX CANYON
Targhee National Forest

Location: Eastern Idaho northeast of Idaho Falls.

Access: From U.S. Highway 20 at milepost 386 (0.2 mile south of Island Park, 26 miles north of Ashton, 31 miles southwest of West Yellowstone, Montana), turn west onto a gravel access road and continue for 2 miles to the campground.

Facilities: 19 campsites; sites are medium to medium+, with minimal to fair separation; parking pads are gravel, and many have adequate space for larger rv's; some good spots for tents on the grassy slope;

fire rings, plus some barbecue grills; a limited amount of firewood is available for gathering in the area; water at several faucets; vault facilities; gas and camper supplies + in Island Park; adequate supplies and services are available in Ashton and West Yellowstone.

Activities & Attractions: Excellent fly fishing on the river (artificial flies or lures only, catch and release); river access via a short trail; boating on nearby Island Park Reservoir; Harriman State Park, 10 miles south, is the center of an extensive wildlife refuge; it has a visitor center, historical exhibits and tours, but no public camping facilities; Yellowstone National Park is 35 miles northeast.

Natural Features: Located near the Henry's Fork of the Snake River; campground vegetation consists of tall grass, aspens and some second growth timber; the Rocky Mountains rise to heights greater than 10,000' to the east; campground elevation 6300'.

Season, Fees & Phone: May to September; $7.00; 14 day limit; Island Park Ranger District (208) 558-7301.

Camp Notes: This relatively secluded camping area is just far enough from the main highway to be usually quiet. Henry's Fork adds to the serene atmosphere by slowly meandering by within a stone's throw (or a fly's cast) of many campsites.

Idaho 86

RIVERSIDE
Targhee National Forest

Location: Eastern Idaho northeast of Idaho Falls.

Access: From U.S. Highway 20 at milepost 375 +.5 (9 miles south of Island Park, 15 miles north of Ashton, 42 miles southwest of West Yellowstone, Montana), turn southeast onto Forest Road 304 (paved); drive 0.7 mile to the campground.

Facilities: 58 campsites in 2 loops, plus a riverside strip of sites; sites are small + to medium-sized, with nominal to fair separation; parking pads are gravel or paved, and are many are pull-throughs or straight-ins spacious enough to accommodate large rv's; some additional leveling may be necessary; fire rings and barbecue grills; some firewood is available for gathering in the vicinity; water at several faucets; vault facilities; paved/oiled gravel driveways; gas and camper supplies + in Island Park; adequate services and supplies are available in Ashton.

Activities & Attractions: Trout fishing; canoeing/floating; Island Park Reservoir, just 8 miles north, also offers most water recreation opportunities; Harriman State Park, with a visitor center and numerous organized activities, is 5 miles north.

Natural Features: Located along and above Henry's Fork of the Snake River; a number of sites are along the riverbank, and they tend to be more open than the sites away from the river on a forested slope; a short, rocky ridge is just across the river, and there's a midstream island for added interest; though mountains are not visible from the campground itself, the Rockies rise just to the east; elevation 6200'.

Season, Fees & Phone: May to mid-September; $9.00; 14 day limit; may be operated by concessionaire; Ashton Ranger District (208) 652-7442.

Camp Notes: Henry's Fork provides some of the West's best fly fishing. If you're into angling, it usually is worthwhile to stop at one of the local sport shops to find out which pattern is currently hot on the river.

Idaho 87

WARM RIVER
Targhee National Forest

Location: Eastern Idaho northeast of Idaho Falls.

Access: From the junction of U.S. Highway 20 at milepost 360 +.6 and Idaho State Highway 47 in Ashton, travel east/northeast on Highway 47 for 8.9 miles; drive east (right) across the Warm River Bridge and turn south (right) onto Fish Creek Road; continue for 0.2 mile on this paved road, then turn south (right) into the campground.

Facilities: 24 campsites, including 6 sites designated for tents; (a group camp is also available, by reservation); sites are average or better in size, with nominal to fair separation; parking pads are paved, level and several are long enough for large rv's; adequate space for most tents; tent pads for some sites; fire rings and barbecue grills; firewood is available for gathering in the vicinity; water at several faucets; vault facilities; paved driveways; adequate supplies and services are available in Ashton.

Activities & Attractions: Stream fishing; an old wooden bridge spans the river between sites; picnic shelter at the day use area; grand views along the highway to the north toward deep, steep Bear Gulch, and to Upper and Lower Mesa Falls.

Natural Features: Located in a narrow, forested canyon along both grassy banks of the Warm River, which flows westward into Henry's Fork of the Snake River; vegetation consists mostly of open grassy areas, with some trees for shelter, especially toward the east end of the campground; campground elevation 5200'.

Season, Fees & Phone: May to mid-September; $9.00 for a standard site, $7.00 for a tent site; 14 day limit; Ashton Ranger District (208) 652-7442.

Camp Notes: Warm River Campground is nestled in a beautiful canyon near a superscenic mountain drive. There are two small campgrounds, called Grandview and Pole Bridge, near Lower Mesa Falls, north of here. They offer super scenery but their facilities are definitely second-best to those at Warm River.

Idaho 88

FALLS
Targhee/Caribou National Forests

Location: Southeast Idaho east of Idaho Falls.

Access: From U.S. Highway 26 at milepost 373 +.6 (3 miles west of Swan Valley, 40 miles east of Idaho Falls), turn south onto a gravel road which crosses a bridge and follows the south-west bank of the Snake River; proceed east for 1.2 miles to a fork; take the left fork and continue for 1.2 miles east along the river; turn left into the campground.

Facilities: 24 campsites; sites are spacious, level, with very good separation; parking pads are gravel, mostly short to medium-length straight-ins; some very nice, large, grassy tent spots; fireplaces or fire rings; firewood is available for gathering in the area; water at faucets throughout; vault facilities; gravel driveways; camper supplies in Swan Valley; complete supplies and services are available in Idaho Falls.

Activities & Attractions: Fishing; river floating (boat ramp nearby off Highway 26 at Spring Creek); Fall Creek Trail leads south along the creek and up into the Caribou Range.

Natural Features: Located on the south bank of the Snake River, just below the confluence of Fall Creek with the Snake; tall cottonwoods, light underbrush, and tall grass are the predominant vegetation in the campground; the river follows several channels along this section, thus forming a number of islands in the river; low ridges with light vegetation border the river on the north and south banks; elevation 5300.

Season, Fees & Phone: May to October; $5.00; 14 day limit; Palisades Ranger District, Idaho Falls, (208) 523-1412.

Camp Notes: Falls Campground is not heavily used. It's tucked away in a very pleasant and secluded spot, and is yet only a couple of miles from a main thoroughfare. A picturesque, multi-stream waterfall is visible from the south bank of the river, just west of the campground. The countryside in this section of the Snake River Valley is a pastoral picture.

Idaho 89

PINE CREEK
Targhee National Forest

Location: Southeast Idaho east of Idaho Falls near the Wyoming border.

Access: From Idaho State Highway 31 at a point 15 miles east of Swan Valley, and 6 miles west of Victor, turn south into the campground.

Facilities: 11 campsites; sites are medium to large and fairly well separated; parking pads are gravel, fairly level, mostly medium to medium+ straight-ins; small to medium-sized tent areas; barbecue grills; firewood is available for gathering in the area; water at several faucets; vault facilities; gravel driveways, with a turnaround loop at the west end of the campground; camper supplies in Victor; nearest source of adequate supplies and services is Jackson, Wyoming, 29 miles east.

Activities & Attractions: Fishing on the creek; short hiking trails; perhaps the most extraordinary attraction is the panoramic view from nearby hilltops.

Natural Features: Located in the Big Hole Mountains, just 0.2 mile east of Pine Creek Pass; sites are sheltered by a stand of pines along Pine Creek; elevation 6600'.

Season, Fees & Phone: June to October; $7.00; 14 day limit; Teton Basin Ranger District, Driggs, (208) 354-2431.

Camp Notes: The campground is situated on a divide between the great Teton Basin to the northeast, and the Swan Valley and vast Antelope Flat to the southwest. (The Teton Basin lies in Idaho between the Big Hole Mountains and the Teton Mountains, and shouldn't be confused with much more famous Jackson Hole on the east side of the Tetons.) The scenery along Highway 31 is pleasant, and sometimes dramatic, as the road winds through the fertile valleys and up into the mountains.

Idaho 90

MIKE HARRIS
Targhee National Forest

Location: Southeast Idaho east of Idaho Falls near the Wyoming border.

Access: From Idaho State Highway 33 at a point 4 miles east of Victor and 19 miles northwest of Jackson, Wyoming, turn south onto a gravel access road and proceed 0.4 mile to the campground.

Facilities: 11 campsites; sites are good-sized with fairly good separation; parking pads are gravel, level, and adequate in size for medium to large vehicles; some good tent spots; barbecue grills; firewood is available for gathering in the area; water at several faucets and a hand pump; vault facilities; gravel driveways; gas and groceries in Victor; nearest source of adequate supplies and services is Jackson.

Activities & Attractions: Possible stream fishing; hiking; the highway leading to this spot from both east and west is superscenic.

Natural Features: Located in a stand of tall conifers on a hillside overlooking Trail Creek on the west slope of the Teton Mountains; campground vegetation consists of fairly dense timber, low-level brush and a forest floor of tall grass and pine needles; elevation 6500'.

Season, Fees & Phone: May to October; $7.00; 14 day limit; Teton Basin Ranger District, Driggs, (208) 354-2431.

Camp Notes: Without the campground sign on the highway, a casual passerby would probably never know that there was this *neat* little campground tucked away up on a pine-covered hillside, just off the highway, near what seems to be the top of the world.

Idaho 91

PALISADES CREEK
Targhee National Forest

Location: Southeast Idaho east of Idaho Falls near the Wyoming border.

Access: From U.S. Highway 26 at milepost 384 +.1 (1 mile north of Palisades, 7 miles south of Swan Valley), turn east onto Forest Road 255; proceed 2.1 miles east to the campground.

Facilities: 7 campsites; sites are medium-sized and fairly well separated; parking pads are gravel, mostly level, short to medium-length, straight-ins or pull-throughs; some good areas for large tents; fire rings or barbecue grills; firewood is available for gathering in the area; water at several faucets; vault facilities; gravel driveways; camper supplies in Palisades and Swan Valley; nearest sources of adequate to complete supplies are Idaho Falls, or Jackson, Wyoming, about 50 miles west and east, respectively.

Activities & Attractions: Hiking; a trail from here follows Palisades Creek to Lower Palisades Lake (4 miles east), and Upper Palisades Lake (7 miles east); trailhead facilities for horseback travel at the campground; for boating and fishing, Palisades Reservoir is about 6 miles south.

Natural Features: Located on a flat in a narrow canyon along small Palisades Creek, which joins the Snake River near the highway turnoff; vegetation in the campground consists of medium-height conifers, hardwoods, some underbrush and grass; sites are on both sides of the creek; a rocky palisade (cliff) borders the campground on the south; limited view to the south of the mountains; elevation 5600'.

Season, Fees & Phone: May to September; $5.00; 14 day limit; Palisades Ranger District, Idaho Falls, (208) 523-1412.

Camp Notes: Most of these secluded sites are creekside. The setting is very pleasant. Palisades Creek Campground serves well and often as a jumping-off point for nearby backcountry trails. Palisades Lakes, mentioned in the Activities section, are small, high mountain lakes, not the expansive Palisades Reservoir along the highway.

CALAMITY
Targhee National Forest

Location: Southeast Idaho southeast of Idaho Falls near the Wyoming border.

Access: From U. S. Highway 26 at milepost 388 (11 miles southeast of Swan Valley, 17 miles northwest of Alpine, Wyoming), turn west onto a paved access road; proceed for 1 mile across the top of the dam and then southerly (left) around to the west lake shore and the campground entrance; campsites are right and left of the entrance.

Facilities: 43 campsites in 2 sections; sites are small to medium-sized, with nominal to fair separation; parking pads are gravel, most are short to medium-length straight-ins; a few sites have very long pull-throughs; many pads will need additional leveling; most tent spots are small and sloped; barbecue grills plus a few fire rings; firewood is available for gathering; water at several faucets; vault facilities; holding tank disposal station below the dam near the highway; gravel driveways; camper supplies in Palisades, 4 miles north; adequate supplies and services are available in Jackson, Wyoming, 53 miles east.

Activities & Attractions: Boating and fishing on the lake and also below the dam on the Snake River.

Natural Features: Located on the northwest shore of Palisades Reservoir, just south of Palisades Dam; fairly dense vegetation in the campground consists of conifers, bushes, grass and a few hardwoods; about two-thirds of the sites are along the lake shore, the balance are on a hillside above the lake; forested mountains and slopes ring the reservoir; elevation 5800'.

Season, Fees & Phone: May to September; $5.00 for a site in the upper section, $7.00 for a lakeside site; Palisades Ranger District, Idaho Falls, (208) 523-1412.

Camp Notes: Calamity Campground is quite densely forested. For a considerably more 'open' campsite, you could look into the Bureau of Reclamation facility just below the dam. It has about a dozen semi-designated sites for self-contained camping on the east bank of the Snake River. It has faucets, vault facilities and no fee. Across from there, on the west riverbank, near the power plant, are day use shelters and restrooms.

BIG ELK CREEK
Targhee National Forest

Location: Southeast Idaho southeast of Idaho Falls near the Wyoming border.

Access: From U.S. Highway 26 at milepost 391 +.2 (13 miles north of the junction of U.S. Highways 26 & 89, 7 miles south of Palisades), turn east onto Forest Road 262 (gravel); proceed 1.4 miles on this single-lane road to the campground.

Facilities: 14 campsites; sites are small to medium-sized, with fair separation; parking pads are gravel, short to medium-length straight-ins; some pads may require a little additional leveling; medium to large areas for tents; water at faucets; vault facilities; gravel driveway; gas and groceries in Alpine, Wyoming, 15 miles south; nearest source of adequate supplies and services is Jackson, Wyoming, 60 miles northeast.

Activities & Attractions: Boating; boat launches near the campground and at Blowout, 3 miles south; fishing; orv possibilities on designated trails in the area.

Natural Features: Located on hilly terrain in a canyon above an inlet/bay on the east shore of Palisades Reservoir; campground vegetation consists of a few tall conifers and a considerable amount of brush; the reservoir is a major impoundment on the Snake River; elevation 5800'.

Season, Fees & Phone: April to October; $5.00; 14 day limit; Palisades Ranger District, Idaho Falls, (208) 523-1412.

Camp Notes: Most sites here have a views of the inlet through the brush. The campground is popular with orv enthusiasts.

ALPINE
Targhee National Forest

Location: Southeast Idaho southeast of Idaho Falls at the Idaho-Wyoming border.

Access: From U.S. Highway 26 at Idaho milepost 402 + .8 and Wyoming milepost 0 (2.5 miles north of the junction of U.S. Highways 26 & 89 near Alpine, Wyoming, 26 miles south of Swan Valley), turn southwest into the campground.

Facilities: 22 campsites; sites are average or better in size, with typically good separation; parking pads are gravel straight-ins or pull-throughs; some units are built for double occupancy and have very large parking spaces; ample space for tents; some table/tent areas are situated on a slope with a terraced arrangement of rails and steps; fireplaces; firewood is available for gathering in the area; water at several faucets; vault facilities; gravel driveways; camper supplies in Alpine, 3 miles south; nearest source of adequate supplies and services is Jackson, Wyoming, 50 miles northeast.

Activities & Attractions: Fishing; boating; some orv travel in the vicinity.

Natural Features: Located in an open forest area at the south end of Palisades Reservoir, a large mountain lake formed by the damming of the Snake River; vegetation in the campground consists of tall grass, some brush, conifers, and a few hardwoods; most sites are nicely sheltered, a few are fairly open; elevation 5700'.

Season, Fees & Phone: May to September; $6.00 for a single unit, $8.00 for a double unit; 14 day limit; Palisades Ranger District, Idaho Falls, (208) 523-1412.

Camp Notes: Some campsites have nice views through the trees of the lake and surrounding forested peaks of the Caribou Range. This campground is located within an easy drive of the very popular Snake River Canyon, just east of here, toward Jackson. River rafters, at times, swarm into Canyon campgrounds, bringing them to overflowing during the peak of the rafting season. Alpine Campground is a good camping alternative that's outside of the mainstream of river activity. It's inside the Idaho State Line by mere inches.

Idaho 95

PINEBAR & TINCUP
Caribou National Forest

Location: Southeast corner of Idaho east of Pocatello near the Wyoming border.

Access: From Idaho State Highway 34 at milepost 104 (10 miles west of Freedom, Wyoming, 45 miles northeast of Soda Springs), turn south into Pinebar Campground; on the same road, except 6 miles east, at milepost 110 + .4, turn south into Tincup Campground.

Facilities: 5 campsites at Pinebar and 4 campsites at Tincup; sites at Pinebar are small to medium-sized, with gravel straight-in parking pads that may require some additional leveling; sites at Tincup are level and better-separated by vegetation, but slightly smaller and closer together; mostly small to medium-sized tent spots in both areas; fire rings; firewood is available for gathering in the area; water at a hand pump at each campground; vault facilities; gravel driveways; camper supplies in Freedom; limited to adequate supplies and services are available in Afton, Wyoming, 20 miles south.

Activities & Attractions: Stream fishing (especially near Tincup); Pinebar is near a trailhead leading south along Lau Creek.

Natural Features: Located along Tincup Creek which flows eastward to the Salt River; sites at Pinebar are on a grassy hilltop overlooking the creek, in an open forest; sites at Tincup are in a grassy creekbed, with more dense vegetation, and situated slightly farther from the highway; rolling, piney hillsides are the prevailing landscape to the west of Pinebar, while level farmland lies to the east of Tincup; elevation 6500' at Pinebar and 6000' at Tincup.

Season, Fees & Phone: May to October; $5.00; 14 day limit; Soda Springs Ranger District (208) 547-4356.

Camp Notes: A number of similarities led us to list these two small campgrounds together. Because they are located along the same highway and the same creek and have the same facilities, it's almost as if they are 2 distinctively different loops of the same campground, just six miles apart. The Lander Cutoff of the Old Oregon Trail passed this way in the mid-1800's.

Idaho 96

EMIGRATION
Caribou National Forest

Location: Southeast corner of Idaho west of Montpelier.

Access: From Idaho State Highway 36 at milepost 23 + .1 (17 miles west of Montpelier, 28 miles northeast of Preston), turn south and proceed 0.2 mile on a paved access road to the campground.

Facilities: 26 campsites in 2 loops; sites are medium to large and fairly well separated; parking pads are paved, most are medium-length straight-ins which may require some additional leveling; some good-sized tent spots in dense vegetation; fireplaces or fire rings, plus a few barbecue grills; firewood is available for gathering in the area; water at faucets throughout; restrooms with service sinks; paved driveways; camper supplies in Ovid, 11 miles east; adequate supplies and services are available in Montpelier.

Activities & Attractions: The drive along the highway offers superscenic views of the northern end of the Wasatch Range; Highline Trail passes along the south and western edges of the campground.

Natural Features: Located high in the northern Wasatch Range just 1 mile east of a 7424' mountain pass; tall conifers, aspens and some underbrush are the predominant vegetation on this heavily forested slope; a small rivulet flows through the campground; elevation 7300'.

Season, Fees & Phone: June to September; $6.00; 14 day limit; Montpelier Ranger District (208) 847-0375.

Camp Notes: When the valleys below are blanketed with midsummer warmth and irrigation humidity, this spot will almost certainly be a haven of coolness. Overall, Emigration is one of the nicest campgrounds in this region.

Idaho 97

MONTPELIER CANYON
Caribou National Forest

Location: Southeast corner of Idaho east of Montpelier.

Access: From U.S. Highway 89 at milepost 29 +.9 (4 miles east of Montpelier, 9 miles west of the Idaho-Wyoming border) turn south into the campground.

Facilities: 17 campsites in 2 loops; sites are small+ to medium-sized, level, with fair to fairly good separation; parking pads are gravel, some are spacious enough to accommodate larger vehicles; some nice grassy tent sites; fireplaces or fire rings; a limited amount of firewood is available for gathering, b-y-o is recommended; water at faucets; (water supply may be unreliable, so b-y-o); vault facilities; gravel driveways; adequate supplies and services in Montpelier.

Activities & Attractions: Fishing opportunities on the creek and in the newly created Montpelier Reservoir to the north; a footbridge crosses over the creek and there are trails in the surrounding area.

Natural Features: Located along the banks of Montpelier Creek at the south tip of the Caribou Range; campground vegetation consists of some conifers, aspens, and dense, high brush; sage-covered canyon slopes border the stream; elevation 6100'.

Season, Fees & Phone: May to October; $5.00; 14 day limit; Montpelier Ranger District (208) 847-0375.

Camp Notes: Caribou National Forest gets its name not from the great deer of the North Country but from a character named Jesse "Cariboo Jack" Fairchild. In 1870 Fairchild, who was a teller of tall tales about the Canadian caribou country, struck pay dirt on what is now Caribou Mountain, about 50 miles due north of this campground. Thousands of fortune-seekers joined the ensuing stampede to riches that produced $50 million in gold over the next two decades. "Cariboo Jack" disappeared into history.

Idaho 98

PORCUPINE
Caribou/Cache National Forests

Location: Southeast corner of Idaho northwest of Bear Lake.

Access: From U.S. Highway 89 at milepost 9 in the community of St. Charles (11 miles south of Ovid, 6.5 miles north of Fish Haven), turn west onto St. Charles Canyon Road (paved); head west for 7.5 miles, then turn south (left) into the campground.

Facilities: 12 campsites; sites are medium to large with average or better separation; parking pads are paved, mostly medium to long straight-ins; some pads may require additional leveling; some nice large tent spots on a grassy slope; fire rings; limited firewood is available for gathering in the area; water at several faucets; restrooms; paved driveways; camper supplies on Highway 89 in St. Charles and Fish Haven; adequate supplies and services are available in Montpelier, 30 miles northeast.

Activities & Attractions: Minnetonka Caves is the main attraction in the area; tours of these limestone caves are conducted on summer weekends; foot trails follow the creek and lead off into the hills; Bear Lake, which straddles the Idaho-Utah border just 10 miles east has boating and fishing.

Natural Features: Located in a narrow canyon along St. Charles Creek, with rocky ridges rising across the canyon to the north; campsites are in a string along the slope of the creekbank; vegetation in the campground consists of medium-dense, tall conifers, hardwoods, and grass; elevation 7200'.

Season, Fees & Phone: June to September; $6.00; 14 day limit; Montpelier Ranger District (208) 847-0375.

Camp Notes: Another national forest campground along this same creek is St. Charles, 4 miles east of here, and only 3.1 miles from Highway 89. It has 6 sites and facilities similar to those at Porcupine.

Idaho 99

CLOVERLEAF
Caribou/Cache National Forests

Location: Southeast corner of Idaho northwest of Bear Lake.

Access: From U.S. Highway 89 at milepost 9 (11 miles south of Ovid, 6.5 miles north of Fish Haven), turn west onto St. Charles Canyon Road (paved); travel westerly for 8.9 miles; turn left (south) into the campground; (St. Charles Canyon Road dead-ends at Minnetonka Caves, just west of the campground).

Facilities: 18 campsites in a complex loop; sites are small+ to medium-sized, with fair to good separation; parking pads are paved, short to long, mostly straight-ins; spots for tents are rather sloped and snug for the most part; fire rings or barbecue grills; firewood is available for gathering in the area; water at several faucets; restrooms; paved driveways; camper supplies on Highway 89 in St. Charles and Fish Haven; adequate supplies and services are available in Montpelier, 30 miles northeast.

Activities & Attractions: Guided tours of Minnetonka Caves are conducted by national forest personnel during the summer; foot trails follow the creek and lead to the Caves; boating and fishing on Bear Lake, 15 miles east.

Natural Features: Located in the narrow St. Charles Canyon along St. Charles Creek near the entrance to Minnetonka Caves; some sites are fairly grassy and open; many sites are engulfed by vegetation; sunlight filters down through the tall conifers and medium-height aspens; elevation 7400'.

Season, Fees & Phone: June to September; $6.00; 14 day limit; Montpelier R.D. (208) 847-0375.

Camp Notes: Campsites at Cloverleaf have certain advantages over those in other area campgrounds. They are within walking distance of Minnetonka Caves and are a bit farther from the roadway than sites at Porcupine and St. Charles, two campgrounds which you'll pass on the way to Cloverleaf and the Caves. (Minnetonka is an Indian word meaning "falling water".)

Idaho 100

BEAR LAKE
Bear Lake State Park

Location: Southeast corner of Idaho at the north end of Bear Lake.

Access: From U.S. Highway 89 at milepost 8 +.8 (9 miles north of the Idaho-Utah border, 17 miles south of Montpelier), turn east onto a paved access road and travel along the north and northeast shores of the lake for 10 miles to the campground.

Facilities: 48 campsites, including 20 with electrical hookups; sites are small+ in size, with minimal separation; parking pads are gravel, short to long straight-ins or medium to long pull-throughs; a bit of additional leveling may be required; adequate space for large tents; fire rings; b-y-o firewood; water at several faucets; vault facilities; hard-surfaced driveways; gas and groceries in Fishaven, 6 miles south of the highway turnoff.

Activities & Attractions: Large swimming beaches and boat launches at both North Beach and East Beach; fishing.

Natural Features: Located on a sage flat above the east shore of Bear Lake; the camp area has been planted with numerous small hardwoods, evergreens and junipers; long, dry-looking, partially forested mountains rise to nearly 10,000' both east and west of the lake; elevation 6100'.

Season, Fees & Phone: May to October; please see Appendix for standard Idaho state park fees; park office (208) 945-2790.

Camp Notes: Bear Lake is a sun-and-sand-lovers park. This campground is located in the park's East Beach area. You'll pass the North Beach day use unit on the way to the campground. North Beach has 1.8 miles of sandy beach; there's "only" a half mile of beach at East Beach.

SPECIAL SECTION:

Jackcamping and Backpacking in the West's Parks and Forests

In addition to camping in established campgrounds, as do the majority of visitors, thousands of campers opt for simpler places to spend a night or a week or more in the West's magnificent parks and forests.

Jackcamping

"Jackcamping", "roadsiding", "dispersed camping", or "siwashing" are several of the assorted terms describing the simplest type of camp there is: just pulling a vehicle a few yards off the main drag, or heading up a gravel or dirt forest road to an out-of-the-way spot which looks good to you. Sometimes, especially when the "Campground Full" plank is hung out to dry in front of all the nearby public campgrounds, or there *aren't* any nearby public campgrounds, it might be the only way to travel.

From what we can determine "jackcamping" is an extension of the Medieval English slang word "jacke", meaning "common", "serviceable" or "ordinary". The explanations of "roadsiding" and "dispersed camping" are self-evident. "Siwashing" is an old term from the Southwest. It apparently refers to the practice of cowboys and other travelers making a late camp by just hunkering-down in an *arroyo* or 'dry wash'. After hobbling your horse, the saddle is propped-up against the *side* of the *wash*, (hence *si'wash* or *siwash*), forming a leather 'recliner' of sorts in which to pass the night out of the wind and cold. It may not be the most comfortable way to spend the night, but by two or three a.m. you get used to the smell of the saddle anyway.

As a general rule-of-thumb, jackcamping isn't allowed in local, state and national parks. In those areas, you'll have to stay in established campgrounds or sign-up for a backcountry site.

However, jackcamping is *usually* permitted anywhere on the millions of road-accessible acres of national forest and BLM-managed federal public lands, subject to a few exceptions. In some high-traffic areas it's not allowed, and roadside signs are *usually* posted telling you so. ("Camp Only in Designated Campgrounds" signs are becoming more common with each passing year.) In certain high fire risk zones or during the general fire season it may not be permitted. For the majority of areas in which jackcamping is legal, small campfires, suitably sized and contained, are ordinarily OK. All of the rules of good manners, trash-removal, and hygiene which apply to camping anywhere, regardless of location, are enforced. (Would *you* want to camp where someone else had left their "sign"?) For off-highway travel, the "Shovel, Axe and Bucket" rule is usually in effect (see below).

Since you don't want the law coming down on you for an unintentional impropriety, it's highly advisable to stop in or call a local Forest Service ranger station or BLM office to determine the status of jackcamping in your region of choice, plus any special requirements (spark arrestors, the length of the shovel needed under the "Shovel, Axe and Bucket" rule, campfires, stay limit, etc.) Local ranchers who have leased grazing rights on federal lands are sensitive about their livestock sharing the meadows and rangelands with campers. So it's probably best to jackcamp in "open" areas, thus avoiding leaseholder vs taxpayer rights confrontations altogether. (Legalities notwithstanding, the barrel of a 12-gauge or an '06 looks especially awesome when it's poked inside your tent at midnight.) Be sure to get the name of the individual in the local public office who provided the information "just in case".

If you're reasonably self-sufficient or self-contained, jackcamping can save you *beaucoups* bucks--perhaps hundreds of dollars--over a lifetime of camping. (We know.)

Backpacking

Take all of the open acres readily available to jackcampers, then multiply that figure by a factor of 100,000 (or thereabouts) and you'll have some idea of the wilderness and near-wilderness camping opportunities that are only accessible to backpackers (or horsepackers).

Backpackers usually invest a lot of time, and usually a lot of money, into their preferred camping method, and perhaps rightfully so (timewise, anyway).

Planning an overnight or week-long foot trip into the boondocks is half the work (and half the fun too!). Hours, days, even *weeks*, can be spent pouring over highway maps, topographic maps, public lands/BLM maps, and forest maps looking for likely places to pack into. (We know!)

219

Backpacking in Western National Forests

To be editorially above-board about this: Of all the possible federal and state recreation areas, your best opportunities for backpack camping are in the national forest wilderness, primitive, and wild areas. Prime backpacking areas in most state parks and many national park units are measured in acres or perhaps square miles; but the back country in the national forests is measured in tens and hundreds and thousands of square miles. Here's where planning really becomes fun.

Backpacking in Western National and State Parks

Finding a backpack campsite in the West's *parks* is relatively straightforward: much of the work has been done for you by the park people. Most state and many national parks which are large enough to provide opportunities for backcountry travel have established backcountry camps which are the *only* places to camp out in the toolies. Yes, that indeed restricts your overnight choices to a few small areas in many cases; but you can still enjoy walking through and looking at the rest of the back country.

Throughout this series, designated backpack campsites and other backpacking opportunities are occasionally mentioned in conjunction with nearby established campgrounds.

Backpacking in Pacific Northwest National Parks

In the Pacific Northwest, the opportunities for backcountry exploration have been maintained at a somewhat more liberal level than farther south along and near the West Coast. From a practical standpoint, significant trail and campsite use is limited to a relatively few short months because of the harsh weather during much of the year, and the wilderness renews itself during each long, snowy and rainy winter.

North Cascades National Park perhaps offers the ultimate backpacking experience in the Pacific Northwest. North Cascades has a half-dozen small 'hike-in/bus-in' backcountry camps, all of them in Stehekin Valley. (You either hike in all the way, or take a combination of boat or floatplane and a 23-mile shuttle bus ride to the campsites.) In *Olympic National Park* are several large, central backcountry campgrounds. North Cascades and Olympic NP's also have a 'limited' number of dispersed areas available. *Mount Rainier* and *Crater Lake National Parks*, and *Craters of the Moon National Monument* list 'various locations' available on a 'limited' basis. Backcountry camping is allowed during most or all of the year in all of these national park units, but late-autumn through early-spring weather may be a discouraging factor in many locations. On the other hand, you'll have the Great Northwest Wilderness pretty much to yourself during the "off" season. Most backcountry sites throughout the region are available on a first-come-first-served basis. Backcountry permits from park headquarters or a major ranger station are required in all areas.

Use the *Phone* information in the text to contact your selected park's headquarters and ask for the "wilderness office" or "backcountry ranger" to initialize your trip planning. In virtually every case, they'll be able to provide detailed information and maps--at no charge, or at most a couple of bucks for first-rate maps. The majority of the backcountry people are enthusiastic boondockers themselves, and they'll generally provide sound, albeit conservative, suggestions. Let's face it: they don't want to have to bail anybody out of a tough spot by extracting them on foot, in a green, muddy, government-issue jeep, a helicopter--or by what they call at Grand Canyon an "emergency mule drag-out". (Try living *that one* down when you get home, dude!)

River Running and Boat Camping

River running and floating are well-established pastimes on the Rogue and Umpqua Rivers of Oregon, and the renowned Salmon River--the "River of No Return"--in Idaho. A river permit is required for float trips on the Salmon, as well as other wilderness rivers under federal management.

Flatwater boat camping is permitted in *Coulee Dam, Lake Chelan, and Ross Lake National Recreation Areas*, plus more than a dozen islands in the San Juans and on the south end of Puget Sound which are part of the Washington State Park System. Standard boat-in campsites have been established in all of these areas. Obtaining the 'regs' for their use is mandatory because of restrictions and limitiations you might not ordinarily expect, (such as an alcohol embargo on Squaxin Island SP in Washington). Topographic maps or hydro charts are really helpful for inland waters, and standard navigation charts and tables obviously are a 'must' for tidewater passages.

At the risk of demagoguery: We can vouch that it really pays to start planning months in advance for a backcountry trip. Besides, planning *is* half the fun.

Creative Camping

In their most elementary forms, outdoor recreation in general, and camping in particular, require very little in the way of extensive planning or highly specialized and sophisticated equipment. A stout knife, some matches, a few blankets, a free road map, a water jug, and a big sack of p.b. & j. sandwiches, all tossed onto the seat of an old beater pickup, will get you started on the way to a lifetime of outdoor adventures.

Idyllic and nostalgic as that scenario may seem, most of the individuals reading this *Double Eagle*™ Guide (and those *writing* it) probably desire (and deserve) at least a few granules of comfort sprinkled over their tent or around their rv.

There are enough books already on the market or in libraries which will provide you with plenty of advice on *how* to camp. One of the oldest and best is the *Fieldbook*, published by the Boy Scouts of America. Really. It is a widely accepted, profusely illustrated (not to mention comparatively inexpensive) outdoor reference which has few true rivals. It presents plenty of information on setting up camp, first aid, safety, woodlore, flora and fauna identification, weather, and a host of other items. Although recreational vehicle camping isn't specifically covered in detail, many of the general camping principles it does cover apply equally well to rv's.

So rather than re-invent the wheel, we've concentrated your hard-earned *dinero* into finding out *where* to camp. However, there are still a few items that aren't widely known which might be of interest to you, or which bear repeating, so we've included them in the following paragraphs.

Resourcefulness. When putting together your equipment, it's both challenging and a lot of fun to make the ordinary stuff you have around the house, especially in the kitchen, do double duty. Offer an "early retirement" to servicable utensils, pans, plastic cups, etc. to a "gear box".

Resource-fullness. Empty plastic peanut butter jars, pancake syrup and milk jugs, ketchup bottles, also aluminum pie plates and styrofoam trays, can be washed, re-labeled and used again. (The syrup jugs, with their handles and pop-up spouts, make terrific "canteens" for kids.) The lightweight, break-resistant plastic stuff is more practical on a camping trip than glass containers, anyway. *El Cheapo* plastic shopping bags, which have become *de rigueur* in supermarkets, can be saved and re-used to hold travel litter and campground trash. When they're full, tie them tightly closed using the "handles". In the words of a college-age camper from Holland while he was refilling a plastic, two-liter soft drink bottle at the single water faucet in a desert national park campground: "Why waste?".

Redundancy. Whether you're camping in a tent, pickup, van, boat, motorhome or fifth-wheel trailer, it pays to think and plan like a backpacker. Can you make-do with fewer changes of clothes for a short weekend trip? How about getting-by with half as much diet cola, and drink more cool, campground spring water instead? Do you really *need* that third curling iron? Real backpackers (like the guy who trimmed the margins off his maps) are relentless in their quest for the light load.

Water. No matter where you travel, *always* carry a couple of gallons of drinking water. Campground water sources may be out of order (e.g., someone broke the handle off the hydrant or the well went dry), and you probably won't want to fool around with boiling lake or stream water. (Because of the possibility of encountering the widespread "beaver fever" (*Giardia*) parasite and other diseases in lakes and streams, if treated or tested H_2O isn't available, boil the surface water for a full five minutes.)

(Reports from the field indicate that extremely tough health and environmental standards may force the closure of natural drinking water supplies from wells and springs in many campgrounds. The upside to this situation is that, if the camp itself remains open, chances are that no fees will be charged.)

Juice. If you're a tent or small vehicle camper who normally doesn't need electrical hookups, carry a hotplate, coffee pot, or hair dryer when traveling in regions where hookup campsites are available. The trend in public campground management is toward charging the full rate for a hookup site whether or not you have an rv, even though there are no standard sites available for you to occupy. In many popular state parks and Corps of Engineers recreation areas, hookup sites far outnumber standard sites. At least you'll have some use for the juice.

Fire. Charcoal lighter fluid makes a good "starter" for campfires, and is especially handy if the wood is damp. In a pinch, that spare bottle of motor oil in the trunk can be pressed into service for the same purpose. Let two ounces soak in for several minutes. Practice the same safety precautions you would use in lighting a home barbecue so you can keep your curly locks and eyebrows from being scorched by the flames. Obviously use extreme caution--and don't even *think* about using gasoline. A really handy option to using wood is to carry a couple of synthetic "fire logs". The sawdust-and-paraffin logs are made from byproducts of the lumber and petroleum industries and burn about three hours in the outdoors. The fire logs can also be used to start and maintain a regular campfire if the locally gathered firewood is wet.

Mosquitoes. The winged demons aren't usually mentioned in the text because you just have to *expect* them almost anywhere except perhaps in the driest desert areas. Soggy times, like late spring and early summer, are the worst times. If you're one of us who's always the first to be strafed by the local mosquito squadron, keep plenty of anti-aircraft ammo on hand. The most versatile skin stuff is the spray-on variety. Spray it all over your clothes to keep the varmints from poking their proboscis through the seat of your jeans. A room spray comes in handy for blasting any bugs which might have infiltrated your tent or rv. Fortunately, in most areas the peak of the mosquito season lasts only a couple of weeks, and you can enjoy yourself the rest of the time. Autumn camping is great!

Rattlers. Anywhere you go in the Desert Southwest, expect to find rattlesnakes, so place your hands and feet and other vital parts accordingly. (While preparing the *Double Eagle*™ series, one of the publishers inadvertently poked her zoom lens to within a yard of a coiled rattler's snout. The photographer's anxieties were vocally, albeit shakily, expressed; the level of stress which the incident induced on the snake is unknown.)

Bumps in the night. When you retire for the night, put all your valuables, especially your cooler, inside your vehicle to protect them against campground burglars and bruins. While camping at Canyon Campground in Yellowstone National Park more than two decades ago, a pair of young brothers unwittingly left their stocked cooler out on the picnic table so they had more room to sleep inside their ancient station wagon. Sometime after midnight, they were awakened by a clatter in the darkness behind the wagon. After they had groggily dressed and crept out to investigate, the sleepy siblings discovered that a bear had broken into their impenetrable ice chest. Taking inventory, the dauntless duo determined that the brazen backwoods *bandito* had wolfed-down three pounds of baked chicken breasts, a meatloaf, one pound of pineapple cottage cheese, four quarters of margarine, and had chomped through two cans of *Coors*--presumably to wash it all down. The soft drinks were untouched. (We dined sumptuously on Spam and pork 'n beans for the rest of the trip. Ed.)

Horsepower. Your camping vehicle will lose about four percent of its power for each 1000′ gain in altitude above sea level (unless it's turbocharged). Keep that in mind in relation to the "pack like a backpacker" item mentioned previously. You might also keep it in mind when you embark on a foot trip. The factory-original human machine loses about the same amount of efficiency at higher elevations.

Air. To estimate the temperature at a campground in the mountains while you're still down in the valley or on the plains, subtract about three degrees Fahrenheit for each 1000′ difference in elevation between the valley and the campground. Use the same method to estimate nighttime lows in the mountains by using weather forecasts for valley cities.

Timing. Try staying an hour ahead of everyone else. While traveling in the Mountain Time Zone, keep your timepiece ticking on Central Time. That way you'll naturally set up camp an hour earlier, and likewise break camp an hour prior to other travelers. You might be amazed at how much that 60 minutes will do for campsite availability in the late afternoon, or for restrooms, showers, uncrowded roads and sightseeing in the morning.

Reptile repellant. Here's a sensitive subject. With the rise in crimes perpetrated against travelers and campers in the nation's parks and forests and on its highways and byways, it's become increasingly common for legitimate campers to pack a 'heater'--the type that's measured by caliber or gauge, not in volts and amps. To quote a respected Wyoming peace officer: "Half the pickups and campers in Wyoming and Montana have a .45 automatic under the seat or a 12-gauge pump behind the bunk". If personal safety is a concern to you, check all applicable laws, get competent instruction, practice a lot, and join the NRA.

Vaporhavens. Be skeptical when you scan highway and forest maps and see hundreds of little symbols which indicate the locations of alleged campsites; or when you glance through listings published by governmental agencies or promotional interests. A high percentage of those 'recreation areas' are as vaporous as the mist rising from a warm lake into chilled autumn air. Many, many of the listed spots are actually picnic areas, fishing access sites, and even highway rest stops; dozens of camps are ill-maintained remnants of their former greatness, located at the end of rocky jeep trails; many others no longer exist; still others *never* existed, but are merely a mapmaker's or planner's notion of where a campground *might* or *should* be. In summation: Make certain that a campground exists and what it offers before you embark on 20 miles of washboard gravel travel in the never-ending quest for your own personal Eden.

We hope the foregoing items, and information throughout this series, help you conserve your own valuable time, money, fuel and other irreplaceable resources. ***Good Camping !***

Appendix

Washington

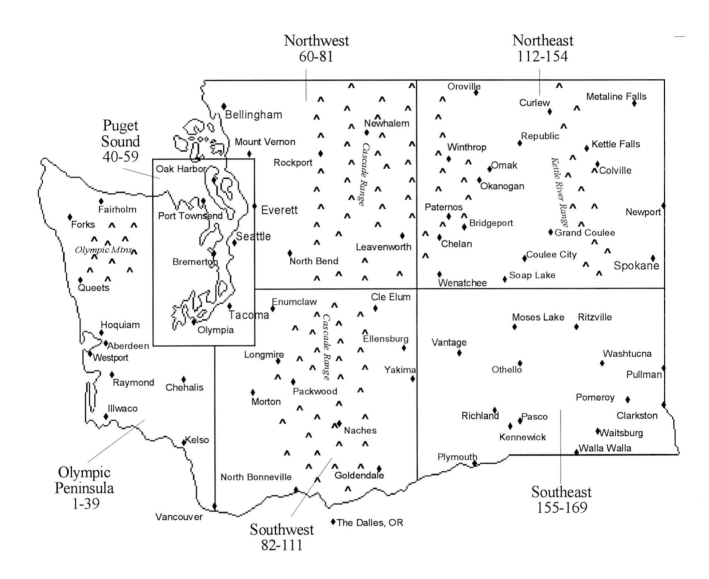

Northwest
60-81

Northeast
112-154

Puget
Sound
40-59

Olympic
Peninsula
1-39

Southwest
82-111

Southeast
155-169

Bellingham
Newhalem
Mount Vernon
Rockport
Cascade Range
Oak Harbor
Fairholm
Forks
Port Townsend
Everett
Olympic Mtns
Seattle
Bremerton
North Bend
Leavenworth
Queets
Hoquiam
Aberdeen
Westport
Tacoma
Enumclaw
Cle Elum
Olympia
Raymond
Chehalis
Longmire
Cascade Range
Ellensburg
Yakima
Illwaco
Packwood
Morton
Kelso
Naches
North Bonneville
Goldendale
Vancouver
The Dalles, OR

Oroville
Curlew
Metaline Falls
Republic
Winthrop
Kettle Falls
Omak
Colville
Okanogan
Kettle River Range
Paternos
Newport
Bridgeport
Chelan
Grand Coulee
Coulee City
Spokane
Wenatchee
Soap Lake
Moses Lake
Ritzville
Vantage
Washtucna
Othello
Pullman
Pomeroy
Richland
Pasco
Clarkston
Kennewick
Waitsburg
Plymouth
Walla Walla

Oregon

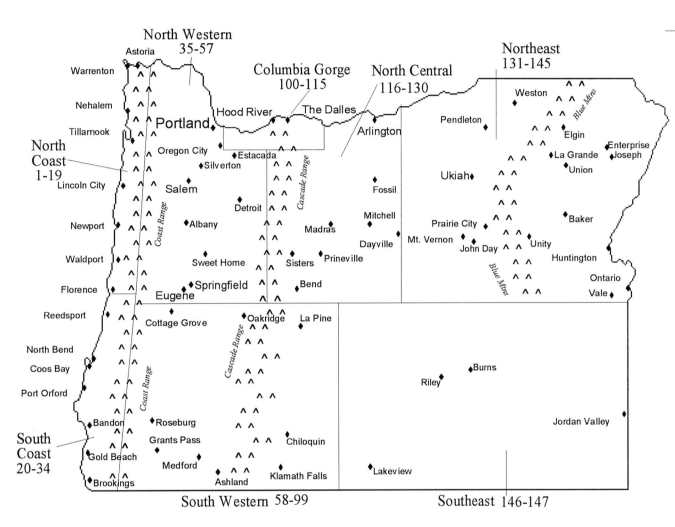

North Western
35-57

Astoria

Warrenton

Nehalem

Tillamook

North
Coast
1-19

Lincoln City

Newport

Waldport

Florence

Reedsport

North Bend

Coos Bay

Port Orford

South
Coast
20-34

Bandon

Gold Beach

Brookings

Portland

Oregon City

Silverton

Salem

Albany

Sweet Home

Springfield

Eugene

Cottage Grove

Roseburg

Grants Pass

Medford

Ashland

Hood River

Estacada

Detroit

Sisters

Oakridge

La Pine

Chiloquin

Klamath Falls

Columbia Gorge
100-115

The Dalles

Madras

Prineville

Bend

Coast Range

Cascade Range

North Central
116-130

Arlington

Fossil

Mitchell

Dayville

Northeast
131-145

Weston

Pendleton

Ukiah

Mt. Vernon

Prairie City

John Day

Blue Mtns

Elgin

La Grande

Union

Baker

Unity

Huntington

Ontario

Vale

Enterprise

Joseph

Riley

Burns

Jordan Valley

Lakeview

South Western 58-99

Southeast 146-147

Idaho

Sandpoint

Coeur d'Alene

Kellogg

Wallace

St. Maries

Lewiston

Kooskia

Bitterroot Range

Lolo, MT

Panhandle
1-32

Bitterroot Range

Salmon

Challis

New Meadows

McCall

West Yellowstone, MT

Cascade

Stanley

Salmon River Mtns.

Weiser

Banks

Lowman

Ashton

Salmon River Mtns.

Victor

Boise

Idaho Falls

Ketchum

Arco

Swan Valley

Mountain Home

Pocatello

Twin Falls

Snake River Plain

Montpelier

Southwest
33-71

Southeast
72-100

PACIFIC NORTHWEST STANDARD STATE PARK FEES

Washington

Primitive campsite	
w/motorized vehicle	$7.00
w/non-motorizid vehicle	$5.00
Standard/developed campsite	$11.00
Hookup campsite	$16.00

Oregon

Primitive campsite (i.e., no showers)	$9.00
Standard/developed campsite	$15.00
Partial hookup campsite	$16.00
Full hookup campsite	$17.00
Designated hike/bike campsite	$5.00
Daily park entry fee for certain parks	$3.00
(Add 3%-9% 'lodging tax to campsite fees.)	

Idaho

Primitive campsite	
(vaults, no water)	$6.00
Basic campsite	
(vaults, central water)	$8.00
Standard/developed campsite	
(flush restrooms, central water)	$9.00
To standard site fee, add for:	
Electrical hookup	$3.00
Sewer hookup	$1.00

Please remember that all fees are subject to change without notice.

PACIFIC NORTHWEST CAMPSITE RESERVATIONS

Reservations may be made for certain individual and group campsites in national forests and state parks in Washington, Oregon and Idaho. As a general rule-of-thumb, reservations for midsummer weekends should be initiated at least several weeks in advance. Reservation fees are charged.

National Forest Reservations

The USDA Forest Service has established a reservation system which affects hundreds of national forest campgrounds nationwide. Continuous changes can be expected in such a large system as campgrounds with reservable sites are added or removed from the list. For additional information about campgrounds with reservable sites, and to make reservations, you may call (toll-free) the independent agent handling the reservation system.

800-280-CAMP   (800-280-2267)

(National Forest Reservations, continued)

Reservations can be made from 10 days to 120 days in advance. It is suggested that you take advantage of the full 120-day period for any medium-sized or large forest camp associated with a lake or sizeable stream, or near a national park, if you want to be assured of a campsite there on a summer holiday weekend.

A fee of $6.00-$7.50 is charged for a campsite reservation. In addition to the reservation charge, the standard campground user fees for all nights which are reserved also need to be paid at the time the reservation is made. (Reservations for consecutive nights at the same campground are covered under the same fee.) If you cancel, you lose the reservation fee, plus you're charged a cancellation fee. Any remainder is refunded. They'll take checks, money orders, VISA or MasterCard, (VISA/MC for telephone reservations).

Reservable campsites in national forest campgrounds are assigned, but you can request an rv or a tent site; rv sites are generally a little larger and most will accommodate tents. When making a reservation, be prepared to tell the reservation agent about the major camping equipment you plan to use, (size and number of tents, type and length of rv, additional vehicles, boat trailers, etc.). Be generous in your estimate. In most cases, a national forest campground's *best sites* are also those which are *reservable*. Most of the national forest campgrounds which have reservable sites still can accommodate a limited number of drop-ins on a first-come, first-served basis.

National Park Reservations

As of this edition, reservations are not available for national park campgrounds in the Pacific Northwest, as they are in some other Western regions. You may want to periodically check with MisTix to determine if national park reservations are being taken for Northwest parks. The MisTix toll-free reservation number for national parks is 800-365-CAMP (800-365-2267).

State Park Reservations

Reservations may be made for individual and group campsites at certain state parks in Washington, Oregon and Idaho, as indicated in the text. As a general rule-of-thumb, the parks will accept reservations after January 1 in the year for which the site is requested. Reservations should be initiated *at least* several weeks in advance of the date requested. A reservation fee of $5.00-$6.00 is charged.

Reservation forms for individual campsites in Washington and Oregon parks may be obtained from the selected park or from the state park office; forms for group sites in Washington and Oregon and for any type of site in Idaho must be obtained directly from the selected park. Additional specific information and procedures are sent with the reservation form. In all three states, the completed reservation form must be sent with the required reservation fees, site fees, and deposits directly to the park at which the reservation is requested. Cancellation fees are usually charged, or deposits are forefeited, if you bow out.

For additional information about campsite reservations, availability, current conditions, or regulations about the use of campgrounds, we suggest that you directly contact the park or forest office in charge of your selected campground, using the *Phone* information in the text.

Please remember that all reservation information is subject to change without notice.

INDEX

Important Note:

In the following listing, the number to the right of the campground name refers to the Key Number in boldface in the upper left corner of each campground description in the text.

(E.G. **Washington 89** is **Alder Lake**. The number does *not* indicate the page number; page numbers are printed in the text only as secondary references.)

* A thumbnail description of a campground marked with an asterisk is found in the *Camp Notes* section of the principal numbered campground.

WASHINGTON

OREGON

IDAHO

Other volumes in the *Camping* series:

The Double Eagle Guide to

CAMPING *in* WESTERN PARKS *and* FORESTS

__Volume I Pacific Northwest   ISBN 0-929760-27-1
        Washington*Oregon*Idaho   Hardcover 8 1/2x11 $18.95^
        (Also in paper cover 6x9 (C) 1992 $12.95)

__Volume II Rocky Mountains   ISBN 0-929760-22-0
        Colorado*Montana*Wyoming   Hardcover 8 1/2x11 $17.95^

__Volume III Far West   ISBN 0-929760-23-9
        California*Nevada   Hardcover 8 1/2x11 $18.95^

__Volume IV Desert Southwest   ISBN 0-929760-29-8
        Arizona*New Mexico*Utah   Hardcover 8 1/2x11 $17.95^
        (Also in paper cover 6x9 (C) 1992 $12.95)

__Volume V Northern Plains   ISBN 0-929760-25-5
        The Dakotas*Nebraska*Kansas   Hardcover 8 1/2x11 $16.95^

__Volume VI Southwest Plains   ISBN 0-929760-26-3
        Texas*Oklahoma   Hardcover 8 1/2x11) $17.95^

^^^ Softcover, spiral-bound editions are also available. Recommended for light-duty, personal use only.
    Subtract $3.00 from standard hardcover price and check here _____ for *Special Binding*.

Available exclusively from: *Double Eagle* camping guides are regularly updated.

Discovery Publishing

P.O. Box 50545   Billings, MT 59105   Phone 1-406-245-8292

Please add $3.00 for shipping the first volume, and $1.50 for each additional volume.
Same-day shipping for most orders.

Please include your check/money order, or complete the VISA/MasterCard
information in the indicated space below.

Name_____

Address_____

City_____ State_____ Zip_____

For credit card orders:

VISA/MC #_____ Exp.Date_____

Prices, shipping charges, and specifications subject to change.

Thank You Very Much For Your Order!

(A photocopy or other reproduction may be substituted for this original form.)